LITERAL IMAGINATION

NELSON HILTON

LITERAL IMAGINATION

Blake's Vision of Words

UNIVERSITY OF CALIFORNIA PRESS

BERKELEY   LOS ANGELES   LONDON

University of California Press

Berkeley and Los Angeles, California

University of California Press, Ltd.

London, England

© 1983 by

The Regents of the University of California

Printed in the United States of America

1 2 3 4 5 6 7 8 9

For
Mary N. Hilton
long-time Deputy Director of the Women's Bureau
United States Department of Labor
and
Howard J. Hilton, Jr.
Foreign Service Officer, Professor of Economics, and
creator of HUC, a concept and code for
universal access to all recorded information

on their fortieth wedding anniversary

Contents

List of Illustrations

UNNUMBERED ILLUSTRATIONS IN THE TEXT

A Note on References and Abbreviations

IN GENERAL, I QUOTE WILLIAM BLAKE from *The Complete Poetry and Prose of William Blake*, ed. David V. Erdman, abbreviated as E. Additional references, where noted, are to *N: The Notebook of William Blake: A Photographic and Typographic Facsimile*, ed. David V. Erdman. For convenience, hard-to-locate references are followed by the appropriate page number in E. Other references to Erdman give the title and page or plate number of Blake's original, followed by a line number. The following abbreviations for some of Blake's titles are used:

Am	*America, a Prophecy*		plate numbers for chapter 2
ARO	*All Religions are One*		are supplied in brackets
AugI	*Auguries of Innocence*		where necessary)
BA	*The Book of Ahania*	M	*Milton, a Poem*
BL	*The Book of Los*	MHH	*The Marriage of Heaven and Hell*
BU	*The [First] Book of Urizen*	NNR	*There is No Natural Religion*
DC	*A Descriptive Catalogue*	PA	*[Public Address]*
EG	*The Everlasting Gospel*	SE	*Songs of Experience*
Eur	*Europe, a Prophecy*	SI	*Songs of Innocence*
FR	*The French Revolution*	SL	*The Song of Los*
FZ	*Vala, or The Four Zoas*	Thel	*The Book of Thel*
GP	*For the Sexes: The Gates of Paradise*	Tir	*Tiriel*
IM	*[An Island in the Moon]*	VDA	*Visions of the Daughters of Albion*
J	*Jerusalem* (the alternative	VLJ	*[A Vision of the Last Judgment]*

All emphasis in Blake quotations, except in the case of textual revisions pointed up by Erdman, is my own.

The Complete Poetry of John Milton, ed. John T. Shawcross, is the edition quoted throughout; *Paradise Lost* is abbreviated as *PL.*

Edward Young, *The Complaint, and the Consolation; or Night Thoughts (NT),* is quoted from the pages of the first and second editions (1743–45) pasted into the sheets of Blake's illustrations to the poem (British Museum Print Room); I have usually trusted the line numbering that was added in by hand.

The Bible is quoted from the Authorized King James Version (AV).

The Compact Edition of the Oxford English Dictionary (New York: Oxford University Press, 1971) is cited as *OED*.

Full bibliographic information for short (author-title) references here and in the notes will be found in the bibliography.

Acknowledgments

THIS WORK OWES ITS BEING to the love, example, encouragement, and support of my parents and of my sister and brother, Dede and Ricko. The book also takes its life from ten luminous years at the University of California, Santa Cruz. I am grateful, first and foremost, to Tom Vogler, dean of the Santa Cruz Blake school and "damned good to steal from." As teacher, friend, and colleague, he has borne with these pages from the beginning. The book was deeply influenced in its early stages by Laura Mikkelson Hilton and by Morton D. Paley, Norman O. Brown, John Lynch, Harry Berger, Jr., Ron Martinez, and Paul Mann. For later comments, questions, and guidance I thank W. J. T. Mitchell, Robert Gleckner, Doris Kretschmer at the University of California Press, *et ma chère* Sherrie.

An award from the United States–United Kingdom Educational Commission helped me spend the year of 1976–77 writing the first draft amid the inspiring resources of the British Library and the British Museum's Department of Prints and Drawings. Summer grants from the School of Criticism and Theory and from the Henry E. Huntington Library assisted my efforts, as did the research time liberally provided by the University of Georgia, Athens.

Chapter 4 first appeared in *The Eighteenth Century: Theory and Interpretation* and part of Chapter 9 in *Philological Quarterly;* both are adapted here with the permission of the respective editors.

Where I have erred, as Urizen says, "my Error remains with me"—as do the infelicities, excesses, and connections not adequately made. The portions of chapter titles in brackets, for example, are offered only to point to a deep drift of the argument. Indeed, there remain so many difficulties, Reader, that to whatever extent this book may succeed, I gratefully acknowledge and thank you, whose work this now is.

CHAPTER ONE

In Words into the Worlds of Thought

To Understand literally these metaphors
. . . seems . . . absurd . . .

Sir Joshua Reynolds, *Discourses on Art*

*The Ancients did not mean to Impose when they affirmd their belief in Vision
& Revelation Plato was in Earnest. Milton was in Earnest. They believd
that God did Visit Man Really & Truly & not as Reynolds pretends*

William Blake, annotations to Reynolds

THIS BOOK IS ABOUT some of Blake's words. As such it is about an imagination I
will call literal, invoking Yeats's profound characterization of Blake as a
"literal realist of the imagination"[1] and, no less, Blake's own vision of achieving
"Divine Revelation in the Litteral Expression" (*M* 42.14). These two uses of
"literal" both point toward the particular naked intensity we often sense rather
than grasp in Blake. Usually, the "literal" bows before some supposed more
complex and mysterious "symbolic" meaning: but enough has been written
about Blake's symbols and images to show that to generalize about them is to
be an idiot. Most readers today will no doubt join in applying to Blake's critics
the *desiderata* that he put to historians:

> All that is not action is not worth reading. Tell me the What; I do not want you to
> tell me the Why, and the How; I can find that out myself, as well as you can, and
> I will not be fooled by you into opinions, that you please to impose, to disbelieve
> what you think improbable or impossible.
>
> [*DC*, E544]

Fewer readers, perhaps, would second the next step of the argument: "His opinions, who does not see spiritual agency, is not worth any man's reading." My concern here is to explore the "what" of Blake's symbols and images, beginning with Northrop Frye's observation at the conclusion of *Fearful Symmetry* that "Behind the pattern of images in poetry . . . is a pattern of words."[2] It is in this pattern of words that we discern "spiritual agency" and through literal meanings the most explicit imagination of literature itself. Blake's text is not strange, rather the reader is a stranger; the vision is literal, its criticism has too often been abstract.

What I intend here is a revaluation of the term "literal" through that standard trope of reversal employed to stir up the water of standing perceptions. To describe someone as possessing a "literal imagination" has often been to suggest that that person sees only the banal surface of things, the letters of the law; at the same time, "literal imagination" can suggest an industrial-strength, hard-core version of the faculty that has in fact opposed literalism ever since the discovery of its own pleasures. "Literal" can thus be brought to resonate through "imagination," literally naming two different contexts. And this, perhaps, is to create a third meaning, another context: that of the state in which *literal* imagination would be literal *imagination*. Such an imagination would, in keeping with its etymology (*littera*), identify itself in letters, that is to say, in the word and in writing.

Although Blake once describes himself as born and bound into language by a "gross tongue that cleaveth to the dust" (*M* 20.15), the bardic voice says, more emphatically, "Mark well my words" (*M* 2.25, and elsewhere). Blake's select vocabulary expresses not conceptual limitation but the deliberate intent to stress certain words to the point where they break their husks and reveal, in the word that appears most frequently in the *Blake Concordance*, "all."[3] All Blake's words can be appreciated in their aural, graphic, contemporary, and historical-etymological associations—each has its fourfold vision. The word "veil," to be discussed in a later chapter, assimilates in sound with "vale," in sound and graphics with "vein" and "vile," in literal similarity and reversal with "live" and "evil,"[4] and in semantic association with "tabernacle," "chastity," and "nature." I do not suggest that Blake was conscious of all these factors; I do argue that all are present in "the source . . . the Poetic Genius" (*ARO*).

Blake had a relationship with words in their literal being that is unique in literature. His sensitivity to the bearing of letter configuration—after changing from a leftward pointing serif on the letter *g* to a rightward one, he would even alter previously etched serifs[5]—offers tangible evidence that "every word and every letter is studied and put into its fit place" (*J* 3), that "poetry admits not a Letter that is Insignificant" (*VLJ*, E560), or that "ideas cannot be Given But in their minutely Appropriate Words" (*PA*, E576). In the careful work of re-touching, in the continual awareness of mirror-writing, Blake participated in, and manifested, a vision of the word as object, as other, and as divine, that stretches our imagination to its limits. The word becomes more than the mark of an idea; it becomes an eternal living form with its own personality, family, and destiny. John Wright concludes his study of "Blake's Relief-Etching Method" with the observation that Blake's "minutely expressive forms became known to their painstaking and inspired creator as a family of visionary figures whose real life is by no means confined to the illusive heaven of his problemat-ical 'meaning.'"[6] That these "minutely expressive forms" include and revolve around words may be seen everywhere in Blake's illuminated work. At times, as in *The Marriage of Heaven and Hell*, pl. 25 (copy C), words strain to become pure graphic form,

jealousy among the flaming hair.

and sometimes they succeed. The reader of Blake must acquire new sensitiv-ities to read the graphic signifiers identified as "words" on plate 22 (copy C) of *The Marriage*.

these words .

Plate 86 of *Jerusalem* (fig. 1), one of the very few plates Blake engraved without any "illumination," offers a different kind of literal picture. The text cannot be seen as a totality—viewed as a whole the lines seem almost to melt together, while at the same time particular words emerge as beacons or win-dows. As an experiment, figure 2 shows the same plate stripped to only a few words, including some I will emphasize in this study. To someone who has never read Blake, it will perhaps occasion no less confusion than the full plate. The point is that each word signifies so amply that even so skeletal a structure begins to bear (bare) meaning as each word finds relation to another. While this relational process occurs initially in the mind of the perceiver, it can develop through and toward structures in the "mind" of the text, and then further to relations in the "mind," or *episteme*, of English and collective imag-ination. For example, we note the repeated pairs "Spectres-cloud" and "clouds-Spectre," and mark the spectral nature of clouds and the cloudy nature of spectres not as a case of mimetic similarity, but as an instance of two words sharing in the same misty reference. Continuing each set, we might compare "Spectres-cloud-veil" with "Fibres-clouds-Spectres," thus relating "veil" to "Fibres" and hinting at a spectral, cloudy veil of clothing woven on cloud looms. We might continue indefinitely through various combinations: "cloud . . . Suns" transforms to "cloud . . . Sons," the "sandals" on Jerusalem's feet seem to turn into "seas roll" beneath the feet of Los. These constructions, of course, do not disclose anything about the narrative, but they do create aspects of the background and frame—the universe in which the narrative action (such as it is in this multistoried text) takes place. And, in large part, the reader's re-creation of that context is the purpose of the text and the way it is presented: the words of the plates have their own plots.

Blake's printing, his expansive meter, his punctuation, and his syntax ensure that his line will not be grasped at once. These conditions force the reader back to the individual words and syntagms, breaking up the line so that it may be reconstituted out of our associations. The rewritten text becomes an original one, since "all are alike in the Poetic Genius" (*ARO*) and able to join in the literal imagination of the Word.

> *And I heard the Name of their Emanations they are named Jerusalem*
>
> [*J* 99.5, the last line of the poem]

This *name* and its permutating *emana*tions are like "the *Amen*, the faithful and true witness" that tells John to "write: for these words are true and faithful" (Rev. 3:14, 21:5). At the beginning of *The Four Zoas*, Blake quotes John 1:14: "And the Word was made flesh, *and dwelt among us*" (καιˑ εσκηνωσεν ενˑ ημιν [Blake's punctuation]). Already, here are the grounds for a myth of logos. If the Spirit has been incarnated in language, then it should be possible to move through the corporality of the word back to the Spirit, to recognize—to name—the Word in the word. At the end of *Milton*, as at the close of *Jerusalem*, Blake again hears the name. Jesus is seen coming in "The Clouds of Ololon folded as a Garment [a gArMENt] dipped in blood" (42.12), a description returning us to the Revelation of John, where one who is "called Faithful and True"—the Amen—comes "clothed in a vesture dipped in blood: And his name is called the word of God" (19:11, 13). This name is the process, the idea, the being of naming with "a name written [inscribed], that no man knew" (19:12); for Blake it is

I see thy Form O lovely mild Jerusalem, Wing'd with Six Wings
In the opacous Bosom of the Sleeper, lovely Three-fold
In Head & Heart & Reins three Universes of love & beauty
Thy forehead bright: Holiness to the Lord, with Gates of pearl
Reflects Eternity beneath thy azure wings of feathery gold
Ribb'd delicate & clothd with feather'd gold & azure & purple
From thy white shoulders shadowing, purity in holiness!
Thence feather'd with soft crimson of the ruby bright as fire
Spreading into the azure wings which like a canopy
Bends over thy immortal Head in which Eternity dwells
Albion beloved Land; I see thy mountains & thy hills
And valleys & thy pleasant Cities Holiness to the Lord
I see the Spectres of thy Dead O Emanation of Albion.
Thy Bosom white, translucent coverd with immortal gems
A sublime ornament not obscuring the outlines of beauty
Terrible to behold for thy extreme beauty & perfection
Twelve-fold, here all the Tribes of Israel I behold
Upon the Holy Land: I see the River of Life & Tree of Life
I see the New Jerusalem descending out of Heaven,
Between thy Wings of gold & silver feather'd immortal
Clear as the rainbow, as the cloud of the Suns tabernacle

Thy Reins coverd with Wings translucent sometimes covering
And sometimes spread abroad reveal the flames of holiness
Which like a robe covers: & like a Veil of Seraphim
In flaming fire unceasing burns from Eternity to Eternity
Twelvefold I there behold Israel in her Tents
A Pillar of a Cloud by day: a Pillar of fire by night
Guides them: there I behold Moab & Ammon & Amalek
There Bells of silver round thy knees living articulate
Comforting sounds of love & harmony & on thy feet
Sandals of gold & pearl, & Egypt & Assyria before me
The Isles of Javan, Philistea, Tyre and Lebanon

Thus Los sings upon his Watch walking from Furnace to Furnace
He siezes his Hammer every hour, flames surround him as
He beats: seas roll beneath his feet, tempests muster
Aroud his head, the thick hail stones stand ready to obey
His voice in the black cloud, his Sons labour in thunders
At his Furnaces; his Daughters at their Looms sing woes
His Emanation separates in milky fibres agonizing
Among the golden Looms of Cathedron sending fibres of love
From Golgonooza with sweet visions for Jerusalem, wanderer

Nor can any consummate bliss without being Generated
On Earth of those whose Emanations weave the loves
Of Beulah for Jerusalem & Shiloh, in immortal Golgonooza
Concentering in the majestic form of Erin in eternal tears
Viewing the Winding Worm on the Desarts of Great Tartary
Viewing Los in his shudderings, pouring balm on his sorrows
So dread is Los's fury, that none dare him to approach
Without becoming his Children in the Furnaces of affliction

And Enitharmon like a faint rainbow waved before him
Filling with Fibres from his loins which reddend with desire
Into a Globe of blood beneath his bosom trembling in darkness
Of Albions clouds, he fed it, with his tears & bitter groans
Hiding his Spectre in invisibility from the timorous Shade
Till it became a separated cloud of beauty grace & love
Among the darkness of his Furnaces dividing asunder till
She separated stood before him a lovely Female weeping
Even Enitharmon separated outside, & his Loins closed
And heald after the separation: his pains he soon forgot:
Lured by her beauty outside of himself in shadowy grief.
Two Wills they had; Two Intellects: & not as in times of old.

Silent they wanderd hand in hand like two Infants wandring
From Enion in the desarts, terrified at each others beauty
Envying each other yet desiring, in all devouring Love

1. *Jerusalem*, pl. 86.

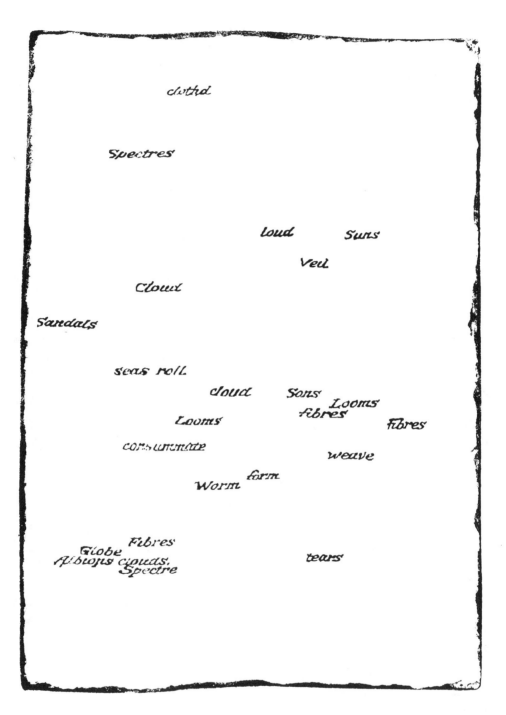

2. *Jerusalem*, pl. 86, edited.

Written within & without in woven letters: & the Writing
Is the Divine Revelation in the Litteral expression:
A Garment of War, I heard it namd the Woof of Six Thousand Years

[*M* 42.13–15]

Blake writes "Litteral" deliberately—that spelling was already an anachronism,[7] and he himself is fully aware of the accepted form for "literal fact" (*DC*, E546). "Litteral" emphasizes the "letter" that is its etymon, yet the poet "heard it"—the Writing—"namd"; and what is heard here is not an entity, but a process, a "going forth & returning" (*J* 99.2), a textual weaving. What Blake *does* hear (here) destroys the fiction of single-minded literalism and asserts instead the war/p and woof, the textuality and "fabric of Six Thousand Years" (*M* 22.19–20). Literal, again, does not mean actual, straightforward, or reduced:[8] to see or hear a word in or through its literal expression is not to see some single meaning, any more than meeting a friend is to see the letters of his or her name. Seeing and hearing the word is meeting it alive in its force-field of sound, etymology, graphic shape, contemporary applications, and varied associations.[9] This kind of attention, physically insisted upon by Blake's text, reveals that the keys to the gates of that text lie in its language: "its most *literal* aspect," as Maureen Quilligan says of allegory, "not in a translation of the story's events to a different (metaphorical) set of terms."[10]

The more deliberately the word is perceived, the more it begins to assert itself—to spell itself out—in all its associations and etymology, its eternal human form. Ratified and amended by generations of imagination, the word continually extends a covenant to inform us of its universe of signification. Every word is a parable about linguistic structure as incarnate human imagination:

every Word & Every Character
Was Human according to the Expansion or Contraction, the Translucence or
Opakeness of Nervous fibres such was the variation of Time & Space
Which vary according as the Organs of Perception vary

[*J* 98.35–38]

The word depends on how it is perceived. We do not create it, but rather reveal or limit it according to our own Translucence or Opakeness. Every word has unlimited potential ("In the beginning was the Word . . . and the Word was God"). It follows, as much psychoanalysis and structural anthropology suggest, that every time we use a word (or any other sign) we cannot possibly truly

know all we are saying—or, put another way, we always mean more than we
think and read more than we see. The word has a spirit of its own, more
expansive than the individual mind through which it speaks or is read. Like
Jesus—the Divine Imagination, Blake would say—the word is the reality in the
midst of us sent to reintegrate our fallen and disparate identities: "For where
two or three are gathered in my name, there am I in the midst of them" (Matt.
18:20). In reading or prayer or conversation or writing, the word is the medium
of communion.

For Blake, the "spirit of the word" is "the Poetic Genius," "genius" then still
implying an engendering, disseminating spirit:

> Principle 1st: That the Poetic Genius is the true Man. and that the body or
> outward form of Man is derived from the Poetic Genius. Likewise that the forms
> of all things are derived from their Genius. which by the Ancients was call'd an
> Angel & Spirit & Demon.
>
> *[ARO]*

The poet close to the Poetic Genius gives the message of words—his words
summon a response from knowledge stored up in the reader's words. Hence the
common impression on first reading Blake that "it makes sense"—though
exactly what sense is difficult to say. In this connection, one thinks of Blake's
repeated statements about the inspired source of his poetry: "I have written
this Poem from immediate Dictation, twelve or sometimes twenty or thirty
lines at a time, without Premeditation & even against my Will" (E729), or
again, "I dare not pretend to be any other than the secretary the Authors are
in Eternity" (E730). Some Other speaks through Blake, whether we call that
other God, the Poetic Genius, or the Word. To be sure, whatever may be made
of his claim to be a mere "secretary," the extensively revised manuscripts and
carefully altered plates show that Blake was critically aware of the language
and words he transcribed. Still, these and other forceful statements concerning
external or eternal authors may stand as Blake's comment on his status as
"subject"—his identity is subject to "Litteral Expression." Though he could
lightly label himself "a Mental Prince" and wonder "what he might do if he sat
down to write" (E580, 501), Blake annihilates his (and thus the reader's)
"authority": he will not be a selfhood talking to itself or to other selfhoods
while there is the waiting (self-)communication of Albion and Jerusalem, of
language and Divine Imagination. The power of "his" words bears witness to
the reality of his belief in the socializing and sacralizing power in language.

Applying Blake's statements on vision semantically, one expects the word to
be minutely organized, with a firm "bounding outline" (E550). For all his

disgust with John Locke, Blake mirrors his concern for "clear and distinct" ideas and for words to best express those ideas. But Blake must reject Locke's contention that words are the arbitrary "signs of our ideas only,"[11] since for Blake words are living beings:

> *The Holy Word,*
> *That walk'd among the ancient trees*
>> ["Introduction," *SE* 4–5]

or again:

> *But first they said: (& their Words stood in Chariots in array*
> *Curbing their Tygers with golden bits & bridles of silver & ivory)*
>> [*J* 55.34–35]

Words have the power of life—or death to those who misuse them:

> *What have I said? What have I done? O all-powerful Human Words!*
> *You recoil back upon me in the blood of the Lamb slain in his Children.*
>> [*J* 24.1–2][12]

and:

> *such are the words of man to man*
> *In the great Wars of Eternity, in fury of Poetic Inspiration*
> *To build the Universe stupendous: Mental forms Creating.*
>> [*M* 30.18–20]

Words (we begin to circle around the literally obvious) are the building-blocks of Blake's "Universe stupendous"—which is language. The words are not signs for what is seen (*idea*); rather, what appears is a *phainomenon* or showing-forth of words, a *logosophany.* Since Blake's work follows (individual and collective) mental life and perception, it must of necessity focus on language as "that system of signs which retrieves for us the process of intellection."[13] Blake's words are the foundation of his work, which is an exploration of what it is possible to say, of how directly the Poetic Genius can speak and of how directly the Poetic Genius/Imagination/Los can speak through a language that is itself his creation:

> *(I call them by their English names: English, the rough basement.*
> *Los built the stubborn structure of the Language, acting against*
> *Albions melancholy, who must else have been a Dumb despair.)*
>> [*J* 36(40).58–60]

Blake's language clearly intersects with ours at some level, and that common ground is "the rough basement" from which we build Jerusalem. For Blake, as for Heidegger, "language is the house of Being" in which we live; Los is its guardian. There are many avenues of "signification" or "meaning" (e.g., history, psychology, gnosticism, science) by which we may follow our language into Los's stubborn—unyielding, untamable—structure, but only when we become its subject, when we have joined in its building, can we begin to live that language in its own terms. As Yeats in the end realized about Blake: we must ourselves remake.[14]

Many labels have been given to the quality of Blake's language that will be emphasized throughout this study. Perhaps the most venerable and entrenched is "ambiguity"[15]—but one should feel some reluctance at applying it to a poet who in his single use of the concept condemns "ambiguous words blasphemous" (*FZ* 53.26, E336). "Tell him to be no more dubious: demand explicit words" (*J* 17.60), Blake writes, and he repeatedly states that "the Infinite alone resides in Definite & Determinate Identity" (*J* 55.64). On the other hand, Blake creates verbal contexts that some call ambiguous ("That which can be made Explicit to the Idiot is not worth my care" [E702]). The issue, evidently, is not the context but the kind of perception brought to bear by the reader. The reader's perception must educate itself through the multiple possibilities of a context that continually attempts to raise the reader to its expanding field of reference. Ambiguity is not an appropriate word to apply to Blake because the very word and its associations presuppose the binary logical thought process that Blake targeted for transformation: ambiguity is in the mind of the beholder. More recent terms for the quality of unambiguous multiple possibilities we are examining are "concomitant meaning" (O. Barfield), "plurisignation" (P. Wheelwright), "extralocution" (W. Nowottny), manifold meaning, multivalent meaning, holophrase, and connotation. My preferences are "polysemy" and "multidimensionality."

For Paul Ricoeur, "polysemy" is mediate between "word" and "metaphor" and thus the means of "creativity in language." Polysemy "is a universal feature of words in natural languages" and ordains the two functional traits of such languages: "economy at the level of the code, and contextual dependence at the level of the message."[16] The polysemous word is "economical" in that it permits a condensed vocabulary and expression, and contextually dependent, according to Ricoeur, in that it relies on the speech situation to point up the pertinent *seme*, or unit of meaning. Context thus emerges as the controlling limit on meaning, and struggles over context lead to the fact, announced by Northrop Frye, of "the principle of manifold or 'polysemous' meaning": "The thing that has established it is the simultaneous development of several different schools of modern criticism, each making a distinctive choice of symbols in its analysis."[17] So each of the various influential interpretations of Blake shows us that the other critical contexts are incomplete and that the text that prompted them all is polysemous. Rather than add to the infinitely proliferating possibilities of symbolic commentary, we might strive instead to study how Blake's polysemous words and context support each other. For, at least in part, how his text works is what it means. Understanding this process depends upon recovering a literal imagination and refusing to read in symbols, metaphors, or figurative language in general—if we encounter something "burning bright," we should at least admit its fiery body.

I introduce the term "multidimensional" for its suggestion of varied spatial fields: it joins "polysemy" to suggest an idea of the word as space in which each *seme*, each golden "bit" of information, opens a dimension, making the word like the rugged diamond "open all within" (*M* 28.37). Each one of these openings into the word represents the passageway for one fibre traversing the text—the polysemous word can thus also be compared to the "nodal point" (*Knotenpunkt*) Freud saw constituted, or "over-determined," by (or at) the intersection of various lines of association, or chains of meaning.[18] We shall have to wrestle with the interchange between "chains" and "fibres" in later chapters. The concept of the nodal point, like Ricoeur's characterization of the economy and contextual dependence of the polysemous word, presents two different approaches. Focusing outward on context, the critic can, in effect, unravel individual threads passing through the point, stringing the text's words in order along a line of thought. Focusing inward on the condensed economy of the polysemous word, the student enters the space of the sign to see the various lines crossing through it, to enumerate its valences, to trace its configuration: the sign becomes "a sensuous idea." This is to enter "inwards into the Worlds of Thought: into Eternity" (*J* 5.19), into the words that form the synapses of imagination's divine body, into the germ of vision, the *semes* that form the seams of Blake's fourfold textuality.

This book studies a few of the polysemous words that best seem to suggest the process of Blake's language: words that join together the converging folds, words that carry the burden of his vision. Many terms perhaps to be expected in a consideration of Blake's significant words are not discussed here, but I believe that the discussions that are offered describe an approach applicable to many of those unexamined. I consider words that seem particularly "literal," so most readily told, and so, I hope (trusting to pertinent Proverbs of Hell), imagined, understood, proved.[19] Some of these words, like "fibre," "lamentation," and "mourning," are not entered in S. Foster Damon's *A Blake Dictionary* or the extensive "Index of Symbols" compiled by D. J. Sloss and J. P. R. Wallis for their 1926 edition of *The Prophetic Writings*: all are words that seem unexceptional in English and, at first, in Blake; but it is precisely such polysemic "ordinary language . . . into whose deepest recesses the *episteme* plunges."[20]

We might consider briefly the examples of two other poets. "There is ample evidence," writes Peter J. Gillett, "that Tennyson's poems often grew out of 'germ-phrases,' groups of words the denotation of which might be unclear but which seemed to him important, pregnant, and poetic."[21] Gillett cites F. T. Palgrave's report that "'more than once [Tennyson] said that his poems sprang from a "nucleus"; some one word, may be, or brief melodious phrase which had floated through the brain, as it were unbidden.'" And, Gillett notes, Dylan Thomas described how, beginning with his hearing of nursery rhymes, his "'love for the real life of words increased'" until he knew that he must "'live *with* them and *in* them always.'" Thomas added that the first thing was to feel and know the sound and substance of words; "'what I was going to do with those words . . . , what I was going to *say* through them, would come later.'" These accounts may be linked to Freud's belief that

> in schizophrenia *words* are subjected to the same process as that which makes the dream-images out of latent dream-thoughts—to what we have called the primary psychical process. They undergo condensation, and by means of displacement transfer their cathexes to one another in their entirety. The process may go so far that a single word, if it is specially suitable on account of its numerous connections, takes over the representation of a whole train of thought.[22]

Perhaps one link between the "poet" and the "madman" is just such a literal imagination that treats even single words in earnest. Anthony Wilden argues that "we might even say that the 'schizophrenic' is responding to a pathological environment" of empty, purely informational speech "by trying to BE the analogue. . . . The 'schizophrenic' is most concerned to break the pathological boundaries (oppositions) which are regarded as 'adequate' and 'normal' in our culture."[23] Annotating J. G. Spurzheim's *Observations on Insanity* sometime in the last years of his life, Blake reports that the dead William Cowper came to him and said, "O that in the bosom of God I was hid. You retain health & yet are as mad as any of us all—over us all—mad as a refuge from unbelief—from Bacon Newton & Locke" (E663).

The classical and Renaissance organization of verbal ambiguity within various systems of rhetoric accompanied the general concern for "argument" ("making clear") or correct reasoning from fixed and established terms. Interested in "proving" their positions, philosophers and rhetoricians had little tolerance for the various equivocations or grammatical ambiguities knowingly or unwittingly employed to hinder the argument. While the use of such figures as amphibology and syllepsis was labeled "fallacious reasoning," the figures or words in themselves were of no particular concern. But beginning with Bacon in the early seventeenth century, ambiguity in words themselves was actively condemned as a major offender in the "false appearances that are imposed upon us by words."[24] Bacon introduced a new attitude (cf. Wilden's "pathological boundaries") in which language was no longer valued as the medium of argumentation, but distrusted as an impediment to the discovery and communication of information about things, or *scientia*. Words are only tokens for the things that make up reality, so it is "the first distemper of learning, when men study words and not matter." Hobbes, Locke, and Hume each amplified this attitude in the ensuing generations. Indeed, one basic concern that joins *Jerusalem*'s infernal trinity of "Bacon, Newton & Locke" is their shared mistrust of verbal reality and their desire for a pure mimesis through unambiguous, univocal language based, implicitly, on the idea of the arbitrary signifier. These desires prompted the century's fantasies of a "universal character" with a word for every thing and their practical application, as urged for the Royal Society, in "Mathematical plainness" of speech.[25] This outlook, despite Swift's parody and the Scriblerus Club's dedicated study of "the Abuse of Words," governed the eighteenth-century's aesthetic rejection of the pun; Johnson, sympathetic and sensitive reader though he was, criticized wordplay in Shakespeare as possessing "some malignant power over his mind. . . . A quibble was for him the fatal Cleopatra for which he lost the world and was content to lose it."[26]

The acceptance of polysemy did not end, of course—as Sterne's popularity illustrates—but it was a polysemy cut off from any possible sacred or numinous potency of language. In the domain of the plain style, *nomen* has nothing to do with *numen*. The ineffability invoked by polysemous language was, however, strongly asserted by two writers whose early influence Blake variously acknowledges: they are Jacob Boehme, with his conception of "the Language of Nature," and Emanuel Swedenborg, with his more diffuse system of "Correspondences." Boehme believed that the revelation of "the Language of Nature" given to him was an insight into the language of Adam. The revelation consisted "in comprehending the expressive value of the sounds making up the word."[27] Boehme imagined a sense of the *process* for recovering the Language from the traces left in various languages, not the Language itself. William Law explained in a preface to his edition of Boehme:

> And as one Jot or Tittle of the Word of God shall not pass away, till all be fulfilled, so there is no Tittle of any Letter, that is proceeded from that eternal essential Word, as all things are, but has its weighty Signification, in the deep Understanding, in that Word from whence it came, even in the Voices of all Men and Sounds of all other Creatures . . . that Language shows the greatest Mysteries that have ever been in the Nature of any Thing, in the Letters of that Word by which it is expressed. . . .[28]

The word is polysemous in its very constitution. In the *Mysterium Magnum*, Boehme stated that "man has God's Word *in him*, which created him; understand, the Word has imprinted and formed itself with the Creating." The outward world, Earth itself, he continues, "was amassed and compacted through the Word" (3:95). The very idea of language is the metaphor. "All Words and Names that are in every Language of every Nation," he writes, must be considered "every one according to its own understanding [and meaning]"; the actual languages may differ, but their operation according to the Language of Nature remains constant. For Boehme, "language is the agent of man's likeness to God."[29]

Swedenborg is not as much concerned with words and language at large as with making his case for the natural and spiritual polysemy of each word in the Bible. "The Stile of the Word is of such a Nature, as to contain what is Holy in every Verse, in every Word, and in some cases in every Letter; and hence the Word joineth Man with the Lord, and openeth Heaven."[30] For Swedenborg every word offers a literal meaning and an "internal" one, which in turn consists of a spiritual meaning and a celestial meaning inaccessible to human intelligence; this idea that "the Word of the Lord is Holy" and contains "a three-fold Sense . . . united by Correspondences" was part of the Swedenborgian manifesto signed by W. Blake and C. Blake on April 13, 1789.[31] "A correspondence," Blake might have read, "is the actual relation subsisting between a *natural* object and a spiritual subject," though the exact operation of this "actual relation" ("as the ectype to its prototype, or as a face to face in a glass") is a mystery.[32] For example, in the Spiritual Sense of the Word, "by a Garden, a Grove, and a Woods, are meant Wisdom, Intelligence, Science."[33] This language of correspondences is the language of God that has been lost and corrupted. Nonetheless, the premise of this symbol-laden science of correspondence is the literal meaning, for which Swedenborg expresses great re-spect: "Without the letter, the Word would be like a body without skin or bones, like a brain without membranes and skull."[34] "It appears," he writes in *Arcana Coelestia*, "as if the literal sense vanishes or dies through the internal sense; but on the contrary it does not vanish, still less dies; but through the internal sense it lives."[35] For Blake—to anticipate the argument—the internal sense lives through the literal. Also significant for Blake, Swedenborg imagines that "the literal sense" when it is being read ("especially by a little boy or girl") becomes "more beautiful and delightful by degrees as it ascends, and at last it is presented before the Lord as the image of a human being, in which and by which heaven is represented in its whole complex, not as it is, but as the Lord wills it to be, namely, a likeness of Himself" (*Arcana Coelestia*, n. 1871).

"W. B. *was* mad about languages," wrote Samuel Palmer;[36] that is to say, mad about words, translations of the spirit into the flesh. Gilchrist tells us that Blake "was always willing to apply himself to the vocabulary of a language for the purpose of reading a great original author," and would learn the language "substantially, if not grammatically."[37] Unlike other great English poets, Blake does not seem to have been taught foreign languages in his youth. In the languages he acquired—French, Latin, Greek,[38] and Hebrew by 1804 (when he was forty-seven), and Italian in old age—he was largely self-taught: his was an individual appropriation rather than an inscribed, rote memorization of for-eign letters. His desire for vocabularies and his application suggest a mind extraordinarily attuned to the richness of the word as sign.[39] For example, "Heshbon," the name of a town built by "the children of Reuben" (Num. 32:37) also signifies "reasonings" in Hebrew. In *Jerusalem* Blake draws on both these significations, revealing "Heshbon" as the polysemous name of an inter-related psychological state and historical reality: "In reasonings Reuben re-turns / To Heshbon" (32[36].9–10).[40] This kind of play underlies the much-discussed names of many of Blake's characters—Palamabron, for example, whose connection with the Greek *palamā* (hand, palm) appears in the formula "the hand(s) of Palamabron." In the privacy of the *Notebook*, we see Blake creating his own puns: the artistic connoisseurs and amateurs are "the Cun-ning sures & Aim at yours," Tom Cooke's poor rendering of Hogarth is con-demned from "Skumference to Center," and the aesthetic cant of the "je ne sais quois" is transformed into the injunction to "never flinch but keep up the Jaw / About freedom & Jenny suck awa'" (E510; E505; E510, cf. E869).

The inspiring word, the epic-making "winged word," was for Blake far more than convention: according to Crabb Robinson, "his books—(& his MSS. are immense in quantity) are dictations from the Spirits—he told me yesterday that when he writes—it is for the Spirits only—he sees the words fly about the room the moment he has put them on paper And his book is then published."[41] The *concordia discors* of such flying words can be studied not only in Blake's text, but through the discourse of the *Blake Concordance*. As every reader will soon realize, these pages depend heavily on that valuable work, the ultimate Blake dictionary. Words fly about—each like Blake's image of "every bird" as a "world of delight, clos'd by your senses five"—but through the *Concordance* we may trace the worlds in their trajectories. The *Concordance* gives literal evidence for polysemy, the world in every word, the steps of its dance. The implicit assumption here is that, just as "not one Moment / Of Time is lost, nor one Event of Space unpermanent" (*M* 22.18–19), so each word in Blake's text recalls its earlier uses, associations, and contexts, and foreshadows the later ones. Let the reader be warned once before continuing this road of synchronic excess, such an attitude risks doing violence to the diachronic aspect of Blake's vocabulary, to the real movements in the development of his thought. Still, the lifelong development of an individual's thought takes place against a nearly synchronous moment in the life of language, so that the movement of individual thought can in part be described as the selective development of the network already latent in those particular words—nodal points—that thought has taken to organize its perceptions. The network, the text, grows from the available nodal points, not the other way around.[42] Polysemy is always available, words and their meanings are always flying about, though it has long been necessary for some to deny this for fear they themselves will fly apart. At the turn of the century the founder of "semantics," Michel Bréal, wrote, "We are not even troubled to suppress the other meanings of the word: these meanings do not exist for us, they do not cross the threshold of our consciousness. It is bound to be so, since happily the association of ideas is for most men based on essentials of things, and not on the sound."[43] Closed to our senses five, other meanings "do not exist for us." The opposing tack is to fathom, to sound the mute: tracing the phonemic, semantic, and graphic concord; assimilating the winged, reverberating joy of the polysemous word. "We look for resolution of the vibrations," writes one student of Blake's style, "and find none."[44]

In recent years a number of critics have sensed or pointed to the polysemous verbal play in the Blakean text: one notes "his varied verbal manipulations, which include puns or plays on words; contradictory yoking of two unlike words . . . and ultimately a vast, seemingly endless equation of nouns and adjectives"; another sees "an almost Joycean awareness of the manipulability of words." A third is "convinced that Blake delighted to use a number of quite different lines of thought, cultures and aspects of life, just as he enjoyed a play on words, as James Joyce did later on." A fourth concludes that "apart from Spenser and Shakespeare there have been few writers in our language more verbally inventive than Blake." Another, discussing Blake's use of word histories, argues that "his exploitation of etymology owes . . . much to his conviction that wisdom comes from penetrating to the inner workings of phenomena"; and yet another describes his "flexible or multiple exploration of the word."[45] But, as Swedenborg warned, accepting the polysemous, counter-logical figure can be a demanding experience:

> If any Person who is under the Influence of Falses, looketh at the Word, as it lieth in its holy Repository, there ariseth a thick Darkness before his Eyes, in Consequence whereof the Word appears to him of a black Colour, and sometimes as if it was covered with Soot; but if the same Person toucheth the Word, it occasioneth an Explosion, attended with a loud noise, and he is thrown to a Corner of the Room where he lieth, for about the Space of an Hour, as if he was dead.
>
> [*True Christian Religion*, 1:282–83]

This was not peculiar to Swedenborg. A 1795 tract on language, "founded on the Association of Words and Ideas" as proposed by David Hartley, observes that "the task is extremely dangerous to the inquirer, if fully and fairly performed, for when the light first breaks in upon the long-concealed sense of any interesting word, it is like the explosion of gunpowder."[46] The realization of interrelations unperceived before explodes the reader's sense of self and context in the experience of literal imagination. Appendix 1 catalogues some Blakean detonations.

An example illustrative of Blake's polysemous and multidimensional practice may be found toward the bottom of *Jerusalem*, plate 21: it suggests the heading WAR-WORSHIP and requires that the category of "graphic polysemy" be added to the discussion of Blake's verbal effects.

I see them die beneath the whips of the Captains, they are taken
In solemn pomp into Chaldea across the bredths of Europe
Six months they lie embalmd in silent death: war-shipped
Carried in Arks of Oak before the armies in the spring
Bursting their Arks they rise again to life: they play before
the Armies: I hear their loud cymbals & their deadly cries

Editions before 1982 transcribe the final word of line 44 as "worshipped," though any close consideration of the plate's lettering finds the word "warshipped" inscribed as well. A comparison of the "worshipped" *o*'s in *Jerusalem* plates 77 and 29[33] shows how differently the shape of the letter in that word can be crafted. The context creates another instant in Blake's identification of early Jewish history and contemporary Britain using the multiple reference of "the Ark": the "Arks of Oak" or Arks Royal of the British Navy, which go "before the armies" (21.45), and the "golden ark" of Israel carried, again, "before the Armies" (22.5). One "intertext" is the story of David bringing the Ark to Jerusalem, as twice told in the Old Testament. The account in Chronicles begins with David consulting "the captains," the standard Biblical word for "generals," but neatly applicable to Blake's plural context. David and all the house of Israel play before the Ark "on all manner of instruments . . . on timbrels, and on coronets, and on cymbals" (2 Sam. 6:5). Both these accounts are remembered for the story of Uzzah, who "put forth his hand to the ark of God" to steady it, but incurred the wrath of God and was smitten "for his error; and there he died by the ark of God."[47] It is clear, particularly considering a later context (*J* 65.33–36) that those "warshipped" are sailors, so "their deadly cries" should be the naval cheer "huzza!".[48] Such "deadly cries" could perhaps be discussed as the loud (verbal) symbols Blake hears and plays on. Whatever else we may bring to this complex passage, we have been given a parable in "one" word: here to worship is to warship; that which should be most precious is embalmed in a body of death, in a grave the reader must enter to burst.

CHAPTER TWO

Entering the Grave

(Grave the sentence deep)

William Blake,
"The Little Girl Lost"

AMONG HIS FEW EXAMPLES "in regard of Equivocals" in *Essay towards a Real Character and a Philosophical Language* (1668), John Wilkins notes that, "The word Grave signifies both Sober, and Sepulcher, and to Carve, etc."[1] The "etc." no doubt includes the verbal sense of "inter" or "entomb," for which Johnson's *Dictionary* cited *Timon of Athens*: "And ditches grave you all!" To grave, Wilkins says, is to carve. Hence, to sculpt, as in Milton's image of a "Freeze, with bossy Sculptures graven" (*PL* 1.716). The word in its sculptural sense remains memorialized in the Authorized Version, with its description of the infamous "graven image," the free-standing golden calf (Ex. 32:4, Deut. 4:16). Sculpting, as the engraver's Latin tag "sculpsit" suggests, was very much a part of the engraver's idiom. But, by the early eighteenth century, the sculptural implication of the original French loanword *graver* seems to have bowed before the powerful descendant of Old English *grafan*, "to dig." To grave became to carve downward into a surface: "Grave in the tables of your heart," says Locke. As a result, the second loanword, "engrave," became the dominant term for the graphic art, further distancing it from the sepulchral taint of "inter." The history of "grave" manifests unconscious associations by which engraving may be perceived as digging and burying as much as sculpting. With the conscious poet and engraver these associations proliferate.

We enter the secrets of the word "grave" with "The Little Girl Lost" (originally in *Songs of Innocence*, later transferred to the other state):

> *In futurity*
> *I prophetic see*
> *That the earth from sleep*
> *(Grave the sentence deep)*
>
> *Shall arise. . . .*
>   [1–5]

For whom is this coffin of parentheses intended, and what does it hold? Does the engraving "I" wish to etch the plate of its as yet incomplete sentence more deeply? Such a need, with its interrupting importance, hints at some doubting hesitation—or perhaps the prognosticated outcome is felt to be so distant that, like a tombstone placed under the open sky, the prophecy must be designed to withstand the elements. Perhaps it is aimed at the reader whom the poet wishes to impress profoundly: "Then hear my words, and grave them in thy mind!"[2] On the other hand, it may retrospectively be perceived that while "grave" offers no imperative, "the sentence" offers another kind of command. As Robert Essick notes, "it is a simple pun converting 'grave' from verb to noun that transforms graphic reference into prophecy."[3] Graves, like sleep, are to be risen from: for the "bodies of the saints which slept" until Jesus' resurrection and then "arose" (Matt. 27:52); for the Youth and the pale Virgin who "Arise from their graves and aspire" ("Ah! Sunflower"); and for the reader-"spectator," who, if he entered Blake's "images of wonder . . . then would he arise from his Grave" (*VLJ*, E560). So the vision that the Earth "shall arise," indicates that she is at present in the deep sleep of the grave. Earth's grave sentence was, then, the "sentence of death"—in Blackstone's words, "the most terrible and highest judgment in the laws of England."[4] This most grave judgment may be one form of "the terrible Sentence" referred to in an early opening to *The Four Zoas*: "Whosoever reads / If with his Intellect he comprehend the terrible Sentence / The heavens quake" (E819). Comprehending our own sentence to the grave entails a transformation in the mind's understanding of itself and its relation to the world. But the deep sentence engraved on Earth's grave—that she from sleep shall arise—emphasizes its own transitory status; as in 1 Corinthians: "Behold, I show you a mystery: We shall not all sleep. . . ." (15:51).

So, sleeping words are laid in order into the "silent repositories" (James Hervey's image)[5] of sentences or verses, or—for the poet who "would have all the writing Engraved instead of Printed" (*IM*, E465)[6]—laid deeply into the "ground" of the plate to await their sure resurrection in our eyes and minds. In luxurious eighteenth-century quartos and folios, one reader observes, "the individual words stand out in bold relief, defined against the expanse of white which surrounds them." This urges the reader "to linger over the images evoked by the printed characters."[7] But Blake's reader is able to linger over characters—engraved marks, χαρακτήρες—themselves, like Hervey in his *Meditations among the Tombs* approaching the funeral marks to "inquire of the stone, 'Who or what, is beneath the surface?'" One of Blake's illustrations to Gray's "Elegy in a Country Church-Yard" (no. 8) shows a figure studying a gravestone "spelt by th'unletter'd"—the lying inscription reads, "DUST THOU ART / HERE LIETH / Wm. Blake," with his age indistinctly added. The quintessential signifier—the *sēma* (or σῆμα, "tomb," "grave")—is the grave-marker, words written to signify what is beneath. Who or what, the reader may inquire of the page, lies beneath or behind its inscriptions? In the *Notebook*, Blake imagines epitaphs etched, like copper plates, "with tears of aqua fortis."[8] *King Henry IV, Part 2* presents books turned to graves and ink to blood (IV.i.50), while Henry Vaughan sees, in the "curious book" of time, "in that same page thy humble grave."[9] In Pope's *Dunciad*, Dulnesse urges her critics to attack the "standard-Authors" and "Leave not a foot of verse, a foot of stone, / A Page, A Grave, that they can call their own" (4.127–28). Swift, more direct, suggests that we "for Learning's mighty Treasures look / In that deep Grave a Book," since "she there does all her Treasures hide" and "her troubled Ghost still haunts there since she dy'd."[10] As the work of the grave is corruption of the body, Blake anticipates and hastens the process "by printing in the infernal method, by corrosives" (*MHH* 14). While the printed word dies in its superficiality, the word etched in relief arises, aspiring to display "the infinite which was hid."[11] Indeed, its aspiration is the guarantee of its resurrection.

To engrave is to dig in words, so to bury them. This in turn makes words into seeds, the emblems of resurrection from earth: to engrave is to sow. Theodore Thass-Thienemann discusses at length the "unconscious identification of 'word' and 'seed,'" showing, in particular, their connection by the multiple reference to "gathering, picking fruit" and "speaking" or "reading" of the Greek λέγω, Latin *legō*, and Germanic *lesan*.[12] The association was readily available in the Bible; in the parable of the sower, "the seed is the word of God" (Luke 8:11), for "the sower soweth the word" (Mark 4:14), and Peter urges his readers to love one another, "being born again, not of corruptible seed, but of incorruptible, by the word of God" (1 Peter 1:23). So Blake links "the Seed of

Contemplative Thought the Writings of the Prophets" (*VLJ*, E555). Like engraved bodies of the dead, seeds first sleep in the earth; the "Wild Flower" sings:

> *I slept in the earth*
> *In the silent night*
> [E472]

If the song that is the germ of the "Introduction" to *Songs of Innocence* could speak in the first person, it might recount a similar tale: paradoxically, now that it is written down in a book, "every child may joy to hear." Containing literal seeds, the grave produces "blossoms sweet" (E480).

The engraved line is hollow until filled with the body of ink (as is the "hollow reed" of the "Introduction"), for which it offers an all-too-transient resting place. Thel—"listning to the voices in the ground"—comes "to her own grave plot" and hears the "voice of sorrow breathed from the hollow pit" (6.8–10). The hollowness of the grave is also that of the womb, waiting to be filled:

> *The Grave shrieks with delight, & shakes*
> *Her hollow womb, & clasps the solid stem:*
> *Her bosom swells with wild desire*
> [*SL* 7.35–37]

The identification of tomb with womb is long standing: "The earth that's Nature's mother is her tomb; / What is her burying grave that is her womb."[13] For Blake, too, the images are closely bound, as in the following lines, which also make clear their association with engraving ("impressions of . . . the plates," as Blake wrote in 1804 [E745]):

> *. . . the Caverns of the Grave & places of Human Seed*
> *Where the impressions of Despair & Hope enroot forever*
> [*FZ* 44.3–4, E329]

The grave, as "Death's Door," offers a passageway leading from above to underground. To inter is to "enter," a word repeated four times in as many lines as Thel enters "the eternal gates" (5.15–6.2); once "enter'd," Thel sees "the couches of the dead." Crossing that door of perception effects a total transformation:

For God himself enters Death's Door always with those that enter
And lays down in the Grave with them, in Visions of Eternity
[*M* 32.40–41]

Such visions are the subject and object of Blake's engraving. *Jerusalem* opens
with a depiction of Los stepping over the threshold of an arched version of
"Death's Door"—entering the page and the underlying poem—which is
inscribed on one proof sheet as "the Void . . . which if enterd into /
Englobes itself & becomes a Womb, such was Albions Couch." Los is entering this
written crypt to unearth "the secrets of the grave," "the secrets of Eternity,"
"the Wonders of the Grave": "the wond'rous art of writing," which man
received "in mysterious Sinais awful cave."[14]

Milton similarly opens with its protagonist entering the dark ground—the
"plot"—of the plate and poem (fig. 3). Milton, not surprisingly, is a graver
matter;[15] the white-line technique seems designed to insist that the spectator
perceive the skein of lines that engrave Milton's naked body at the same time as
the figure itself rises bodily from the grave.[16] With its strongly articulated lines,
Blake's figure stresses his rejection of standard convention as stated by the
Encyclopaedia Britannica in 1771: "The engraver must avoid making very acute
angles, especially in representing flesh, when he crosses the first strokes with the
second, because it will form a very disagreeable piece of tabby-like lattice-
work" (s.v. "Engraving"). The cross-hatching offers, instead, a literal version of
"the Grave, / Dark Lattice! Letting in Eternal Day."[17] Plate 9 of *America* offers
another striking example of the grave disclosing itself (fig. 4); here, as Essick
notes, "The supine child almost disappears beneath the vegetation surrounding him, but the lines used to suggest vegetation can more immediately be
recognized as constituting a linear web that develops into crosshatching on the
right and up the left margin. The technique used to create the lines is at the
heart of the design's iconography."[18] The child is a kind of engraved seed, a
sign—like Milton's body—that institutes context and information; it recalls,
perhaps, John 12:24: "Except a corn of wheat fall in the ground and die, it
abideth alone; but if it die, it bringeth forth much fruit." An equally dramatic
example of engraving discourse is the title page to *The Book of Urizen* (fig. 5).
Here Urizen sits with (in some versions) a quill in one hand and an etching
needle in the other, writing on a tombstone.[19] Behind him, as a double
headstone, are the graven tablets of the law, while beneath him is a large open
book ("that deep Grave a Book"). Urizen, himself sitting in a vault, writes the
epitaph of the arts in their contemporary forms of reproductive engraving

3. *Milton*, pl. 1.

4. *America,* pl. 9, detail.

and imitative poetry—the grave of imagination at the hands of the law. The illustration seems to ask the viewer to "awake beyond the Grave!" (*J* 31[35].10), that is, for Urizen arisen. The "net of Religion" entangling Urizen on the final plate of his book may, however, be seen as another version of the linear web he was engraving on the first, reiterating the point that Urizen and his reader are equally caught in his grave condition.

"The Grave," writes Blake, "is Heaven's golden Gate" (E480). The "gates of the Grave" (*SL* 7.8) lead to "the Caverns of the Dead," one of the important settings for the Blakean drama. A "Memorable Fancy" of *The Marriage of Heaven and Hell* suggests that printing takes place in a cave (pl. 15), the cave that may then also lie behind as well as beneath the page. So in "Night the Ninth" of *The Four Zoas*, the "odors of life" (like vocative doors of perception) arise and sing about wine/print making: "O terrible wine presses of Luvah O Caverns of the Grave / How lovely the delights of those risen again from death" (136.1–2, E404). A notebook poem on "The Caverns [Visions, *deleted*] of the Grave" points to the relation between Eternity and the graves of print:

Reengravd Time after Time
Ever in their youthful prime
My Designs unchangd remain
Time may rage but rage in vain
For above Times troubled Fountains
On the Great Atlantic Mountains
In my Golden House on high
There they Shine Eternally
[E480, E858]

5. *The Book of Urizen*, pl. 1.

"Engraving," Blake wrote Hayley, "is Eternal work" (E743).

The wonder of the grave is the secret of spiritual transformation. Believing such transformation to be possible and necessary in life, Blake found in the rich vocabulary dealing with the grave one way of envisioning the reader's experience with his etchings and engravings. Words are to be "laid in." The spectator is to "enter into" the engraving. The engraved page may prompt several reactions. We may ("God us keep!") be put to sleep in a single vision of the embedded lines. Or we may enter the page, but, like Thel overcome with fear, refuse to die—to give up our preconceptions—and so flee out of the book. For, in entering the grave, we cross over to our own "land unknown," approaching the hollow pit of print from which any voice whatever may at first emerge. That voice may be the reader's own, fearfully projected on the text; or it may be one that speaks not from a repressed unconscious but from a realm outside our comprehension, a realm that, being entered, cannot be denied. We all know the desire not to know, to misread, or, having read, to forget. Sometimes we enter, but cannot lie down in the grave. A third reaction is one of surprise and wonder, indicative perhaps of our need to know more. This response leads further into Blake and the grave, leaving the Earth behind. For the "desire to know" is none other than that "God" or Divine Imagination who "lays down in the Grave . . . in Visions of Eternity." Blake says that his "images of Wonder" are always entreating the spectator "to leave mortal things as he must know" (*VLJ*, E560). The etched and engraved poem is the setting for the death of the reader, a death synonymous with imaginative transformation and rebirth, lamentation and morning.

CHAPTER THREE

Lamentation, Mourning, and Morning

> *And when I looked, behold, an hand was sent unto me; and, lo, a roll of a book was therein;*
>
> *And he spread it before me; and it was written within and without: and there was written therein lamentations, and mourning, and woe.*
>
> *MOREOVER he said unto me, Son of man, eat that thou findest; eat this roll, and go speak unto the house of Israel.*
>
> *. . . Then did I eat it; and it was in my mouth as honey for sweetness.*
>
> Ezekiel

IN LINES HE PRINTED only in the first and last copies of *America, a Prophecy*,[1] Blake suddenly reveals the dark side of the forceful "voice of one crying in the Wilderness" (*ARO*) which he had taken up with his earliest illuminated declarations:

> *The stern Bard ceas'd, asham'd of his own song; enrag'd he swung*
> *His harp aloft sounding, then dash'd its shining frame against*
> *A ruin'd pillar in glittring fragments; silent he turn'd away,*
> *And wander'd down the vales of Kent in sick & drear lamentings.*
>
> [*Am* 2.18–21]

And indeed, "lamentation" becomes a mode more common to Blake than to any other important English poet or to the Bible (see Appendix 2). What fascinates in plate 2 of *America* is the picture of the self-divided Bard. Because he is a stern judge and his song evidently does not measure up, he is ashamed; because of his shame, he is enraged. George Quasha suggests that the Bard's shame stems from "recognizing . . . that the poet of Experience can become his own lamenting song and close himself within it."[2] One may see in the lines the Bard's reaction to the growing discrepancy between the vision of the poetic genius and historical reality. The poetic genius has seemingly proved false, America is not fulfilling its prophecy, and the Bard, like Jonah, appears "displeased . . . exceedingly" and "very angry" (4:1). His ultimate reaction is to *turn away* and wander aimlessly through the vales lamenting, a "state" that here seems almost as earthly as Lambeth and the Old Kent Road. Lamenting is, almost by definition, a state in which one wanders because nothing more purposeful offers itself: "The Prophet *Jeremiah* (if he could) would have prevented the ruine of the Church; but all endeavours being ineffectual, because carnal confidence is always an enemy to faithful obedience, therefore nothing is left now but to lament what cannot be help'd."[3] So Thel "wanderd in the land of clouds thro' valleys dark, listning / Dolours & lamentations"(6.6–7)— the omission of a preposition after the participle indicates that what she hears and the state in which she hears it are one and the same: the voice she will hear is her own. The year after *America*, the stern Bard confirms *his* own lack of faith and "turning away," as his "voice" introduces the *Songs of Experience* in a lament:

> *Calling the lapsed Soul*
> *And weeping in the evening dew;*
> 　　　　[6–7]

"O Earth O Earth return! . . . Turn away no more," he continues. The powerful echoes of Jeremiah and Hosea[4] blind us to the fact, which "EARTH'S Answer" reiterates, that it is the Bard—as we shall see later—who has turned away to his own words to lament and mourn Earth's condition.

The basic state of lamentation appears in Blake's most famous study of one who turned away, *The Book of Thel*. The poem begins by emphasizing how "her soft voice is heard" (1.4). After a line that serves to describe her action throughout most of the poem, "And thus her gentle lamentation falls like morning dew," Thel gives voice to her plaint:

> *O life of this our spring! why fades the lotus of the water?*
> *Why fade these children of the spring? born but to smile & fall.*
> *Ah! Thel is like a watry bow, and like a parting cloud,*
> *Like a reflection in a glass. like shadows in the water.*
> *Like dreams of infants. like a smile upon an infants face,*
> *Like the doves voice, like transient day, like music in the air*
> 　　　　[1.6–11]

Thel begins with a fount or "water spring,"[5] so identifying herself as a naiad or nymph and securing a place in the tradition of pastoral elegy. Her central vision, like that of the wilderness voice crying in Isaiah 40, is of a life that "fades away": "The grass withereth, the flower fadeth" (Isa. 40:7, 8). Thel never grasps the other half of the message, ". . . but *the word* of our God shall stand forever" (Isa. 40:8, italics added). "The fading cry is ever dying" we read in *The Four Zoas* (34.76, E324), and such is Thel's lot. Vividly comparing herself in quick succession to nine transient phenomena, she disintegrates as a personality, becoming only a voice living from one simile to the next. The fact that she does not speak of the transience of her own voice is an index of her problem. Thel displays an essential aspect of lamentation: not going anywhere, not standing firm, but assimilating everything to its vision. Narcissus-like, lamentation centers on itself and so defeats its fulfillment.

Thel cannot connect to any consoling vision, to another realm of discourse that could explain the sense of loss that is now herself. She sees, but in her intense self-consciousness imposes her own perception: "ah Thel is like to Thee," she complains to the reader, adding (truthfully), "and no one hears my voice" (3.3–4). Thel has, ultimately, nothing to say, since she can only complain—that is, lament and bewail (*Thel* accounts for half of Blake's poetic uses of "complain" and its cognates). Faced with the Worm, image of an infant (*in-fans*, "not speaking"), Thel offers this ineffectual communication:

> *Ah weep not little voice, thou can'st not speak. but thou can'st weep;*
> *Is this a Worm? I see thee lay helpless & naked: weeping,*
> *And none to answer, none to cherish thee with mothers smiles.*
>
> [4.4–6]

In Thel's retreat from articulation, speaking and weeping become alternate aspects of the same expression, one that leaves "none to answer." The only response is action, and the Clod of Clay points up Thel's inability and erroneous vision as it hears the Worm, bows over it, and feeds it "in milky fondness." The Clod cannot verbalize its understanding—"I know not, and I cannot know, / I ponder, and I cannot ponder; yet I live and love" (5.5–6)—nevertheless, Thel is reassured enough to go to her own self-encounter in "the land unknown." There she does not confront, but only hears, herself:

> *. . . listning*
> *Dolours & lamentations: waiting oft beside a dewy grave*
> *She stood in silence. listning to the voices of the ground,*

Till to her own grave plot she came, & there sat down.
And heard this voice of sorrow breathed from the hollow pit.

[6.6–10]

The voice and voices are Thel's own sighs, complaints, and moans "heard" and "call'd down" by the matron Clay.

While we can point to evident sexual anxiety prompting "the voice," it may also be heard, like Thel's initial "soft voice," as a merely rhetorical reality. Its following nine questions offer not ineffable images of transience, but various unanswerable and paradoxical questions—"the voice" beginning, suitably, with the ear: "Why cannot the Ear be closed to its own destruction?" (6.11). This again is lamentation, somewhat more intense (even "hysteric," given Thel's psychological state). The truly lamentable aspect of Thel is that, in the vales of Har, as well as in the land unknown, she hears only her own voice: her lot joins that of Echo and Narcissus. Caught in the wilderness of herself she vacillates, as her palindromic Greek name suggests, between wishing or willing (*thelō*) and forgetfulness (Lethe). Frye's description of Thel as a "rococo china shepherdess"[6] aptly fixes the static fragility of her self-fulfilling lamentation, unable to break out of its own categories and find another voice. She has fallen into the state or voice of seeking but not finding: "Then we shall seek thee but not find" (3.3). Just as her earlier vision of "fading" missed Isaiah's emphasis on the permanence of the word of God, so now Thel ironically fulfills Jesus' prophecy to the Pharisees, "Ye shall seek me, and shall not find me: and where I am, thither ye cannot come" (John 7:34).

The Visions of the Daughters of Albion wanders further into the mire of lamentation. Not only is the word used to describe the monologues of different characters, but its appearance in the first line of the poem proper serves to characterize the poem as a whole and to direct the reader's response:

Enslav'd, the Daughters of Albion weep: a trembling lamentation
Upon their mountains; in their valleys. sighs toward America

[1.1–2][7]

The daughters present an unchanging chorus behind their sister Oothoon, and again one senses the presence of Echo and Narcissus, for every morning the daughters "hear her woes & eccho back her sighs."[8] Oothoon, like Thel, "wanderd in woe, / . . . seeking flowers to comfort her" (1.3–4). Instead of Thel's silver-shrined Lily, Oothoon speaks to the Marigold in "her golden shrine" (1.10) and receives explicit reassurance that "the soul of sweet delight / Can never pass away" (1.9–10). The story of Oothoon's Passion is in some ways extraneous to the inviting rhetorical morass of her words—her rape becomes the reader's rapture as Oothoon, like Thel, runs along the surface of her speech in her one defense against despair. While Thel sought "to fade away like morning beauty," the more experienced Oothoon regrets that "beauty fades from off my shoulders" (7.14) as she becomes

> *A solitary shadow wailing on the margin of non-entity.*
>
> [7.15]

This realization—to dispute received interpretation—pushes the manic Oothoon to greater excesses, as she cries in the wilderness her message of "happy happy Love!" (7.16). She never connects with the psychic reality (barren though it is) of Bromion and Theotormon, and so becomes a contradiction in terms, forfeiting her possibility of instigating change. They, in turn, never speak to her or to each other, which accounts for Bromion's speech being labeled explicitly a "lamentation" (4.12), while Theotormon's words, coming from "one o'erflowd with woe" (3.22), are even more lamentable.

One significant aspect of Oothoon is the way that her lamentation turns outward to a stirring condemnation of eighteenth-century sexual politics, rising to the same conclusion as "A Song of Liberty" in *The Marriage of Heaven and Hell*: "for everything that lives is holy!" (*VDA* 8.10; *MHH* 27). Yet these glorious cries are finally heard as Oothoon's "morning wails" (8.11), and we feel that they represent a logical emotional conclusion to her earlier desperate condition, "incessant writhing her soft snowy limbs" (2.12). In this juxtaposition of frustrated desire and intellectual vision, we see Blake's analysis of, and compassion for, Mary Wollstonecraft, the seemingly "liberated" authoress of the recently published *A Vindication of the Rights of Woman*, who was, at the same time, enthralled by her neurotic and unsatisfied desire for Blake's then best friend, Henry Fuseli. This disjunction between desire and vision, with its fall into "the World of Loneness" (*BA* 4.64), is one root of lamentation. Ahania, cast out by Urizen, continues Oothoon's situation:

> *The lamenting voice of Ahania*
> *Weeping upon the void.*
> . . . .
> *Her voice was heard, but no form*
> *Had she: but her tears from clouds*
> *Eternal fall round the Tree*

And the voice cried: Ah Urizen! Love!
Flower of morning! I weep on the verge
Of Non-entity;

[*BA* 4.45–46, 49–54]

Cut off from the realm of form and substance, Ahania comes closer to being only a voice in the void.

This disembodied, lamenting feminine voice finds its apotheosis in *The Four Zoas*:

For now no more remaind of Enion in the dismal air
Only a voice eternal wailing in the Elements

[46.6–7, E331]

Lamentation is the initial identifying expression of an emanation, which is, in turn, the embodiment of lamentation—the emanations first appear with the wailing feminine voices in *The Four Zoas*. Lamentation is assimilated into the structure of a feminine, uncomprehending Nature, a motif mirrored in the constant of "mother's grief," which the caterpillar on the leaf memorializes. Maternal nature does not comprehend or accept change—it is, in one sense, a radical innocence destined to become embittered in the face of experience. Becoming embittered, it also becomes a spurious and deadly innocence, blind to the facts before it. The delineation and interrelation of these states is a key concern of Blake's vision, involving the transition from emotion to intellect: from Beulah to Eden, or, negatively, from an embittered Nature to the despairs of Vala and the Ulro. At the wedding feast of her children, Enion asks in her too-touching "lamentation":

Why is the Sheep given to the knife? the Lamb plays in the Sun
He starts! he hears the foot of Man! he says, Take thou my wool
But spare my life, but he knows not that winter cometh fast.

The Spider sits in his labourd Web, eager watching for the Fly
Presently comes a famishd Bird & takes away the Spider
His Web is left all desolate, that his little anxious heart
So careful wove; & spread it out with sighs and weariness.

[18.1–7, E310]

Like Oothoon, and Thel before her, Enion sounds the Siren-call of wistful sadness. Her lament is unanswerable; rooted in an excess of anthropomorphism and emotional sympathy, it reveals finally a base in self-pity. She dwells on the "tears in the nature of things" in order to avoid a self-awareness of her true position.

Modulation out of the lament calls for self-consciousness and a vision that encompasses and moves beyond that consciousness. It calls, most of all, for effective words—Enion embodies the uncreative alternative as she regresses to the non-verbal basis of lament and wanders in *Milton* "like a weeping inarticulate voice" (19.42). In prophetic speech, words are actions, but the words of lamentation are idle because they are ultimately self-referential. The degree to which Blake continually attempts to verbalize lamentation is an index of its great temptation, particularly in an age of "sensibility," with its "exaltation of unhappiness."[9] The printing history of *America* 2.18–21, referred to at the beginning of this chapter, points to Blake's complex feelings on the matter. On the one hand, the poem is felt to fail, so the poet, "enraged," writes his own self-condemnation; but this soon seems an attempt to have it both ways, an indulgence at odds with the poem's activity. One of the prophet's duties is not to despair; but that, as Blake knew, is sometimes beyond human control.

It is as if, in writing so many varied lamentations, Blake exorcises his doubts and despairs in order to hold on to a larger perspective. We can see this process working itself out in *The Four Zoas*, which Blake at some point was going to characterize as a "dirge."[10] After multiple lamentations by Enion, Ahania, Tharmas, Vala, and Urizen,[11] Night the Fifth retells the story of the chaining of Orc. Los and Enitharmon are overtaken with "Despair & Terror & Woe & Rage," and as they revive from a faint, we read in one of Blake's direct comments:

> *all their lamentations*
> *I write not here but all their after life was lamentation*
> [63.8–9, E343]

This is the end of one road, and had it indeed proved the case, there would have been nothing left to say. But instead, "when satiated with grief," they return to the newly created Golgonooza, and Enitharmon, on "the road to Dranthon" (like Paul outside Damascus), has the "heart attack" that opens her perception to the "dreary Deep" containing Ahania and the roots of the chain of Jealousy. Here, finally, lamentation touches ground and finds the possibility of conversion in the self-annihilation of absolute despair. This same realization governs Albion's conversion when he admits that "hope is banish'd from me" (*J* 47.18): the dark night of the soul is the necessary prologue to illumination. While the incident occurs without great ado in Night the Fifth, one may see in it the dynamic that prepares the way for the redemptive imagery of Jesus and Golgonooza. It is striking that, while earlier lamentations are "gentle" (*Thel*) or "trembling" (*VDA*), after the crisis in Night the Fifth they may be identified as "selfish" or "jealous" (73.26, E350; 81.22, E357).

The increasing awareness of different kinds of lamentation finds its full expression in *Milton*, which asks us to consider three distinct, mutually exclusive "lamentations" and has lamentation embodied in its heroine. The first lamentation is that of the Sons of Albion, who sing as they create "the Three Classes" of Men, "lamenting around the Anvils":

> *Ah weak & wide astray! Ah shut in narrow doleful form*
> *Creeping in reptile flesh upon the bosom of the ground*
> *The Eye of Man a little narrow orb closed up & dark*
> *Scarcely beholding the great light conversing with the Void*
> ·
> *The Tongue a little moisture fills, a little food it cloys*
> *A little sound it utters & its cries are faintly heard*
> *Then brings forth Moral Virtue the Cruel Virgin Babylon*
> ·
> *Can such a Tongue boast of the living waters? or take in*
> *Ought but the Vegetable Ratio & loathe the faint delight*
> *Can such gross Lips perceive? alas! folded within themselves*
> *They touch not ought but pallid turn & tremble at every wind*
>
> [5.19–22, 25–27, 34–37]

The second tells how "the Shadowy Female seeing Milton, howl'd her lamentation"; she "howls in articulate howlings":

> *I will lament over Milton in the lamentations of the afflicted*
> *My Garments shall be woven of sighs & heart broken lamentations*
> *The misery of unhappy Families shall be drawn out into its border*
> ·
> *I will have Writings written all over it in Human Words*
> *That every Infant that is born upon the Earth shall read*
> *And get by rote as a hard task of a life of sixty years*
> *I will have Kings inwoven upon it & Councellors & Mighty Men*
> ·

For I will put on the Human Form & take the Image of God
Even Pity & Humanity but my Clothing shall be Cruelty
. . . .
And all my ornaments shall be of the gold of broken hearts
And the precious stones of anxiety & care & desperation & death
And repentance for sin & sorrow & punishment & fear

[18.5–7, 12–15, 19–20, 22–24]

Finally, there is the pathetic lamentation of Beulah:

Thou hearest the Nightingale begin the Song of Spring
The Lark . . .
. . . .
Mounting upon the wings of light into the Great Expanse:
Reecchoing against the lovely blue & shining heavenly Shell:
. . . .
All Nature listens silent to him & the awful Sun
Stands still upon the Mountain looking on this little Bird
With eyes of soft humility, & wonder love & awe.
. . . .
This is a Vision of the lamentation of Beulah over Ololon!

Thou percievest the Flowers put forth their precious Odours!
And none can tell how from so small a center comes such sweets
. . . .
First eer the morning breaks joy opens in the flowery bosoms
Joy even to tears, which the Sun rising dries; . . .
. . . .
The Jonquil, the mild Lilly opes her heavens! every Tree,
And Flower & Herb soon fill the air with an innumerable Dance
Yet all in order sweet & lovely, Men are sick with Love!
Such is a Vision of the lamentation of Beulah over Ololon

[31.28–29, 32–33, 36–38, 45–47, 50–51, 60–63]

Each of these lengthy lamentations has its errors or limitations, which may be explored by setting one against another. Through their regular progression, the reader is given the possibility of seeing them all in a vision that realizes the full nature of the word/world "lamentation" and the selfish structure of the "World of Sorrow."

The Furnaces and Anvils around which the Sons of Albion work belong to Los:

In Bowlahoola Los's Anvils stand & his Furnaces rage;
Thundering the Hammers beat & the Bellows blow loud
Living self moving mourning lamenting & howling incessantly

[24.51–53]

Lamentation is built into the system in its physical nature, for "the Bellows are the Animal Lungs: the Hammers the Animal Heart / The Furnaces the Stomach for digestion. terrible their fury" (24.58–59). The body may be seen to live the pain of vegetable existence, ever suffering decay, and the mind predisposed to that conception quickly comes to believe that its experiences are illusory, or at least hindrances on the path to the spiritual absolute of death. The lamentation of the Sons of Albion is a type of mystical lament over the dross of nature—a distancing perception that perpetuates the very condition it laments. The Sons of Albion exhibit more intellectual vision than the other lamenting voices (they recognize "Moral Virtue the Cruel Virgin Babylon"), yet the regretful and stoic vocabulary they use indicates that they have lost perception of the possibility of change. Having chosen to see an irrevocably fallen world, they are limited by their condescension. The best they can do is to create the three classes, hoping that from the resulting internecine strife something may emerge. Unfortunately, their creation of the new, rising class of the "reasoning negative" undermines the possibility that progress may emerge from the conflict of the two contrary classes also created.

The description—"in articulate howlings"—of the Shadowy Female's speech comments on the nature of her lamentation and supplies one of the poem's subtle verbal and ideational oppositions. The key here is that the Authorized Version occasionally collocates "lamentation" and "howl."[12] So Jeremiah 4:8, "gird you with sackcloth, lament and howl: for the fierce anger of the LORD is not turned back from us." Howlings are the most visceral form of lamentation. The word is common in Blake, its forms appearing more than twice as frequently as those of lamentation (again, far more than in the AV or in other English poets), though generally with the sense of "uttering brute sounds"[13] of sorrow or torment. The Shadowy Female's lamentation is brutish enough in its attempt to project a Hobbesian awe of power and necessity, but the manner in which her speech vacillates between howl and lament, represented by the ambiguous "in articulate," bespeaks its origins in an almost incoherent despair. Having lived in cruelty, she can only speak cruelly for fear of losing what control and order she has established. In 1798 Blake wrote that "the Beast & the Whore rule without controls" (E611), and with the lamentation of the Shadowy Female, he enters the psychology of that state. She must, in effect, argue (with Hobbes) that "all that is real is material, and what is not material is not real"[14] in order to preserve her existence. She is the "cruel Virgin Babylon" whom the Sons of Albion correctly, but impotently, perceived clothed in the ornaments and precious stones of the unrealized dreams of selfhood, the philosophy of possessive individualism. Without these dreams and their concomitant guilt and repentance, life would seem devoid of experience—yet within that system, experience will be a continual cruelty and unanswered lamentation. The end of *Milton* sees "One Man Jesus the Saviour" appear in a different version of the Shadowy Female's Garment, woven of lamentations and with "writings written all over it in Human Words." His is

> . . . *a Garment dipped in blood*
> *Written within & without in woven letters: & the Writing*
> *Is the Divine Revelation in the Litteral expression*
>
> [42.12–14]

The expression "written within & without" occurs only once in the Bible, not in Revelation, but in Ezekiel's vision of the book of "lamentation, and mourning, and woe," quoted as the epigraph to this chapter. The robe of the Shadowy Female is obscured with "writings written all over," and they are "human words" to be learned "by rote," suggesting that the letter without the spirit killeth, as does the lamentation without God, or self-pity without forgiveness.

Beulah voices the third lamentation as it sees Ololon descend through its "moony shades & hills" of mild love, seeking a darker reality. The orientation and values of Beulah are evidenced by its presence in maternal love:

> . . . *Beulah to its inhabitants appears within each district*
> *As the beloved infant in his mothers bosom round incircled*
> *With arms of love & pity & sweet compassion.*
>
> [30.10–12]

Like the "mother's grief" that embodies a certain kind of lamentation, Beulah possesses a reserve of potential lament to inflict on its wayward children. "Mother" here is also Mother Earth, the realm of natural love that is "from Great Eternity a mild & pleasant Rest" (30.14). The lamentation has been neatly discussed by Harold Bloom, who finds it one of Blake's unparalleled achievements, depending on "the subtle paradox . . . that it is a lamentation which we, men of Generation, hear as a rejoicing Song of Spring."[15] "To rise from Generation free" (as the speaker hopes in "To Tirzah"), Beulah's speech must be heard and understood as lamentation; the real mother must be seen as material. Seeing Ololon descend, Beulah laments—hoping in paradoxical fashion that the reader may still be coaxed into regarding Beulah as the highest good. Beulah has a maternal and material interest in maintaining its status as a special state, the value of which the boundary-crossing Ololon will diminish by revealing Beulah's "soft sexual delusions" (2.3); the "married land" does not want anything divorced from it. Beulah identifies its bias—and our grounds for ultimately rejecting it—by concluding with a vision of its most intense offering to human experience, "Men are sick with Love!" In *The Pilgrim's Progress*, Christian and Hopeful "solaced themselves" for a season in a somewhat similar Beulah, where they "heard continually the singing of birds, and saw everyday the flowers appear in the earth." The resolution of Bunyan's vision foreshadows that of Blake's, for, catching a glimpse of the Heavenly City:

> . . . *Christian*, with desire fell sick, *Hopeful* also had a fit or two of the same Disease: wherefore they lay by it a while, crying out because of their pangs, *If you see my Beloved, tell him that I am sick of love* [Song of Songs, 5:8].
>
> But being a little strengthened, and better able to bear their sickness, they walked on their way. . . .[16]

The countryside, the mother, must be left behind if they (or Ololon) are to enter the city of fellowship and activity, the world to come. Love-sickness, like lamentation, is another essentially passive relationship to the world, another melancholy and narcissistic fixation. For Christian and Hopeful, falling sick is a step on their pilgrimage—but, lovesickness is introduced at the end of Beulah's "vision of the lamentation," and is sealed off by the *fiat* "such is," leading us to see that Beulah has no awareness of the larger journey.

Ololon, who occasions Beulah's lament, is a remarkable presence, appearing only in *Milton*. Variously "she," "they," or, implicitly, "it," and including Milton's "six-fold emanation" of his three wives and three daughters, Ololon is generally feminine, though at odd moments she crosses with Jesus into the androgyny of "One Man" (21.59). Her identity is best approached through her name, which in part evidently derives from the Greek ὀλολύζω (cf. "ululation"), used in classical Greek of women's crying, *mostly jubilant*, to invoke the gods, but by the Septuagint to translate the Hebrew *hi* ("howl" or "wail" in the AV).[17] Ololon first appears on plate 21:

> *There is in Eden a sweet River, of milk & liquid pearl.*
> *Named Ololon; on whose mild banks dwelt those who Milton drove*
> *Down into Ulro: and they wept in long resounding song*
> *For seven days of eternity, and the rivers living banks*
> *The mountains wail'd! & every plant that grew, in solemn sighs lamented.*
>
> [21.15–19][18]

Ololon is thus also a river of tears ("pearly tears," as in *The Four Zoas* 130.21, E399) and maternal milk, evoking the twice repeated image that "tears run down like a river" for the Prophet of Lamentations (2:18; cf. 3:48). The progression from Thel's lamentation and the "voice of sorrow" through "the lamenting voice of Ahania" and the disembodied, wailing voices of *The Four Zoas* suggests that Ololon may be seen as "Lamentation" personified—analogous, say, to Milton's "Mirth" or Shakespeare's "Pity," which Blake could depict so "literally." As a personification or "intellectual ideograph,"[19] she is, unlike the ordinary states, herself able to pass through individuals; Ololon seems to exemplify Donald Ault's intriguing remark that "Blake's characters are relationships between events which are named and then proceed to act as if they were independent characters with lives of their own."[20] Ololon names the dynamic of conversion that operates when lamentation touches ultimate despair—here the resonance of her name with "all alone" is appropriate. As one who has come through the wilderness of solitude, Ololon joyfully offers the message fearfully broached by Thel that,

> *In Selfhood, we are nothing: but fade away in mornings breath.*
>
> [*J* 40(45).13]

A few lines after her introduction Ololon begins her mysterious transformation:

> *. . . at this time all the Family*
> *Of Eden heard the lamentation,* and Providence began.
> *But when the clarions of day sounded they drownd the lamentations*
> *And when night came all was silent in Ololon: & all refusd to lament*
> *In the still night fearing lest they should others molest.*
>
> [21.23–27]

Hearing that Milton has descended "to Eternal Death" to redeem his sixfold emanation,

> *. . . Ololon said, Let us descend also, and let us give*
> *Ourselves to death in Ulro among the Transgressors.*
> *. . . . .*
> *Or are these the pangs of repentance? let us enter into them*
>
> [21.45–46, 50]

All this is cryptic in the extreme, but as it reflects on one contemporary issue in Blake studies, namely his attitude toward woman, it deserves extended consideration. The Divine Family says to Ololon:

> *. . . now you know this World of Sorrow, and feel Pity. Obey*
> *The Dictate! Watch over this World, and with your brooding wings,*
> *Renew it to Eternal Life: . . .*
> *. . . . .*
> *So spake the Family Divine as One Man even Jesus*
> *Uniting in One with Ololon & the appearance of One Man.*
> *Jesus the Saviour appeard coming in the Clouds of Ololon!*
> *. . . . .*
> *And Ololon lamented for Milton with a great lamentation.*
>
> [21.54–56, 58–60, 22.3]

As the lamentation of Milton, the goading divine spirit that ever knew the truth and so made him "unhappy tho in heav'n" (2.18), Ololon laments her incarnation in domestic and poetic femininity. She laments for Milton and for herself, since she is part of Milton (as Robert is of William in the poem's illustrations). She represents an instinctual fund of energy that ever hopes for integration—that can occasion "Providence" because at any moment hope may appear. Providence begins when we realize that there is something other than ourselves to attend to. Ololon appears to Blake as a "Virgin of Providence" (36.28) and, in one of the poem's several echoes of Paul's experience on the road to Damascus, she is identified as the agent of Blake's conversion.[21] In the drama of the poem, Milton sees the error of his ways and descends to self-annihilation in order to remove the curse he placed on women. On one level, Milton's spirit descends to be "stained" with—for example—Johnson's memorable image of Milton's "Turkish contempt of females, as subordinate and inferior beings."[22] But greater than the act of Milton's descent is the sacrifice of Ololon. Not only will she forgive Milton but, reminiscent of the Creation in *Paradise Lost* ("Dove-like satst brooding," 1.21), Ololon will obey that epic poem's dictate (its letter, not its spirit) and renew the world, making it a place where the new Milton might live and be read.[23] This will also mark the end of the "brooding Melancholy" that has occasioned so much lamentation. With Ololon, lamentation for self becomes lamentation for another—an other greater self, for which the basic example is not the mother's instinctive regard for her child, but the growing child's understanding sympathy with its mother. If "the Catterpiller on the Leaf / Reminds thee of thy Mother's Grief,"[24] that act of sympathy simultaneously opens the way for the acceptance of change and history, confirming the reality of greater-than-individual experience and thus offering liberation from "weeping over the Web of life" (E269).

Ololon appears to Blake on his garden path:

And as One Female, Ololon and all its mighty Hosts
Appear'd: a Virgin of twelve years nor time nor space was
[36.16–17]

Much has been written on this passage, the general suggestion being that, in S. Foster Damon's unfortunate phrase, Ololon is "on the point of fecundity," or that she is the "breastless 'little sister'" of the Song of Songs.[25] But Ololon's name, age, and situation join her to Mark's story of the ruler of the synagogue's dead daughter. Jesus came to the house,

> . . . and seeth the tumult, and them that wept and wailed greatly.
>
> And when he was come in, he saith unto them, Why make ye this ado, and weep? the damsel is not dead, but sleepeth. . . .
>
> And he took the damsel by the hand, and said unto her, Talitha cumi; which is, being interpreted, Damsel, I say unto thee, arise.
>
> And straightway the damsel arose, and walked; for she was of the age of twelve years. And they were astonished with a great astonishment.
>
> [Mark 5:38–39, 41–42]

This is an emblem of the central, indescribable event, the conversion of lamentation into joy. Here finally we must agree with the Clod of Clay, "how this is sweet maid, I know not, and I cannot know" (*Thel* 5.5). At the heart of lamentation, one finds a limit or built-in reversal point; lamentation, as Shelley puts it, itself is mortal—not divine (cf. Shelley's *Adonais*, line 183). This seemingly antithetical movement can be seen in language: Latin *miseror* signifies "to lament, bewail," and also "to have or feel compassion." Discussing the Greek "ololuge," *Paulys Real-Encyclopädie* offers the poetic suggestion Ololon also embodies, that the word is "vielleicht auch hebr. halelujah."[26]

A discussion of Ololon and lamentation would be incomplete without accounting for one of the most important and misunderstood passages in *Milton*. Shortly after the lamentation of Beulah, we hear an apparently new voice, which needs to be considered closely and in its evasive entirety:

And the Divine Voice was heard in the Songs of Beulah Saying

When I first Married you, I gave you all my whole Soul
I thought that you would love my loves & joy in my delights
Seeking for pleasures in my pleasures O Daughter of Babylon
Then thou wast lovely, mild & gentle. now thou art terrible
In jealousy & unlovely in my sight, because thou hast cruelly
Cut off my loves in fury till I have no love left for thee
Thy love depends on him thou lovest & on his dear loves
Depend thy pleasures which thou hast cut off by jealousy
Therefore I shew my Jealousy & set before you Death.
Behold Milton descended to Redeem the Female Shade
From Death Eternal; such your lot, to be continually Redeem'd
By Death & misery of those you love & by Annihilation
When the Sixfold Female percieves that Milton annihilates
Himself: that seeing all his loves by her cut off: he leaves
Her also: intirely abstracting himself from Female loves
She shall relent in fear of death: She shall begin to give
Her maidens to her husband: delighting in his delight
And then & then alone begins the happy Female joy
As it is done in Beulah, & thou O Virgin Babylon Mother of Whoredoms
Shalt bring Jerusalem in thine arms in the night watches; and
No longer turning her a wandering Harlot in the streets
Shalt give her into the arms of God your Lord & Husband.

Such are the Songs of Beulah in the Lamentations of Ololon

And all the Songs of Beulah sounded comfortable notes
To comfort Ololons lamentation, for they said
Are you the Fiery Circle that late drove in fury & fire
The Eight Immortal Starry-Ones down into Ulro dark
Rending the Heavens of Beulah with your thunders & lightnings
And can you thus lament & can you pity & forgive?
Is terror changd to pity O wonder of Eternity!   [33.1–34.7]

Some readers have found this passage troubling and even offensive. Harold Bloom gives it five lines of comment, explaining that "the speaker . . . is the unfallen Man-God, and he addresses what will become . . . the aggregate Female Will, ironically called 'Virgin Babylon'" (E924). It seems clear, however, that the speech is neither the true utterance of the Divine Voice (which has been mentioned only once previously in the poem, when Satan created "moral laws and cruel punishments . . . to pervert the Divine Voice in its entrance to earth" [9.22–23]) nor a manifestation of the Divine Voice in the Songs of Beulah; rather, it is both, a perverted and Beulahized divinity subsumed under "the lamentations of Ololon." It is the Divine Voice Moses heard, now re-presented by Ololon. Many details ask for closer consideration. By beginning with the one overt reference to marriage in the poem, the Divine Voice shows his strictly Beulah-oriented philosophy. He states redundantly that he gave "all my whole soul," which is just as quickly revealed as no gift at all, but a series of expectations; just so one imagines Milton regarding his first wife, who, unfortunately for his high arguments, "seems not much to have delighted in the pleasures of spare diet and hard study."[27] Lacking even the generosity of the Mosaic God, who "set before thee this day life and good, and death and evil" (Deut. 30:15), this Divine Voice sets before us only Death. The intimidating inference, however, remains the same: "I command thee this day to love the LORD thy God, to walk in his ways" (Deut. 30:16). The Divine Voice then labels the "Virgin Ololon" (whose lamentation this is) as "Virgin Babylon"[28] and imagines her as God's procuress—all this so that it may be "as it is done in Beulah." As Ololon is the mature form of Oothoon (their names link them together, and at the end of the poem Oothoon seems suddenly to appear as a stand-in for Ololon), she is forced to hear Oothoon's misdirected offer to "catch for thee girls" thrown back in her face as a different Theotormon's (now a tormenting theology's) perverted command.[29]

Ololon's vision is far different from that of Beulah and its Divine Voice. In effect, the entire passage, "the Songs of Beulah *in* the Lamentations of Ololon," is her perspective on "the lamentations of Beulah *over* Ololon" presented two plates previously; completing the insight of the Bard's song, she sees that lamentation is not beyond the imputation of guilt. Ololon (like Thel) does not wish to be married to the Beulah world of beauty and polygamy, a false version of a Divine Voice that has for millennia been used to subjugate women. She knows (unlike Thel) that "In Eternity they neither marry nor are given in marriage" (*J* 30[34].15), and, as Beulah dimly perceives, that she herself is one "wonder of Eternity." The fate and standing of Beulah is bound to that of lamentation—Ololon, being greater than Beulah, can "thus lament" yet "pity & forgive."

In *Jerusalem's* diminished recourse to lament and lamentation, Blake passes beyond the temptation of bardic sorrow, jeremiad, or lament to the intellectual vision of Ezekiel. Jeremiah and Ezekiel are apt metaphors for states in Blake's career, since in Jeremiah we may see, according to Gerhard von Rad, the lamentable figure of a prophet who suffered "an increasing inability to see where he was going. It was not merely that he pondered on the lack of success which attended his work. The failure was not only an outward one, stemming from the people, it was also personal, in that the prophet was no longer at one with his office or his tasks."[30] This is the psychology of the self-enraged Bard of *America* and the poet who conceives his epic as a "dirge"; little wonder that Lamentations was attributed to Jeremiah. Ezekiel offers a different alternative and becomes the model for "Albions Watchman";[31] it was Ezekiel who ate the book of lamentations, and mourning, and woe, and found it "as honey for sweetness," a response Blake might have come to feel was as effective as Ezekiel's eating dung for "raising other men into a perception of the infinite" (*MHH* 13). Ezekiel "individualizes the prophetic alternative" in which, writes Martin Buber, "no one has to answer for his fellow, but each one has to answer fully for himself. . . . This is the special character of the time of great transition."[32] In *Jerusalem* lamentation moves toward the background as part of the given state of things, a state from which individuals may be redeemed even if the nation as a whole cannot. The Daughters of Albion speak blankly of "our World of Cruel / Lamentation" (like "this World of Sorrow" in Ololon's charge), such that infants prefer to "flee back & hide in Non-Entitys dark wild" (56.15–16). So are Thel and Ahania and Enion given their due as voices crying in the dark wilderness, with no language but a cry. In the world of nature, "lambs bleat to the sea-fowls cry, lamenting still for Albion."[33] They may be lamenting still and perhaps indefinitely, but while Los hears the "lamentations in the deeps afar!" (*J* 5.66), he sees now the Divine Analogy of Six Thousand Years, the creation of Time and Space, the world of sorrow and the seeds of beauty:

> *. . . listning to their lamentation*
> *Los walks upon his ancient Mountains in the deadly darkness*
> *Among his Furnaces directing his laborious Myriads watchful*
> *Looking to the East: & his voice is heard over the whole Earth*
> [85.9–12]

Like Thel, he is "listning" to "dolours & lamentations," but unlike her he can reply from his experience of passing through loss of Eden, loss of unity, loss of love, and loss of the past underlying all lamentation to the discovery of Los's voice, which in its articulation fills the void, the whole ear. Such language changes mourning to morning.

The first poem of the Blakean canon, "To Spring," progresses from "morning" to "morn" to "mourns" (lines 2, 11, 12) and shows the germ of the idea that "morning dew" may be seen on another level as the "dewy tears" of mourning:

> ... *let us taste*
> *Thy morn and evening breath; scatter thy pearls*
> *Upon our love-sick land that mourns for thee.*
> [lines 10–12]

The "pearly dew" (*Eur* 14.15) embodies some sort of consolation or affirmation for the mourning land.[34] *Tiriel* brings the two concepts explicitly together for the first time:

> ... *all the sons & daughters of Tiriel*
> *Chaind in thick darkness utterd cries of mourning all the night*
> *And in the morning Lo an hundred men in ghastly death*
> [5.27–29]

This deliberate association leads us toward an understanding of *The Book of Thel*'s description of how its heroine sought

> *To fade away like morning beauty from her mortal day:*
> *Down by the river of Adona her soft voice is heard:*
> *And thus her gentle lamentation falls like morning dew.*
> [1.3–5]

The magic of these lines comes not only from the limpid music of morning beauty : mortal day : morning dew but also from the manner in which Blake plays the sense of transience into a sadness of morning, the sense that one might "fade away in mornings breath" (*J* 40[45].13). "Morning dew," by its close position to "lamentation" succumbs to the expected association "lamentation and mourning," a standard figure found in various combinations in Spenser, Shakespeare, the Bible, and Blake: "They return with lamentations mourning & weeping" (*FZ* 93.31, E365). One suspects that the mourning beauty Thel, like Romeo, "many a morning hath . . . been seen, / With tears augmenting the fresh morning's dew," making a "dew of lamentations."[35] Tears fall, but "morning dew" should be "arising." The Cloud tells Thel that he passes away "unseen descending" to

> . . . court the fair-eyed dew. to take me to her shining tent;
> The weeping virgin, trembling kneels before the risen sun,
> Till we arise link'd in a golden band, and never part;
>
> [3.13–15][36]

"The Little Boy lost" in the *Songs of Innocence* offers the antithesis of Thel's self-mourning. After he tries bravely to convince himself of his father's presence, we read:

> The night was dark no father was there
> The child was wet with dew.
> The mire was deep, & the child did weep
> And away the vapour flew.

The vapour is the damp dew—as in Blake's associations of vapor with cloud (*BU* 3.17) and "cloud of dew" (*BA* 5.13)—and it remarkably evaporates with the child's own weeping or dew-making. The moment foreshadows the later one on the banks of the Ololon when "all the Family / Of Eden heard the lamentation, and Providence began." As the child is wet with the dew of his material birth, so must he be reborn in the tears of his separateness and need, becoming a son of loss.

Weeping naturally associates with mourning: in *The French Revolution*, the "vineyards weep, in the eyes of the kingly mourner; / Pale is the morning cloud in his visage" (6–7); to the mourner the morning cloud is mourning. Similarly, morning becomes a signal for weeping; in the *Visions of the Daughters of Albion*:

> . . . when the morn arose, her lamentation renew'd,

for,

> Thus every morning wails Oothoon.
>
> [5.1, 8.11]

Here again the close association to "lamentation" and "wailing" links morning to mourning (she wails every mourning of the Daughters). The "Introduction" to *Experience* has "the voice of the Bard":

Calling the lapsed Soul
And weeping in the evening dew;

. . . .

O Earth O Earth return!
Arise from out the dewy grass
            [6–7, 11–12]

"Arise," he seems to say unawares, "from this dew I am weeping for you." The nature of the morning promised in the poem is less than obvious, since the Bard weeps "in the evening" as he declares, "Night is worn / And the morn / Rises"; more curious still, he pleads with Earth to remember that her condition (wearing Night?) is "giv'n thee till the break of day," indicating that this event is in the indefinite future and unrelated to the morn he alleges rises already through the evening dew. There seems to be an implicit distinction between morning and the break of day that is the end of mourning. Earth is not breaking out—she would lament, with Dowland, "Day breaks not, it is my heart." "EARTH'S Answer" in fact sees no light; for her, the "weeping" is "cold and hoar," and rather than scattered poetic dew, she asks for a "sower" and a "plowman." The Bard and Earth enact the Romantic dilemma that presents itself when nature and nature spiritualized are not enough: the Bard wants Earth to change her natural existence ("controll / The starry pole / And fallen fallen light renew!") but knows not how to realize it, while Earth sees the physical reality, but cannot imagine more ("her light fled"). "The Sky rejoices in the morning's birth," wrote Wordsworth:

But, as it sometimes chanceth, from the might
Of joy in minds that can no further go,
As high as we have mounted in delight
In our dejection do we sink as low;
To me that morning did it happen so;[37]

Tied to natural imagery the mind "can no further go," and each morning introduces another day of incomprehension and growing sadness.

For Blake, inner life does not correspond to the natural world, but to the imagination that, speaking through language, says that morning denotes not only dawn and expected light, but also sadness.[38] This mourning leads in turn to the everlasting day of spiritual light. Page 10 of *The Four Zoas* shows Enitharmon, "with a dropping tear & frowning / Dark as a dewy morning when the crimson light appears" (1–2). After she speaks, Los answers:

Why is the light of Enitharmon darken'd in dewy morn

. . . .

Why dost thou weep as Vala? & wet thy veil with dewy tears,
In slumbers of my night-repose, infusing a false morning?

[10.17, 20–21, E306]

"Dewy" here coordinates the elements of tears as dew, *lacrimae rerum*, the veil as the damp ground, and identifies Enitharmon's false weeping as a "false morning." Like Dalila with Samson, Enitharmon "in false tears" oppresses the soul of Los ("Samson," E443), emulating the "false self-decieving tears" of Tirzah. The perceived "falseness" of these tears and mornings underlies Blake's attack on the self-dramatizing sentimentality and melancholy of the age—both Young and Hayley were prime examples—which he saw darkening the true light of imagination and real sympathy.

Morning dews reappear in the closing pages of *The Four Zoas*. Harkening back to *Thel* and the "Introduction,"

Luvah spoke
With voice mild from his golden Cloud upon the breath of morning

Come forth O Vala from the grass & from the silent Dew
Rise from the dews of death for the Eternal Man is Risen

[126.29–32, E395]³⁹

Vala does rise; "her hair glistens with dew,"⁴⁰ and she says, "but for thee / I must have slept Eternally nor have felt the dew of thy morning" (127.1–2). That dew, emphasized a few lines later by "the dew of morning" and "the morning dew" (127.9–10) offers another form of the weeping of "The Little Boy lost." The real morning dew shows the weeping of the sun of love, love that begins, as ours toward the little boy, or Luvah's toward Vala, "in the Pity of others Woe" ("William Bond," E498). Vala's is the earthly version of what *Jerusalem* describes when "the Divine Vision wept / Like evening dew on every herb upon the breathing ground" (*J* 42.7–8). In contrast to the case of the Bard, who weeps in the evening dew, the dew here represents the mourning of the Divine Vision—that is, earthly morning and birth into limited natural referents.

But, as we also first learn in the *Poetical Sketches*, "pleasing woe," or mourning of one's own lot, can be an agreeable end in itself. In one of the manuscript sketches we read:

There is a Melancholy, O how lovely tis whose heaven is in the heavnly
Mind for she from heaven came, and where She goes heaven still doth follow
her. She brings true Joy once fled. & Contemplation is her Daughter. Sweet
Contemplation.

[E447]

Thomas Warton's earlier discussion of "The Pleasures of Melancholy" opens
typically with an apostrophe to "Contemplation," who is there, as more
often than not she was, "the sister of Melancholy."[41] However, the curious
variation in another pensive poetical sketch gives us "Contemplation,
daughter of the grey Morning!" (E442). "Melancholia," writes Freud,
"borrows some of its features from mourning, and others from the process of
regression . . . to narcissism."[42] The melancholic mourns narcissistically for
him- or herself, for the passing of some earlier fixation is seen as a death or loss
of the precious self: the intellectualized version of this self-indulgence hides
itself as "contemplation," and thought becomes the precipitation of mourning.
The intuitive perception of such "narcissism" underlies the embarrassment
most readers feel at Frederick Tatham's account (ca. 1832) of Blake relating to
his future wife the "lamentable story" of a lost love, "upon which Catherine
expressed her deep sympathy, it is supposed in such a tender & affectionate
manner, that it quite won him, he immediately said with the suddenness
peculiar to him 'Do you pity me?' 'Yes indeed I do' answered she. 'Then I love
you' said he again."[43] The account offers, at any rate, an apt prologue to the
sorry picture of courtship in the notebook poem, "The Birds":

> She.   *Yonder stands a lonely tree*
> *There I live & mourn for thee*
> *Morning drinks my silent tear*
> *And evening winds my sorrows bear*
>
> He.   *O thou Summers harmony*
> *I have livd & mournd for thee*
> *Each day I mourn along the wood*
> *And night hath heard my sorrows loud*
>
> [5–12, E478]

Here Venus's doves and the loves of night appear as "mourning doves," though
this mutual melancholic mourning leads to the happy outcome that "sorrow is
now at an End" (line 15). *Poetical Sketches* also depict the morning that is the

cruelest time. In the "Mad Song," "morning peeps / over the eastern steeps," but the singer cries that,

> *Like a fiend in a cloud*
> *With howling woe,*
> *After night I do croud,*
> *And with night will go;*
> *I turn my back to the east,*
> *From whence comforts have increas'd;*
> *For light doth seize my brain*
> *With frantic pain.*
>   [17–24, E415]

"Howling woe" identifies the speaker's condition as melancholy—"howling melancholy" (*FZ* 94.48, 55, E367)—not the pleasing contemplative variety, but the kind Samuel Johnson knew and defined as "A kind of madness, in which the mind is always fix'd on one object." It was a condition Blake knew when he wrote in a letter to Cumberland, "I begin to Emerge from a Deep pit of Melancholy, Melancholy without any real reason for it, a Disease which God keep you from & all good men" (E706), and later in a cryptic notebook entry: "Tuesday, Janry. 20, 1807, between Two & Seven in the Evening—Despair."[44]

A passage in *The Four Zoas*, repeated with slight additions in *Jerusalem*, associates "melancholy" and "morning" in the figure of Vala:

> *O Melancholy Magdalen behold the morning breaks*
> *Gird on thy flaming Zone. descend into the Sepulcher*
>   [93.2–3, E365; cf. *J* 65.38–39]

The breaking of morning is an image of the *crise de coeur*, the breaking (fever-like) of mourning. Vala, however, breaks into "howling in discontent black" (93.34; etymologically, of course, *melan*choly is "'black' [-bile]"), or "dark despair. the howling Melancholy" (94.55). The light she is to bring is another false morning, scattering the blood of battle instead of dew or seed—a parody of the morning promised in the beginning. The "demons of the deep" hear her melancholy sighs "in trumpets shrill when Morn shall blood renew" (93.19), and the morrow finds her strewn through the abyss:

> *Like clouds upon the winter sky broken with winds & thunders*
> *This was to her Supreme delight The Warriors mournd disappointed*

They go out to war with Strong Shouts & loud Clarions O Pity
They return with lamentations mourning & weeping

[93.28–31]

The end of the night shows Vala pervading the natural world of Urizen's journey:

the howling Melancholy
For far & wide she stretchd thro all the worlds of Urizens journey
And was Ajoind to Beulah as the Polypus to the Rock
Mo[u]rning *the daughters of Beulah saw nor could they have sustaind*
The horrid sight of death & torment But the Eternal Promise
They wrote on all their tombs & pillars

[94.55–95.5, E367]

Editors emend 95.3, but a consideration of what sense that emendation is designed to save offers tangible evidence of Blake's manner of expanding a line's reference. Do the daughters see "Mourning," instead of "howling Melancholy" (as "death & torment")? If the daughters themselves are "Mourning," what did they see, and how are they able, a few lines later, to wait "with Patience" and to sing "comfortable notes"? Perhaps the daughters see a morning that lightens the horrid sight of night of "black melancholy." This ambivalence over the quality of morning in Beulah suggests the formula "solemn mourning" with which it is four times associated, as when Jerusalem "descended / With solemn mourning out of Beulahs moony shades and hills."[45] If critics are correct in feeling that the passage calls for emendation, it seems more likely—especially considering the context—that "Morning the daughters of Beulah saw [*not*] nor could they have sustained . . ." (see 93.19, above).

The association of mourning and melancholy was a familiar feature in eighteenth-century England's "Age of Melancholy"; melancholy was "the English Malady" often thought to end in suicide (that classic object of "contemplation").[46] "Albion's Malady" asks, we might say, for some kind of psychoanalytic therapy, and Blake's analysis in effect envisions a form of pre-Freudian "talking cure": Los "built . . . the Language, acting against / Albion's melancholy, who must else have been a Dumb despair" (*J* 36[40].59–60). Language is the base because it is the medium of communication, the medium of under-standing, and the only cure for Albion is to talk everything out; where dumbness was, there shall language be, or, in place of the void of loss, Los's voice. Here again Blake sets himself against the splenetic, fashionable, melancholic inwardness that is, at heart, an expression of the self's despair at its "dumbness"—its inability to connect to another or to a medium of connection. Blake must supply a language with which to break down the rising prison walls of bourgeois individualism and self-sentimental narcissism. The dynamic of the problem appears in yet another popular "Ode to Melancholy," this one dating from the year of Blake's death:

> *All things are touched with Melancholy,*
> *Born of the secret soul's mistrust*
> *To feel her fair ethereal wings*
> *Weighed down with vile degraded dust;*
> [109–112][47]

A "secret soul" already predestines melancholy and the narcissistic mistrust of a vile reality; so Blake must first give it a language, and by that the conviction that it is not alone and not to be "degraded." Freud's discussion of "Mourning and Melancholia" develops the point that while mourning (ostensibly) involves the loss of an other, melancholy reflects a division within the self: "the conflict due to ambivalence gives a pathological cast to mourning and forces it to express itself in the form of self-reproaches to the effect that the mourner himself is to blame for the loss of the loved object, i.e., that he has willed it" (p. 251).

Man's "fall into division," one of the central themes of the Blakean epic, is his fall into melancholy, a story that begins in the mourning. The first chapter of *Jerusalem* states at the outset as one evidence of Albion's "souls disease" that "a black water accumulates" (4.13, 10). *The Four Zoas* opens with Tharmas crying out, "Lost! Lost! Lost! are my Emanations," and continues with his repeated plea to Enion, "O Pity Me." Enion answers in an accusatory manner, saying that she has found "Sin" in "the secret soul" of Tharmas. With that, Tharmas gives his blackening vision of the human psyche,

> *The infant joy is beautiful but its anatomy*
> *Horrible Ghast & Deadly nought shalt thou find in it*
> *But Death Despair & Everlasting brooding Melancholy*
> [4.31–33, E302]

and falls into pathological self-reproaches: "Yea I know / That I have sinnd & that my Emanations are become harlots" (4.35–36). He concludes with the epitome of the melancholic stance, "Despair will bring self murder on my Soul" (4.38). The aetiology of this event is a topic the whole poem pursues—but the disease is plain enough.

The straightforward sense of morning as sunrise to eternity may be exemplified by Vaughan's lines,

> Mornings *are mysteries; the first world's* Youth,
> *Man's* Resurrection, *and the future's* Bud,
> *Shrowd in their births.* . . .
>
> ["Rules and Lessons," 25–27]

or in the variations Boehme brought to the title of his first work: *Aurora: The Day Spring, or, Dawning of the Day in the East, or, Morning-Redness in the Rising of the Sun.* Despite such grandeur, we ought to feel that nature writ large cannot overcome natural associations. "The same dull round even of a universe" is soon loathed (*NNR*b). Wordsworth can tell the leech-gatherer that "this morning gives us promise of a glorious day," but even in such a fine morning cannot banish his "longing to be comforted," the "dim sadness—and blind thoughts, I knew not, nor could name."[48] So Blake saw "in Wordsworth the Natural Man rising up against the Spiritual Man Continually" (E665): that is, saw him using an imagery focused on natural objects that binds the perceiver to nature's wheel. "In Nature there is nothing melancholy," wrote Coleridge to Wordsworth, adding that he would make his child Hartley "Nature's playmate . . . that with the night / He may associate joy."[49] This is the crystallization of what Blake calls "the night of Nature," an attitude that in Coleridge's poem leads to a Hartleian vision of behavior-modification by "association" and "influxes" in an attempt to "share in Nature's immortality." This implicit fear of loss and its compensatory, self-deceiving desire to repose in the impersonal night of Nature, reveals again the basis of mourning and melancholy, the refusal or inability of the natural man to die to, or pass through, the things of this world, a refusal that is the "Death Despair" Tharmas finds already in the infant joy.

Born into a world initially imaged from nature, a world that must be conceived in terms "of somewhat on earth" (E600), Blake moves beyond nature by the greater nature literally available in language (see Appendix 3). Susan Fox offers a nice confirmation of this in the language she uses to analyze simultaneity in *Milton*: "The moment includes also the seven thousand years, the 'Day of Mourning' Los establishes in the Bard's Song, the millennium before Judgment. The action of *Milton*, in the historical scale, is the ending of mourning."[50] That is to say, the Day of Mourning—our history of loss and lamentation—is the Morning of Eternity, the real breaking of day:

> *I will arise and look forth for the morning of the grave.*
> *I will go down to the sepulcher to see if morning breaks!*
>
> [*M* 14.20–21]

Our world represents the mourning and morning of Eternity. But if one end of lamentation, one more-than-human consolation of "language, acting against Albions melancholy," is the association of morning and mourning, another is the changing nature of such chains of association.

CHAPTER FOUR

Chains of Being [The Line, 1]

Break this heavy chain
William Blake,
"EARTH'S Answer"

FOR THE POET WHO HEARS "mind-forg'd manacles" and who describes our planet Earth pleading for someone to break her heavy chain, such devices assume more than material reference; they present themselves as key links in the linear, univocal speech and lockstep thought process that Blake strives to replace by the four folds of his vision. A "chain" is not simply a chain,,but also an instance of what it refers to and (as a word) itself participates in: an image of order variously epitomized as the "great chain of being" and its double the "chain of discourse," with its verbal "links." These formulations and assertions of the intelligibility of world and communication are bound together through the sign of the chain; this sign Blake seizes on in order to explore its nature and unlock the reader from its implications. Though perception necessarily begins enchained, linked to a past and context, in realizing the nature and operations of its restraint—the psychic and cultural fetters, locks, and manacles—perception may to some extent unchain itself. Or, in Max Weber's terms, from being "enchanted" (another term for enchainment, as in Milton's *Comus* 659–60), we raise ourself to the freedom of "disenchantment." Fully to appreciate Blake's subversive activity, it will be useful first to recall the power of the eighteenth century's manifold chains.

The background of "the Great Chain of Being" needs little comment after A. O. Lovejoy's seminal study of what he saw as "the sacred phrase of the eighteenth century."[1] The chain originates in the *Iliad* (8.19), is adapted and expanded by Macrobius and others, approved by Bacon, and memorialized in Milton's picture of our pendant world, "hanging in a golden Chain" (*PL* 2.1051). A passage from Pope sets the tone for the century's sense of the image:

> *Vast chain of being! which from God began*
> *Natures aethereal, human, angel, man,*
> Beast, bird, fish, *insect, what no eye can see*
>
> ·
> *From Nature's chain whatever link you strike,*
> *Tenth, or ten thousandth, breaks the chain alike.*[2]

Samuel Johnson, by contrast, was not at all comfortable with the "presumptuous" notion or doctrine of the "chain of nature." He saw in it "infinite vacuities," each of which gave room for the "infinite exertion of infinite power": "no system can be more hypothetical than this, and perhaps no hypothesis more absurd."[3] Blake would perhaps have agreed; Northrop Frye finds, for example, that "there is no 'chain of being' in Blake and no trace of any of the creatures invented by those who believed in a chain of being."[4] But, though there is certainly no positively valued chain, one can, remembering the lines from Pope, still see its presence in Blake: the icon cannot be broken without having been recognized. In *The Book of Urizen* it begins not "from God" but as "the linked infernal chain" (10.35) given Urizen for a backbone after he disintegrates in

> *unseen conflictions with shapes*
> *Bred from his forsaken wilderness,*
> *Of* beast, bird, fish, *serpent & element*
> *Combustion, blast, vapour and cloud.*
>
> [3.14–17]

Blake transposes "Beast, bird, fish," from Pope's series of nine links but completes Urizen's "ninefold darkness / Unseen" (3.9) by breaking down Pope's "Natures aethereal" into the infinite vacuities of "combustion, blast, vapour and cloud." Urizen is in the state—or rather, is the state—where Nature's chain is being (mentally) created: in "an unform'd / Dark vacuity: here Urizen lay"

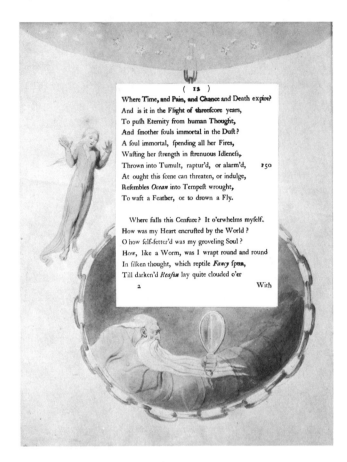

(12)

Where Time, and Pain, and Chance and Death expire?
And is it in the Flight of threescore years,
To push Eternity from human Thought,
And smother souls immortal in the Dust?
A soul immortal, spending all her Fires,
Wasting her strength in strenuous Idleness,
Thrown into Tumult, raptur'd, or alarm'd,   150
At ought this scene can threaten, or indulge,
Resembles *Ocean* into Tempest wrought,
To waft a Feather, or to drown a Fly.

Where falls this Censure? It o'erwhelms myself.
How was my Heart encrusted by the World ?
O how self-fetter'd was my groveling Soul ?
How, like a Worm, was I wrapt round and round
In silken thought, which reptile *Fancy* spun,
Till darken'd *Reason* lay quite clouded o'er
    2   With

6. *Night Thoughts,* design no. 15.

(*BL* 5.49–50). Blake's intimate contact with the eighteenth-century image and its permutations is graphically evident in his illustrations to *Night Thoughts.* Visualizing and reinterpreting Young's paradigmatic and chain-surfeited imagery, Blake produced what must be the most exhaustive catalogue ever made of the illustrative possibilities for chains of being, of the world and self (fig. 6), of death, of pleasure, of ambition, of light (fig. 7), of Providence, of Darkness (fig. 8), of Ages (fig. 9), and of Reason.

The Chain of Being is only the most memorable instance of Being in chains: "Our thoughts are link'd by many a hidden chain," wrote Samuel Rogers,[5] while for Burke, "There is a chain in all our sensations." The French jurist J. M. Servan gave the power of association even more dramatic expression in 1767:

7. *Night Thoughts,* design no. 454.

When you have . . . formed the chain of ideas in the heads of your citizens, you may then boast of leading them and being their masters. A stupid tyrant can restrain slaves with chains of iron, but a real politician fastens them much more strongly by the chain of their own ideas; it is to the firm ground of reason that he attaches the first end, a link all the stronger because we ignore its composition, and because we consider it our own work: despair and time corrode links of iron and steel, but they can do nothing against the habitual association of ideas, except to strengthen it further, and on the soft fibres of the brain is founded the inalterable base of the firmest empires.

Hume wrote of "that chain of causes and effects which constitute our self or person"; Berkeley drew on the Greek word for chain (*seira*) in the title of his

8. *Night Thoughts,* design no. 154.

Siris: A Chain of Philosophical Reflexions; and Alexander Campbell's discussion of Newton was presented as a *Chain of Philosophical Reasoning.* Young wrote of *"Reason's* Golden Chain," and, according to Erasmus Darwin, "Love and Sympathy . . . bind Society in golden chains," while "thoughts to thoughts are link'd with viewless chains." Hannah More felt in 1782 that the essence of sensibility still eluded "the chains / Of Definition," and Boswell, saying that Johnson's understanding was cramped by "his supposed orthodoxy," wrote, "He was confined by a chain which early imagination and long habit made him think massy and strong." Hobbes spoke of "the chayn of a mans Discourse," which was for Albrecht von Haller an intrinsic aspect of human communication: *Natura in reticulum sua genera connexit, non in catenam: homines non possunt nisi catenam sequi, cum non plura simul sermone exponere* [*sic*]. Little wonder that Rousseau's famous words found such resonance; as Blake may have read in the 1791 translation of *The Social Contract,* "Man is born free, and

9. *Night Thoughts,* design no. 322.

yet we see him everywhere in chains: and those who believe themselves the masters of others, cease not to be even greater slaves than the people they govern. How this happens I am ignorant." William Godwin's answer, two years later, was that "the chains fall off of themselves when the magic of opinion is dissolved."

Bacon, seen as having liberated science from the tyranny of scholastic rhetoric by realizing "the false appearances that are imposed upon us by words," is praised by James Thomson as the one who

Led forth the true philosophy . . . long
Held in the magic chain of words and forms
And definitions void . . .

. . . .

Investigating sure the chain of things.[6]

The intense concern for making words adequate to things is mirrored in an ongoing discussion of the "bondage of Riming," which included both cognates, rhyme, and rhythm. Rhyme is in one sense the highest expression of its proverbial complement, reason (precisely *because* it offers "a kind of fixative counterpattern of alogical implication"),[7] so that criticism of rhyme unavoidably involves a conception of reason and its link to words, and the relation of words to things. The discussions of rhyme are particularly interesting since, with the growing power of the doctrine of "association," rhyme was, as it were, an assertion of the operation of *verbal* association opposed to connections "really" in the world. Criticism of rhyme is then part and parcel of the attack on the pun, the concern over "the abuse of words," and is expressed even by Pope:

> *We ply the Memory, we load the brain,*
> *Bind rebel wit, and double chain on chain*
> *Confine the thought, to exercise the breath;*
> *And keep them in the pale of Words till death.*
> *Whate'er the talents, or howe'er design'd,*
> *We hang one jingling padlock on the mind*
> (*The Dunciad* 4.157–62)

Mark Akenside's Shakespeare justifies his "hardy style" and locates its possibility in politics: "I saw this England break the shameful bands / Forg'd for the souls of men by sacred hands"; England has spurned "her Gothic chain" and so, turning again to style, should cease to regard as a model the French language "which fetters eloquence."[8]

Both the chain of association (via the physiological psychology of David Hartley) and its analogue, the chain of discourse or language (implicit in the concern with versification), lead back to book 3 of Locke's *Essay Concerning Human Understanding*, "Of Words." Here the first link of these chains is discovered to be *"a perfect arbitrary imposition"* in which "such a word is made arbitrarily the mark of such an idea" (3.2.8, 3.2.1). This arbitrariness, however, far from being weak or random, is supported by a great and continuing power: "But so far as Words are of Use and Signification, so far is there a constant connexion between the Sound and the *Idea* . . . without which . . . they are nothing but so much insignificant noise" (3.2.7). The "sound annexed" to a collection of ideas must serve "as the sign of that precise determined Collection, and no other. This is very necessary" (3.9.9). The relation between word and referent is arbitrary but "very necessary," reflecting an enforced "constant connexion." The resulting links in the chains of association and language are thus the instruments of an arbitrary, dictatorial power that in its political form was "an eighteenth-century obsession"[9] but that in its invisible semiotic (the word proposed by Locke [4.21.4]) or psycholinguistic expression passed with less regard.

Reporting that he read Locke "when Very Young," Blake declares that "Lockes Opinions of Words & their Fallaciousness are Artful Opinions & Fallacious also" (E659). Blake's rape of Locke begins with *An Island in the Moon*; there Scopprell takes up a book and reads the following passage to his friend Obtuse Angle: "An Easy of ⟨Huming⟩ Understanding by John Lookye Gent   John Locke said Obtuse Angle. O ay Lock said Scopprel" (E456). Hence Urizen, who perhaps makes a cryptic appearance in the exclamation "Your reason Your reason . . . I'll give you an example for your reason" (E450), ends "In chains of the mind locked up" (*BU* 10.25, et al.); so also the speaker of "The Crystal Cabinet" is seized by the Maiden, put "into her Cabinet"—like Locke's "empty cabinet"[10]—and "Lockd" (significantly capitalized) up to consider *reflections* that are moonlight. Locke's "nominal essence" is, for Blake, no different than his "real essence" (cf. Locke's *Essay* 3.14.2), and so it stands as the terminal element of the infernal trinity "Bacon & Newton & Locke" pointed to throughout *Jerusalem.*

"King Edward the Third," in *Poetical Sketches,* opens with the king commending "Liberty, the charter'd right of Englishmen." He exhorts the troops before Cressy, telling them that "The enemy fight in chains, invisible chains, but heavy: / Their minds are fetter'd" (E424). After listening to Blake's eponymous character, "William, Dagworth's Man," identify the king's expedition as sinful ambition (scene 4) and Dagworth in turn label the field of battle as "this prison house" (scene 5), we arrive at the obvious question: how do the king's auditors know that they, too, are not invisibly bound? And what is the nature of such unseen but heavy chains that fasten in the mind?

In "London" we experience these questions for ourselves. Here chartered rights have produced "charter'd streets" and a "charter'd Thames," and are revealed through "marks of weakness, marks of woe," marks that testify to an "arbitrary imposition" based on some mysterious charter or "any writing bestowing privileges or rights." To gloss this definition, Johnson's *Dictionary* cites Sir John Denham: "Here was that *charter* seal'd, wherein the crown / All marks of arbitrary power lays down";[11] but "London" sees that power taken up again, as the chains binding the earlier "enemy" are spoken by fellow-travelers who have also lost the ability to hear themselves:

In every cry of every Man
In every Infants cry of fear,
In every voice: in every ban,
The mind-forg'd manacles I hear

                    [5–8]

The closing line of the stanza first read, "The german forged links I hear"
(E796), referring more to the national ties of the Hanoverian king than the
strength of German iron. The final version, a uniquely Blakean line, moves
beyond the hint of simple political oppression to question the structure of our
experience and our response to it. "I hear," implicitly asks, "do you hear?" "He
that hath ears to hear, let him hear," is the repeated refrain of Jesus, Blake's
"Divine Vision." What do we hear? "Forg'd" or "fraudulent"? Mine or mind?
Man in manacles? Whatever it is, it is everywhere mined and forged in the
hearth of what is heard and seen. In this dungeon of London, Blake's strategy
for unlocking the reader is the multiplication of significance, breaking the
vocal chain at its weakest link, the univocal sign.[12] This deconstruction involves
reorienting logic according to synaesthetic relations of eye and ear. Thus we are
urged to hear here ("hear" is everywhere in this poem) the soldier's sigh
running in blood, while the chimney-s/weeper's cry casts a pall over St.
Paul's:

H*ow the Chimney-sweepers cry*
E*very blackning Church appalls,*
A*nd the hapless Soldiers sigh*
R*uns in blood down Palace walls*
              [9–12, emphasis added]

Thus the opening line of the final stanza again emphasizes "I hear":

But most thro' midnight streets I hear
How the youthful Harlots curse
Blasts the new-born Infants tear
And blights with plagues the Marriage hearse

What is heard is not the "curse" ending the second line, but how it blasts the
"tear" ending the third line and rhyming back to "hear." These words, hear-
curse-tear, bring to bear the contradictions of sight and sound as we hear/see
them coalesce in the final word, "hearse." The oxymoronic image of the
"marriage hearse" points to the impossibility of imagining that sight and

sound, signified and signifier can be eternally "linkd in a marriage chain" (*FZ* 58.13, E339), wedlocked. Gavin Edwards points to this impossibility in connection with stanza 3, seeing that the lines "themselves join sound and sight, voice and matter, but in such a way as to suggest their radical *dis*junction." Edwards also notes the "very complex relations between reading, and hearing, and seeing" in the poem, and continues his discussion of the third stanza in terms particularly appropriate for our purpose: "Blake links 'sigh' and 'blood' as immediately and magically correlative in a way that suggests the active exclusion of chains of cause and effect that might *really* link them." What *really* links is, of course, the question. We do indeed "converge on the final word [of the poem] like a Greek tragedy on its recognition-scene," not simply to encounter "hearse" for an expected "bed," but rather to experience "litterally" what Edwards himself senses, "a liberating movement from off-stage, as a work of scription and vocalization, an inscription of written characters."[13] The importance of the word "marriage" in this general context of hearing and seeing is observed by W. J. T. Mitchell; he notes that in Blake's art, "at one extreme, visual form is constructed in accord with what is, from the point of view of the visual arts, a completely arbitrary, abstract, nonsensory system (language); at the other extreme, the picture is designed as an immediate, synaesthetic presentation of primitive sensory elements. The union of these two concepts of form is embodied, appropriately enough, by the word 'marriage' on the title page of *The Marriage of Heaven and Hell,* which unites the abstraction of typography with the flowing, organic forms of Blake's pictorial style."[14] The univocal signifier, whether Lockean precision, instinctual cry, or unquestioned daily hearsay, is the curse of imagination, its hearse "vehicle"; this poem literally marks and mars our single-visioned dreams of "spousall verse" celebrating the mind fitted to the external world.

For Harold Bloom, "'London' centers itself upon an opposition between *voice* and *writing* . . . [and] offers us a terrifying nostalgia for a lost prophetic *voice,* the voice of Ezekiel and religious logocentrism, which has been replaced by a demonic *visible trace,* by a mark."[15] But Blake, who took more care than most poets with the "visible traces" of his writing, hardly offers a compelling example of nostalgia for voice. As the example of "hearse" illustrates, the "Spirit of Prophecy," which is "the Poetic Genius" (*ARO*), particularly manifests itself in language by using the additional freedom found at the intersection of voice and writing. The achievement of this transcendence of either category makes it impossible to consider "London" an "altogether negative and self-destructive . . . text." We might rather conclude that "London" offers an affirming and self-deconstructing text, one that implicitly urges the reader to allow his or her eye to wander through its chartered lines, marking its marks, and hearing its "every voice." These invitations are conveyed through the contradictions in logic mentioned above and by dint of repetition: we simply cannot encounter "charter'd . . . charter'd," "mark . . . Marks . . . marks," and "every" six times in five lines without being driven to wonder what the words mean and *how* they mean. Our delight as these questions, and then their several "answers," come to light at once proves and loosens "the mind-forg'd manacles." The poem's self-unchaining does not, of course, usher the delighting reader into any realm of absolute free-play, that "allegorical abode where existence hath never come" (*Eur* 6.7). One could characterize the "liberated" version of "London" as merely proliferated chains of association, but such prolific "chains" are no longer limiting, enslaving, "devouring"; they become—the subject of the next chapter—"fibres . . . a living Chain" (*FZ* 63.3, E342).

In addition to expressing her desire for morning, "EARTH'S Answer" asks for someone to

> *Break this heavy chain,*
> *That does freeze my bones around*
> *Selfish! Vain,*
> *Eternal bane!*
> *That free love with bondage bound.*
> [21–25]

Her chain appears to be the creation of a Zeus-like "Starry Jealousy . . . Cold and hoar," who keeps her "prison'd on watry shore." The coldness of her keeper and the freezing power of the chain invoke the common poetic conception of winter locking everything in ice, and remembering the first lines, "Earth raisd up her head," we are led to believe that the rest of her body is restrained by chains of "the darkness dread & drear." Similarly the children of Tiriel are "chaind in thick darkness" and Ahania, like Earth, asks "how can delight, / Renew in these chains of darkness" (*BA* 5.42–43). So the last line in the first stanza, "And her locks cover'd with grey despair," involves more than the image of "grey hairs" on Earth's head. Despair, in the *Visions,* is "cold," while "grey" associates "hoary" (4.2, 7.19) and "the grey hoar frost" (*FZ* 138.9, E406). Her "locks," then, also form part of the cold, frost-covered chain; her hair represents her "mind-locks" (cf. *Eur* 10.29). This identity of Earth, linked to the Homeric and Miltonic golden chain, and the englobed, enchained

mind—like Prometheus ("Forethought") in the original "adamantine chains"—
is also evident in Samuel Rogers's *Ode to Superstition* (1786): "Thy chain of
adamant can bind / That little world, the human mind" (1.1). The serpent
pictured at the bottom of "EARTH'S Answer" shows another chain. It is the
bound form of free love: "men bound beneath the heavens in a reptile form,"
"Like a serpent! like an iron chain" (*Tir* 8.10, *BL* 5.16). Earth is held by chains,
which jealously attempt to limit her to monogamous meaning and prohibit the
free intercourse of signification. But it seems to be the nature of Earth and
language not to endure restraint; her very locks transform themselves. The
language of the third stanza manifests the earth's potential liberation from
univocal syntax and meaning, as the various constructions in themselves contest the heavy chain:

> *Selfish father of men*
> *Cruel jealous selfish fear*
> *Can delight*
> *Chain'd in night*
> *The virgins of youth and morning bear.*
> > ["EARTH'S Answer," 11–15]

The Marriage of Heaven and Hell goes into the nature of the chains in greater
detail.

> The Giants who formed this world into its sensual existence and now seem to
> live in it in chains, are in truth. the causes of its life & the sources of all activity,
> but the chains are, the cunning of weak and tame minds. which have power to
> resist energy, according to the proverb, the weak in courage is strong in cunning.
> Thus one portion of being, is the Prolific. the other, the Devouring: to the
> devourer it seems as if the producer was in his chains, but it is not so, he only takes
> portions of existence and fancies that the whole.
> > [pl. 16]

This recapitulates plate 11, which tells how "the ancient Poets animated all
sensible objects with Gods or Geniuses, calling them by the names." However,
"a system was formed, which some took advantage of, & enslav'd the vulgar by
attempting to realize or abstract the mental deities from their objects." Hazard
Adams has pointed out that the activity of "the ancient poets" was "the
creation of language," but that "the poetic verbal universe that holds subject,
deities, and object together is destroyed by a competing idea of language that
claims for itself only the power to point outward toward *things*."[16] This is the

language-chain, which limits us to "portions of existence"; the chains in which the Giants "seem" to live are, similarly, only our devouring perception. This relation between language, perception, and the giant man enchained underlies Blake's exclamation at the beginning of *Jerusalem* that "Poetry Fetter'd, Fetters the Human Race!" (*J* 3). Such fetters, the chains of uninspired language and quotidian association, "the soft fetters of easy imitation,"[17] are like those binding the inhabitants of the cave in Plato's *Republic*. As presented by Blake's acquaintance Thomas Taylor, "Suppose them to have been in this cave from their childhood, with chains both on their legs and neck, so as to remain there, and only able to look before them, but by the chain incapable to turn their heads around."[18] So, in *Europe,*

> *With bands of iron round their necks fasten'd into the walls*
> *The citizens: in leaden gyves the inhabitants of suburbs*
> *Walk heavy . . .*

[12.29–31]

while *The Book of Los* shows "the Eternal Prophet bound in a chain / Compell'd to watch Urizens shadow" (3.31–32).

The ground of perception, like language, generally goes unperceived, and this ignorance is an intrinsic attribute of chains, an aspect of the invisibility of the determining dimension of language that Ferdinand de Saussure called *langue.* Thus Milton "wrote in fetters when he wrote of Angels & God" because "he was a true Poet and of the Devils Party without knowing it" (*MHH* 5). Religion with its laws and mysteries is an instrument restraining awareness; its popular etymology, "to bind back" (*re-ligiare*), testified to its enchaining function.[19] *America* sees "the female spirits of the dead pining in bonds of religion; / Run from their fetters reddening" (15.23–24). The liberating message of Jesus was hampered by his disciples' fantasies of "chains of darkness" and "everlasting chains" to bind fallen souls until Judgment; but true language and true perception are of the Devil's Party, itself ultimately Jesus', because they reject writing in fetters and urge instead, as the "Proverbs of Hell" witness, the free flow of significance. Both the concept of "energy" in Blake's early poetry and that of "imagination," which dominates the longer poems, are expressions of the desire to soar above a common bound, to copulate as freely as possible. The transition between these two terms marks Blake's realization that such polymorphous, polysemous desire is to be acted and answered in unrestrained language: "If in the morning sun I find it: there my eyes are fix'd / In happy copulation" (*VDA* 6.23–7.1).

The Book of Urizen tells the story of the binding of its subject like this:

Forgetfulness, dumbness, necessity!
In chains of the mind locked up,
Like fetters of ice shrinking together
Disorganiz'd, rent from Eternity,
Los beat on his fetters of iron
        [10.24–28; cf. *FZ* 54.4–5, E336]

Urizen's chains are made by Los, "the eternal Prophet." Urizen having separated from Eternity through his mournful discovery of self-love, Los must for the time being bind him back by whatever means possible—any Urizen being better than none. Los must bind himself to Urizen, and it is precisely this act of sacrifice that holds the key to their mutual resurrection. So, as things get worse before they get better, "the terrible race of Los & Enitharmon gave / Laws & Religion to the sons of Har` binding them more / And more to Earth."[20] As part of his (Los/Urizen's) binding, Urizen is given a body consisting of the chained changing world. The pun is evidently intended since:

[Los] watch'd in shuddring fear
The dark changes & bound every change
With rivets of iron & brass;

And these were the changes of Urizen.
        [*BU* 8.9–12]

Later Los sees Urizen, "in his chains bound." Perhaps the most intriguing and spectacular aspect of this bound creation is the first "change," Urizen's backbone:

Like the linked infernal chain;
A vast Spine writh'd in torment
Upon the winds;
        [*BU* 10.36–38]

or, as *The Book of Los* sees it, "Like a serpent! like an iron chain / Whirling about in the Deep." These connections disclose the underlying identification that:

[Urizen's] *spine* = *serpent* [worm] = *chain* [gravity].

Links here are the idea that the spinal marrow of a dead man turns into a snake,[21] the classical and Norse conception of the serpent wound around the earth (Blake labels his title-page illustration to Gray's *The Descent of Odin*, "The Serpent who Girds the Earth"), and the Homeric and Miltonic golden chain of being that binds the earth. After Newton the image of gravity as a chain became common; so James Thomson apostrophizes the Sun in *Summer*:

> *'Tis by thy secret, strong, attractive force,*
> *As with a chain indissoluble bound,*
> *Thy system rolls entire.*
>
> [97–99]

In a footnote on the "golden everlasting Chain" of Jove in book 8 of the *Iliad*, the original source for chain-of-being imagery, Pope suggested that "the *Aegyptians* understood the true System of the World," so that "it will be no strained Interpretation to say, that by the Inability of the Gods to pull *Jupiter* out of his Place with this *Catena*, may be understood the superior attractive Force of the Sun, whereby he continues unmoved, and draws all the rest of the Planets toward him."[22] This is the "Back bone of Urizen," which appears in "the dark void" as an iron chain "whirling about in the Deep." "Chain'd to one centre whirl'd the kindred spheres, / And mark'd with lunar cycles solar years," wrote Erasmus Darwin of the earth and its newly created moon.[23]

Los makes the Sun "the chaind Orb" (*BL* 5.40) and casts it "down into the Deeps." Then

> *He the vast Spine of Urizen siez'd*
> *And bound down to the glowing illusion*
> [*BL* 5.46–47][24]

Urizen's sevenfold "chainges" produce the biological body (*BU* 10.36–13.19), which we may describe today as bound in links of stimulus-response, tethered to the history of its evolving mutations. This is one aspect of the body "obscuring the immense Orb of fire" as it encases Energy and Imagination in material forms—including language—necessary to prevent Urizen from disintegrating into the void he created. So the other spiritual suns ("sons of Eternity," *BU* 5.34) were changed to material stars:

> *Thus were the stars of heaven created like a golden chain*
> *To bind the Body of Man to heaven from falling into the Abyss*
> [*FZ* 33.16–17, E322]

At the same time, the perceptual "Abyss" and the Body of Man are maintained in their present state by the chain; it is, after all, the mind of man that "created" the images of the golden and other chains. They came into being with the cosmic fall from "Unity" into the present ontological realities, or chains, of gravity, time, the nervous system, and language; and, having securely instituted these basic parameters, they cannot of themselves unlock their prisoners. Like the image of the golden chain, these seemingly steadfast realities must also be understood in terms of their having been created and imposed, if not by an evil or naive fabler then by some earlier and different form of consciousness. The further back we trace a chain (to the imposition of gravity, say), the more free of it we become. In the end, or beginning, our chains will be seen as vestigial appendages helping "two Eternities meet together" (*M* 13.11).

On one level, for example, the existence of the astronomical orbs "creates" time (e.g., moon: month); but for Blake, their existence is a function of our perception: *we* established them as markers of time:

> *The Eternal Prophet heavd the dark bellows,*
> *And turn'd restless the tongs; and the hammer*
> *Incessant beat; forging chains new & new*
> *Numb'ring with links. hours, days & years*
>
> *The eternal mind bounded began to roll*
>   [*BU* 10.15–19; cf. *FZ* 52.29 ff., E335][25]

Here again the (eternal) mind has forged its manacles, now as bonds of linked time. Eternity is no longer (the) present; all that remains for most is the unquestioning acceptance offered by one of Blake's contemporaries in 1790: "The change of seasons, and the golden chain / That links the year, and leads the ages on / And joins them to eternity."[26] The "golden chain" points to the creation of time; one part of that chain began when the stars and planets became primary objects of speculation (hence "the stars of Urizen," *Eur* 14.33; *FZ* 93.26, E365), leading to the development of abstract reasoning ("*Reason's* golden chain," as Young wrote). Reasoning in turn created the clock and chain of linear, sequential time (tame time as opposed to Los's "messenger to Eden," the deliciously synchronic, synaesthetic, polysemous "Wild Thyme").[27] This process produced Stonehenge, already hypothesized by the mid eighteenth century as an instrument based on, and intended for, the measurement of time.[28] Blake erred with his contemporaries in attributing Stonehenge to the

Druids, but was correct in identifying it as a temple to time and astronomical reasoning built by Newton's forebears:

> *They build a stupendous Building on the Plain of Salisbury; with chains*
> *Of rocks round London Stone: of Reasonings: of unhewn Demonstrations*
> *In labyrinthine arches. (Mighty Urizen the Architect.) thro which*
> *The Heavens might revolve & Eternity be bound in their chain.*
>
> [*J* 66.2–5]

So, in *The Four Zoas,* Urizen tries to make "another world better suited to obey," where he would be king and "all futurity be bound in his vast chain" (73.20, E350).

The Book of Urizen also tells for the first time the story of the chaining of Orc. After Orc's birth, Los's jealousy appears as a girdle tightening around his own bosom. For a while his sobbings nightly break the girdle:

> *The girdle was form'd by day;*
> *By night was burst in twain.*
>
> *These falling down on the rock*
> *Into an iron Chain*
> *In each other link by link lock'd*
>
> *They took Orc to the top of a mountain.*
> *O how Enitharmon wept!*
> *They chain'd his young limbs to the rock*
> *With the Chain of Jealousy*
> *Beneath Urizens deathful shadow*
>
> [20.16–25]

Plate 21 (fig. 10) shows the chain of jealousy emerging from Los's chest, dropping past his loins to assimilate his erect penis as one of its rigid links, and disappearing into the ground at the base of an improvised anvil. The chain of jealousy mirrors the chain of generations (as the pictured chain mirrors the relation of Orc to Enitharmon), and again we witness the forging of a primal link, the enslavement of the child (and ensuing generations) to the psychosexual conflict his existence occasions.[29] This struggle, like that for the realization of language, may be seen as a contest over "perfect arbitrary imposition": a struggle, that is, for the unequivocal, unilateral possession (enchainment) of the signifier. "The chains are, the cunning of weak and tame minds, which

10. *The Book of Urizen*, pl. 21.

have power to resist energy" (*MHH,* above). The father's resentment of filial desire or energy comes to be internalized by the son, who so perpetuates "the Links of fate link after link an endless chain of sorrows" (*FZ* 53.28, E336). The oedipal chain doubles the body's biological one, and sexuality, cut off from its polymorphous, polysemous free expression, becomes another form of enslavement; Albion sees "his Sons assimilate with Luvah, bound in the bonds / Of spiritual Hate, from which springs Sexual Love as iron chains" (*J* 54.11–12). The story of the chaining of Orc is retold and continued in "Night the Fifth" of *The Four Zoas*. There "Los & Enitharmon / Felt all the sorrow Parents feel," and return to release their son only to find that "fibres had from the Chain of

Jealousy inwove themselves / In a swift vegetation" (62.23–24, E342) around Orc and the rock. Their attempt is in vain, since they cannot

> . . . *uproot the infernal chain. for it had taken root*
> *Into the iron rock & grew a chain beneath the Earth*
> *Even to the Center wrapping round the Center & the limbs*
> *Of Orc entering with the fibres. became one with him a living Chain*
> *Sustained by the Demons life*
>
> [62.32–63.4, E342]

Darwin's *Zoonomia* also suggests that the body's living fibres and nerves can themselves be seen as chains: "This perpetual chain of causes and effects, whose first link is rivetted to the throne of GOD, divides itself into innumberable diverging branches . . . like the nerves arising from the brain" (p. 393).

The fiery form of Orc merges into the energy of nature; the life-force repressed and used by the reasoning mind itself represses and uses the reasoning mind. The Earth has become a "chained Orb"—Orc-sustained—like "the terrible Sun clos'd in an orb" (*FR* 211). As Los offers an anagram of "sol," so fiery red Orc may be his orb, his terrible son. In "Night the Sixth" of *The Four Zoas,* Orc is explicitly represented as a sun, the focus of the comets' "excentric paths" (75.28 ff., E345), further developing his role with *revolution* and its portents. The chain of jealousy becomes a feature of Blake's cosmography; *Milton* emphasizes twice the old prophecy that its protagonist will "ascend forward from Felpham's Vale & break the Chain / Of Jealousy from all its roots" (23.37–38; cf. 20.59–61). This same section of *Milton* tells of "the fires of youth / Bound with the Chain of Jealousy by Los & Enitharmon," a formulation resonating with their having given "Laws & Religion" to bind the sons of Har "to Earth." The chain of jealousy is more than Los's fear of loss of love. Though the chain belongs to Los, it exists *sub specie* Urizen, first appearing "beneath Urizens deathful shadow." Orc, in fact, confronts Urizen as "the cold attractive power that holds me in this chain," so identifying him as gravity in the standard metaphor and also as the cold or gelid chain of "Starry Jealousy." The Sun, then, is jealous of its planets as Los is jealous of his fiery son. "Ocalythron binds the Sun into a Jealous Globe" (*M* 10.19), that is, one imposing a gravitational chain; and "EARTH'S Answer" from her chained condition has already been presented.

The astronomical bodies in their chains are an expression of the enslavement of Orcean energy. A mundane analogue for Blake was the slave trade, rooted in white ethnocentric claims for profit. Radical humanitarian though he was, we ought to recognize that for Blake, as in the following passage, the slave trade showed only another aspect of the universe in chains: "And slaves in myriads in ship loads burden the hoarse sounding deep / Rattling with clanking chains the Universal Empire groans" (*FZ* 95.29–30, E361). Here, for example, the deep becomes "the Deep" of Urizen in the following line, the abyss in which is hung the Sun. "Universal Empire" reflects back eleven lines to the "Universal Ornament . . . the ends of heaven" and still further to the one other instance of the imperial root in the poem, "a bright Universe Empery" (3.10, E301). The "slaves in myriads" are another vision of Urizen's Sons or suns, "his myriads" of two lines following. In this passage, the slave trade figures largely as yet another rattle of the "clanking chains" from which the whole creation groans to be delivered (cf. *J* 16.26); such expanding cross-reference mocks the chains of criticism.

Orc contained his chains from the beginning. He cannot consume all since the structure that allowed his conception—language and imagination—cannot be burned away. His serpent form in *America* is but a step toward the "living chain" of jealousy sustained by his life; similarly his binding, beginning with *The Book of Urizen,* must be seen as the complement to Urizen's. The only other instance of "the infernal chain" rooting Orc to the Earth is "the linked infernal chain; / A vast Spine" made for Urizen. To say that Orc is Urizen's spine or that Urizen is Orc's chain is to suggest the reciprocity (like the id and the superego, signifier and signified) that is both the backbone and chain of human experience. Confronting Urizen, Orc realizes, "now when *I* rage my fetters bind me more," yet at the same time he accuses Urizen: "*Thou* dost restrain my fury. . . . *Thou* wilt not cease from rage" (*FZ* 80.36, E356). Frye hints at the common chain when he observes that as early as *The Book of Ahania* (itself dated a year after *The Book of Urizen*), "Blake is becoming increasingly aware that by 'Orc' he means something inseparably attached to Urizen."[30]

Jealousy is like a chain in that it will not release its object, its "signified." While Orc flames and Urizen freezes through *America* (1793), with the first appearance of Los in 1794 (*The Book of Urizen*) both are enchained; Orc is tied down with the chain of jealousy under the auspices of the already chain-linked Urizen. Los seems as jealous for himself as the newborn infant or ego; he chains Urizen to give him form and restrains Orc to give *him* form. Rather than a figure of prolific inspiration, Los looks very much like one of the "devourers" described in *The Marriage;* he is, in effect, the source of the "chains" circumscribing his experience, Urizen and orbed Orc. As Being, Los—the self-realization of being lost—must first institute the chains of being to halt the fall into disunity, for "Truth has bounds. Error none" (*BL* 4.30). But then the poet must grasp these chains as openly and clearly as possible. For while "Deceit," especially self-deceit, "forges fetters for the mind," "Love . . . breaks all chains from every mind" (E472). Accepting the burden of incarnation/incarceration[31] is the first step toward freedom:

> *So Orc became*
> *As Los a father to his brethren & he joyd in the dark lake*
> *Tho bound with chains of Jealousy*
>
> [*FZ* 90.47–49, E371]

The ultimate of love is forgivingness, which also embraces our own being linked to a situation (language, world, body) not knowingly self-created, though in good measure we are created by it. To forgive, for Blake, is the way to understand.

In "Night the Ninth Being the Last Judgment," the shackles fall from Urizen as he realizes that the binding power of his chains was a function of his having failed to see them. The image offers a cracking mirror in which the reader may catch a glimpse of his or her individual, chained experience:

> *Urizen said. I have Erred & my Error remains with me*
> *What Chain encompasses in what Lock is the river of light confind*
> *That issues forth in the morning by measure & the evening by carefulness*
> *Where shall we take our stand to view the infinite & unbounded*
> *Or where are human feet for Lo our eyes are in the heavens*
>
> *He ceasd for rivn link from link the bursting Universe explodes*
>
> [122.21–26, E391–392]

Urizen has taken that step so evidently feared by Edmund Waller, where, "one link dissolved, the whole creation ends."[32] Precisely this image of a chain that guards and overvalues its every link must be broken; chains, connections of some sort there will undoubtedly be, but provision must be made for those "links," like the incarnate word, that "pass the limits of possibility, as it appears / To individual perception" (*J* 62.19–20). Blake would call Urizen's self-recognition a beginning of true creation, destroying the separate and separating links of the chain of being, the isolated moments of the seriatim progression of time, and the attractive, compelling power of gravity and reason. The chain's logic of restraint is finally located and manifested in the prison of prosaic language continuously forged by reason and memory (Samuel Rogers, praising *The Pleasures of Memory* in 1792, writes, "Hail,

MEMORY, hail! thy universal reign / Guards the least link of Being's glorious chain" [1.358–59]). But this chain is always ready to be snapped by the divine or polysemous character of poetic, prophetic language. Urizen's confession explodes, as if deliberately, one of the most pertinent examples Samuel Johnson offers for "chain": "A line of links with which land is measured. A surveyor may as soon, with his chain, measure out infinite space, as a philosopher, by the quickest flight of mind, reach it, or, by thinking, comprehend it. Locke."[33] In "The Last Judgment," "our eyes are in" Urizen; "our" becomes "are," and being "Lo" we are nonetheless "in the heavens," as our feet are no longer human but poetic. Locke's "candle of understanding"—the regular canals[34] and channels of knowledge—has become a "river of light," which in full flood rives the torch links and chain links of the Uni-verse.

Blake at once announces and surpasses the Romantic and modern concern with liberation, or naive unchaining. In the sonnet prefixed to *The Prisoner of Chillon*, Byron praises the "eternal spirit of the chainless mind," but returns at once to the actual prison and fetters prompting the expression. Shelley imagines more profoundly a break in "the links of the great chain of things" that have hitherto weighed upon "every thought within the mind of man."[35] These broken links are reconstituted almost immediately as a "chain of linked thought," leading one observer to comment, "that chains binding and chains linking may be the same thing does not occur to Shelley."[36] Indeed, Shelley's pained cry at the end of *Epipsychidion* that his "winged words" are themselves "chains of lead" is emblematic of his final failure of vision. But Blake's treatment of chains directs itself toward an apocalyptic uncovering of language, an unchaining of thought and association: phonetic, semantic, and historical associations are stressed past their breaking points (the unchaining text bursts its semes). From being what we beheld—a link in the chain of being or discourse—we must become what we now behold: polysemous consciousness (fourfold perhaps) creating and created in, going forth and returning to language.

Such a consciousness will be still chained; but, using one chain to contest and transform another, it will find the validation of freedom, presence, and imagination in the moment of transition from one to another across the chain-strung void. Unchaining, like disenchantment, is finally relative; as "it is impossible to think without images of somewhat on earth" (E600), so there are links that cannot be broken while we are as we are. Blake offers instead an experience of "words of Eternity," a language not of puns mocking or amusing, but one where plural meanings, image of the infinite, are equally present in finite words. Such proliferation of meaning points toward a state where the chains begin to dissolve and melt together, where, rather than a universe interlinked and netted with univocal lines of discourse, each in its very existence bespeaking absence or loss, we participate in the plenum of being-presence, "the Universal Brotherhood of Eden." By his chains, Blake gives us to understand that man serves as his own jailer, imprisoned by his vocabulary, culture, and perception; that the inexorability of a "chain of events" derives from our labeling it so, the logic in a "chain of reasoning" from our being bound to its premise. Neither reason nor understanding can wholly lift us from the realm of human bondage. Yet, though we ourselves are the chain of jealousy and the mind-forg'd manacles, already inscribed (as some might say) in the chains of signification, it is in an imaginative vision of the nature of those chains and fetters, the nature of present perception and its transmission, that we find the key to our release: a release when we shall again "be changed, In a moment, in the twinkling of an eye" (1 Cor. 15:51–52) and see instead of chains, fibres.

CHAPTER FIVE

Fibres of Being [The Line, 2]

. . . the interiors of Albions fibres & nerves were hidden
From Los; astonishd he beheld only the petrified surfaces
William Blake, *Jerusalem*

G. S. ROUSSEAU HAS RECENTLY SUGGESTED that the origins, "at the deepest levels," of the pervasive eighteenth-century concern with "sensibility" are to be located in Locke and, more particularly, in the paradigm of cerebral and neurological organization expounded by Thomas Willis, one of Locke's teachers. Willis "was the first scientist clearly and loudly to posit that the seat of the soul is strictly limited to the brain," so laying the ground for Locke's intuitive realization "that the whole argument about knowledge pivots upon the concept and definition of 'sensation.'" As a result of the late seventeenth-century "revolution in brain theory," it became possible "to expect the totality of human feeling to be nothing but motion in the nerves." Rousseau concludes that the "Age of Sensibility," with its omnipresent nervous maladies and emphasis on sentiment and sensation, is heir to a preceding philosophic concern with "internalization," which found expression in "the new science of man, directing thought about man from his visible eyes and expressive face to his unseen nerves and controlling brain."[1]

These remarks can apply with special force to Blake, who declares his purpose "to open the immortal Eyes / Of Man inwards into the Worlds of Thought," and who, alone among major poets, dwells on "nerves" and "fibres."[2] Moreover, Blake's use of these terms, especially "fibre," proves far from simple. Even the transparency of the memorable couplet in *Auguries of Innocence*

Each outcry of the hunted Hare
A fibre from the Brain does tear
[13–14]

becomes problematic if the nature of the "fibre" is questioned, not to mention its subliminal gloss as a "hair." Urizen uses the word in a different fashion, lamenting to Ahania that:

Vala shall become a Worm in Enitharmons Womb
Laying her seed upon the fibres soon to issue forth
[FZ 38.8–9, E326]

Here "the fibres" refer to Orc in his embryonic state of development. The fetal connotations do not, however, seem to apply to the description of

the Ulro: a vast Polypus
Of living fibres down into the Sea of Time & Space growing
A self-devouring monstrous Human Death
[M 34.24–26]

And none of these associations explain Los's injunction to Enitharmon:

How then can I ever again be united as Man with Man
While thou my Emanation refusest my Fibres of dominion?
When Souls mingle & join thro all the Fibres of Brotherhood
Can there be any secret joy on Earth greater than this?
[J 88.12–15]

Fibre, it is evident, offers an important example of the polysemous words constituting Blake's vision.[3] Moreover, an examination of Albion's fibres will perhaps discover one clue to his "souls disease," his nervous disorder—for, as Pope's physician, William Cheselden, argued, it is the "exquisite state of the nerves that leads to melancholy, to madness, and finally of necessity to suicide."[4]

Brought into English from the Latin *fibra*, fibre did not find any strong specific signification and so became a "concept" word, representing, as it had in antiquity, "a basic unit of animal and plant life."[5] The word was initially employed directly from Latin, with its senses of living string or filament, and, in an expansion of the idea, entrails. The first sense moved into both the vegetable world, where it became an aspect of root structure—"*Fibres*, the smal threads, or hair-like strings of roots"[6]—and the animal world, where it became associated with veins, and to a lesser extent at first, sinews and nerves; Edward Topsell says of the hart, "his blood . . . hath no Fibres or small veins in it" (1658, *OED*, s.v.). The second Latin sense finds its greatest use in Blake's favorite Roman poet, Ovid, as in the *Metamorphoses* 15.136–37, which tells of a sacrificed ox:

> *Protinus ereptas viventi pectore fibras*
> *Inspiciunt, mentesque deum scrutantur in illis.*

The word is sometimes "Englished" by Ovid's first and best translator, George Sandys, as "the threads of Life, his fivers [sic]."[7]

Blake along with the age believed that such searching of the fibres was practiced by the Druids on human victims; Thomas Pennant quotes Tacitus in reporting that "the Britons held it right to sacrifice on their altars with blood of their captives, and to consult the gods by the inspection of human entrails."[8] This practice was for Blake an epitome of man's fall into division, representing the depersonalization of the human being and mystification of the body to the point that the configuration of the fibres was more regarded than being itself. Plate 25 of *Jerusalem* (fig. 11) offers an explicit image of the process and plays on the various sense of "fibre." Vala, Rahab, and Tirzah (perhaps the one with false tears) watch as they eviscerate Albion—winding his fibres into a ball—while at the same time Vala's fingers and hair trail off in fibres; as Morton Paley notes, "the bowels and the umbilical cord are equally manifestations of those fibres of vegetation which play so large a thematic role in Blake's later works."[9] Tharmas's melancholy outcry to Enion at the beginning of *The Four Zoas* presents another version of the same sacrifice:

> *Why wilt thou Examine every little fibre of my soul*
> *Spreading them out before the Sun like Stalks of flax to dry*
> [4.29–30, E302]

This image of a fibrous soul reflects an appropriate eighteenth-century modification of haruspication by locating the divine information in the "fibrillous" brain and its "fibrillary matter."[10]

From his earliest uses, Blake seizes on the word as a means of connecting human and vegetable life, micro- and macrocosm. On her subterranean voyage, Thel sees

> . . . *the couches of the dead, & where the fibrous roots*
> *Of every heart on earth infixes deep its restless twists*
> [*Thel* 6.3–4]

11. *Jerusalem,* pl. 25, detail.

We begin underground looking at plant roots (a motif repeated in the *Marriage*, pl. 17) and are led by the associative overlap of "fibre"—which had on occasion been rendered by Sandys as "heart-strings" and used by Young in describing "the tender tyes, / Close-twisted with the fibres of the heart" (*NT* 5.1058–59)—to bind together the "nature" of the heart and its anagram, earth. The conception of human fibres growing up from fibrous roots in the earth is the first instance of what later becomes one of Blake's pervasive graphic images: human forms seen in roots, growing out of roots, or with extremities disappearing into fibres of vegetation or flames of fi(b)re. In plate 1 of *America* (fig. 12), "root-bound" figures writhe in the roots, while a worm weaves through the space beneath the text.[11] The total effect suggests a sequence similar to that represented on plate 15 (fig. 13), where spiritual life changes—attenuates—into vegetation: fires rise to fibres and physical forms and finally a phoenixlike eagle ready to take flight. In plate 19 of *Milton* (fig. 14), we see Los when "in fibrous strength / His limbs shot forth like roots of trees" (lines 34–35). In plate 36[40] of *Jerusalem* (fig. 15), vines and leaf stems replace his left arm—representing here, perhaps, the artist's connection to, and creation of, these forms. Throughout Blake's illuminated work, tendrils or fibres of vegetation merge and weave into the words of the text (fig. 12 again), offering a paradoxical comment on the ultimately vegetable nature of writing, or the written structure of nature. Such graphic effect literally anticipates Jacques Derrida's pronouncement "that a text is never anything but a *system of roots*"[12]—it is what we might expect to see, entering the grave where "tangled roots perplex our ways."

The presence of fibres at the root of human physical existence is evident in the creation of "the first female":

> *The globe of life blood trembled*
> *Branching out into roots;*
> *Fibrous, writhing upon the winds;*
> *Fibres of blood, milk and tears;*
> [*BU* 18.1–4]

Carmen S. Kreiter observes that "Blake's choice of 'fibres' is not fortuitous, it refers poetically to the three kinds of vessels anatomists had discovered in the body, the last two only recently—vessels conveying blood, milky chyle (lacteals), and tears (lacrymals)."[13] Kreiter's transition from "fibres" to "vessels" glosses over the vexing problem of the structure of fibres—"lacteals" and "lacrymals" were generally classed as ducts, while fibres were the subject of a long and intense debate over the solidity or hollowness of nerves. Appearing the same year as *Urizen*, the first volume of Erasmus Darwin's *Zoonomia* presented another version of fibrous conception: "I conceive the primordium, or rudiment of the embryon, as secreted from the blood of the parent, to consist of a simple living filament as a muscular fibre; which I suppose to be an extremity of a nerve of loco-motion" (1:489). The ensuing embryological development had already received Darwin's poetical treatment: "First in translucent lymph with cobweb-threads / The Brain's fine floating tissue swells, and spreads; / Nerve after nerve the glistening spine descends."[14]

The shadowy daughter of Urthona stood before red Orc.
When fourteen suns had faintly journeyd oer his dark abode;
His food she brought in iron baskets, his drink in cups of iron:
Crownd with a helmet & dark hair the nameless female stood;
A quiver with its burning stores, a bow like that of night.
When pestilence is shot from heaven; no other arms she need:
Invulnerable tho' naked, save where clouds roll round her loins,
Their awful folds in the dark air; silent she stood as night;
For never from her iron tongue could voice or sound arise;
But dumb till that dread day when Orc assayd his fierce embrace.

Dark virgin; said the hairy youth, thy father stern abhorr'd;
Rivets my tenfold chains while still on high my spirit soars;
Sometimes an eagle screaming in the sky, sometimes a lion,
Stalking upon the mountains, & sometimes a whale I lash
The raging fathomless abyss, anon a serpent folding
Around the pillars of Urthona, and round thy dark limbs,
On the Canadian wilds I fold, feeble my spirit folds.
For chaind beneath I rend these caverns: when thou bringest food
I howl my joy: and my red eyes seek to behold thy face
In vain! these clouds roll to & fro, & hide thee from my sight.

12. *America*, pl. 1.

Blake's biological image appears again in *The Book of Los*, which describes "organs like roots / Shooting out from the seed" (4.64–65). The age-old association of conception and planted seed is bound into the language, and Swedenborg's use, in a passage Blake annotated, is standard: "Seeds are Beginnings, the Womb or Ovum is as the Earth, the State before Birth is as the State of Seed in the Ground while it puts forth its Root."[15] For Blake, the state after birth is usually governed by the same vegetable imagery, and indeed the human form can all too easily revert to fibrous nature, as when

> . . . *Enitharmon pale & cold in milky juices flowd*
> *Into a form of Vegetation living having a voice*
> *Moving in rootlike fibres trembling in fear upon the Earth*
>   [*FZ* 107.28–30, E383]

The analogy of conception to a seed planted in the ground, however, came to be challenged by the different associations of a scientific discourse that saw the embryo "swimming in water" (*liquor amnii*).[16] This may serve to account for the aquatic environment surrounding the organ-shooting seed in *The Book of Los* mentioned above, and Blake's conception of the "Polypus"—which is, essentially, the aqueous version of a mass of living fibres. Chapter 3 of *The Book of Los* begins:

> *The Lungs heave incessant, dull and heavy*
> *For as yet were all other parts formless*
> *Shiv'ring: clinging around like a cloud*
> *Dim & glutinous as the white Polypus*
> *Driv'n by waves & englob'd on the tide.*
>   [4.54–58]

Discussing these lungs, Paul Miner observes that "the contraction and dilation of the Medusae, called by the ancients *Sea Lungs*, resemble closely the action of respiration in the human chest."[17] The ultimate reference, as we shall see, is far more profound; for instance, the Greek word for lungs, πλευμόνες (as in Latin *pulmo* and its English derivatives), "implies 'floating' [as in the] English 'lights,' now confined to the lungs of beasts."[18] In the mid eighteenth century, "Sea Lungs" were identified as "a very singular and odd animal; it seems a mere lump, of whitish semi-pellucid jelly" (1752, *OED*, s.v.). But Blake's image also suggests the placenta in its first stages of growth, characterized—in the *Encyclopaedia Britannica*'s early articles on "Generation," for example—as being

14. *Milton*, pl. 19, detail.

13. *America,* pl. 15, detail.

15. *Jerusalem,*
pl. 36(40), detail.

"like a little cloud."[19] As for the cloud's "glutinous" nature, William Harvey had long since stated that "the first rudiment of the body is onely a *similar soft gluten*, or *stiff substance*, not unlike a *spermatical concernment*, or *coagulated seed*."[20]

None of these associations offer any rationale for why, in this instance, the lungs are the first organs to form—the only primacy possessed by the lungs is that they are the organs effectively initiating our postnatal interaction with the world. But in *The Wisdom of Angels Concerning Divine Love and Divine Wisdom*, Blake would have encountered Swedenborg's involved physiological and spiritual imagery, in which the lungs correspond to "understanding."[21] The lungs, or understanding, Swedenborg says, "depend upon the Blood from the Heart," which represents "love" and "affection"; so, "understanding does nothing from itself," a sentiment Blake underlined. According to Swedenborg, "*thought corresponds to respiration*," and "the Ramifications of the Bronchia of the Lungs correspond *to perceptions and Thoughts* from . . . Affections." In *The Book of Los*, however, Blake is not so much interested in spiritual love and affection as in the phenomenon of how "*incessant* the falling *Mind* labour'd / *Organizing* itself "[22] when it was itself "like the babe / New born into *our* world" and when "contemplative thoughts first arose" leading, in particular, to brachia, or "branchy forms: *organizing* the Human" (4.38–39, 40, 44). So the mind is the lungs floating by thought over the chaotic waters; but as the organization of thought requires "finite inflexible organs" (4.45), the lungs sink, "over-weigh'd,"[23] and create a body suitable for submarine existence in the sea of time and space:

> *his spent Lungs*
> *Began intricate pipes that drew in*
> *The spawn of the waters. Outbranching*
>
> *An immense Fibrous form*
>
> [4.68–71]

Miner's linking of the lungs and the Polypus via "Sea Lungs" seems mis-placed, though, for it is the "other parts formless . . . clinging around" to which the Polypus is compared on its first appearance in Blake's work. S. Foster Damon is also taken with the image of ocean coelenterates, concluding that Blake's Polypus "seems to be . . . a jellyfish."[24] In the late eighteenth century, "polypus" had two primary meanings. In the first it denoted "a species of hydra, which, although cut in a thousand pieces and in every direction, still exists and each section becomes a complete animal."[25] This had been a topic of considerable fashionable interest, crystallized by Henry Baker's *An Attempt toward a Natural History of the Polype* (London, 1743), which dwelt with loving concern over the "mill-like" motion of the polyp's arms, setting up a current to draw in objects; the instant death of prey on being bitten; the polyp's manner of giving birth by budding off; and its regeneration if severed. Henry Fielding, for one, was moved to write a satire in the style of *Philosophical Transactions*, which replaced the polypus with a "Chrysipus," or English guinea, possessing similar powers of reduplication.[26] Baker felt he had proved that the polyp was an animal, but this remained a much-debated point; significant for Blake's conception is Buffon's judgment later in the century that "the polypi . . . may be regarded as the link which connects the animal and vegetable Kingdoms."[27] The polyp's regenerating power fascinated observers, and scientific discussion continued through the remainder of the century. In France, the image influenced La Mettrie's argument for *L'Homme Machine*, and in Diderot's *Rêve de D'Alembert* (1769), the dreamer asks, "Well, philosophers, you then conceive of polyps of all types, even human polyps?"[28] Blake might have seen a larger jellyfish or starfish type of "polypus" at William Hunter's famous Anatomical Theatre, since one description of its holdings mentions "those which are simply a bag or stomach, with one opening, as the polypus, having no organs of generation, as every part of the bag is endowed with that power."[29] The polypus also offers associations of an octopus-like "Devouring Power" (George Sandys glossed it as "a ravenous fish: so called of his many feet where with he catches his prey")[30] and of almost indestructible life (Richard Payne Knight noted in 1786: "It is also observed, that animals of the Serpent kind retain life more perticiniously than any others except the Polypus, which is sometimes represented upon Greek medals, probably in its stead.").[31] This biological polypus seems to underlie Blake's image of "the Great Selfhood Satan," characterized as

> *Having a* white *Dot calld a Center from which branches out*
> *A Circle in continual gyrations. this became a Heart*
> *From which sprang numerous branches varying their motions*
> *Producing many Heads three or seven or ten, & hands & feet*
> *Innumerable at will of the unfortunate contemplator*
> *Who becomes his food such is the way of the Devouring Power*
>
> [*J* 29(33).19–24]

The second sense of "polypus," which was then limited to that form of the word exclusively,[32] was popularized by Matthew Baillie in *The Morbid Anatomy of Some of the Most Important Parts of the Body*, published in 1793 by Joseph

Johnson. Baillie uses "polypus" extensively for what we would now call a tumor or clot: "It consists in a mass of coagulable lymph filling up some of the large cavities of the heart . . . in the ventricles it shoots out processes between the fasciculi of the muscular fibres";[33] the polypus is sometimes found in "the trachea and its branches," and is "a very common disease of the uterus."[34] The uterine polypus is "a diseased mass . . . of different kinds: the most common kind is hard, and consists evidently of a white substance, divided by a very thick membranous septa. Another sort of polypus . . . consists of a bulky, irregular, bloody mass, with a number of tattered processes hanging down from it." The usual lymphatic whiteness, "without any admixture of the red globules of blood," suggests that the term could be over-interpreted as "much [poly-] pus." Blake did not need to make up the deadly consequences of the "devouring" or "*glut*inous" polypus:

> *Then all the Males combined into One Male & every one*
> *Became a ravening eating Cancer growing in the Female*
> *A Polypus of Roots of Reasoning Doubt Despair & Death.*
>
> [*J* 69.1–3]

Returning to the passage from *The Book of Los* with the uterine reference to the polypus in mind, it is evident that the "waves" and "tide" that "englobe" the polypus are, in part, the ebb and flow of pulsing, circulating blood[35] around a diseased, embryonic, "fibrous form." The Polypus in the body's ocean is a version of the branching "Polypus nam'd Albions Tree" that is "a Mighty Polypus in the Deep" (*J* 66.48, 53). The association between the sea-tree and the diseased fibres of the polypus may be seen in figure 16, which—according to Abram Trembley in his influential French study—illustrates "a piece of wood . . . covered with long-armed Polyps"; the connection is stated explicitly in Darwin's *Zoonomia*: "Those who have attended to the habits of the polypus . . . affirm that the young ones branch out from the side of the parent like the buds of trees." As "Albions Tree," the Polypus becomes the vegetable cross on which man is crucified, or the net in which he is caught.[36]

The Polypus represents the unorganized (in all respects) proliferation of fibres:

> *No Human Form but only a Fibrous Vegetation*
> *A Polypus of soft affections without Thought or Vision*
>
> [*M* 24.37–38]

Against this formless background, the organized fibres of the human body exist in a continual state of tension in order to maintain their differentiation. George

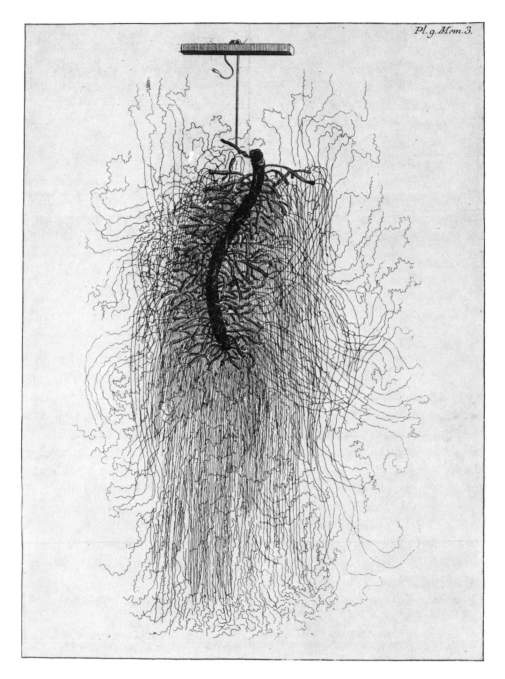

Pl. 9. Mem. 3.

16. Abram Trembley, *L'Histoire d'un Genre de Polypes*, vol. 2, pl. 9 (1744).

Cheyne's popular study of *The English Malady; or, A Treatise of Nervous Diseases of all Kinds* presents the case for the fibrous structure of the body:

> All solids of the Body, when duly prepar'd, resolve themselves, or may be separated into such *Fibres* at last. They are probably platted and twisted together . . . to make the larger sensible *Fibres*; And these again are united in Bundles to form the *Muscles, Tendons, Ligaments*, &c. or woven into a fine Web, like cloth, to make the *Membranes*, the coats of the vessels, &c.[37]

The sense of "muscular fibres" (*FZ* 55.28, E338) joined with tree-fibre seems to contribute to Blake's formula "fibrous strength" and its concomitant image of "upfolding," "condensing," "collecting" fibres into "impregnable strength" (*BL* 5.18–19; *M* 37.5–6, 38.5–6). Considering the generally negative implications of the latter condition for Milton, pregnable strength would be more productive. As Cheyne also illustrates, the fibrous conception of the body naturally leads to the image of the "woven body" (discussed in the following chapter); we see it in Cambel's unraveling of Hand:

> *drinking his sighs in sweet intoxication:*
> *Drawing out fibre by fibre: returning to Albions Tree*
> *At night: and in the morning to Skiddaw; she sent him over*
> *Mountainous Wales into the Loom of Cathedron fibre by fibre:*
> *He ran in tender nerves across Europe to Jerusalems Shade,*
> *To weave Jerusalem a Body repugnant to the Lamb.*
>
> [*J* 80.60–65]

This offers the depressing possibility that the woven body, far from being the organized opposite of the Polypus (or, in this passage, "Albions Tree"), is just another unconscious web or net. *Jerusalem*, plate 40[45] (fig. 17), shows Albion entrapped in such a net, which seems at the same time, along with Vala, to be extruded from his vegetable body. Human bodies are often a source of the fibres rewoven according to the designs of Female Will: plate 74 of *Jerusalem* (fig. 18) shows Reuben giving off fibres (notably from his head and loins) and enrooting, while plate 57 (fig. 19) shows three Female Wills themselves trailing fibres that, in effect, connect with and compact into the ball of our Earth—an expanded version, perhaps, of the ball they wind on plate 25 (fig. 11, above).

Late in *Jerusalem* the Daughters are still pulling fibres from Albion:

> *Conwenna sat above: with solemn cadences she drew*
> *Fibres of life out from the Bones into her golden Loom*
>
> [*J* 90.21–22]

17. *Jerusalem*, pl. 40(45), detail.

The clear sexual connotation of these lines suggests that fibres are related to semen.[38] It was known that the testes consisted of "a vast number of whitish tubes, folded and twisted in different manners,"[39] and commonly believed that the brain was connected to the testes by the nerves, which transmitted "the white or spermatic components."[40] Fibre's near synonym, "nerve," was frequent in Latin for the penis (*nervus*), and so used in English by Dryden; this sense seems to creep into Urizen's address to his "bowstring" (one of the word's other meanings): "O nerve of that lust form'd monster!" (*BA* 3.27). In effect, the lamentable creation of the (s-)emanation, or separated female, testifies to the fact that the fibres of the loins have assumed an independent existence and become an embodied fallacy, as happened to Los when

> . . . *Enitharmon like a faint rainbow waved before him*
> *Filling with Fibres from his loins which reddend with desire*
> *Into a Globe of blood beneath his bosom . . .*

Los "fed it . . . Till it became a separated cloud of beauty grace & love," and then

> *She separated stood before him a lovely Female weeping*
> *Even Enitharmon separated outside, & his Loins closed*
> [*J* 86.50–52, 55, 57–58]

This gives us yet another vision of the fibrous "globe of life blood" that led to "the first female" in *The Book of Urizen*. Once separated, the disseminated fibres are even more difficult to control, as Los discovers when he utters his love, "intoxicated":

18. *Jerusalem,* pl. 74, detail.

> *my wild fibres shoot in veins*
> *Of blood thro all my nervous limbs. soon overgrown in roots*
> *I shall be closed from thy sight. sieze therefore in thy hand*
> *The small fibres as they shoot around me draw out in pity*
> *And let them run on the winds of thy bosom: I will fix them*
> *With pulsations. we will divide them into Sons & Daughters*
>
> [*J* 87.5–10]

Los is being enclosed in genitality, becoming a sort of polyphallos with additional "nervous limbs" and "roots," [41] as the Daughters coalesce into their own polypus. Los's fibres on the sinuous winds of Enitharmon's bosom offer another vision of Orc lying "like a worm . . . on her bosom" all day, and "All night within her womb" (*BU* 19.21, 24–25). Orc changes to a serpent and at length there is "brought forth an Infant form / Where was a worm before (19.35–36). This suggests that Orc, as burning sexual energy "within the vegetated mortal Nerves" (*M* 29.30) is one materialization of (Los's) spermatozoa, the "simple living filament . . . an extremity of a nerve" that Erasmus Darwin saw as the mysterious generative secretion; the moving fibres are in turn "the seminal worms, now so well known," which, Blake could have read in 1786, "were first observed in the male seed by the help of the microscope."[42]

At some stage, remarkably, human fibres become nerves and consciousness. Nerves had long been seen as a species of fibre, though their manner of operation was unknown: Cheyne wrote that "the *nerves* being only some of these Fibres the most susceptible, by their Structure of communicating Action and Motion, made use of to convey such Impression, as they receive from

And the voices of Bath & Canterbury & York & Edinburgh. Cry
Over the Plow of Nations in the strong hand of Albion thundering along
Among the Fires of the Druid & the deep black rethundering Waters
Of the Atlantic which poured in impetuous loud loud, louder, & louder.
And the Great Voice of the Atlantic howled over the Druid Altars:
Weeping over his Children in Maiden & Colchester.
Round the Rocky Peak of Derbyshire London Stone & Rosamonds Bower

What is a Wife & what is a Harlot? What is a Church? & What
Is a Theatre? are they Two & not One? can they Exist Separate?
Are not Religion & Politics the Same Thing? Brotherhood is Religion
O Demonstrations of Reason Dividing Families in Cruelty & Pride!

But Albion fled from the Divine Vision, with the Plow of Nations enflaming
The Living Creatures maddend and Albion fell into the Furrow, and
The Plow went over him & the Living was Plowd in among the Dead
But his Spectre rose over the starry Plow. Albion fled beneath the Plow
Till he came to the Rock of Ages. & he took his Seat upon the Rock.
Wonder seizd all in Eternity: to behold the Divine Vision. open
The Center into an Expanse, & the Center rolled out into an Expanse

19. *Jerusalem*, pl. 57, detail.

outward Objects, as the other Fibres (however this Intercourse is carried on between them, whether by Engrafting, like Blood Vessels, or otherwise, I shall not determin)." The brain was imagined to consist of "infinite Windings, Convolutions, and complications" of nerves.[43] Tirzah thus "ties the knot of nervous fibres, into a white brain!" and hence, also, "the knot of milky seed" (*M* 19.55, 60).[44] The white color here identifies Tirzah's handiwork with the Polypus. But the brain, as the seat of consciousness, must also have some positive valuation; so Los can threaten Enitharmon saying:

> *Tho in the Brain of Man we live, & in his circling Nerves.*
> *Tho' this bright world of all our joy is in the Human Brain.*
> *Where Urizen & all his Hosts hang their immortal lamps*
> *Thou neer shalt leave this cold expanse where watry Tharmas mourns*
>
> [*FZ* 11.15–18, E306]

The distinction between "this bright world" and "this cold expanse" appears to be in the mind of the beholder.

One problem that emerges from all this is the description of differing relationships between the individual fallen brains comprising Albion—an issue that seems to depend on the kind of nervous fibres envisaged. On the one hand,

> *Orc incessant howls burning in the fires of Eternal Youth,*
> *Within the vegetated mortal Nerves; for every Man born is joined*
> *Within into One mighty Polypus, and this Polypus is Orc.*
>
> [*M* 29.29–31]

Yet this same Polypus can become the "ravening eating Cancer growing in the Female." Swedenborg, however, suggested "that all Things of the Body are formed in the Womb, and that they are formed by Fibres from the Brains and . . . that all Things of Man exist from the Life of the Will, which is Love, from its Principles from the Brains by Fibres."[45] From this Blake could construct the different vision of fibrous connection that Jesus urges at the beginning of *Jerusalem*:

> *I am in you and you in me, mutual in love divine:*
> *Fibres of love from man to man thro Albions pleasant land.*
>
> [4.7–8]

In carrying communication, what were before chains of information become living fibres that incarnate the spirit, the language, and the play of the imagination. Thus, expanding the formula given for "chains" in the preceding chapter, we now have:

$$\frac{\text{chain} = \text{spine} = \text{worm}/\text{serpent} = \text{(penis)} = \text{root} = \text{nerve} = \text{fibre}}{\text{line}}$$

As we are members of one body ("The IMAGINATION" [E273]), fibres—lines of text, for example—are the means by which we communicate with one another; this in turn accounts for the danger to all created by any sick or vegetating member, and for the continual attempts of Tirzah et al. to cut, tie, and reweave the fibres. The fibres' real function as the representation of the intangible pathways of ideas may be hardened or "opaked" into single vision, trade routes, and troop movements, a hardening embodied linguistically in the common English (from Latin) metaphors of money as "the sinews of war" or "the nerves of worldly power."[46] Fibres may represent the system of economic relations through which currency "circulates." The (de-)generated or diseased mass of such fibres constitutes one aspect of the Albionic polypus (the polyp: us) Blake saw enveloping the world, expressing not only British economic imperialism, but its trade and roots in Druidic human sacrifice as well:

> *his Heart beat strong on Salisbury Plain*
> *Shooting out Fibres round the Earth, thro Gaul & Italy*
> *And Greece, & along the Sea of Rephaim into Judea*
> *To Sodom & Gomorrah: thence to India, China & Japan.*
> [*J* 67.37–40]

On the organic level, fibres encompass the continuum from sensitive, semi-liquid nerves to the hardened "fibres of the Bones" (Cheyne, p. 64). Robert Burton believed that "nerves, or sinews, are membranes without, and full of marrow within,"[47] and it is the solidifying transformation to marrow and bone we see throughout *The Book of Urizen*:

> *And bones of solidness, froze*
> *Over all* [*Urizen's*] *nerves of joy.*
> . . . .
> *Then the Inhabitants of those Cities:*
> *Felt their Nerves change into Marrow*
> *And hardening Bones began*
> [10.40–41; 25.23–25]

The operating principle of the nerves, Cheyne suggested, might be "a subtile spirituous, and infinitely elastick Fluid, which is the *Medium* of the Intelligent Principle" (p. 89). "This subtile fluid," to quote again from the first *Encyclopaedia Britannica* (1:288), "commonly called *animal spirit, nervous juice,* or *liquor of the nerves,* is continually forced into the medullary fibres." The fluid was on occasion identified with the mysterious powers and presence of aether, and was also seen to be, as mentioned above, the major constituent of semen. Just as the mind, or "fountain of thought," became enclosed in the cave of the skull in the Fall, so in the first condensation, "the void shrunk the lymph into Nerves" (*BU* 13.56; "lymph," appearing only once in Blake's work, here has the sense of pure, limpid, energized water[48]). The Resurrection restores the fibres to "the Rivers" from which they were cut (*J* 90.14 ff.) and the nerves to their rushing, spirited vitality:

And the dim Chaos brightend beneath, above, around! Eyed as the Peacock
According to the Human Nerves of Sensation, the Four Rivers of the Water of Life

South stood the Nerves of the Eye. East in Rivers of bliss the Nerves of the
Expansive Nostrils West, flowd the Parent Sense of the Tongue. North stood
The labyrinthine Ear.

[*J* 98.14–18]

The connection of nerves with the water of life harks back to the ancient belief that the cerebrospinal fluid was the "stuff of life."[49] This may lead in turn to a further understanding of Ololon's strange initial appearance as "a Sweet River, of milk & liquid pearl"[50] and Milton's resolution at the end of the poem, "to bathe in the Waters of Life; to wash off the Not Human"—the "Not Human" being, in part, a nervous disorder. Another aspect of the cerebrospinal connection is reflected in the belief that wine was a "life-fluid," classically thought "to go to the brain and the *genius*" and "to stimulate and feed sexual appetite."[51] Most curious in this respect is the marriage banquet of Los and Enitharmon, where Los "felt love / Arise in all his Veins he threw his arms around her loins," and (instead of the original "bloody wine"),

They eat the fleshly bread, they drank the nervous wine
[*FZ* 12.44, E307]

"Nervous" was standard eighteenth-century diction for "strong" or "potent," but Blake's considered use of it here points to the position of wine in the older conception of the vital cerebrospinal fluids: "milk & blood & glandous wine / In rivers rush" (*SL* 7.38–39).[52]

The importance of fibres lies in their being the conducting passageways of the vital *spirits* of imagination (spirits that, as Los says, live *in* the brain and nerves). Richard Blackmore's *Creation* supported just such an image of the "subtle channels (such is every nerve!)":

Arterial streams through the soft brain diffuse,
And water all its fields with vital dews:
From this o'er flowing tide the curious brain
Does through its pores the purer spirits strain;
Which to its inmost seats their passage make,
Whence their dark rise th' extended sinews take;
With all their mouths the nerves these spirits drink,
Which through the cells of the fine strainer sink,
These all the channel'd fibres every way
For motion and sensation still convey.

[6.368–77][53]

From such conceptions it is but a small step to the "fibres of love" or "a fibre / Of strong revenge" (*J* 15.1–2). Vegetable fibres carry sap,[54] which explains how after Orc's chaining:

Lo the young limbs had strucken root into the rock & strong
Fibres had from the Chain of Jealousy inwove themselves
In a swift vegetation round the rock . . .
. . . .
. . . Orc entering with the fibres. become one with him a living Chain

[*FZ* 62.22–24, 63.3, E342]

So it is that Orc may also be "burning . . . within the vegetated mortal Nerves"[55] and this similarity between men become fibres binding them:

By invisible Hatreds adjoind, they seem remote and separate
From each other; and yet are a mighty Polypus in the Deep!

[*J* 66.53–54]

It follows that one liability of human fibres is that the vital perceptual fluids—or the milk of loving-kindness—may be squeezed out of them, leaving only a woody denseness behind: hence the danger for Milton in "condensing" and "collecting" his fibres. Hardening of the nerves seemed a real possibility, and, not surprisingly to Blake, had its exemplary exponent in Isaac Newton. In the closing "queries" that were considered the most important feature of the *Opticks*, Newton speculates that "rays of light in falling upon the bottom of the Eye excite Vibrations . . . which Vibrations, being propagated along the solid Fibres of the optick Nerves into the Brain, cause the Sense of seeing." The fibres would be "solid" and "dense," because in such bodies "the Vibrations of their parts are of a lasting nature, and therefore may be propagated along solid Fibres of uniform dense Matter to great distance, for conveying into the Brain the impressions made upon all the Organs of Sense."[56] Newton returns to this idea in several subsequent "queries," suggesting that "the harmony and discord of Colours" arise from "the proportions of the Vibrations propagated through the Fibres," and that "the Species of Objects seen with both Eyes" are "united where the optic nerves meet before they come into the Brain." Newton concludes by imagining "solid, pellucid and uniform Capillamenta of the optick Nerves," though the nerve as a whole may "appear opake and white."[57]

But, for Blake,

The Sons of Ozoth within the Optic Nerve stand fiery glowing
And the number of his Sons is eight millions & eight

[*M* 28.29–30]

These sons may represent the millions of spirits or nerve endings thought to constitute the retina and optic nerve.[58] "They give delights to the man unknown"—that is, to "the poor indigent" who has no time to lose in Newtonian conceptual mazes. For,

> *artificial riches*
> *They give to scorn, & their posessors to trouble & sorrow & care,*
> *Shutting the sun. & moon. & stars. & trees. & clouds. & waters.*
> *And hills. out from the Optic Nerve & hardening it into a bone*
> *Opake. and like the black pebble on the enraged beach.*

[*M* 28.31–35]

This warning is only a prelude to the history of catastrophic events before our birth, for

> *in the Optic vegetative Nerves Sleep was transformed*
> *To Death in old Time by Satan the father of Sin & Death*
> *And Satan is the Spectre of Orc & Orc is the generate Luvah*

[*M* 29.32–34]

Earlier in the poem, it is revealed that Satan is "Newtons Pantocrator" and that at present the spectres "take refuge in Human lineaments" (*M* 28.28); so Orc in the vegetative nerve is the same as the Newtonian despiritualized, linear fibre. The energies of corporeal vision, which are at best a kind of sleep—seeing through a glass, darkly—in the natural world, have been laid to rest in the vision of Newton's solid fibres. Indeed, the "Web of Urizen," or Newtonian science, which "vibrated strong" with its all too solid fibres in Night the Sixth, seems the reason why "the wing like tent of the Universe"

> *Vibrated in such anguish the eyelids quiverd*
> *Weak & Weaker their expansive orbs began shrinking*
> [74.5–6, E351][59]

The leading theoretician of the Newtonian nerve was David Hartley, whose doctrine of vibrations and associations in his *Observations on Man* needed "rather solid capillaments, according to Sir Isaac Newton, than small tubuli."[60] By introducing "aether . . . a very subtle and elastic Fluid" and "the uniformity, continuity, softness, and active Powers of the medullary Substance of the Brain, spinal Marrow, and Nerves," Hartley believed he could accommodate the older spiritual nervous system to "the *Newtonian* hypothesis of vibrations." Donald Ault relates *Jerusalem*'s image of all things being "human according to the Expansion or Contraction, the Translucence or / Opakeness of Nervous fibres" (98.36–37) to "later eighteenth-century 'Newtonian' doctrines about the vibrations of ether in the nerves, where healthy continuous nerves are 'pellucid' or 'translucent.'"[61] But when Bishop Watson recommended Hartley's judgment, Blake wrote, "Hartley a Man of Judgment then Judgment was a Fool what Nonsense" (E619), and Alexander Monro, writing on the nervous system in 1783 summarizes the dominant conception, remarking, "most authors have supposed that the nerves are tubes and ducts conveying a fluid secreted in the brain, cerebellum and spinal marrow."[62] "Translucence and Opakeness," as well as "Time & Space," the passage from *Jerusalem* goes on to say, "vary according as the Organs of Perception vary" (98.38). A vision of solid fibres reflects a solidified perception, blind to the "spirits" and the "Spiritual Cause" (*M* 26.44) that determine life. The "nature" of that cause may explain the curious examples with which Blake concludes his statement that "we who dwell on Earth can do nothing of ourselves, every thing is conducted by Spirits, no less than Digestion or Sleep" (*J* 3). So Los's fall from insight into Albion's spiritual condition is plainly evident when we read that

. . . the interiors of Albions fibres & nerves were hidden
From Los; astonishd he beheld only the petrified surfaces

[*J* 46(32).4–5]

But even when we cannot see into the fibres and nerves, we may still trace them into their woven forms of text and tissue.

CHAPTER SIX

Spinning and Weaving [The Text, 1]

Shall we tremble before clothwebs and cobwebs, whether woven in Arkwright looms, or by the silent Arachnes that weave unrestingly in our imagination?

Thomas Carlyle, *Sartor Resartus*

THE "WEAVING SPIDER" GOES TO THE ROOTS of the imagination. In English the primary signification of "spinner" is, simply, "spider," and the Indo-European *webh*, from which are derived "weave" and "web" among other words, shows itself in Sanskrit as *ūrṇavābhi*, or "spider" (literally, "wool-weaver"). Extensive mythological, allegorical, and psychological associations surround the Arachnida and their webs. Closer to the present, the spider's "filamental" secretion was used by some critics to epitomize a certain type of abstract thought. In *The Advancement of Learning*, Bacon criticizes the "schoolmen," whose contemplation, "if it work upon itself, as the spider worketh his web, then it is endless, and brings forth indeed cobwebs of learning" (1.4.5). Sandys notes in his translation of the *Metamorphoses* that "uselesse and worthless labors are expressed by the spiders web."[1] In *The Battle of the Books*, Swift makes the spider the representative of the moderns, whose skill in "the Mathematicks" is manifest in his web, built with "Materials extracted altogether out of my own Person."[2] Young develops the same image, warning against the danger when we,

> *spider-like, spin out our precious All,*
> *Our more than Vitals spin (if no regard*
> *To great Futurity) in curious Webs*

Of subtle Thought, and exquisite Design;
(Fine Net-work of the Brain!)

[*NT* 6.208–12]

But at the same time, as Georges Poulet writes, "the symbol of the spider in its web . . . greatly pleases the thinkers of the eighteenth century." It offers an image, he continues, "of an external peripheric world, incessantly felt and rethought by a central consciousness. The spider not only devours, in a literal sense, the insects that it captures; it absorbs them also figuratively."[3] So, the *Essay on Man*, using an already traditional image, describes

The spider's touch, how exquisitely fine!
Feels at each thread, and lives along the line.

[1.217–18]

Blake knows this imagery and says of "each mortal brain": "here is the Seat / Of Satan in its Webs" (*M* 20.37–38). According to the second edition of the *Encyclopaedia Britannica* (1778), the membranous *pia mater* surrounding the brain "is usually described as being composed of two laminae, of which the exterior one is named *tunica arachnoides*, from its supposed resemblance to a spider's web" (1: 391); Walter Shandy, of course, worries continually over "the fine network of the intellectual web."[4] The filaments making up the sensory or mental web are another instance of the "fibres" of sensation, threads of discourse, lines of text.

The spider in its web is also, Poulet tells us, a type of the sun, "ornamented with rays."[5] Just such a webbed sun, together with a spider comet, appears on plate 85 of *Jerusalem* (fig. 20). Joseph Priestley offers an even more dramatic image in *A Comparison of the Institutions of Moses with Those of The Hindoos:*

The production of all things from the substance of the Divine Being is thus represented by some of the Bramins. Comparing the first cause to a spider, they say the universe was produced by that insect spinning out of its entrails and belly; so that it brought forth first the elements, and then the celestial globes, & c., and that things are to continue in this state till the end of ages, when this spider will draw into its body the several threads, which had issued from it, when all things will be destroyed, and the world no longer exist, but as in the belly of the spider.[6] [cf. fig. 21]

Blake's spider-man is, naturally, Urizen; in *The Book of Urizen,*

20. *Jerusalem*, pl. 85, detail.

And where-ever he wanderd in sorrows
Upon the aged heavens
A cold shadow follow'd behind him
Like a spiders web, moist, cold, & dim
Drawing out from his sorrowing soul
                    [*BU* 25.7–11]

Urizen does achieve a kind of parturition, for "the Web is a Female in embrio," soon to become the "Shadowy Female," or vague material-maternal world organized through and structured by his network of perception: "So twisted the cords, & so knotted / The meshes: twisted like to the human brain" (*BU* 25.20–21).

   One curious version of the web has gone seemingly unnoticed, except as an instance of "the fallen world as seen through the natural veil of mystery."[7] Toward the end of Night the Sixth of *The Four Zoas*, Urizen tries to bind "all futurity . . . in his vast chain," and, as part of this attempt, he again appears:

Travelling thro darkness & whereever he traveld a dire Web
Followd behind him as the Web of a Spider dusky & cold
                    [73.31–32, E350]

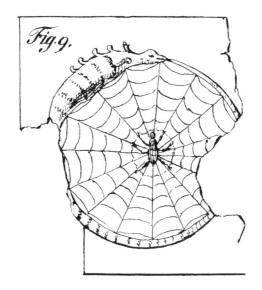

21. A Hindu emblem (published 1822).

He goes to visit the Vale of Urthona but is forced to retreat, and the image spins out as he goes:

Then Urizen arose upon the wind back many a mile
Retiring into his dire Web scattering fleecy snows
As he ascended howling loud the Web vibrated strong
From heaven to heaven from globe to globe. In vast excentric paths
Compulsive rolld the Comets . . .
. . . .
Slow roll the massy Globes at his command & slow oerwheel
The dismal squadrons of Urthona. weaving the dire Web
In their progressions & preparing Urizens path before him
[75.25–29, 32–34, E352][8]

This strange web is part of the conceptual vocabulary of anyone who has seen a schematic diagram of the planetary orbits around the sun, especially if the orbits of some comets were also represented. Blake would have seen such a diagram in John Bonnycastle's popular *Introduction to Astronomy*, first published by Joseph Johnson in 1786—plate 15 of that work offers a plenitude of stellar cobwebs (fig. 22). And early on, in *The Marriage of Heaven and Hell*, Blake sees the planets or "massy Globes" as spiders that plan nets:

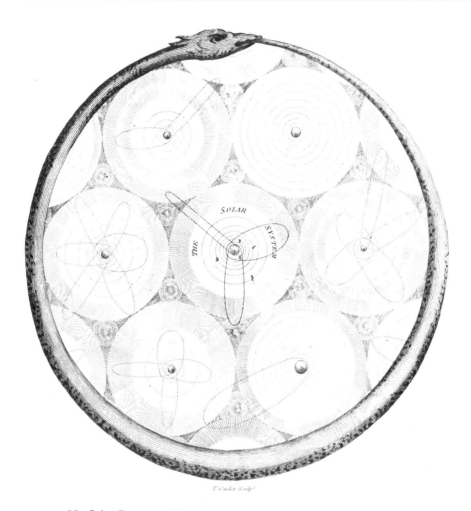

22. John Bonnycastle, *An Introduction to Astronomy*, pl. 15 (1786).

. . . beneath us at an immense distance was the sun, black but shining round it
were fiery tracks on which revolv'd vast spiders, crawling after their prey

[pl. 18]

The spider, given the skill in mathematics attributed to it by Swift, has an
objective correlative in the astronomical orbs whose movements are traced out
in the void; its diagrammatic creation offers a modern instance of "the Direful
Web of Religion" whose gravity collapses in Night the Eighth of *The Four Zoas*,
"misplacing every Center . . . till Urizen / Sitting within his temple furious felt
the num[m]ing stupor / Himself tangled in his own net" (103.26, 29–31,

E376). Located "within his temple," we again find the mental spider lurking in the skull, the cerebral "Seat / Of Satan in its Webs."

The wide range of these associations may serve as a useful introduction to the nature of things woven, for, as Morton Paley notes, "when Blake employs the imagery of weaving, it usually has a literal referent."[9] These images also confirm the generally negative associations of webs (and their lines, fibres, or chains), identified by Poulet: "Even in imagining a mobile or indefinitely extensible web, or an infinity of webs, one is only able to conceive in this way a universe which at most is furrowed with the strands of spirit; not the plenary movement by which reality converges into consciousness, by which consciousness extends itself into reality" (p. 67).

The Industrial Revolution, practically coterminous with Blake's life, was nowhere so evident as in the textile industry. Its rapid transformation wrought by a succession of technological inventions make it, as Paul Mantoux says, "the earliest and also the classical example of modern large-scale industry."[10] Mechanical inventions and improvements began with the "flying shuttle" in 1733, and appeared in ever-increasing numbers during the final decades of the century: Richard Arkwright's and James Hargreaves's "spinning jennies"[11] in the 1760s; Arkwright's carding, drawing, and roving machine, 1775; Samuel Crompton's "mule" (so called as it "mixed" different technologies), 1779; Edmund Cartwright's first power loom, 1785; Arkwright's "scutcher" (which flailed the fibres), 1797; and the bobbin-and-fly frame, 1815.[12] We can sense the scope and rapidity of the textile expansion in the rocketing volume of raw cotton imports: over five million pounds in 1781; over eleven million in 1784; over thirty-two million in 1789; forty-three in 1799; fifty-six million the next year; and over sixty million pounds in 1803.[13] Little wonder that, as early as 1788, one pamphlet exclaimed, "The cotton manufacture . . . has burst forth, as it were, upon the country in a moment." One consequence of the spreading "revolution" was not far to seek, for by the end of the century anyone could see "cart-loads of London pauper children . . . being packed off to work in the cotton mills of the industrial north."[14] Or, as Blake saw it, to "the Looms & Mills & Prisons & Work-houses of Og & Anak" (*J* 13.57). Blake, whose hosier-family background gave him a good practical knowledge of weaving (cf. fig. 23), must have felt some irony reading in Thomas Taylor's early translation of Porphyry's "Concerning the Cave of the Nymphs" that, "to souls that descend into generation and are occupied in corporeal energies, what symbol can be more appropriate than those instruments pertaining to weaving?"[15]

23. Advertisement for Moore & Co. (engraved by Blake, 1797?).

The invention of spinning and weaving has traditionally been attributed to women. Freud, acknowledging his own *idée fixe*, attributes it to a desire to weave the pubic hair to conceal the lack of a penis.[16] But the back-and-forth movement of the shuttle and the spinning of the distaff would seem to manifest sexual potency rather than lack of it, as Shakespeare hints in *Twelfth Night*, when Sir Toby Belch says of Aguecheek's hair: "It hangs like flax on a distaffe: I hope to see a huswife take thee between her legs; and spin it off " (1.3.102–4). Geoffrey Keynes notes "the phallic nature of the distaff of Phorcys" at the bottom center of the Arlington Court picture[17] (fig. 24)—its fibres are "drawn out" or spun by female figures in evident sexual "intoxication." In particular, "they cut the Fibres from the Rocks groaning in pain they Weave" (*J* 67.11). The once common substantive "rock" (*OED*, sb. 2) signifies "the distaff," together with the wool or flax attached to it (depicted, for example, on the title page to the engraved edition of Young's *Night Thoughts*). Thus may the fibrous mass of flax or wool be called "Rocks Atomic Origins of Existence" (*J* 67.12). Blake's spinning Daughters often appear in threes, as representations of the Fates who spin our conceptions and destinies. In the illustrations to *Night Thoughts*, Blake shows the three Destinies as "Time's Daughters," who "spin our Hours" (fig. 25); three women appear around Albion drawing out his life's cord in *Jerusalem*, plate 25 (fig. 11, above);[18] and three Fates handle the fibre from Phorcys very much after the fashion of "Time's Daughters" in the Arlington Court picture. The Greek names of the Fates (or Moirai) personify their respective textile functions in the making of destiny: Lachesis, from λάχος, is simply the allotted "wool" to be spun; Klotho is "the spinner"; and Atropos ("she who cannot be turned") represents the merciless course of the shuttle weaving in the pattern—like Enion weaving the nerves and veins of the spectre of Tharmas "in her shining loom / Of Vegetation" (*FZ* 6.1–2, E303). Atropos was later imagined with shears to cut the individual's (spinal) life-cord, so determining the length of earthly existence.[19] Blake's interest in the Moirai, at least with Plato's version in Book 10 of the *Republic*, is made evident by their gratuitous presence in his illustration of the line "The Spirit of Plato to unfold" in "Il Penseroso." Blake describes this picture thus: "The Spirit of Plato unfolds his Worlds to Milton in Contemplation. The Three destinies sit on the Circles of Platos Heavens weaving the Thread of Mortal Life" (E685).

Closer to home, in the northern mythology that fascinated Blake and his contemporaries, fate is *wyrd*, coming from "turn," as in the case of a spindle, and often thought of as woven: "me þaet wyrd gewâf."[20] The word owes its continued existence largely to the "weird sisters" in *Macbeth*, though Blake

24. The Arlington Court picture.

notes that "those who dress them for the stage, consider them as wretched old women, and not as Shakspeare intended, the Goddesses of Destiny" (*DC*, E535; Blake evidently determines Shakespeare's "intention" from one opinion concerning the sisters offered in the source, Holinshed's *Chronicles of Scotland*). Although unrelated etymologically, the closeness of *word* to *wyrd* is provocative—as in the proverb, "after word comes weird"—for *fate* ("wyrd," "weird") itself is strictly derived from Latin *fatum*, "that which is spoken." The point here is that words are often woven together; we "weave a spell," Pindar "wove" a hymn; a reconstructed Indo-European designation for the poet is *wekwom teksos*, "word weaver";[21] and the Latin for weaving, *texere*, appears in its woven derivatives, *tissue* and *text*. We can see how deeply Blake was struck by these possible associations in the account he wrote of his painting, "The Bard, from Gray": "Weaving the winding sheet of Edward's race by means of sounds of spiritual music and its accompanying expressions of articulate speech is a bold, and daring, and most masterly conception, that the

[7]

Man is the Tale of narrative old *Time*;
Sad Tale! which high as *Paradise* begins;
As if, the Toil of Travel to delude,
From Stage to Stage, in his eternal Round,
The *Days*, his Daughters, as they fpin our Hours
On *Fortune*'s Wheel, where Accident unthought
Oft, in a Moment, fnaps Life's ftrongeft Thread,
Each, in her Turn, fome tragic Story tells,
With, now-and-then, a wretched Farce between;
And fills his Chronicle with human Woes.

TIME's Daughters, True as thofe of Men, deceive us;
Not One, but puts fome Cheat on all Mankind;
While in their *Father*'s Bofom, not yet *Ours*,
They flatter our fond Hopes; and promife much
Of Amiable; but hold him not o'er-wife,
Who dares to truft them; and laugh round the Year,
At ftill-confiding, ftill-confounded, Man:
Confiding, tho' confounded; hoping on,
Untaught by Trial, unconvinc'd by Proof,
And Ever looking for the Never-feen.
Life, to the laft, like harden'd Felons, lyes;

Nor

25. *Night Thoughts,* design no. 353.

public have embraced and approved with avidity. Poetry consists in these conceptions" (*DC*, E541). More daring is Blake's bold transposition,

> *The Harlots cry from Street to Street*
> *Shall weave Old Englands winding Sheet.*
> [*AugI*, 115–16]

As "Every Harlot was a Virgin once," perhaps in their sacrificed virginities and midnight curses they are to be equated with "the Spirits of the murdered bards" whom Blake also summons up for his painting, quoting Gray's lines,

> *With me in dreadful harmony they join,*
> *And weave, with bloody hands, the tissue of thy line.*

The multiple implications of "fate" and weaving are neatly brought together in another of Gray's poems that evidently impressed Blake, "The Fatal Sisters."[22] That poem in fact stems from the most striking example of fatal weaving in Norse mythology, a chapter in *Njals Saga*, which Gray knew from a Latin translation.[23] Gray's "Preface" sets the scene: "A native of *Caithness* in Scotland saw at a distance a number of Persons on horseback riding full speed towards a hill & seeming to enter into it. Curiosity led him to follow them, till looking thro' an opening in the rocks he saw twelve gigantic figures resembling women: & as they wove, they sang the following dreadful song." One of Blake's illustrations to the poem depicts the song's graphic lines:

> *Glitt'ring lances are the loom,*
> *Where the dusky warp we strain,*
> *Weaving many a Soldier's doom,*
> Orkney's *woe*, & Randrer's *bane.*
> *See the griesly texture grow,*
> *('Tis of human entrails made)*
> *And the weights, that play below*
> *Each a gasping warriours head.*
> *Shafts for shuttles, dipt in gore,*
> *Shoot the trembling cords along.*
> [5–12][24]

Here the loom is the battlefield itself, and the weaving is the actual fighting—the forays and retreats, preemptive raids and retaliatory strikes—whose product is death. The poem closes as the sisters rejoice in their "web of war . . . web of death," and "songs of joy & triumph sing."

The loom can also be the womb. *Jerusalem* repeats on three occasions that "the Female is a golden Loom," and looms are the main feature of "Cathedron," the textile-mill district of Golgonooza. Cathedron, with its domes and spires, obviously owes something of its name to "cathedral"—which as a "holy place" is a type of the female genitalia—but more suggestive is the word's closeness to the given name of the women in Blake's life: his mother, sister, and wife were all called Catherine.[25] Enitharmon erected looms, "And calld the Looms Cathedron in these Looms She wove the Spectres / Bodies of Vegetation" (*FZ* 100.3–4, E372; cf. fig. 26). There,

> *The Daughters of Enitharmon weave the ovarium & the integument*
> *In soft silk drawn from their own bowels in lascivious delight*
> *With songs of sweetest cadence to the turning spindle & reel*
> *Lulling the weeping spectres of the dead. Clothing their limbs*
>
> [113.9–13, E376]

The surprising technical term, "ovarium," and the heady image of "lascivious delight" show what diverse discourses Blake asks us to join together to see that in weaving the daughters are doing more than making garments for the spectres: they are perpetrating the whole system of generation. As in the beginning of *Milton*, "they Built the Looms of Generation" (3.38). "Lulling" is inevitably associated with putting to sleep, and just so the spectres "put on their sweet clothing" until "the dread Sleep of Ulro is past." This would seem fairly straightforward neo-Platonic imagery but for the picture of the daughters' masturbatory ("drawn from their own bowels") delight, which tells us that we are in the realm of instinct, like Erasmus Darwin's "Silkworm-Nymphs" who "begin,"

> *Attach'd to leaves, their gluten-threads to spin;*
> *Then round and round they weave with circling heads*
> *Sphere within Sphere, and form their silken beds.*[26]

It is the spectres and themselves whom the daughters would clothe, but the more powerful company of "Satan Og & Sihon" has built mills ("around the roots of Urizen's tree") to unravel the spectres' clothing, and—as was done with cocoons to make silk—the wheels of the mills "unweave the soft threads then they weave them anew" (*FZ* 113.29, E377). This local struggle of unraveling and reweaving is all part of the warped battle of Ulro weaving out "webs of torture / Mantles of despair girdles of bitter compunction"—and with those girdles, chains of jealousy—and "veils of ignorance" (113.19–21). And from this

26. "Theotormon Woven."

system, "none from Eternity to Eternity could Escape / But thou O Universal Humanity" (113.30–31), the humanity (literally, we, the readers) that receives the body, the text, "the Integuments woven."

Milton restates all this very concisely. Ololon descends to Chaos, the Or-Ulro, "where the Contraries of Beulah *War* beneath Negations Banner" (34.23). War, it should be clear by now, forms the greatest part of our "warp." Then,

> *they see the Ulro: a vast Polypus*
> *Of living fibres down into the Sea of Time & Space growing*
> *A self-devouring monstrous Human Death Twenty-seven fold*
> Within it *sit Five Females & the nameless Shadowy Mother*
> Spinning it *from their bowels with songs of amorous delight*
> *And melting cadences that lure the Sleepers of Beulah down*
>
> [M 34.24–29]

"Around this Polypus," the passage concludes, "Los continual builds the Mundane Shell" (34.31). This world, then, is the ovarium and the ovum, the weaver and the woven. But the formless, many-fibred Polypus begins to have some strange shape; in particular, *Milton* goes on to say, "the Great Polypus" is "woven by Urizen into Sexes" (38.2, 4) and sexual strife. The history of the Polypus, then, includes the biological origin of life (or, death) as a primordial spinning and weaving of its fibres; similarly, for Erasmus Darwin life issues from the strife of "Repulsion" and "Attraction" acting through fibres:

> *Last, as fine goads the gluten-threads excite,*
> *Cords grapple cords, and webs with webs unite;*
> *And quick CONTRACTION with ethereal flame*
> *Lights into life the fibre-woven frame.—*
> *Hence without parent by spontaneous birth*
> *Rise the first specks of animated earth;*
> *From Nature's womb the plant or insect swims,*
> *And buds or breathes with microscopic limbs.*
> *In earth, sea, air, around, below, above,*
> *Life's subtile woof in Nature's loom is wove;*
>
> [*The Temple of Nature*, 1.243–52]

What should be emphasized here is not the garment, or woven result—which may appear either benevolent or false—but the process of physical creation: spinning a fibre and then weaving it into fabrication. In *The Spinning Aphrodite*,

Elmer G. Suhr notes "the importance of spinning as analogous to the process of creation in the cosmos."[27] He shows how "*alma* Venus," Aphrodite *genetrix*, originally occupied a central position in the classical mythology of the creation and economy of the world. In particular, she spun the "fleecy," "woolly" clouds into the threads of life or rain; a mythic function reenacted by Vala when "the Souls of those who sleep / Were caught into the flax of her Distaff, & in her Cloud" (*J* 80.33–34). The action is one instance of the spinning that attenuates the *pneuma* of the Sun down to the Earth. Discussing one representation of heavenly Aphrodite on a coin, Suhr observes that "the symbol of the sun, placed where the Greek would normally look for the distaff of wool or flax, supplied the *pneuma* of creation which was spun into the thread of life." However valid his interpretation may be, Suhr's image does offer an analogy for the mysterious object that Enitharmon holds in her left hand in the striking final plate of *Jerusalem* (fig. 27). David Erdman calls it a "shuttle," and so argues that Enitharmon "unwinds" its fibre.[28] But its size, spiral grooves, and the fact that there is no "eye or cavity, wherein is enclosed the spoul with the woof,"[29] suggest that it is a spindle. In this case, Enitharmon is twisting fibres from the Moon with her right hand, and winding them on to her spindle—the general movement is then counterclockwise. The Moon may supply fibres since it has the power to draw up cloudy ("fleecy") vapor to itself. This moisture, according to Suhr, "the moon then mixes with the generating light of the sun in such a way that early man thought of it as a spinner."

Plate 100 not only presents the logical process of ascending fibres being wound on to a spindle: there is also clearly a clockwise movement, which results in what Erdman calls "red rain, veins of mortal life immortal" descending from Enitharmon's spindle or the Moon.[30] But to conceive of this as "unwinding" hardly seems satisfactory. The spiral grooves, which we have seen before (fig. 24, above), tell us that Enitharmon's spindle may also be a distaff.[31] The "rock" of fibres to be spun from the head of the distaff is supplied by Los's hair, itself a materialization of the rays of the Sun, toward which we are directed by Enitharmon's gaze and the tilt of the spindle (urging the eye to continue the thread's serpentine curve, the mirror of that below). This aspect of the picture has been neglected because it is not (and cannot be) illustrated. But just as the bottom of the picture is connected by the symmetry of the temple, so the top presents the less tangible, but equally real and reciprocal, connection of energy from the Sun to the matter constituting the fibres of life.[32] The "red rain" is not an "unwound" version of the single fibre running from the distaff to Enitharmon's right hand (which is not shown in a position to "unwind"),

27. *Jerusalem*, pl. 100.

but is, rather, a close-up, expanded vision of the woven atmosphere, the medium of materialization.[33] As the movement or energy circuit around the picture is both clockwise and counterclockwise ("going forth & returning"), Enitharmon holds a spindle or a distaff, or both, depending on the beholder's point of view.

At the end of "The Keys of the Gates," the speaker looks down through the Gate or plate or "Door of Death," and finds "the Worm weaving in the Ground." He continues, again evoking the associations of "Cathedron" by expanding Job 17:14 to include all possible primary feminine relations,

> *Thou'rt my Mother from the Womb*
> *Wife, Sister, Daughter to the Tomb*
> *Weaving to Dreams the Sexual strife*
> *And weeping over the Web of Life*
> [*GP*, "Keys," 47–50]

Or, as N. O. Brown summarizes, "woman, wife, thy name is weaving (*Weib, weben*)."[34] "The web of our life," we read in Shakespeare, "is of a mingled yarn, good and ill together,"[35] a sentiment echoed in *Auguries of Innocence*:

Joy & Woe are woven fine
A Clothing for the Soul divine
                    [59–60][36]

The (caterpillar-) worm's weeping must be an expression of the "Mother's Grief" it memorializes at the beginning of "The Keys." Her melancholy, narcissistic grief is that the web or clothing assumes an existence of its own, leaving its moth-mother-maker as it left Enion at the beginning of *The Four Zoas*:

Wondring she saw her woof begin to animate. & not
As Garments woven subservient to her hands but having a will
Of its own perverse & wayward
                    [5.20–22, E302]

Her *dream* is that it could be otherwise; a dream of intoxicating, unchanging woven bliss. Dreams, like reasonings, are already weavings. As early as "A Dream" in *Songs of Innocence* we read: "Once a dream did weave a shade," while "A Cradle Song," asks for "Sweet sleep" to "weave." The sexual strife woven to such dreams is again that battle woven by, and weaving out, fate—the back-and-forth movement of woof into warp, producing a compaction of itself.

These associations may account for the central importance of the weaving "worm." We have largely lost sight of how commonplace this imagery was for Blake's contemporaries, together with the fact that "worm" and "silkworm" were interchangeable.[37] Blake knew from the Bible that "man is a worm"; but equally important was the fact that the worm, for "reasons" unknown to itself, at a certain moment, begins to weave itself a chrysalis for transformation: it embodies an intruding communication from a higher level of organization. This imagery is developed in connection with Beulah, the land where souls are married to bodies. These body–souls are "females," who "sleep the winter in soft silken veils / Woven by their own hands" (*FZ* 5.1–2, E298). *Jerusalem* speaks of "the woven Veil of Sleep / Such as the Flowers of Beulah weave to be their Funeral Mantles" (90.6–7), identifying it with the "Veil & Net / Of veins of red Blood" (90.4–5) that grow "as a scarlet robe" around the feminine and the masculine when separated "both from Man." Porphyry explained "the purple webs" woven by the nymphs in Book 13 of the *Odyssey* as "the flesh which is woven from the blood," forming "a garment with which the soul is invested." For Blake, if man is a worm, then his body can become a cocoon.

But not only is the body woven, the world and the mind's thoughts about it are as well. So, in *Jerusalem*, corresponding to passages from *The Four Zoas* and *Milton* quoted above, a confident Los urges:

> *Let Cambel and her Sisters sit within the Mundane Shell:*
> *Forming the fluctuating Globe according to their will.*
> *According as they weave the little embryon nerves & veins*
> *The Eye, the little Nostrils, & the delicate Tongue & Ears*
> *Of labyrinthine intricacy: so shall they fold the World*
> *That whatever is seen upon the Mundane Shell, the same*
> *Be seen upon the Fluctuating Earth woven by the Sisters.*
>
> [83.33–39]

The product is fallacious—"An outside shadowy Surface superadded to the real Surface" (*J* 83.47)—for woven senses perceive only a woven superficial world. It is fallacious, but it is necessary. Los can afford to encourage this weaving because he knows that, like the worm, the sisters are, unawares, acting in accordance with a larger plan:

> *Weaving the Web of life for Jerusalem. the Web of life*
> [83.73][38]

Several times Blake speaks of "weaving a bower," and one instance in particular, "Weaving bowers of delight" (*J* 83.50), makes it clear that mazes and bowers are formulaically interchangeable. In *Milton*, after seeing ("Thou seest") "the *Constellations*," we see ("Thou seest") "the gorgeous clothed Flies," every one of which "the dance / Knows in its intricate mazes of delight artful to weave" (25.66; 26.2, 3–4). In the first night of *The Four Zoas*, the interplanetary Los and Enitharmon "delighted in the Moony spaces" and "nine bright Spaces [i.e., "spheres"] wanderd weaving mazes of delight" (9.21, E305; cf. 34.62, E323). So, in another of Blake's far-reaching associations,[39] we can see the Mundane Shell—"heavens high bower" ("Night," *SI*)—as woven by the dancing flies or fates or planets or spiders or Sons of Urizen[40] from the less visible fibres of the Tree of Mystery (or Polypus), making a "garment" of the world (cf. Ps. 104:2), which Urizen thinks he can wear (*FZ* 42.20, E328; 95.20, E360). It is, in fact, another chrysalis. Among the Sons of Los, "these are the Visions of Eternity / But we see as it were only the hem of their garments" (*M* 26.10–11)—we see, as it were, only the woven weaving, not the weaving itself. The Tree of Mystery, which exists "in intricate labyrinths [like the planetary dance] oerspreading many a grizly deep" (*FZ* 78.8, E353), appears in *The Book of Ahania* and in *Jerusalem* as "an endless labyrinth of *woe!*" (*BA* 4.4, *J* 28.19). In another form, it is seen as the "*woven* labyrinths" of snares and physical bodies (*J* 13.48–49, 87.3–6).[41] These labyrinths are woven by thought from its seat in "the infinite labyrinth" of the "brain," which, like Rahab's "enlabyrinths the whole heaven" (*FR* 190, *J* 70.29). "Reason weaves," says Pope; while, according to Swift, "Wit and Weaving had the same beginning."[42] The fibber fabricates a cover-up, a tissue of lies (the *OED*'s first citation of "fabrication" as "forgery" is 1790): "The web of social action. The complexities of intellectual systems; a web of deceit. . . . the complexes, or complications."[43] We are born "warped" into the world and so woven on by accepted ideas from birth that we can scarce see through their web:

> *I turn my eyes to the Schools & Universities of Europe*
> *And there behold the Loom of Locke whose Woof rages dire*
>
> [*J* 15.14–15]

The product is a black cloth that "folds over every nation." So, in *The Book of Urizen*, when the Eternals "weave curtains of darkness" to bind in "the Void," our world, they "a woof wove, and called it Science" (19.9).

The previous chapter pointed out the place of "fibre" in representing the different kinds of connection in the world. On one level, the fibres make up the woven fabric of national and international life. But whether as web of commerce or mantle of war, the result is much the same, for in Albion's sleep, "his machines are woven with his life" (*J* 40[45].25). We can even see the British merchant fleet as so many shuttles (which are shiplike in appearance, cf. Ger. *weberschiff*, Lat. *navicula*, and, of course, our own "space shuttle") plying the designs of the increasingly dominant textile industry. Trade, even before the cotton explosion, was tying the world's markets to England, like "rising Petersburg, whose splendid streets / Swell with the webs of Leeds."[44] But, by the time *Jerusalem* was being built, Blake had seen fate's weaving goddesses· lead England into several wars to protect or open up markets, blast the established craft organizations, lower workers' wages, and execute workers for breaking (knitting) frames:

> *The Shuttles of death sing in the sky to Islington & Pancrass*
> *Round Marybone to Tyburns River, weaving black melancholy as a net,*
> *And despair as meshes closely wove over the west of London*
>
> [*J* 37(41).7–9]

The prime weavers are Vala and the twelve Daughters of Albion, who sometimes transform into Rahab and Tirzah; between them they weave "webs of
War & of / Religion, to involve all Albions sons" in a continual effort "to
weave Jerusalem a body" according to their will. Gray's mythological exercise
pales before the scope and intensity of Blake's vision, which sees "Gwendolen
cast the shuttle of war: as Cambel returnd the beam," "the Distaff & Spindle in
the hands of Vala with the Flax of / Human Miseries turnd fierce with the
Lives of Men," and "the stamping feet of Ragan upon the flaming Treddles of
her Loom / That drop with crimson gore with the Loves of Albion & Canaan" (*J* 66.62; 64.32–33, 36–37).

The goddesses have their unwilling representatives in English women, and
we see their enthrallment in the exceptional number of women weavers in
London's silk trade, its major textile industry: "In the expansion of trade that
began about 1798 or 1800," relates Dorothy George, "enough women could not
be found to wind the silk, as so many had taken to weaving."[45] Their full
employment did not enrich the local economy, for as Francis Place noted later,
"It is the ease with which women and children can be set to work that keeps
these weavers in poverty and rags and filth and ignorance." But there was no
alternative:

> *O dreadful Loom of Death! O piteous Female forms compelld*
> *To weave the woof of Death, On Camberwell Tirzahs Courts*
> [*M* 35.7–8]

The situation exemplified the way in which the "Opressors of Albion" were
setting to work all over England: "They buy his Daughters that they may have
power to sell his Sons: / They compell the Poor" (*J* 44[30].29–30). Such economic rape led to an impossible contradiction, for the women had to work
twelve- to thirteen-hour days, shredding the fabric of the traditional social-
sexual possibilities they dreamed of participating in. For a variety of reasons,
marriage was often impossible, and the woman was left to her own support, so
becoming, in the term that legally designated an unmarried woman (like
Catherine Boucher in Blake's own marriage bond), a "spinster." Throughout
the eighteenth and early nineteenth centuries, these unmarried women were
caught in an increasingly dire web.[46]

The attitude that "normally weaving was man's work"[47] has often blinded
us to the real conditions behind Blake's female weavers. A pamphlet of the
mid-1780s pointed out the growing significance of muslin weaving, which in
1783 occupied 1,000 looms in Glasgow alone, noting that it "is of the greatest

importance from a national point of view, because the whole process consists of labour alone, in many instances performed by women and children."[48] In 1816 there was the following exchange between a parliamentary select committee and a Glasgow manufacturer:

> Some part of your works are employed in weaving by power?—Yes.
>
> Do you employ generally men, or women?—Women, or, more properly speaking, girls from twelve to sixteen or eighteen, and probably twenty years of age.
>
> What is the nature of their employment?—The nature of the employment is to attend the loom, and to mend the threads when they break down.[49]

What happens to the vast, frustrated feminine power channeled into "attending" the loom and spinning wheel? In searing lines, *Jerusalem* maps out the daughter's torment:

> *And one Daughter of Los sat at the fiery Reel & another*
> *Sat at the shining Loom with her Sisters attending round*
> *Terrible their distress & their sorrow cannot be utterd*
> *And another Daughter of Los sat at the Spinning Wheel*
> *Endless their labour, with bitter food. void of sleep,*
> *Tho hungry they labour: they rouze themselves anxious*
> *Hour after hour labouring at the whirling Wheel*
> *Many Wheels & as many lovely Daughters sit weeping*
>
> [59.26–33]

The accompanying design shows the daughters bound to, if not on, their wheels of fire. "It is not in the power of language to describe their long and continued miseries not brought on by idleness, intemperance, or a dissolute course of life," read an account in *The European Magazine* in 1802.[50] Their condition hardly improved in the ensuing years. Hence the history of oppressed humanity in the grip of fallen Albion's exploitative power:

> *Yet the intoxicating delight that they take in their work*
> *Obliterates every other evil; none pities their tears*
> *Yet they regard not pity & they expect no one to pity*
> *For they labour for life & love, regardless of any one*
> *But the poor Spectres that they work for, always incessantly*
>
> [*J* 59.34–38]

This poisoning of human potential is the greatest evil, and the Daughters of Albion, the oppressed, are little to blame, caught as they are in the vicious circle of "the omissions of intellect springing from poverty" (E601). The "lascivious delight" and "amorous delight" that motivated Blake's other weaving daughters has become a masochistic, compulsive "intoxication." The spectres they were previously moved to clothe and embody have now become their "poor" employers (and consumers)—"the Reasoning Power in every Man" as the spectres are called a few plates earlier (54.7). The daughters are deluded by their "own" hopes and dreams, which are themselves the woven texts of the social order's power looms.

Weaving, then, offers a quintessential example of human activity changed into impersonal production—the cause of "alienated labor" is, first and foremost, the production of "other" than human material, invested with only a shadowy existence. But the Daughters of Los or of Beulah are far from such perception, naively and pathetically operating on the "innocent" assumption that "if all do their duty, they need not fear harm."

> *Other Daughters weave on the Cushion & Pillow, Network fine*
> *That Rahab & Tirzah may exist & live & breathe & love*
> *Ah, that it could be as the Daughters of Beulah wish!*
>
> [*J* 59.42–44]

They weave the costly cushion and pillow for the sleep and dreams of high-fashion ladies of luxury, thinking that their effort and sacrifice will be appreciated. But their products are as taken for granted as their labor, and the daughters remain entirely blind to any vision of class, sexual, or mental struggle. Doing "their duty" consists in attempting to weave a covering for "sin," that indeterminate, free-floating quality used by those with a profitable position in the system of morality to impute guilt to the powerless. So Albion in the depths of shame hopes for an easy way out:

> *That the deep wound of Sin might be clos'd up with the Needle,*
> *And with the Loom: to cover Gwendolen & Ragan with costly Robes*
> *Of Natural Virtue*
>
> [*J* 21.13–15][51]

Like the Daughters of Beulah, Albion thinks to appease the angry weaving goddesses with an offering of their kind, oblivious to the fact that the four natural virtues are "the four pillars of tyranny" (*M* 29.49).

Having established the human situation of oppressor and oppressed, *Jerusalem* plate 59 then reaches out to the natural world:

> *Other Daughters of Los, labouring at Looms less fine*
> *Create the Silk-worm & the Spider & the Catterpiller*
> *To assist in their most grievous work of pity & compassion*
> *And others Create the wooly Lamb & the downy Fowl*
> *To assist in the work: the Lamb bleats: the Sea-fowl cries*
> *Men understand not the distress & the labour & sorrow*
> *That in the Interior Worlds is carried on in fear & trembling*
> *Weaving the shuddering fears & loves of Albions Families*
> *Thunderous rage the Spindles of iron. & the iron Distaff*
> *Maddens in the fury of their hands, weaving in bitter tears*
> *The Veil of Goats-hair & Purple & Scarlet & fine twisted Linen*
>
> [59.45–55]

The external world itself—that is, our perception of it—is also an offering, a woven covering produced out of seeming necessity. The wider implications of "veil" will be discussed in the next chapter, but for the moment Exodus 35 may be noted; there, just such a veil is spun by women as an offering for the tabernacle—along with contributions from "the weaver, even of them that do any work, and of those that devise cunning work" (35.25–26, 35). As we saw in an earlier portion of the text, what is seen is woven, resulting from the simple fact that all souls or spirits or essences must be clothed in form in this world, and that the activity of clothing is weaving. The complex fact is that we sanctify such a thing.

Form, in the linear universe, is fabricated by the crossing of lines: of sight, of ink, of thought, of discourse. The principle of a "web" (and of "weaving") is the intersection of lines, as is evident in the word's reference both to "nets," with open meshes, and to tightly woven "cloth." This intersection, the crisscross, is Christ's Cross and the crucifixion of the plenary interrelation of reality and consciousness.[52] Even the cross-hatching of engraving may be seen as weaving a form into the plate, a worm into a word. At worst, the images are trapped and encased, as in a spider's web (fig. 28); at best, they may be imagined as sleeping in a woven cocoon (fig. 29). They are, in either event, only "embo*died* semblances in which the *dead* / May live" (*FZ* 90.9–10, E370). Weaving itself is merely the most practical way of utilizing the fibrous nature of the vegetable world; its positive or negative value depends on the "uses" to which perception puts it. A mechanical and made thing, the frame of the loom

28. *Europe,* pl. 12, detail.

29. *Jerusalem*, pl. 45(31), detail.

cannot produce anything greater than itself, unlike Los's furnaces, which can occasion essential transformation. So Enitharmon's terror toward the end of *Jerusalem* as she realizes that Albion, uncovered and inconceivable, will rise:

> *For if he be that Albion I can never weave him in my Looms*
> *But when he touches the first fibrous thread, like filmy dew*
> *My Looms will be no more*
>
> [*J* 92.9–11]

Enitharmon's natural looms/loins and wondrous net, "thin, as the filmy threads the spider weaves,"[53] will be transformed by the intrusion of a different order of being. But Los, in a lovely and profound touch—for the weaving is still going on, only changed into some process rich and strange—"answerd swift as the shuttle of gold." Los speaks literally as "the voice of the shuttle," and his "textorial"[54] answer, "sexes must vanish & cease / To be, when Albion arises" (92.13–14), looks forward to the end of the limiting feminine warp and masculine woof, "weaving to Dreams the Sexual strife." Spinning and weaving will not end, as the end of *Jerusalem* demonstrates, but textile and textual production are now revealed as manifestations of the "going forth & returning" of eternal life. It is from such weaving that we ourselves may be "clothd,"

> *With fortitude as with a garment of immortal texture*
> *Woven in looms of Eden, in spiritual deaths of mighty men*
> *Who give themselves, in Golgotha, Victims to Justice*
>
> [*J* 34(38).52–54]

The spirits of mighty men die into immortal texts—but for weaker souls these are too often only other veils.

CHAPTER SEVEN

Veil, Vale, and Vala [The Text, 2]

The analysis would be unsatisfactory if it failed to explain the phrase used by the patient for summing up the troubles of which he complained. The world, he said, was hidden from him by a veil; and our psychoanalytic training forbids our assuming that these words can have been without significance or chosen at haphazard.

Sigmund Freud, "From the History of an Infantile Neurosis"

IN A FAMOUS PASSAGE, Saint Paul claims for Christianity: "great plainness of speech: And not as Moses, which put a vail over his face" so that "until this day remaineth the same vail untaken away in the reading of the old testament; which vail is done away in Christ" (2 Cor. 3:12–14). But, in his earlier letter to the Corinthians, Paul used the same imagery to state that women should not pray or prophesy "uncovered" i.e., unveiled; moreover, he says that a woman's long hair is her glory, since it "is given her for a covering," which the Authorized Version glosses, "Or, veil" (1 Cor. 11:13, 15). Through Saint Paul's letters, women become unreadable, unapproachable, at the same time that Christ brings a new reading with "great plainness." Covering herself, a woman shows "that she is under the power of her husband" (1 Cor. 11:10, gloss), man thus showing his power by making woman take the veil.

This dynamic appears in many guises. Plutarch tells of a statue of Isis in Egypt inscribed, "I am everything that has been, that is, and that shall be: nor has any mortal ever yet been able to discover what is under my veil."[1] According to Cudworth, that veil—similar to one given Minerva at Athens—was "hieroglyphically to signifie, that the Deity was invisible and incomprehensible to mortals, but had veiled it self in this Visible corporeal World, which is . . . the exteriour variegated or embroidered Vestment of the Deity."[2] In a note to his translation of the Orphic Hymn "To Nature" (1787), Thomas Taylor also says that Minerva, representing wisdom and mind, "fabricated the variegated veil of Nature."[3] This veil becomes a type of the book or woven "text" of Nature fabricated by God (forged by the mind) to organize the unknown, "invisible and incomprehensible" aspects of Nature, an ignorance centering on vegetative fertility, reproduction, and the operation of desire. The attempt to objectify and so displace this ignorance leads to such idols as the famous many-breasted "Diana of Ephesus," Paul's most difficult pagan opponent in the New Testament: "the great goddess Diana . . . whom all Asia and the whole world worshippeth" (Acts 19:27 ff.).[4] Her many breasts, symbolic of nature's nourishment, are always bare, but her engendering loins are invariably veiled. So the author of a seventeenth-century alchemical tract reverses the received conception to claim that "many men both of high, and low condition in these last years, have to my knowledge seen Diana unveiled."[5]

The increasingly carnal image of veiled Nature may perhaps be related to the slow rise of "scientific" investigation, so that, by the end of the eighteenth century, it is not a Minerva-like spirit but the body of Nature that is sought. Cowper's anticipation of the physical world at the Last Trump is orthodox enough, but the image seems oddly embarrassed:

> *In that blest moment Nature, throwing wide*
> *Her veil opaque, discloses with a smile*
> *The author of her beauties, who, retir'd*
> *Behind his own creation, works unseen*
>
> [*The Task*, 5.891–94]

Erasmus Darwin, who delighted the public with the sexual side of botany in *The Loves of the Plants*, sees a "Majestic NATURE" ("births unnumber'd milk her hundred breasts") from whose "brows a lucid veil depends / O'er her fine waist the purpled woof descends." Uninterested in any "retir'd" or "unseen" author, Darwin hopes to see more and prays,

> *PRIESTESS of NATURE! while with pious awe*
> *Thy votary bends, the mystic veil withdraw;*
> *Charm after charm, succession bright, display,*
> *And give the GODDESS to adoring day!*
>
> [*The Temple of Nature*, 1.167–70][6]

Blake himself uses the motif to illustrate "the mighty mother," Nature, unveiling "her awful face" in a design for Gray's "The Progress of Poetry." At the
same time, as Florence Sandler observes, many writers of the Enlightenment
saw themselves engaged in "iconoclastic 'unveiling'"; Christianity or antiquity
"unveiled" recurs as a favorite title, "often a prelude to the proclamation of the
triumphant Reign of Reason."[7] A remarkable example of such unveiling only
to reveal new idols was the "lewd ritual" of the Goddess of Reason in Notre
Dame, November 10, 1793, often referred to in English anti-Jacobin propa-
ganda. According to one account, the ceremony included the following: "'We
do not,' said the high priest, 'call you to worship of inanimate idols. Behold a
masterpiece of nature (lifting up the veil which concealed the naked charms of
the beautiful Madms. Barbier): This sacred image should inflame all hearts.'
And it did so; the people shouted out, 'No more altars, no more priests, no God
but the God of Nature.'"[8] Reliable or not, for Blake this might have served to
signify another revelation of the growing solidification of error.

While Nature "herself" became more sensuous, the nature of language
became less accessible. No longer the "dress," language now turned into the
veil of thought. This change may be studied at length in Shelley, where the veil
offers "one of the most subtle and complex of all [his] poetical concepts."[9]
Earlier critics were content to see these veils as "symptomatic of a fundamental
dualism in Shelley's conception of the relationship between mind and nature,"
but Jerome J. McGann goes further to argue that, for Shelley, "language is a
veiled vision, and the poet's veil of imagery" must be continually worked on by
the imagination, which is "both a veiling and an unveiling power."[10] The veil
of language appears associated with the veiled female, perhaps most dramatically in Shelley's *Alastor*, with its picture of the youthful poet who

> dreamed a veilèd maid
> Sate near him, talking in low solemn tones.
> Her voice was like the voice of his own soul
> Heard in the calm of thought; its music long,
> Like woven sounds of streams and breezes, held
> His inmost sense suspended in its web
> Of many-coloured woof and shifting hues.
>
> [151–57]

Here we sense that the poet has himself veiled the maid, clothed her in a text,
unconsciously desiring to conceal from himself an awareness of the "made"
(poetic) nature of the work and the annihilating consequences for the al-

ready-made self that its true perception would entail. The poet, he says in
Adonais, who "Actaeon-like" gazes on "Nature's naked loveliness" ends fleeing
astray, pursued by "his own thoughts" (275–79). The fearful implication seems
to be that Nature's loveliness is (or was) merely the product of his
thought—there is no real other, hence no real self, only veil after veil. For
Shelley, "the Spirits of the human mind" come "wrapped in sweet sounds, as in
bright veils,"[11] and must therefore finally be inaccessible, hence mysterious,
hence threatening behind their veils, sounds, letters; in another instance, life
itself is seen as "the painted veil" behind which "lurk Fear / And Hope, twin
Destinies, who ever weave / Their shadows, o'er the chasm, sightless and
drear" (for Blake, "Fear & Hope are—Vision" [*GP* 13]). The deep romantic
chasm, the feminine abyss (the maid, the making), is veiled with texts inspired
by the fear and hope it occasions.[12]

Why the female genitals would pose such a mystery to men proves a
question leading far into the nature of veils. We could speculate on fear of
castration, or womb-envy, or the essential "uncanniness," *unheimlichkeit*, of "the
entrance to the former *Heim* (home) of all human beings,"[13] but all these, in
Blake's vision, are ancillary to the existence of

> *the Sexual Garments, the Abomination of Desolation*
> *Hiding the Human Lineaments as with an Ark & Curtains*
> . . . .
>
> *that veil which Satan puts between Eve & Adam*
> *By which the Princes of the Dead enslave their Votaries*
>
>   [*M* 41.25–26; *J* 55.11–12]

Thel's memorable complaint

> *Why a tender curb upon the youthful burning boy!*
> *Why a little curtain of flesh on the bed of our desire?*
>
>   [*Thel* 6.19–20]

has long been given a physical reference by readers who see the "curtain"
or veil as some significant part of her virginal body. But this is worth ponder-
ing—if by "our" Thel includes herself and "the youthful burning boy" of
the previous line, does she objectively view her own vagina as "the bed"?[14] Or
is it, rather, that her hymen, offered on the desired bed, is lamented as representing the oxymoronic "tender curb" to the boy? Curbs are products of reason and "Councellors" (E429; *SL* 6.15). Thel laments not the curtain of flesh
in itself, but the significance *invested* in it; as with Ona, as she becomes "A Lit-

tle Girl Lost" in the system (*SE*), a "veil of Moral Virtue" descends between Thel and her delight.[15]

"Sexual Organization," contrary to what seems to be the case, is not a given:

> *If Perceptive Organs vary: Objects of Perception seem to vary:*
> *If the Perceptive Organs close: their Objects seem to close also:*
> *Consider this O Mortal Man! O worm of sixty winters said Los*
> *Consider Sexual Organization & hide thee in the dust.*
>
> [*J* 30(34).55–58]

"Sexual organization" equals closed perceptive organs, closed objects; throughout Blake it represents the great closure. Luvah is closed in the furnaces, Enitharmon closes her loins, and, most pervasive, the Gate of the Tongue, or touch, the Western Gate, "Is closd as with a threefold curtain" (*J* 13.23 et al.). This curtained closing becomes clothing (cf. "closd in clouds" and "clothed in Clouds" [*FZ* 129.22, E398; *J* 62.38; *M* 42.20]) or sexual garments sweet. But "Humanity knows not of Sex" (*J* 44[30].33): in imagination is neither male nor female. Blake seconds Mary Wollstonecraft's argument in *A Vindication of the Rights of Woman* (1791) that "the sexual should not destroy the human character," and that, "to give a sex to mind was not very consistent with the principles of . . . the immortality of the soul" (pp. 112, 85–86).

The basic question, more accurately, should be why males have made the female genitals such a mystery, why women are to be veiled, so causing sexuality to veil human possibilities. Take, for example, the idea of "modesty"—which in the eighteenth century also signified "a kind of veil for the concealment of the bosom" (*OED*). William Wollaston's popular *Religion of Nature Delineated* urged typically that "Chastity . . . bids us . . . to participate of the mysteries of love with *modesty*, as within a veil or sacred inclosure."[16] But, as Mary Wollstonecraft saw, the modesty of her contemporaries was often "only the artful veil of wantonness"; and, more particularly, they were made to assume "an artificial character," learning to manipulate a virtue that had "no other foundation than utility, and that utility men pretend to judge, shaping it to their own convenience" (pp. 449, 106). So, in the *Visions of the Daughters of Albion*, Oothoon cuts to the heart of the matter, crying:

> *Who taught thee modesty, subtile modesty! child of night & sleep*
> *When thou awakest. wilt thou dissemble all thy secret joys*
> *Or wert thou not, awake when all this mystery was disclos'd!*
> *Then com'st thou forth a modest virgin knowing to dissemble*
>
> [6.7–10]

"This mystery" is not that of love, but of the origin and practice of *dissembling*, the first veiling.[17]

The veil, as in *Thel*, points not to an actual curtain of flesh, but rather to its investiture with significance as possession, fetish, persona, "selfhood." This creates the blind over the window through which man could "himself pass out what time he please, but he will not; / For stolen joys are sweet" (*Eur* iii.5–6): it exists only in the mind. This illusory veil serves as the magical boundary of separation and division between the introjected "within" and the projected "without." The selfhood's pleasure is no mere "sensual enjoyment" but a perverse delight in asserting its own—the veil's—separating existence. The self's hooded existence is dependent on the continuance of the veil that constitutes it. Blake's fundamental insight here appears in a contemporary psychoanalytic discussion of sexual excitement—after noting that "the mystery being managed emanates from sexual anatomy," Robert Stoller continues, "The point is not simply that in the past a person was frightened by mystery but that, paradoxically, *he or she is now making sure the mystery is maintained. . . .* if the appearance (façade [i.e., veil]) of mystery does not persist, excitement will fade."[18] Such mysterious male excitement, which has at its core hostility, is the origin of sexuality, the "eternal torments of love & jealousy" (*FZ*, title). This organization, the "sexual texture Woven" (*M* 4.4) offers the corollary to "the Veil of Moral Virtue, woven for Cruel Laws" that emerges out of the reciprocal, self-intensifying structures of "jealousy" and fallen "love." The veil is "cast into the Atlantic Deep, to catch the Souls of the Dead" (*J* 23.23, 59.2–3),

> *And now the Spectres of the Dead awake in Beulah: all*
> *The Jealousies become Murderous: uniting together in Rahab*
> *A Religion of Chastity, forming a Commerce to sell Loves,*
> *With Moral Law, an Equal Balance, not going down with decision*
> *Therefore the Male severe & cruel filld with stern Revenge:*
> *Mutual Hate returns & mutual Deceit & mutual Fear.*
>
> *Hence the Infernal Veil grows*
>
> [*J* 69.32–38]

Jealousy leads to chastity, which creates the commerce of prostitution and matrimony as "mattermoney."[19] According to Mary Wollstonecraft, under this system "reputation for chastity, became the one thing needful to the sex," though at the same time, "in proportion as this regard for reputation of chastity is prized by women, it is despised by men: and the two extremes are equally destructive" (pp. 303, 312). It is, Blake also sees, a "mutual" system, a word used in the passage quoted above to harken back to "The Human Abstract" of *Songs of Experience* and its completion of the cycle: "And mutual fear brings peace; / Till the selfish loves increase." The veil represents human blindness to, and participation in, this system, and so is at the same time the covering or cloak for the "sin" it defines. Like snow, the veil is freezing, colorless, odorless, deadly, and descends on a world after the fall.[20]

The important biblical veil is that which God instructs Moses to place in the tabernacle:

> And thou shalt rear up the tabernacle according to the fashion thereof which was shewed thee in the mount.
>
> And thou shalt make a vail of blue, and purple, and scarlet, and fine twined linen of cunning work: with cherubims shall it be made:
> . . . .
> And thou shalt hang up the vail under the taches, that thou mayest bring in thither within the vail the ark of the testimony: and the vail shall divide unto you between the holy place and the most holy.
>
> [Exod. 26:30–31, 33][21]

Already we see a woven "cunning work" curtaining off "holiness," and the veil is, as its etymology reveals, a woven work. It maintains separation: even the High Priest is only to enter behind the veil once a year, on the Day of Atonement. Since the veil, representing distance, boundary, separation, and inaccessibility, comes to characterize Old Testament holiness, one major effect of Christ's crucifixion is that "the veil of the temple was rent in twain from the top to the bottom" (Mark 15:38). In the intertwining of religion and sexuality—as in the idea of chastity—the significance of the veil and tabernacle is projected onto women (so are built "brothels with bricks of Religion" [*MHH* 8]).[22] By the nineteenth century, the vulgarism "hole" included an ironic and psychological reflection on contemporary values, in which the vagina became "the Holy of Holies,"[23] a pun that could be illustrated with designs from *The Four Zoas* and *Jerusalem*. Blake uses this cross-referencing extensively,[24] sometimes in a strikingly "literal" manner:

In Beulah the Female lets down her beautiful Tabernacle;
Which the Male enters magnificent between her Cherubim
[*J* 44(30).34–35]

But in Eden, in *Jerusalem*'s memorable image of at-one-ment,

Embraces are Cominglings: from the Head even to the Feet;
And not a pompous High Priest entering by a Secret Place.

[*J* 69.43–44]

Further drawing on the history of the veil, Blake says of "the beautiful
Daughters of Albion / If you dare rend their Veil with your Spear; you are
healed of Love!" This line, set in the midst of horrific passages devoted to the
Druidic priestesses, introduces a countervailing comment identifying phallic
penetration with the soldier's spear that pierced Christ's side (John 19:34). The
point is to show that the "love" of which one may be healed is, as elsewhere in
the passage, pride and wrath; Los says in *The Four Zoas*: "I also have piercd the
Lamb of God in pride & wrath" (113.52, E380).

The rationale for the tabernacle/secret place/veil *appears* to be that the
feminine cannot live in the floodlight of mental existence. Fearing discorpo-
ration:

We Women tremble at the light therefore: hiding fearful
The Divine Vision with Curtain & Veil & fleshly Tabernacle

[*J* 56.39–40]

Los responds to this in a curious way:

Look back into the Church Paul! Look! Three Women around
The Cross! O Albion why dids't thou a Female Will Create?

[*J* 56.42–43]

Here the three Marys associated with Joseph of Arimathea's wrapping the
body of Jesus in fine linen clothes (like the linen veil of the tabernacle) are
impersonally presented, hinting at yet another image of the Three Fates. It is as
if, having rent the veil, Jesus was to be reveiled immediately.[25] But, more
important, this is Blake's one direct address to Saint Paul. Paul, Los suggests,
never saw the women around the cross (John 19:25–27), representing their
necessary association with the church—illustrated, for example, in the water-
color of the Angel appearing to "The Three Maries at the Sepulcher" or
(apparently) in the lost "Vision of the Last Judgment," which showed "the
Church Universal represented by a Woman" (E559). The implication seems to
be that Paul has made the women tremble; it is he, and in him all men, Albion,
who has veiled them from the Divine Vision, and, in making them veil
themselves, forced the creation of Female Will.[26] Woman, in short, is to be
veiled ("under the power of her husband") because man cannot cope with the

self-loss of anxiety and lust that her reproductive interior and naked beauty inspire—but this, precisely, creates an unbearable imposition on women.[27] Ololon is the crucial figure; "in clouds of despair" she stands before the Pauline Milton as his yet unrecognized equal and says the words of his eternal salvation:

> *Is this our Femin[in]e Portion the Six-fold Miltonic Female*
> *Terribly this Portion trembles before thee O awful Man*
> *Altho' our Human Power can sustain the severe contentions*
> *Of Friendship, our Sexual cannot: but flies into the Ulro.*
> *Hence arose all our terrors in Eternity!*
>
> [*M* 41.30–34]

The redemption of Milton's sixfold Female, of Saint Paul's millionfold Emanation, removing their veil and revealing its sources, is one central task of the Blakean epic.

The fleshly tabernacle or veil in which Jesus, the Divine Vision, was hid, is the body he put on in the womb of Mary. The womb, as discussed in the preceding chapter, functions also as a loom, a veil-making machine ("a Sexual Machine," *J* 39[44].25). In "The Keys of the Gates," the Speaker remembering his conception relates, "She found me beneath a Tree / A Mandrake & in her Veil hid me." So "the Infernal Veil" that "grows in the disobedient Female / Which Jesus rends" (*J* 69.38–39) is also the (internal) womb. The sole appearance of this phrase in Blake is mirrored by its single occurrence in Milton as the "infernal Vale" (*PL* 2.742), the void space where Satan first encounters Sin. This feminine vale/veil—evidently vibrating between at least two or three dimensions[28]—becomes Canaan, "closing," as veils do, Los from Eternity:

> *The nature of a Female Space is this: it shrinks the Organs*
> *Of Life till they become Finite & Itself seems Infinite*
> *And Satan vibrated in the immensity of the Space! Limited*
> *To those without but Infinite to those within: it fell down and*
> *Became Canaan: closing Los from Eternity in Albions Cliffs*
>
> [*M* 10.6–10]

The feminine veil then becomes the Mundane Shell: "Freezing her Veil the Mundane Shell" ("Keys," 19). So, in *Jerusalem*, we see the "Veil of Moral Virtue" or "Veil of Vala" become a "mighty wall" as

Thus in process of time it became the beautiful Mundane Shell,
The Habitation of the Spectres of the Dead & the Place
Of Redemption & of awaking again into Eternity

[*J* 59.7–9]

The veil of the temple, according to commentators Blake probably read, symbolized the elements of the mundane world.[29]

One manifestation of the veil in this world is the vale. The association offers another example of homonyms asserting a shared identity in Blake's discourse, as in his adaption of Milton's "infernal vale" noted just above.[30] In Night the Seventh of *The Four Zoas*, Los says that Enitharmon's roses:

Hid in *a little silken* veil *scarce breathe & faintly shine*
Thy lilies that gave light what time the morning looked forth
Hid in *the* Vales *faintly lament & no one hears their voice*

[82.1–3, E357]

Milton emphasizes the connection, showing "Mystery Babylon" in "Satans Bosom":

Here is her Cup filld with its poisons, in these horrid vales
And here her scarlet Veil *woven in pestilence & war*

[38.25–26][31]

Still more tellingly, "Tirzah & her Sisters":

Weave the black Woof of Death upon Entuthon Benython
In the Vale of Surrey *where Horeb terminates in Rephaim,*

which is linked in a more involved rhyme several lines later to:

The veil of *human miseries . . . woven over the Ocean*

[29.56–57, 62]

As this last example might suggest, Blake's usage of "vale" plays greatly on the quotidian image of "this Earthly vale" as a "vale of misery" or "vale of tears," imagery that begins with the twenty-third psalm and its conception of walking through the valley of the shadow of death. Blake's earliest uses of the word include "the vale of death" and "vales of woe" (*MHH* 2.5, *Tir* 2.3).

Already in *The Book of Thel*, one wonders at the insistence with which Thel, clothed in a "white veil" (5.7), is addressed with reference to her living place,

"The Vales of Har," as "Mistress of the Vales," "Beauty of the Vales," and, twice, "Queen of the Vales." Thel does finally descend into the vale, or "valleys dark" (6.6), which show themselves as a morass of sexual feelings—the topology of her body does not disclose any fertile "sweet valleys of ripe virgin bliss" (*Am* c.30).[32] These associations are evoked again in "The Argument" to the *Visions of the Daughters of Albion*, which opens with Oothoon telling that she "hid in Leutha's vale!"—a location later identified with "valleys of delight" (*SL* 3.28). Oothoon continues:

> *I plucked Leutha's flower,*
> *And I rose up from the vale;*
> *But the terrible thunders tore*
> *My virgin mantle in twain.*

Together with the subsequent information that "Bromion rent her with his thunders," the poem presents a strange version of the crucifixion and the temple veil rent in twain. Oothoon's rising from the vale rends her veil: her Passion begins with her being pierced, as it were, by Bromion's spear (Bromion who is immediately "healed" of his "love"), while her apocalypse exposes the neurotic insufficiency of her virgin love and lover, the torn mantle and Theotormon (the terrible words also must be torn asunder).

From admitting this earth to be a vale of misery, it is only a small step to see mundane existence as a vale of death, a "habitation of the Spectres of the Dead," with the sides of the valley as veils behind which we cannot see (fig. 30). The dead "pass beyond the veil." In Night the Ninth of *The Four Zoas*, the sacrifice of the Lamb causes the Eternal Man to "awake from deaths dark vale" (122.3, E391). On the other hand, as the vale is the vulva, to enter leads to the "englobing" womb, while to exit places one in the Mundane Shell: Blake's soul-making vale/veil has both a biological and a spiritual aspect. The vale also is a function of its silken, woven (textual) wall, or perhaps its copper side, since engraving, the etching or biting of vales into the plate, is Blake's technique for tearing the veil and "displaying the infinite which was hid."

But we have thus far neglected the eponymous creator of vales and veils, Vala.[33] She is both the veiled and the veiler, and the seductive valley transforming, like a womb, those spirits that enter. The image of Vala and the processes that meet in her stand close to one center (or, *knotenpunkt*) of Blake's vision (see Appendix 4). His first long poem was originally titled after her, and Jerusalem may be seen as an anti-type to help in further recognizing, comprehending, and rending this Shadowy Female. She may be called a goddess of

The *Roman?* *Greek?* They ftalk, an empty Name!
Yet Few regard them in this ufeful Light;
Tho' Half our Learning is *their* Epitaph.   *110.*
When down thy Vale, unlock'd by Midnight Thought,
That loves to wander in thy Sunlefs Realms,
O *Death!* I ftretch my View; what Vifions rife?
What Triumphs! Toils imperial! Arts divine!
In wither'd Laurels, glide before my Sight?
What Lengths of far-fam'd Ages, billow'd-high
With human Agitation, roll along
In unfubftantial Images of Air?
The melancholy Ghofts of dead Renown,
Whifp'ring faint Echoes of the World's Applaufe,   *120.*
With penitential Afpect, as they pafs,
All point at Earth, and hifs at human Pride,
The Wifdom of the *Wife,* and Prancings of the *Great.*

    BUT, O LORENZO! far the reft above,
Of ghaftly Nature, and enormous Size,
One Form affaults my Sight, and chills my Blood,
And fhakes my Frame: Of *One* departed World
I fee the mighty Shadow; Oozy Wreath

                              And

30. *Night Thoughts,* design no. 425.

Nature, remembering that "Nature" represents everything that is born (Lat. *natus*), and

> *What'er is Born of Mortal Birth,*
> *Must be consumed with the Earth*
>   ["To Tirzah," 1–2]

Rather than strain to fit Vala into the vaguely similar-sounding names of Northern earth-goddesses,[34] we might more profitably compare her with another goddess whose name also directly relates to veils, Kalypso.

Blake would have known the derivation of Kalypso's name ("she who conceals") from Thomas Taylor's note on Odysseus' wanderings in his translation of "Concerning the Cave of the Nymphs," or perhaps from Fuseli, a thorough classical scholar, who helped with Cowper's 1791 translation of Homer, to which Blake subscribed. He could have relearned it for himself in early 1802, as he was busy reading the *Iliad* and *Odyssey* in Greek with William Hayley. We also know that Blake owned a copy of Chapman's *Homer*, and it seems probable that he read (or reread) Pope's translation at Hayley's side, since Hayley felt that "Homer is very much improvd by Pope" (E505). Even for the student with little Greek, Kalypso is a most memorable character, with her intriguing name and dominating appearance fourteen lines into the *Odyssey*:

> νύμφη πότνι' ἔρυκε Καλυψώ, δῖα θεάων,
> ἐν σπέσσι γλαφυροῖσι, λιλαιομένη πόσιν εἶναι.

> *The nymph Kalypso, supreme, shining among goddesses,*
> *detained him in hollow caves, longing to make him her husband.*

Pope noted of this "amorous delay" that "residing seven years in the caves of Calypso (the Goddess of Secrecy) may only mean that [Odysseus] remained so long hid from the knowledge and inquiry of all men, or that whatever befel him in all that time was lost to History, or made no part in the Poem." He later notes that because of this delay, Kalypso "is the cause of all his calamities."[35] Blake would probably have noted her epithet of Ἄτλαντος θυγάτηρ ὀλοόφρονος, "the daughter of wise Atlas" (*Odyssey* 1.52). Chapman explains the mysterious ὀλοόφρων as "qui universe mente agitat" ("who drives everything by mind"), while Pope's comment holds even greater interest:

It implies either, *one whose thoughts are full of terrible and dismal things*, or *one who has infinite knowledge and unbounded views*, and 'tis doubtful which of them *Homer* means. To reconcile both, may we not think our Author has heard something of the ancient tradition which makes *Atlas* the same person with *Enoch*, and represents him as a great Astronomer, who prophesy'd of the universal deluge . . .?

The Atlantic memorializes the name of Atlas and the universal deluge, and Blake joined both to the history of England: "The giant Albion, was Patriarch of the Atlantic; he is the Atlas of the Greeks" (*DC*, E543). *Jerusalem* twice identifies the "Veil of Vala . . . cast into the Atlantic Deep" as the "Atlantic Vale" (4.9, 48.32) in which we are caught. So it could have been of more than passing interest to imagine, as did Pope's translation, that "*Calypso's* Court" was "th' *Atlantic* isle" (1.105–6).

Another consideration: in the cave Kalypso works "a curious web" (Chapman, 5.85) on her loom with a "golden shuttle." The exterior of the cave offers a beautiful "sylvan scene . . . and groves of living green," of which Pope remarks:

> It is impossible for a Painter to draw a more admirable rural Landskip: The bower of *Calypso* is the principal figure, surrounded with a shade of different trees: Green meadows adorn'd with flowers . . . vines loaded with clusters of grapes, and birds hovering in the air. . . . But whoever observes . . . will find . . . the whole scene drawn, agreeable to a country situate by the sea.
>
> [5.80–81, and note]

We may be reminded, perhaps, of Hayley's repeated, sweet descriptions of Felpham as a little "marine village," and Blake's initial feeling that Felpham was "a dwelling for immortals" and "the sweetest spot on Earth."[36] Here Kalypso offers Odysseus "garments . . . from Her fair hand" and an enticing sexuality, seen in Pope's version of the lines that gloss her name:

> *The nymph's fair head a veil* [καλύπτρην] *transparent grac'd*
> *Her swelling loins a radiant zone embrac'd*
> *With flow'rs of gold: an under robe, unbound,*
> *In snowy waves flow'd glitt'ring on the ground.*
>
> [5.295–98]

Kalypso's offer of immortality shows that she retains some vestige of her earlier role as a death-goddess.[37] But, like Odysseus (only after three years instead of seven), Blake forgoes the natural and sexual attractions of the vale/veil in favor of the mental traveling that passes through the Cave of the Nymphs (fig. 24) and through the vision of Vala. Figure 31 shows us Vala in her glory and power attempting—in the name of all whoring, self-concealing vested interests—to cover up the naked form of Jerusalem. The veil trails off in fibres that merge and diverge from her body, revealing her to be, in fact, the veil she and we hold up.

Veils, like "the curtains of the sky" creating the Mundane Shell, constitute our vale: Jerusalem speaks of "my curtains in all their vales" (*J* 79.46). These various associations underlie Blake's common use of "vale" to qualify real geographic sites—"Lambeth's Vale" and "the Vale of Felpham" both evoke terrain that would not ostensibly warrant that description. "Felpham's Vale," in particular, is emphasized by its sixfold appearance in the penultimate plate of *Milton*. Since Blake repeatedly described his stay in Felpham as a "three years' Slumber," and sleep is also a woven veil, so "to go forth" from there (*M* 43.1) was to rend the veil. Blake's stay at Felpham led him to recognize nature's seduction: so, when one daughter draws aside her veil "from Mam-Tor to Dovedale / Discovering her own perfect beauty" (*J* 82.45–46), we see an instance of Vala's erotic display—and, indeed, since the time of Izaak Walton, "the valley of Dovedale . . . has been a favorite theme for painters and poets."[38] It is only a short step to the vales, glens, dells, nooks, crannies, and chasms of Romantic nature worship. But the revelation Blake experienced on his garden path seems to have led him to see in lovely FELPHAM the shadowy suggestion of REPHAIM (which in turn brings in EPHRAIM), the valley near Jerusalem where the Philistines camped, and also a word for "ghosts," "shades." So, one theme through four plates of *Milton* is the progression of Milton and his wives and daughters (their bodies "clos'd / In the dark Ulro") "wandering thro *Death's Vale*," to the academies of learning, lamenting "upon the winds of Europe in *Rephaims Vale*," to the old prophecy that Milton/Blake "should up ascend / Forwards from Ulro from the *Vale of Felpham*" (17.5, 19.40, 20.59–60).

So Blake moves from his first union with Los, "trembling I stood / Exceedingly with fear & terror, standing in the Vale / Of Lambeth" (22.9–11), to his final vision at the rending of Felpham's Vale: "Terror struck in the Vale I stood at that immortal sound / My bones trembled" (42.24–25). To emphasize that the veil as sexual boundary has been taken away, Catherine also "stood trembling by my side." Rending the veil (terrorizing [tearing] it is one sublime way), as the last plate illustrates, is what the poem asks for. That image (fig. 32) is particularly relevant, for as the central feminine figure throws

31. *Jerusalem*, pl. 46(30), detail.

off the veil with Christ-like outstretched arms, she at the same time steps forth out of a tree trunk that is the root of the veil and her body. Vegetable tree and human thigh meet in her loins. This figure might be seen as "Apo-Kalypso" taking off the veil of mystery, stepping out from the Tree of Mystery and the stem of generation, reversing the history of root-bound Daphne. She is the text, no longer veiled (no longer lamenting) and with great plainness of speech coming to reveal the reader as a garment of Jesus:

Written within & without in woven letters: & the Writing
Is the Divine Revelation in the Litteral expression

[*M* 42.13–14]

A drawing presenting the "negative" of *Milton*'s revelation shows how essential are the particulars of "litteral expression" (fig. 33). Here a deathly female with snaky, fibrous hair and a cloven foot, far from leaving the veil, seems the form of the veil ready to go forth and re-veil.

In *Jerusalem*, prime components of veils are tears (not rendings), reflecting the vale-of-tears imagery and the "weaving in tears" of feminine characters like Tirzah (condition becomes actuality as tears are woven in). So Jerusalem and Vala:

But when they saw Albion fall'n upon mild Lambeth's vale:
Astonish'd! Terrified! they hover'd over his Giant limbs.
Then thus Jerusalem spoke, while Vala wove the veil of tears:
Weeping in pleadings of Love, in the web of despair.

[20.1–4]

Similarly the Daughters of Albion take their victim and "cause / Lids to grow over his eyes in veils of tears" (66.30–31). Weeping and wailing are another aspect of veiling—they may produce "lovely forms," but Blake's double-edged line still applies: "O what *avail* the loves & tears of Beulahs lovely Daughters" (5.54). They avail little, but they veil much. A "tear" also names the finest fibre (or "marrow") of flax, making it particularly available for weaving. This gives another version of the creation of the body out of fibres,[39] for the Daughters of Los, as seen in the conclusion of the last chapter, weave, "in bitter tears / The Veil of Goat's hair & Purple & Scarlet & fine twined Linen"—that is, the veil of mystery that is also our flesh. The "purple & scarlet" veil is intimately connected to the body by the "bloody veins" (60.3) of Luvah, so that "a *Veil* & Net / Of *Veins* of red Blood grows . . . like a scarlet robe" (90.4–5): a version of the "scarlet robe" the soldiers put on Jesus (Matt. 27:28). But the crucifixion at "the place of a skull" (John 19:17) and the rending of the temple (of the skull) veil is also the revelation of the body's veil of mystery. Los sees that "as a Man / Is born on Earth so was [the Lamb of God] born of Fair Jerusalem / In mysterys woven mantle & in the Robes of Luvah" (*FZ* 104.33–35, E378). A revision immediately following gives some insight, for the Lamb descends "to rend the veil of mystery," or, as Blake rephrased it: "to give his vegetated body / To be cut off & separated that the Spiritual body may be Reveald."

32. *Milton*, pl. 50.

33. An untitled sketch.

Revelation, Apocalypse, is ending or "rending the veil" ($\dot{\alpha}\pi o\text{-}\kappa\alpha\lambda\acute{\nu}\pi\tau\epsilon\iota\nu$), which can happen at any moment:

> Having therefore, brethren, boldness to enter unto the holiest by the blood of Jesus,
> By a new and living way, which he hath consecrated for us, through the veil, that is to say, his flesh;

> [Heb. 10:19–20]

The veil of the body epitomizes the other veils and their common function of dividing inside from outside, mind from brain and body, I from us, good from evil, woman from man: "Such are the Feminine & Masculine when separated

from Man . . . clothed in the bloody Veil. / Hiding Albions Sons within the
Veil, closing Jerusalems / Sons without;" (*J* 67.14, 16–18). But, for Blake (and
this may further distinguish him from the Romantic poets), the veil is not an
inherent aspect of experience—it is itself mentally created to hide us, not from a
neo-Platonic "One" of Truth or Beauty, but from the ecological and social
reality that we are one body. We desire to conceal the fact of this relation because, like the female genitals reminding us all of our origin or the text bespeaking our own inscription, it tells of our apparent end and replacement,
which is an awareness that rends our veiling hoods of self.

CHAPTER EIGHT

Spectres [The Text, 3]

Every Thing has its Vermin O Spectre of the Sleeping Dead!
William Blake, *Jerusalem*

ONE CRITIC, remarking a "curious literalness" in Blake's "redefinitions," offers a brief explanation of the "spectre" as "no less an incorporeal ghost in Blake than it would be in any Gothic novel, but it is only an incorporeal ghost as defined from eternity." She continues, "Blake is not being perverse when he calls our hard live flesh a ghost, he is being literal to his vision."[1] But it is hardly being literal to Blake, who uses the word "ghost" only once in the poetry after *Poetical Sketches*.[2] Spectres, while indubitably "Gothic,"[3] are of an order very different from ghosts: in 1796, as today, "the spectre of democracy" and its "ghost" would have elicited different responses. The incorporeal, as our reaction to the two words indicates, presents itself in more and less affecting forms. Blake's spectre offers special interest as a "concept" that crosses over directly from poetic text to biography, for the reenlightenment Blake announces in 1804 is explicitly equated with a victory over such a being: "For now! O Glory! and O Delight! I have entirely reduced that spectrous Fiend to his station, whose annoyance has been the ruin of my labours for the last passed twenty years of my life" (E756). Moreover, the metamorphoses of the spectre take it through several different forms of existence[4]—by the end of *Milton* and *Jerusalem* it has one manifestation as "the Reasoning Power in every Man."

A "spectre," its Latin etymology indicates, is a thing seen. An early treatise on the matter states that "*a Spectre, or Apparition, is an Imagination of a substance wi[t]hout a Bodie, the which presenteth itself sensibly unto men, against the order and course of nature, and maketh them afraid.*"[5] The close connection of "spectre" and imagination arises in part from the Latin term having been used to translate an aspect of the physical theories of perception and memory taught by Democritus and Epicurus. "They held," Thomas Reid explains, "that all bodies continually send forth slender films or spectres from their surface, of such extreme subtilty, that they easily penetrate our gross bodies, or enter by the organs of sense, and stamp their image upon the mind."[6] The semi-material existence of the spectre was intensified by the elevation of the kindred word "spectrum"—which had been used synonymously for "a thing seen"—into the center stage of Newtonian optics.[7] At any moment, the eighteenth century came to understand, the light of day and vision could be divided into the spectrum. The disquieting perceptual and conceptual problem raised by the spectrum finds an analogy in that of one "Gothic" hero, who is told of his haunting "spectre" that, though only visible to him for one hour in twenty-four, "neither by day or night does She ever quit you."[8] Blake's spectre, like the Newtonian spectrum, represents a new order of knowledge and a new kind of reason bent on possessing it.

A study of "spectre" and its immediately related forms (all of which go unused by the Authorized Version, Shakespeare, and, with a couple of minor exceptions, Milton) as represented in dictionary citations reveals a tremendous surge in usage through the eighteenth century, culminating in the first half of the nineteenth. The widespread literary adoption of "spectre" followed the example of Dryden, who used the word in his translation of the *Aeneid*, and Pope, in his translations of Homer. Visiting the underworld in the *Odyssey*, Pope's Ulysses sees "ten thousand thousand spectres stand / Thro' the wide dome of *Dis*, a trembling band" (11.699–700). Another great input to the word's evocative power resulted from its use by conservatives to characterize the Jacobin threat. It became a standard metaphor to condemn and describe an "inhuman" social force ever to be repressed lest, unleashed, it establish itself as "the Terror." Burke, writing in 1796, epitomizes this propagandistic appropriation:

> . . . out of the tomb of the murdered monarchy in France has arisen a vast, tremendous, unformed spectre, in a far more terrific guise than any which ever yet have overpowered the imagination, and subdued the fortitude of man. Going straight forward to its end, unappalled by peril, unchecked by remorse, despising all common maxims and all common means, that hideous phantom overpowered those who could not believe it was possible she could at all exist.[9]

A complementary aspect of this political personification was the prominent role of "spectres" in experiments with "the use of supernatural imagery as a mode for expressing psychological truth," which seems quickly to have become a convention.[10] It is evident that when Blake picked out the term it was nearing its point of greatest currency.

Disregarding a few early, conventional apparitions of "spectres," it seems that Blake's spectre first appears in Night the Fourth of *The Four Zoas* and was only later incorporated into a revision of Night the First:[11]

> *And Tharmas calld to the Dark Spectre who upon the Shores*
> *With dislocated Limbs had falln. The Spectre rose in pain*
> *A Shadow blue obscure & dismal.*
>
> [49.11–13, E333]

The scene, as is evident from this and following passages, borrows in considerable measure from the Hell of *Paradise Lost*, though Blake has replaced the Miltonic "spirit" with "spectres" from other underworlds.[12] This initial image recalls Satan's encounter with Beëlzebub (*PL* 1.76 ff.) though, by the end of Night the Sixth, Tharmas and the Spectre of Urthona resemble "Sin and her shadow Death" (*PL* 9.12) awaiting the arrival of the Satanic explorer, Urizen, as

> *Striding across the narrow vale the Shadow of Urthona*
> *A spectre Vast appeard whose feet & legs with iron scaled*
> *Stampd the hard rocks expectant of the unknown wanderer*
>
> [75.6–8, E352]

Just so Death, "that shadow seem'd," comes on toward the adventuring Satan "with horrid strides" (*PL* 2.669, 676). The description then shifts to associate the Spectre of Urthona with Hercules: "Round his loins a girdle" and "in his hand a knotted Club" (75.13–14). This points to Pope's image of Hercules in the underworld of the *Odyssey*: "A tow'ring spectre of gigantic mold, / A shadowy form!" (11.742–43).[13] The fascinating aspect of Hercules is that "high in heav'n's abodes / Himself resides, a God among the Gods," whereas "here" ghosts surround "his shade" (11.743–44, 747). Pope observes in a note that the passage offers "full evidence of the partition of the human composition into three parts: The body is buried in the earth; the image or $\epsilon\emph{i}\delta\omega\lambda o\nu$ descends into the regions of the departed; and the soul, or the divine part of man, is receiv'd into heaven." Needless to say, this conception nicely fits *Milton*; that Blake was taken with it is evident in the *Descriptive Catalogue*, where we read that "the Plowman of Chaucer is Hercules in his supreme eternal state, divested of his spectrous shadow"—this shadow, curiously enough, appears in the engraving as another character, "the Miller, a terrible fellow" (E536). "Characters," it would seem, "remain unaltered" only if we limit ourselves to a constant, single frame or state. These associations may help us to locate the confused genesis of "spectre," like so many of Blake's terms, in a tangle of individual vision and intertextuality.

Blake inserted a description of the spectre's origin early in the manuscript of *The Four Zoas*; Tharmas

> *sunk down into the sea a pale white corse*
> *In torment he sunk down & flowd among her filmy Woof*
> *His Spectre issuing from his feet in flames of fire*
> [5.13–15, E302]

The "filmy" woof suggests the "filmy dew" of Enitharmon's looms and the Epicurean "slender films or spectres" of matter,[14] while the curious birth of the spectre may echo the superstition that the soul left the body through the feet (so in *Milton* 15.50: "from my left foot a black cloud redounding").[15] Another image of the spectre's birth tells that "a spirit springs from [a] dead corse" (34.36, E323). But the fate of Tharmas signals another origin: just as the Spectre of Urthona later "sinks down" to "the place of *seed* (84.18–21, E359) so Tharmas sinks to the "*sea*" (cf. Urizen, whose "loins wavd like the sea" [*FZ* 55.29, E338]). The spectre's association with the genitals relates to two aspects of its existence. Physically, the spectres wait there to be "drawn out" (or, in the Latinate equivalent, *abstracted*) and incorporated; the loins are an energy source (Hell is another version) engendering the "terrific Passions & Affections" that characterize spectres and fallen existence.[16] As these sexual energies become abstracted or rationalized, the spectre is shown to draw its imaginary existence out of our "reasoning from the loins in the unreal forms of Ulros night" (*FZ* 28.2, E318).

One early characteristic of the spectre is the unreal form of "indefinite lust" (*FZ* 107.20, E382). "The Spectre is in every man insane & most / Deformd," say the Daughters of Beulah, viewing Tharmas's spectre and repeating what the spectre of Urthona says of himself (5.38–39, 85.36–37, E368). The basic "deformity" is identified by Tharmas: "Deformd I see these lineaments of ungratified Desire" (48.1, E332). The Spectre of Urthona also calls himself a "deformed form," now "the Slave of Every passion," "a ravening devouring

lust continually / Craving & devouring" (84.25 ff., E359). With these attributes, the spectre shows some affinity to the eighteenth-century figure of
"Spleen," as in Hayley's *The Triumphs of Temper*:

> *It seem'd all passions melted into one,*
> *Assum'd the face of all, and yet was none:*
> *Hell stood aghast at its portentous mien,*
> *And shuddering Demons call'd the spectre Spleen.*
>
> [1.218–21]

Later in that work (for which Blake engraved six plates dated 1802), the spectre
is defined as "A phantom, never blest with human life, / Tho' oft on earth his
noxious power is rife" (3.160–61).

Blake's intriguing personal references to "spectres" all occur around the
time of *The Four Zoas*. In a letter of 1801, he writes, "my abstract folly hurries
me often away while I am at work, carrying me over Mountains & Valleys,
which are not Real, in a Land of Abstraction where Spectres of the Dead
wander" (E716). Such spectres are referred to several times in the later nights
of *The Four Zoas*, while the opening of *Milton* (dated three years after the letter)
speaks similarly of "the Spectres of the Dead" taking "sweet forms," evidently,
of spirits such as Milton, "in heaven." Blake said he conversed with the spirit
world, and in later life identified some of the "visionary portraits" as being
"Drawn from [the] Spectre" of the sitter.[17] And in 1800 he had written Hayley:

> I know that our deceased friends are more really with us than when they were
> apparent to our mortal part. Thirteen years ago I lost a brother & with his spirit
> I converse daily & hourly in the Spirit & See him in my remembrance in the
> regions of my Imagination. I hear his advice & even now write from his Dictate.
>
> [E705]

When the Spectre of Urthona enters Los's bosom in Night the Seventh, "Los
embracd the Spectre first as a brother / Then as another Self" (85.29–30,
E367). This intimate *doppelgänger*[18] relationship is further suggested by the
mirror-image plates in *Milton* (figs. 63, 64, below), where, if "William" and
"Robert" could be joined face to face or back to back, they would make a
whole (which, appropriately, would be a closed book to us). But Robert was
not Blake's only personal "spectre," for in a poem included in a letter of 1802,
Blake writes of angels and demons, "With my Father hovering upon the wind,"
Robert "just behind," and another brother, "Tho' dead, they appear upon my

path" (E721). This is the one mention by Blake of his father (the image recurs in the same poem), though in Blake's poetry fathers figure more largely than mothers, brothers, or sisters, and poems such as "The Little Boy lost" and "The Land of Dreams" (another version, perhaps, of the "land of abstraction") reveal an acute sense of sons and their fathers.[19]

With these experiences in mind, we may consider the famous letter of October 23, 1804. The account begins, as already quoted, with Blake's delight at having "entirely reduced that spectrous Fiend." Fiends appear to be much like the spectres with which they are sometimes equated, and we can infer the character of their existence from the notebook poem "Mary":

> *Her soft Memory imprinted with Faces of Scorn*

> *With Faces of Scorn & with Eyes of disdain*
> *Like foul Fiends inhabiting Marys mild Brain*
> [40–42, E488]

The letter continues immediately with a description of the "spectrous Fiend": "He is the enemy of conjugal love and is the Jupiter of the Greeks, an iron-hearted tyrant, the ruiner of ancient Greece." The opening reference to "conjugal love" is the first of three instances in which Blake presents his spiritual release as a release for his wife as well, and this solitary emphasis on "conjugal" further hints at domestic, sexual dissensions occasioned by the spectre. *Jerusalem*, plate 88, perhaps offers some background on this—as Los and Enitharmon descend into sexual recrimination,

> *A sullen smile broke from the Spectre in mockery & scorn*
> *Knowing himself the author of their divisions & shrinkings, gratified*
> *At their contentions*
>
> [88.34–36]

Blake continues, comparing his twenty years passed over to Nebuchadnezzer's seven, concluding, "thank God I was not altogether a beast as he was; but I was a slave bound in a mill among beasts and devils; these beasts and these devils are now, together with myself, become children of light and liberty, and my feet and my wife's feet are free from fetters." The Spectre of Urthona was "the Slave of Every passion," and in deleted verses to Night the First, "the Spectre thus spoke. Art thou not my slave" (E821). Like Samson, Blake has been eyeless at the mill, in the spectre's power.

The account now rises to its climax: "Suddenly, on the day after visiting the Truchsessian Gallery of pictures, I was again enlightened with the light I enjoyed in my youth, and which has for exactly twenty years been closed from me." Much has been made of this and of what Blake would have seen in the collection. The general conception holds that the sight of these (mostly copied) "old masters" helped restore Blake "to the light of Art" by either positive or negative reinforcement.[20] But it seems equally possible that Blake's reference to his visit is to some extent a way of dating the event, setting the context. The experience occurred "the day after," indicating that while the gallery played a part, it served more as an incidental trigger to Blake's re-enlightenment, which seems, at heart, a resolution to deep anxieties of self-doubt. Blake explains that everyone "knew my industry and abstinence from every pleasure for the sake of study, and yet—and yet—and yet there wanted the proofs of industry in my works." A uniformly negative word in Blake's vocabulary, "abstinence" here indicates Blake's realization that the pursuit of Puritan ideals and the drive for knowledge and recognition are ultimately self-defeating. The lustful spectre now begins to look, paradoxically, very much like the Freudian image of the superego.[21] Blake again refers to the spectre: "—he is become my servant who domineered over me, he is even as a brother who was my enemy." This echoes again the interview of the Spectre of Urthona and Los, where Los embraces the spectre "as a brother," then, referring to both those "selves," "in Self abasement Giving up his Domineering lust." Another letter, six weeks later, returns to the same theme in language again descriptive of the spectres in *The Four Zoas*: "I have indeed fought thro a Hell of terrors & horrors (which none could know but myself.) in a Divided Existence now no longer Divided. nor at war with myself" (December 4, 1804, E758).[22] The result of all this struggle and enlightenment, Blake concludes in the earlier letter—so revealing the underlying conflict—is that, "In short, I am now satisfied and proud of my work, which I have not been for the above long period." In such triumphant spirit, he may have first envisioned *Milton* and *Jerusalem*, both dated "1804" on the title pages.

What occasioned Blake's dissatisfaction? Where is the genesis of the spectre to be located? The "long period" during which Blake was "closed" (veiled) lasted "exactly twenty years," an amount of time specified twice elsewhere in the letter. Blake set up a print shop with his friend James Parker and entered the world of business in 1784, but he was able to do that only after the more affecting occurrence of the death, in July, of his father, James Blake, Sr.[23] The little that is reported of the latter suggests that he was at least an adequate father, an impression supported by his son's rather liberal upbringing. Alexander Gilchrist says, however, that "to his father, Blake's early and humble marriage is said to have been unacceptable."[24] And it must have been in good bourgeois tradition that James Sr. impressed on his son, perhaps merely through expectation, the virtue of success, particularly for one going outside the family trade.[25] The internalized parent is the Freudian superego, the copied "old master" whom we attempt to please "daily & hourly." In this connection, one of Samuel Palmer's anecdotes about Blake takes on another dimension: "I can yet recall it when, on one occasion, dwelling upon the exquisite beauty of the parable of the Prodigal, he began to repeat a part of it; but at the words, 'When he was yet a great way off, his father saw him,' he could go no further; his voice faltered, and he was in tears." Similarly moving is *Job*, plate 17, which shows God blessing Job and his wife while the bottom text amasses quotations, mostly from John 14, to the effect that "I & my Father are One," "I am in my Father," "He that hath seen me hath seen my Father also." These instances suggest that Blake might have been positively reidentifying himself with his father—never an easy task, since the spectral image can be most cruel in its demands. Critics generally agree in finding in the spectre "a repressive father figure, a selfish old man who moralistically restrains, judges and punishes."[26] It is under this sign (in the name of the father and the holy spectre) that Blake's conception takes shape—from the tension of inhibited, shadowy desires emerges a picture of the inhibiting censorious spectre whose attributes open the path for its later assimilation of rationing "rational power." The connection of the spectre with the physically dead explains their unincarnate state as they await woven vegetable bodies (hence their dwelling place in the "loins"), and also their vicarious existence in the present, in the spirit and imagination of each of us.

The image of an internalized split in the self, represented by conscience, guilt, and the rest, was already axiomatic in Adam Smith's popular and influential study, *The Theory of Moral Sentiments*, which develops the concept of "spectator," especially an inner one. According to Smith, we learn to examine and govern ourselves by transferring our experience as spectators of others' conduct, and others' of ours, to a hypothetical "fair and impartial spectator." This entails, Smith points out, that "I divide myself, as it were, into two persons," the first of whom is "the examiner and the judge . . . the spectator." Not infrequently, this spectator leads us to "the most humbling of all reflections, the reflection of what we ought to be, but what we are not"—that is, "the real littleness of ourselves and whatever relates to ourselves." Smith then gives a memorable homily on how this psychology operates in "the man of real constancy and firmness, the wise and just man":

He has never dared to forget for one moment the judgment which the impartial spectator would pass upon his sentiments and conduct. He has never dared to suffer the man within the breast to be absent one moment from his attention. With the eyes of this great inmate he has always been accustomed to regard whatever relates to himself. This habit has become perfectly familiar to him. He has been in the constant practice, and, indeed, under the constant necessity of modelling, or of endeavouring to model, not only his outward conduct and behaviour, but, as much as he can, even his inward sentiments and feelings, according to those of this awful and respectable judge. He does not merely affect the sentiments of the impartial spectator. He really adopts them. He almost identifies himself with, he almost becomes himself that impartial spectator, and scarce even feels but as that great arbiter of his conduct directs him to feel.

We may feel some trepidation at the power whom "those vicegerents of God within us" serve.[27] The Blakean spectre seems to serve the same authority, saying that its God "is Righteous . . . He cannot feel Distress: he feeds on Sacrifice & Offering" (*J* 10.47–48).[28] This produces states where characters experience "tortures of self-condemnation while their Spectres ragd within" (*J* 37[41].25).[29] Fourteen months after his letter to Butts describing the vision of his spectral father and brothers, Blake wrote that he would yet "make a Figure in the Great dance of life that shall amuse the Spectators in the Sky" (E741). Perhaps reading Smith or Godwin, Blake realized that the "spectator within" was the "spectre," the philosophical *spectator ab extra* that demands intellectual detachment from areas of emotion.[30] This verbal relation leads to the other psychological root of the spectre. It is not merely a thing seen, but something seeing us, the vision of division: "My eyes were fascinated, and I had not the power of withdrawing them from the spectre's."[31]

Milton and *Jerusalem* develop the conception of the spectre considerably. Milton sees that "I in my Selfhood am that Satan: I am that Evil One! / He is my Spectre!" (14.30–31), while in *Jerusalem* Los identifies his spectre as "my Pride & Self-righteousness" (*J* 8.30). One connection between the spectre and Satan is revealed by the meaning of the latter's name, "the accuser," hence, "watch-fiend" (or, spectator-spectre). Reason is the mode of operation for accusation and self-righteousness, in that it presupposes a reification of perception and thought-processes that, divided from the imagination, are open to manipulation:

> *All Quarrels arise from Reasoning. the secret Murder, and*
> *The violent Man-slaughter. these are the Spectres double Cave*
> *The Sexual Death living on accusation of Sin & Judgment*
>
> [*J* 64.20–22]

Jerusalem sees that "man is born a Spectre or Satan . . . & must continually be changed into his direct Contrary" (*J* 52). Victory over the spectre sees it cast "down into the Lake / Of Los, that ever burneth with fire" (*M* 39.11–12), and, in *Jerusalem*'s famous reflection, "Each Man is in / his Spectre's power / Untill the arrival / of that hour. / When his Humanity / awake / And cast his Spectre / Into the Lake" (37[41] in reversed lettering). This lake, like that which encompasses Satan and his cohorts at the opening of *Paradise Lost*, is the melting pool of energy and imagination. When, through the "strength of Art," Los fabricates "forms sublime / Such as the piteous spectres may assimilate themselves into" (*FZ* 90.22–23, E370), he does his work on "flames" drawn "from out the ranks of Urizens war & from the fiery lake / Of Orc" (90.29–30). The "Humanity" that awakes and overpowers the spectre is the same as in Adam Smith's definition "Humanity consists merely in the exquisite fellow-feeling which the spectator entertains,"[32] except that Blake imagines the spectator as consumed in the larger energy-field of fellow-feeling.

We may also study the spectre in terms of the bat wings and frequent sexual suggestiveness that are part of its visual representation. Winged forms often depict psychical existence: "the Soul Expands its wing" (*EG* 68, E522), and Blake seems particularly to have favored the Hellenistic conception in which Psyche is represented with butterfly wings, an image he would have known from Jacob Bryant, Erasmus Darwin, or Richard Payne Knight.[33] A design Blake engraved for George Cumberland, Sr., in 1795 shows the convention (fig. 34—perhaps Blake saw this as a "conjugal union" in which Psyche stretches out Cupid's wing while mocking his loss of liberty). A design for Young's *Night Thoughts* presents a seemingly conventional depiction of "the gliding Spectre" that haunts graveyard poetry (fig. 35). But, on closer consideration, this erect nocturnal apparition may be seen as the terrified Lorenzo's vision of his missing or shadow phallus—a suggestion arising from the way his improbably positioned right foot joins ("roots") his groin and the ground, while his left extends toward the source of the spectre. Also relevant to the later spectres are the bat-winged "passions" that appear in the *Night Thoughts* illustrations (fig. 36). Passions, by inference, are "little devils," though as passions they are clearly personifications of inner or psychic demons. These are such passions as the reader is warned against in the *Auguries of Innocence*: "To be in a Passion you Good may do / But no Good if a Passion is in you."

Bat wings, it need scarcely be observed, were given to Satan and his forces as the antithesis of the angels' feathered glory—they are black, boney, "leathern," and belong to an animal that flies at night, emerging from caves and for-

34. George Cumberland, "Conjugal Union of Cupid and Psyche,"
Thoughts on Outline, pl. 15 (1796), engraved by Blake.

35. *Night Thoughts,* design no. 523.

gotten places. The iconography of the Renaissance identified bats, or "vesper-tiliones," as "cogitationes immundae, quas improbi daemones ingerunt,"[34] while a famous simile in the *Odyssey* compares the souls of the slain suitors to bats:

> Trembling the Spectres glide, and plaintive vent
> Thin, hollow screams, along the deep descent.
> As in the cavern of some rifted den,
> Where flock nocturnal bats, and birds obscene.
>
> [Pope trans., 24.7–10]

"The Bat that flits at close of Eve," says another of the *Auguries,* "has left the Brain that wont Believe." The first clearly identified bat-winged spectre appears in the *Illustrations to Gray,* begun during or directly after the *Night Thoughts*

[37]

Muſt take an Air leſs Solemn : She complies :

Good-Conſcience ! — at the Sound *the World* retires ;

Verſe diſaffects it, and LORENZO ſmiles ;

Yet has ſhe her *Seraglio* full of Charms ;

And ſuch as Age ſhall Heighten, not Impair.

Art thou dejected ? Is thy Mind o'ercaſt ?

Amid her Fair Ones, thou the Faireſt chuſe,

Thy Gloom to chace. — " Go, fix ſome weighty *Truth* ;

" Chain down ſome *Paſſion* ; do ſome gen'rous *Good* ;

" Teach *Ignorance* to ſee ; or *Grief* to ſmile ;

" Correct thy *Friend* ; befriend thy greateſt *Foe* ;

" Or, with warm Heart, and Confidence divine,

" Spring up, and lay ſtrong Hold on *Him* who made Thee."—

Thy Gloom is ſcatter'd, ſprightly Spirits flow ;

Tho' wither'd is thy Vine, and Harp unſtrung.

DOST call the Bowl, the Viol, and the Dance,

Loud Mirth, mad Laughter ? Wretched Comforters !

Phyſicians ! more than Half of thy Diſeaſe :

Laughter, tho' never cenſur'd yet as Sin

(Pardon a Thought that only *ſeems* ſevere),

Is half-immoral : Is it much indulg'd ?

36. *Night Thoughts*, design no. 383.

series and completed before November 1797.[35] It seems, therefore, to predate those of *The Four Zoas* (whose title page suggests it was begun in 1797). On a blank page between the title and text of "The Descent of Odin," Blake lists the illustrations to the poem, including the one surrounding the list itself; it is described laconically as depicting "Spectres" (fig. 37). All three figures are of interest—not least because the poem does not explain their presence. The moth (identified by its setaceous antennae) at the top may remind us of a somewhat similar form in another illustration to Gray, labeled "Angels Riding Flies" (fig. 38). There, however, the fly's body is human, while in "The Descent of Odin" the top spectre's is not. That the insect is clearly a moth may be worth emphasizing, for moths, as *Chamber's Cyclopaedia* defined them in the mid-eighteenth century, are "butterflies which fly *by night* (*OED*)—it thus accompanies "the invisible worm" that flies "in the night." The nocturnal aspect in-

37. *Illustrations to Gray*, design no. 78, "Spectres."

38. *Illustrations to Gray,* design no. 64,
"Fairies Riding on Flies," detail.

forms the left-hand figure, another moth, ridden by a woman and having
the starry heavens on its wings. Wings of heavenly design may be positive or
negative, depending on the possessor: in the partially butterfly-winged forms
of the title page of *Jerusalem,* they offer positive associations, whereas Vala's
starry, black wings halfway through the poem in plate 53 are a negative, over-
shadowing inversion. Toward its close, *Jerusalem* assembles a striking colloca-
tion of starry heavens, moth, and spectre: "The Spectre builded stupendous
Works, taking the Starry Heavens / Like to a curtain," but Los reacts, smit-
ing the spectre, and

> *Then he sent forth the Spectre all his pyramids were grains*
> *Of sand & his pillars: dust on the flys wing: & his starry*
> *Heavens; a moth of gold & silver mocking his anxious grasp*
> *Thus Los alterd his Spectre*

[91.47–50]

Descending the "Spectres" illustration to the lowest and dominant version, we
find the bizarre image of a bat-winged, clawed, demonic face, ridden and
directed by a naked woman. The bat wings immediately distinguish this
creature from the other two, whose contrasting appearance suggests one of the
salient facts the *Encyclopaedia Britannica* singles out in its brief discussion of bats:
"They fly about in the night, and feed upon moths."[36] David Erdman first
noted the evident connection between the spectre's bat wings and A. Smith's

39. "The Vampire or Spectre of Guiana."

engraving (dated 1791) of "The Vampire or Spectre of Guiana" (fig. 39) for
John Gabriel Stedman's *Narrative of a Five Years Expedition . . . in Guiana;*[37] Blake
engraved a number of designs for the work and, as "Stedman's most trusted
friend in London" between 1793 and 1795,[38] might have been able to question
the author directly concerning his strange account. Stedman's design also
seems to underlie the bat-winged face that rules the upper right of Blake's 1795
color print, *Hecate* (fig. 40).

Stedman relates that "on waking about four o'clock this morning in my
hammock, I was extremely alarmed at finding myself weltering in congealed
blood, and without feeling any pain whatever." The "mystery" was that he
had been bitten by "the *vampire* or *spectre* of Guiana . . . this is no other than a
bat of monstrous size, that sucks the blood from men and cattle when they are
fast asleep, even sometimes till they die."[39] Stedman emphasizes that "its
aspect was truly hideous upon the whole, but particularly the head," with
"long, rounded ears," evoking those in Blake's illustrations. The night attack
on a sleeping victim looms large in later appearances of the spectre, which,
according to Stedman, knows "by instinct that the person they intend to attack
is in a sound slumber." This motif appears, for example, in *Jerusalem* 33[37],
where the bat-winged spectre shadows the sleeping, butterfly-winged
Jerusalem (fig. 41). This spectre is, in turn, a version of the winged disc,
perhaps the moon or earth, that overshadows the twelve lines of text and

40. *Hecate* (1795), detail.

marginal stars in the center of the plate.[40] This "blue death in Albions *feet*" and to which Albion's right foot is rooted (33[37].10; "blue," significantly, was with great difficulty mended from the original "pale"), applies both to "the Spectre . . . A Shadow blue obscure & dismal" and "the blue Mundane Shell" or "blue sky spread over with wings" (*FZ* 49.12–13, E333; *J* 13.33, 19.44).

Stedman's account of the spectre's method is remarkable: after alighting "near the feet . . . he bites a piece out of the tip of the great toe, so very small indeed that the head of a pin could scarcely be received into the wound, which is consequently not painful; yet through the orifice he continues to suck blood." This strange scene appears in the detail of plate 71 of *Jerusalem* shown below, where the spectre sucking Vala's great toe[41] is the end result of the fibrous vegetation coming from her mind.

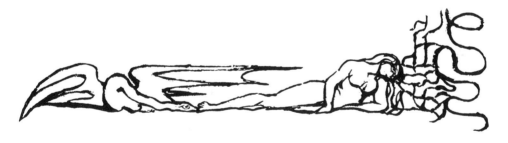

Another connection between spectre and vegetation appears on plate 13 (fig. 42), where fibres of vegetation trail off from a spectre's wing (now a moth-like spectre). A male, who perhaps, like the narrator of *Europe*, seeks to catch a fairy in his hat "as boys knock down a butterfly," is already (through his left arm) part of a spectrous continuum.

The psychoanalytic possibilities of Stedman's image are readily apparent. Ernest Jones observes that "as is well known toes [and] feet . . . are in folklore

And One stood forth from the Divine Family & said

I feel my Spectre rising upon me! Albion. arouse thyself!
Why dost thou thunder with frozen Spectrous wrath against us?
The Spectre is, in Giant Man: insane. and most deform'd:
Thou wilt certainly provoke my Spectre against thine in fury!
He has a Sepulcher hewn out of a Rock ready for thee:
And a Death of Eight thousand years forg'd by thyself. upon
The point of his Spear! if thou persistest to forbid with Laws)
Our Emanations. and to attack our secret supreme delights

So Los spoke: But when he saw pale death in Albions feet,
Again he joind the Divine Body. following merciful:
While Albion fled more indignant: revengeful covering

41. *Jerusalem*, pl. 33(37), detail.

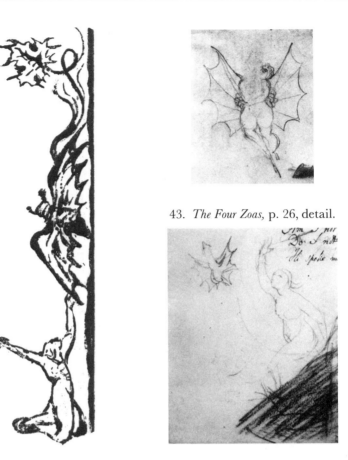

43. *The Four Zoas,* p. 26, detail.

42. *Jerusalem,* pl. 13, detail.   44. *The Four Zoas,* p. 42, detail.

and mythology, as well as in dreams and psychoneurotic symptoms, frequently recurring phallic symbols," and Payne Knight reported in 1786 that "the modern Priapi" were referred to as "the *Great Toe.*"[42] These associations link together the idea of the "spectre issuing from . . . feet" and the several representations of a bat-winged penis, which, like feet, can be imagined as rooting males to earth.[43] Drawings in *The Four Zoas* manuscript show the spectre as a bat-winged genital that dominates the body (fig. 43) or has separated from it and taken flight on its own, becoming a fairy-spectre that another misguided soul wants to make her own (fig. 44). The spectre's generative organization can be either male or female; in *Jerusalem* we see the spectre as an uncanny mix of female holy trinity and winged disc (fig. 45): it represents the gates, not of Paradise, but of sexuality, of the world of generation—and not

45. *Jerusalem,* pl. 58, detail.

only "human" bodies, but also "astronomical" ones like "the revolving Sun and Moon pass thro its porticoes" (*J* 58.27). The spectre's wings of generation are another version of "the wing like tent of the Universe," "dragon wings coverd with stars" (*FZ* 74.3, E351; *J* 54.30).

The operation of such sexual attributes may be seen in two contrasting plates. The "Epilogue" to *For the Sexes: The Gates of Paradise* shows the Satanic spectre "that has resided in [the traveller's] breast" now "rising out of the sleeping traveller"[44] (fig. 46). Commentators seem to have avoided the obvious fact that the starry spectre's foot is drawn so as to suggest the traveller's snaky penis rising in his sleep while the spectre, in effect, emerges from it (again illustrating Blake's equation of foot and penis). We see a spectrogram of the fallen Los ready to copulate ("sleep") with his own nocturnal emission, his dream of the starry universe of generation: "The lost traveller's dream under the hill." This visualization of the sleeper's condition is implicit in earlier references to Luvah's "reasoning from the Loins in the unreal forms of Ulro's night" or that while "Albion slept," his "spectre from his Loins / Tore forth in all the pomp of War! / Satan his name" (*J* 27.37–39). A contrasting scene appears in plate 6 of *Jerusalem,* where Los, apparently unterrified, studies the division of the spectre—who, in turn, re-presents to him one of the most mysterious Blakean moments, plate 17 of *The Book of Urizen* and the spectrous "emanation" ("sending forth") of the globe of blood, the first female, the world of vegetation (figs. 47, 48). Los's ability to face this image of his earlier division and loss comes from his being awake to hold on to, and to take power from, his erect phallos-hammer, a common apotropaic emblem for warding off "the evil eye" and the danger of fascination (the spectre threatens "to punish thee in thy members" [*J* 7.50]). And, though we know the spectre is "hungring & thirsting for Los's life," we have confidence in the outcome from the strange shoes we see when the spectre kneels "before Los's iron-shod feet" (*J* 8.27). The bellows are drawn so as to suggest a spectre wing for Los himself—reminding us again

46. *For the Sexes: The Gates of Paradise,* pl. 19, detail.

of the intimate connection between the spectre and Los, and the spectre's role
in fanning the inner flames of lust and thought. Still, given the spectre of
genital sexuality, it is easy enough to understand Blake's despairing and
radical argument in the notebook poem "My Spectre":

> *Let us agree to give up Love*
> *And root up the infernal grove*
> *Then shall we return & see*
> *The worlds of happy Eternity*
>
> [49–52, E477]

The groves are the sites of genital and generative worship, and, as another
poem asks, "Shall we suffer the Roman & Grecian Rods / To compell us to
worship them as Gods"? (E501).

The beginning of this discussion noted the family resemblance between Milton's "Death" and the Blakean "spectre," a connection that appears explicitly
in *Milton*; Leutha is equated with "Sin" in lines taken directly from *Paradise
Lost*; then, "in dreams she bore the shadowy Spectre of Sleep, & namd him
Death" (*M* 13.40). These two are identified also by Shakespeare, with graphic
detail significant for Blake's spectre: "death-counterfeiting sleep / With
leaden legs and batty wings."[45] To fall asleep recapitulates the fall into division and the double dreamed in the "spectred solitude of sleep."[46] Tharmas's
fall into sleep leads to his spectre issuing from his feet, illustrating Géza
Róheim's later formulation that "the moment of falling asleep is the moment

47. *Jerusalem,* pl. 6, detail.

in which the soul is born, that phallic personification of the body."[47] The "Epilogue" to *For the Sexes* illustrates this same moment—the fall into division was the fall into sleep, the fallacy of dream vision, the phallos mistaken as object of desire, the imaginary taken for real.

Psychologically, the spectre embodies the objectification of desire that arises naturally out of the mind's attempt to order its anxiety over its ignorance; it is "undisguisd desire" (*J* 17.15). As a result of this originary fission, the spectre exists in *despair,* a divided pair[48] ("If any could desire what he is incapable of possessing [e.g., one's self], despair must be his eternal lot" [*NNR*b]). But

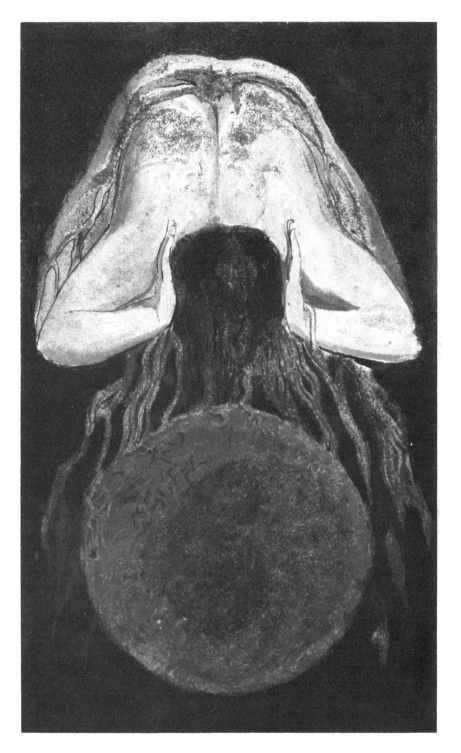

48. *The Book of Urizen*, pl. 17.

conscious despair reflects the (disguised) desire to be whole, to know even as one is known: "I also hope the Reader will be with me, wholly One in Jesus our Lord" (*J* 3). That imaginary desire is "undisguisd" while real motivation is hidden is a tribute to "this world of generation" and the "primeval Priests assumd power." ("Priests," like teachers, are those who dimly realize the real nature of the [imaginary] system but rush to shore it up and secure their own advantage, so showing themselves to be the most enthralled of all to the imaginary.) The confounding despair of the spectre is its subsequent subdivision into "lustful" and "rational" components. In *The Four Zoas*, the spectre knows itself as "a ravening devouring lust continually /Craving & devouring"; in *Jerusalem*, it has become enough a respecter of priestly values to accuse "vain foolish Man" of its own sins and ask why man will bother to build "a World of Phantasy . . . / A World of Shapes in craving lust & devouring appetite" (*J* 54.23–24). Whether the spectre is seen as objectified lust or as "your rational power," however, it represents "energy enslaved"—that is, Albionic, Zoic potentiality distanced, restrained, and bridled by a dividual attempting to define (which is to limit) and to reflect itself. The rational spectre arises dialectically out of the craving lust—the two, like Bromion and Oothoon, are bound "back to back" and feed off one another.

One of Blake's densest comments on spectral interrelation and genesis reads:

> *But in the Optic vegetative Nerves Sleep was transformed*
> *To Death in old time by Satan the father of Sin & Death*
> *And Satan is the Spectre of Orc & Orc is the generate Luvah*
>
> [*M* 29.32–34]

Treating this as a kind of formula, we can substitute some of Blake's other formulations, for we read elsewhere that Satan is the spectre, the selfhood (*J* 27.73; 52, prose) and that Satan is Luvah as both are "the Spectre of Albion" (*M* 32.13; *J* 60.2). So we can construct the following composite:

> *in the Optic vegetative Nerves Sleep was transformed*
> *To the Spectre of sleep by the Spectre the father of Leutha and the Spectre of sleep*
> *And the Spectre is the Spectre of Orc and Orc is a Spectre of Albion.*

In other words, things seen (*spectra*) were transformed by things seen to spectres—and the "cause" of that tautology is the location, "the Optic vegetative Nerves" which cannot behold the complete spectrum of light. If we could envision ourselves literally as spectres, as imaginary (imagined) beings, then a new seer could emerge to open the door beyond our insight: "And what will enter, submerging appearance and breaking its engagement to essence, will be the event; the incorporeal will dissipate the density of matter . . . the actual semblence of the simulacrum will support the falseness of false appearances":[49] the literal will displace the imaginary, the symbolic, the interpretation. Blake's text itself, engraved, is only a dead semblance to spectral eyes. But, in a new beginning, the end of *The Four Zoas* looks back to its text as "the Spectre of Prophecy . . . the delusive Phantom" (139.6, E407), announcing, through these words, its faith in the spectator who has entered its event. The spectre is not a thing or character, but, like Ololon, a mode and ontology of vision—it is aspect. Hence there are different spectres, different aspects, all functions of our sleeping vision, dead to eternal, literal existence.

Here we may begin to understand why there are "spectres of the dead" and a "spectre of the living," why man is "by double Spectres Self Accurst" (*GP*, "Keys," 30). The Keynes proof of the frontispiece to *Jerusalem* outlines the situation with the self-reflexive comment, "*Every Thing* has its Vermin O Spectre of the Sleeping Dead!" This instance of "becoming what you behold"—which we must hold to a mirror to read—reminds the reader-inspector to study, like Edgar in Shakespeare's similarly isolated use of the word, "how to prevent the fiend, and to kill vermin."[50] "Every Thing" in the frontispiece contrasts with the belief expressed in plate 3 that "we who dwell on Earth can do nothing of ourselves *every thing* is conducted by Spirits, no less than Digestion or Sleep." In our fallen spectreship, spirits and everything else are seen as vermin[51]—an appropriately disturbing hallucination for the beginning of a poem with vermicular text and an insect-winged heroine. These contrasting instances of "every thing" may gloss the *Vision of the Last Judgment*, which says that "there Exist in that Eternal World the Permanent Realities of *Every Thing* which we see reflected in this Vegetable Glass of Nature" (E555). Thus every thing seen or felt or thought by us is "as a distorted & reversed Reflexion" (*J* 17.42).[52] But, at the same time, everything is like "all Things . . . comprehended in their Eternal Forms in the Divine body of the Saviour" (*VLJ*, E555). Each of our passions or desires presents a spectre of the already dead, whose longing for form is a longing to be expressed. But once bodied forth, the spectre-passion is "insane," vermin, and intent only on devouring its host. The text is an aspect of vision, a minute particular speck of vision; but, when we forget that, it becomes only a spectre of vision, another aspect of the optical illusion generated in old time.

The "spectre of the Living" (*J* 17.15), on the other hand, reflects imagination, the process of forming itself, the reflection of reflecting: "living going forth & returning wearied." This vision of the identity of change, of our determination by the momentary intersection of various invisible spirits and powers, this aspect of consciousness attempting to recognize itself in its determining frame describes the heroic Eternal Prophet, himself revealed finally as the spectre of Urthona, "*the Great Spectre Los* unwearied & weeping" who "kept the Divine Vision in time of trouble" (*J* 95.18, 20).

CHAPTER NINE

Stars and Other Bright Words

. . . we see their visible body as a shining light, the invisible Astrum or
Syderiall Spirit in the Stars we cannot see; so that not the body of the Sun, but
the Spirit in the body, is the Sun properly; the like may also be said of man.

Oswald Crollius, *Philosophy Reformed*

AMONG THE MOST HAUNTING OF BLAKE'S VERSES are lines seventeen and eighteen of "The Tyger":

When the stars threw down their spears
And water'd heaven with their tears

The many interpretations[1] of these lines indicate that they trigger numerous associations, evoking a powerful, if dimly recognized, frame of reference embedded in our language and in the contextual, nodal relations of stars and words.

In the extensive commentary, one thing seems agreed upon: that there are two sequential actions. But—except for our too-common bias toward linear time—the connecting "and" does not demand that reading. The repetition of "their" sets up a strong identification between "their spears" and "their tears," a kind of repetition with permutation that is a favorite technique of the poem: "What immortal hand or eye" (which first read "&"), "what shoulder, & what art." One of the poem's possible exclamations offers a good example:

In what distant deeps or skies
Burnt the fire of thine eyes!

As an exclamation, what is emphasized is a distance where the difference between "deeps" and "skies" no longer exists. The high sound of "skies" leads the reader to a false opposition and deceptive expectation of meaning: both words refer, separately, to the same cosmological firmament,[2] while together they form a self-cancelling opposition marking the linguistic firmament or distance in which they paradoxically exist. Many editors and critics, however, disagree with D. V. Erdman's (pre-1982) reading and see the wavering line as a question mark—and this plural reading is also part of Blake's design.[3] The "brilliant indeterminacy of origin"[4] in "deeps or skies" is part of a larger indeterminacy of intent that works to deny closure (one "true meaning") and to stress the polysemous possibilities of the text. To such perception, the stars throwing down their spears may be synonymous and synchronous with their watering heaven with their tears.

The liquid associations of "deeps" are not to be forgotten, however, for the "Introduction" to the *Songs of Experience* tells of "the starry floor / The watry shore." These images lead back to several lines in the Bible easily overlooked because of their lack of resonance with contemporary astronomical imagination. The sixth and seventh verses of Genesis 1 relate:

> And God said, Let there be a firmament in the midst of the waters, and let it divide the waters from the waters.
> And God made the firmament, and divided the waters which were under the firmament from the waters which were above the firmament: and it was so.

Verse eight says that "God called the firmament Heaven," and in verse fourteen God establishes "lights in the firmament of the heaven." Jacob Boehme thought profoundly on this sequence of events and concluded that there were two waters: the outward, external, material element water; and an inward holy water. "The stars," he writes, "are nothing else but a crystalline water-spirit; yet not a material water, but powers of the salnitral flagrant in the fire."[5] The stars burn because they stand in the fiery orb that was enkindled, and each star coagulated in its property, by the "Fiat," the Word. The important point is that the stars are chiefly composed of "fire and water."[6] Evidence for this stellar mixture of opposites persisted in ideas of "liquid aether" and of the stars "raining down influences," one of which was dew.[7]

As we have seen, Blake knew the traditional association of dew and tears, so the watering of the stars in "The Tyger" could be imagined as their shedding of "influence" evident in rain and dew.[8] The manner in which the stars operate is clouded in arcana (particularly watering heaven, let alone earth), but all the serious alchemical philosophers agree that the power of the stars is not their own; it is, rather, something they gain from man's fallen imagination: "the external stars do neither incline nor necessitate Man, but Man rather inclines the Stars, and by his Magicall imagination infecteth them, and causeth those deadly impressions."[9] The logical application of this alchemical insight suggests that the stars' tears are what we imagine.

The nature of the starry spears has always been vexing. Many critics, working on the analogy of Satan's starry host, opt for the solid "upright beams innumerable / Of rigid Spears" in *Paradise Lost* (6.83–84). With considerable ingenuity, these angels, "named 'stars' proleptically,"[10] may be seen as weeping at their fall and so creating stars—falling stars, according to Erdman, were called "angels' tears" by children. Frederick A. Pottle hypothesizes that the spears could be rays of light, for "rays of light from heavenly bodies are traditionally arrows. . . . From arrows to spears is an easy step and no doubt traditional."[11] It is without doubt an easy step for Blake; *Milton* asks:

> *Can such an Eye judge of the stars? & looking thro its tubes*
> *Measure the sunny rays that point their spears on Udanadan*
>
> [5.28–29]

and *The Four Zoas* describes "hidden abysses"

> *Wherever the Eagle has Explord or Lion or Tyger trod*
> *Or where the Comets of the night or stars of asterial* [*"eternal" deleted*] *day*
> *Have shot their arrows or long beamed spears in wrath & fury*
>
> [118.14–16, E387, 843]

Jerusalem shows Sabrina and Ignoge sharpening "their beamy spears / Of light and love" (11.19–20).

Having identified the spears as beams of light, we may ask what kind of bodies their possessors have. And it is not surprising that for Blake, as for science and tradition, the bodies of stars are globes—that is, "bound up / Into fiery spheres" (*BL* 4.1–2). To correlate "spears" with "spheres" may seem farfetched, but even Milton toys with the idea, describing the fight between Satan and Michael as if

> *Two Planets rushing from aspect maligne*
> *Of fiercest opposition in mid Skie,*
> *Should combat, and thir jarring Sphears confound.*
>
> [*PL* 6.313–15]

[34]

AND was there need of ampler Field than *This*,
When Giant-Angels Giant-Angels met,
In fiery Conflict, and outrageous Storm,
To controvert the Sceptre of the Skies?
This Prospect vast, what is it? ---- Weigh'd aright,
'Tis Nature's System of Divinity,
And ev'ry Student of the *Night* inspires:
'Tis *elder* Scripture, writ by GOD's own Hand;
Scripture authentic! uncorrupt by Man:
LORENZO! with my *Radius* (the rich Gift
Of Thought nocturnal!) I'll point out to thee
Its various Lessons; some that may surprize
An Un-adept in Mysteries of NIGHT;
Little, perhaps, expected in *her* School,
Nor thought to grow on Planet, or on Star:
Bulls, Lions, Scorpions, Monsters here we feign;
Ourselves more monstrous, not to see what here
Exists *indeed*; ---- a Lecture to Mankind.

WHAT read we *here?* ---- Th' Existence of a GOD
Yes; and of other Beings, Man above;
Natives of *Æther!* Sons of higher Climes!

49. *Night Thoughts,* design no. 452.

In his illustration of this contest as it is evoked in Young's *Night Thoughts*, Blake deliberately shades the shields of the heavenly combatants to resemble spherical planets (fig. 49). Smollett's Winifred Jenkins uses the transposition, writing in her malapropistic manner at the end of *Humphry Clinker* of "being, by God's blessing, removed to a higher spear," while Paul Miner, discussing "the starry, *spear-like globes* of heaven in 'The Tyger,'" shows how a critic can strive, even unconsciously, to mirror Blake's semantic fullness.[12] In a design for *Il Penseroso* (fig. 50), Blake shows "the Suns flaring Beams who is seen in the Heaven throwing his darts & flames of fire" (E685). Here, heavy arrow-points suggest spears, some of which are emerging directly from the sun's sphere; this

50. *Illustrations to Milton's "L'Allegro" and "Il Penseroso,"*
design no. 10 (about 1816).

motif appears again in the *Illustrations to Gray*, no. 46, which shows "Hyperion" shooting down "glittering shafts" from his spherical solar chariot. In *The Fall of Man* (fig. 51) we see, at the middle left and right margins, an even more complex graphic pun as spears are used to drive down spheres somewhat like the spear-holders' shields. Most curious of all these transpositions are the versions of Urizen exploring his dens. In *The Book of Urizen*, he "explor'd his dens . . . with a globe of fire lighting his journey" (20.48). But at the beginning of Night the Sixth of *The Four Zoas*, "Urizen arose & leaning on his Spear explord his dens" (67.1, E344). Two pages on, we see "his gloomy spear / Darkend before him," and the spear disappears altogether on the next page as

51. *The Fall of Man* (1807).

we hear of "Urizen with a Globe of fire"—but, like the spear it still is, "dark grew his globe" (75.5, E352). *The Book of Ahania* shows one way for a spherical star to become a beamy spear:

> *The Globe of Wrath shaking on high*
> *Roaring with fury, he threw*
> *The howling Globe: burning it flew*
> *Lengthning into a hungry beam*
>
> [2.16–19]

This remarkable image deserves further consideration. Coming shortly after "The Tyger" and "the tygers of wrath" of *The Marriage of Heaven and Hell* (pl. 9), it offers a new twist, or wreath: a "Globe of Wrath" that (perhaps along with its possessor) "roars," "howls," "burns," is "hungry," and changes from sphere to spear. This points to a significant sequence of verbal connections and trans-formations. The Ty*ger* is, in part, the creature of wrath and an*ger*, and so associated with flames of *fire*. A characteristic shape of wrath or fire, for Blake, is circular (turn in a gyre: tyger): it makes a *wreath*. So, in *The Four Zoas*, "the Eternal Mind bounded began to roll eddies of wrath" (54.1, E336), a psy-cho-physics somewhat analogous to that in *America*, where "the fires of Orc" play "in wreaths" and the revolutionary flame is seen "rejoicing in its terror / Breaking in smoky wreaths from the wild deep" (15.20–21, 12.10–11). Orc, being wrath, ends wreathed: bound down, closed into the flaming globe of the sun, he becomes one focus of the comets' "excentric paths."[13] The "Orc cycle" begins and ends in an *orb*, a fear-filled symmetry: "I am Orc, wreath'd round" (*Am* 8.1).

These images lead to a question of gravity: how are the globe of wrath, the Sun, and the stars held together, and how did they come to be? *The Book of Los*, dated a year after the *Songs of Experience*, offers this interesting comment: "Light first began; from the fires / *Beams*" (5.10–11). Los seizes these, "condensing / The subtil particles in an Orb" (5.29–30). The striking description that follows contains the only "anvil"—before the longer poems—outside that in "The Tyger" ("What the hammer? . . . What the anvil?"):

> *Roaring indignant the bright sparks*
> *Endur'd the vast Hammer; but unwearied*
> *Los beat on the Anvil; till glorious*
> *An immense Orb of fire he fram'd*
>
> [5.31–35]

So God, in *Paradise Lost*, "of Celestial Bodies first the Sun / A mightie Sphear he fram'd" (7.354–55). "What immortal hand or eye," asks "The Tyger," "dare frame thy fearful symmetry?" The passage from *The Book of Los* continues with Los taking the burning "all-bright" orb and (another pun) "casting / It down into the Deeps"—here the maker does unequivocally smile his work to see: "And Los smild with joy" (5.36, 42–43, 45). Blake's words and images resonate more deeply than we realize: Los, imagination (whose name, again, reflects *sol*), frames a "roaring" Orb of fire: a Tyger, a Globe of wrath, "the fires of Orc a Globe immense" (*FZ* 115.16, E380): sphereful symmetry. The correlation between Tyger and Sun mirrors the standard association of the lion and the Sun: *The Four Zoas* depicts "the terrific orb / . . . The Sun reddning like a fierce lion" (96.10–11, E361), while plate 23 of *The Book of Urizen* remarkably juxtaposes the "globe of light" to an otherwise gratuitously present lion, the theriomorphic form of the sun (fig. 78, below).

Following the old belief that stars represent the souls and seeds of men, we can say that the star enspheres its *spirit*; *Comus* says that "aëreal spirits live insphear'd." The idea is also pictured in *The Fall of Man* (fig. 51) and adds a third term to the graphic pun: spear-sphere-spirit. Breaking the sphere is the prerequisite to releasing the immortal, immaterial reality—so *Il Penseroso* hopes to "unsphear / The spirit of Plato" (88–89). "The Last Judgment" in *The Four Zoas* describes the universe reaped and "the stars threshd from their husks," that is to say, from their mundane shells or spheres. When the spheres are winnowed, the seeds or spirits remain; when the spears are thrown down, the tears are revealed. With these possibilities in mind, we might consider the variations in the formula of stars throwing down/spears thrown down:

> 1. *The millions sent up a howl of anguish and threw off their hammerd mail*
>   *And cast their swords & spears to earth, & stood a naked multitude.*
>   [*Am* 15.4–5]

> 2. *When the stars threw down their spears*
>   ["The Tyger"]

> 3. *The stars threw down their cups & fled*
>   ["When Klopstock," E500]

> 4. *I* [*Urizen*] *calld the stars around my feet in the night of councils dark*
>   *The stars threw down their spears & fled naked away*
>   *We fell.*
>   [*FZ* 64.26–28, E344]

The general sense of (1) and (4) is that spears are in part or in sum a covering without which a star is exposed and naked—which seems to occasion its flight. In example (3) they flee embarrassed by the sight of an exposed Blake. (1) and (4) also point to another important uncertainty operating in "The Tyger": did the stars "lay aside" their weapons and surrender, or did they aggressively "launch"—perhaps "to Earth"—the spears that they "threw down"? Even the subsequent standing or fleeing-away naked is inconclusive, perhaps suggesting only that every available weapon was cast or thrown; "The Tyger"'s dramatic economy allows the stars to lay aside weapons, weeping, or to launch spears and even tears. But the use of "cups" in the third example is a most intriguing substitution in the near formulaic pattern that, like an aberrant instance in some half-understood language, may unlock new dimensions of meaning and association. This image comes some five to seven years after "The Tyger," but fulfills associations latent—via the paronomasia spears/spheres—in the earlier usage.

Piecing together the scattered evidence, it seems that "cups" are, in part, astronomical bodies containing a wine that is in some way related to light and to blood. The image taps traditional ideas of the night sky as a revolving sphere or cup and the Greek myth that the sun makes his nightly journey from west to east across Okeanus in a golden cup, and joins to them the Old Testament metaphor of the stupefying cup of wrath or fury that Yahweh forces in judgment on the idolatrous (Jer. 25:15 and elsewhere). The feast celebrating the marriage of Los and Enitharmon in the first night of *The Four Zoas* finds Urizen, Prince of Light, and his hosts also celebrating:

Rejoicing in the Victory & the heavens were filld with blood

The Earth spread forth her table wide. the Night a silver cup

Fill'd with the wine of anguish waited at the golden feast

But the bright Sun was not as yet; he filling all the expanse

Slept as a bird in the blue shell that soon shall burst away

[12.35–39, E307]

Here again we note Blake's delight in "litteral" transformation as "Sun . . . bird . . . shell" become "soon shall burst." The last two lines are far from transparent, but the great emphasis on things filled or filling suggests that we spread our own table around that action:

> *blood fills heavens*
> *wine of anguish fills cup*
> *sleeping Sun fills expanse.*

So also if "waited" is understood in its dominant sense of "to lie in wait," and "cup" as an appositive for "Night," it appears that the heavens/cup/shell (sphere) contains the sleeping sun/wine/blood. In one evident source for the image, light is first *"sphear'd in* a radiant Cloud, *for yet the Sun / Was not*; shee in a cloudie Tabernacle / Sojourn'd the while" (*PL* 7.247–49, italics added).

The transformation of light is depicted in Night the Seventh, where:

> . . . *Orc began to Organize a Serpent body*
> *Despising Urizens light & turning it into flaming fire*
> *Recieving as a poisond Cup Recieves the heavenly wine*
> *And turning affection into fury & thought into abstraction*
>
> [80.44–47, E356]

The "orcanized" body is like a containing cup (or orb). Though we are not so told, the heavenly wine must be that which changed to "wine of anguish," like the light of love into flames. The poison cup brings in Rahab/Mystery, the Whore of Babylon and her cup of abominations—the "cup which foamd in Vala's hand / Like the red Sun" (*J* 88.56–57)—but the point seems confirmed that spiritual light or illumination may be presented as wine or, remembering interpretations of Genesis 1, heavenly, firmamental water. In an astonishing example of the seemingly boundless cross-reference in Blake's text, after Urizen "arose & leaning on his Spear explord," he comes first to a river, "and taking off his silver helmet filled it & drank" (*FZ* 67.3, E345). The silver helmet becomes another kind of liquid container. *Paradise Lost* speaks of stars "in thir gold'n urns" that draw "liquid light" from the fountain of the sun (7.361–65),[14] and just so the daughter that Urizen encounters at the river, "in sighs & care . . . filld her urn & pourd it forth abroad" (67.10–11). But Urizen can no longer communicate with his daughters, whom he sees as "spirits of darkness," nor can the "bright flood" satiate the physical thirst of a king of light darkening to the visible spectrum: "Then Urizen wept & thus his lamentation poured forth" (68.5, E345). His lamentation is what and how we see: "the overflowing stars rain down prolific pains" (*Eur* 1.15). But, at the end of *The Four Zoas*, a resurrected Urizen is nourished by his daughters who "stand with Cups & measures of foaming wine" (125.15, E394), and the image is continued in *Milton* where "the Constellations . . . rise in order and continue" with heavenly songs and instruments and, again, "with cups & measures filld with foaming wine" (25.66–67, 69). It is this "wine of the Almighty" (*FZ* 65.5, E344) that causes such problems when it gets into the wrong hands—Urizen specifically says that Luvah, who used to "bear the golden cup at the immortal tables," gave him some stolen wine, which he "pourd" and then "drunken with the immortal draught fell" from his "throne sublime" (*FZ* 64.31, 65.7–8, E344). Luvah, in this rehearsal of the Bard's Song in *Milton*, had bartered the wine for the "steeds of Light" to run his golden chariot, and, no sooner than obtained, he "*pourd* / The *spears* of Urizen from Chariots round the Eternal tent" (*FZ* 58.23–24, E339). Urizen, remembering all this, uses the now familiar formula to lament:

> *O Fool could I forget the light that filled my bright spheres*
> *Was a reflection of his face who calld me from the deep*
> [*FZ* 54.19–20, E344]

Our spectrum is but darkness visible, the shadow of its source in "the wine of Eternity," "the wine of ages" (*FZ* 132.11, E400 and elsewhere; 135.22, E403 et al.).

There is another astronomical context for "The Tyger." In February 1791, the renowned astronomer William Herschel announced the existence of "true nebulosity" in the skies—what previously had been perceived only as little milky clouds could, in some instances, now be resolved to show a single star "surrounded with a faintly luminous atmosphere, of a considerable extent."[15] This atmosphere led him to imagine stars "involved in a shining fluid, of a nature totally unknown to us," a curious confirmation of the Miltonic image of light "sphear'd in a radiant cloud." Moreover, he suggests, "particles of light" might provide "the constitution of a shining fluid" produced by "a generating star." These remarks, appearing around the time "The Tyger" was written,[16] offered a new possibility for the older conceptions of stellar operations. Perhaps one might even imagine that when the stars threw down their "spheres" of shining fluid, they diffused through heaven the ethereal luminosity of "Tears of Light."[17]

In "The Tyger," as in all of Blake, words are the stars. But with the question, "Did he smile his work to see?" (line 19), the speaker discloses that he is not one with the creating perception of the work, but lost in a univocal realm seeking unequivocal answers. On one level, "The Tyger" is about this "Questioner who . . . Shall never know how to reply" (*Aug I* 93–94), and at the same time a poem openly exposing that questioner in his desire for closure. As has often been noted, the speaker's questions function rhetorically to "create" the poem—but a more profound message is the sense of rhetorical limitation or "frame" implicit in the speaker's questions. The speaker is not asking real questions, since the possible answers are already constrained by the limitations of his preconceptions, his vocabulary, i.e., the single (for him, un-starry) word "tyger." This may account for the "crisis" or "catastrophe," the crucial strangeness of lines seventeen and eighteen, for here we most clearly sense (though didn't we from the onset of a brightly burning tyger in "forests of the night"?) that the poem is not necessarily about natural tigers, natural stars, or whatever the speaker might think, but that it presents the power of literal imagination that can join the wispy traces in words to evoke part of the history of Western imagining (tygers are not tigers; tygers burn brightly, like the stars). This collective literal imagination goes beyond the speaker's questioning formulations, just as language surrounds and grounds his utterance— the literal his symbolic—in ways he cannot perceive or experience.

After the strange couplet of lines seventeen and eighteen comes the repeated reference to another presence, the evidently "immortal" though lower-case, non-speaking "he," and the only capitalized internal word other than "Tyger": "Did he who made the Lamb make thee?" As true making is *poiesis*, so the maker of "The Lamb" is the poet of "The Tyger," the author of *Songs of Innocence and of Experience*. But that author stated earlier, "The true Man is the source he being the Poetic Genius" (*ARO*). And, with the last stanza, the poem declares its inspiring Poetic Genius: an immortal eye or hand *did* frame— simultaneously constituting and limiting—the fearful symmetry of the poem by moving from "could" to "dare." The off-rhyme of "eye . . . [thy] . . . symmetry" enforces this declaration: as if the Poetic Genius says, "see me try" to frame "like measure"—symmetry (*sum-metros*)—a similitude of what it means to imagine, the relation of a relation. The poiesis enacts an image of recurrence or repetition that also includes (what makes this symmetry eldritch, "fearful") asymmetry through the reflexive awareness of the poet for the speaker, for language. "What immortal hand or eye could/dare frame"—that is, "adapt, enclose, set in a frame" and, what turns into the same thing, "put into words, form and articulate sounds" (*OED*). Framing—as with the "hand" or "eye"—is at once plastic and perceptive, readerly and writerly, expanding and contracting, "continually building & continually decaying": one becomes the other in a reading that experiences the infinite in finite words. In thirteen words of "The Tyger," we thus find the simultaneous conception of stars as spirits or angels (perhaps sphered); the Starry Host of Satan; the starry sphere; the firmament dividing the waters of creation; aggressive or passive stars with astrological, alchemical, and meteorological significance; stars as eyes of light, compassionate or hypocritical, with anagrammatic tears: it is an encyclopedic hologram of Western astral mythologies, imagination in a literal form.

The "cold light of reason" is starlight. When Thomas Taylor argued that Ulysses' passing from Calypso's isle to Phaicia, from darkness to light, was "very properly represented by sailing by the splendour of the stars. . . . For starlight corresponds to the light of the mathematical sciences, which are the proper employment of one who is departing from the sensible phantasy,"[18] he was giving voice to the attitude of millennia. Mathematics is μάϑημα, "that which is learned," and that which is to be learned is the movement of the stars: "Urizen answer'd Read my books explore my Constellations" (*FZ* 79.20, E355).

The relation between stars and consciousness is often attributed to man's need for determining the seasons as he moved from nomadic to agrarian organization—but deeper causes must underlie the fact of whole cultures becoming astrally centered. The notable example is "the astral cult of Babylon," which, Franz Cumont reports, "centered . . . the Divine in those luminous and moving bodies at the expense of the other objects of nature—stones, plants, animals—among which the primitive faith of the Semites had equally dispersed it."[19] Vestiges of "the Babylonian mathematical starlight" (as Yeats saw it) survive unaltered in some of the zodiacal constellations. George Stanley Faber's *The Origin of Pagan Idolatry* cites Herodotus to argue that "Astronomy certainly originated at Babylon. . . . Our present sphere is in the main the same as that of the old Babylonians"[20] (so the Tyger may date back to Mesopotamia, still burning bright through the stars of the Tigris-Euphrates sky). *Jerusalem* tells how "Hand has peopled Babel & Nineveh," and

> *They put forth their spectrous cloudy sails; which drive their immense*
> *Constellations over the deadly deeps of indefinite Udan-Adan*

[7.21–22]

In Blake, "The Abyss of Los" (*BU* 15.5) is "The Void," the "Deeps" where are seen the "dark visions of Los": "the endless Abyss of space" (*BU* 15.10). The structure of the abyss or "distant deeps or skies" may be studied in Blake's illustrations to Young's "space intoxicated" *Night Thoughts*.[21] Like Lucretius' Epicurus, who "extra / processit longe flammentia moenia mundi" ("wandered out beyond the flaming ramparts of the world"), and using the rich eighteenth-century tradition of the scientific intellect voyaging into space ("mental travelling"),[22] Young hopes to explore realms "foreign to the Sun" "in boundless Walks of raptur'd Thought." Blake's illustration to this senti-

(30)

And that a *Self* far more illuftrious ftill.
Beyond long Ages, yet roll'd up in Shades,   *510*
Unpierc'd by bold Conjecture's keeneft Ray,
What Evolutions of furprizing Fate?
How Nature opens, and receives my Soul
In boundlefs Walks of raptur'd Thought? Where Gods
Encounter, and embrace me! What new Births
Of ftrange Adventure, foreign to the Sun,
Where what now charms, perhaps, whate'er exifts,
Old *Time*, and fair *Creation*, are forgot?

Is this extravagant? of Man we form
Extravagant Conception; to be juft: *520*
Conception unconfin'd wants Wing to reach him:
Beyond its reach, the Godhead only, more.
He, the great Father! kindled at one Flame
The World of Rationals; one Spirit pour'd
From Spirits awful Fountain; pour'd Himfelf
Thro' all their Souls; but not in equal Stream,
Profufe, or frugal of th' infpiring God,
As his wife Plan demanded; and when paft

52. *Night Thoughts,* design no. 139.

ment (fig. 52) depicts the voyager setting off into the unknown. While the discrepancy in size emphasizes the imaginary quality of the exploration, we note how carefully the voyager remains attached to the sphere, not only by his left foot, but by the flowing continuation of his aerial robe, which encompasses and/or emanates from its planet of origin. A later illustration (fig. 53) shows the immortal soul leaving behind the earth and its satellite in its cloud or *nebula* (the term popularized by Herschel, though used before) and mounting to "Time's further Shore." The latent aquatic referents are vividly conceived two designs later in the remarkable illustration of the lines:

53. *Night Thoughts,* design no. 229.

In the vast Ocean of unbounded Space,
Behold an Infinite of floating Worlds
Divide the Crystal Waves of Ether pure

(fig. 54)

Young completes the macro-microcosmic connection, suggesting that these worlds may be "as Particles, as Atoms ill-perceiv'd; / As circulating Globules in our Veins." Just so, Blake's "globe of life blood" can be a sun, "a red round globe. hot burning deep deep down into the Abyss" (*BU* 15.13; *FZ* 54.17,

(10)

In full Dimenfions, fwells to the Survey;
And enters, at one Glance, the ravifnt Sight.
From fome fuperior Point (where, who can tell?
Suffice it, 'tis a Point where Gods refide)
How fhall the ftranger Man's illumin'd Eye,
In the vaft Ocean of unbounded Space,
Behold an Infinite of floating Worlds
Divide the Cryftal Waves of Ether pure,
In endlefs Voyage, without Port? The leaft   .*/
Of thefe diffeminated Orbs, how Great?
Great as they are, what Numbers Thefe furpafs
Huge, as *Leviathan*, to that fmall Race,
Thofe twinkling Multitudes of little Life,
He fwallows unperceiv'd? *Stupendous* Thefe!
Yet what are thefe Stupendous to the *Whole*?
As Particles, as Atoms ill-perceiv'd;
As circulating Globules in our Veins;
So vaft the Plan: Fecundity Divine!
Exuberant Source! perhaps, I wrong thee ftill.   .(q)
                                                  If

54. *Night Thoughts*, design no. 231.

E336). The oceanic motif reappears in the fascinating design illustrating the Tygerish lines:

> *Where are the Pillars that support the Skies?*
> *What more than* Atlantean *Shoulder props*
> *The incumbent Load? What Magick, what strange Art,*
> *In fluid Air these ponderous Orbs sustains?*

(fig. 55)

The figure's relation to the ocean is even more problematic than that of the earlier "floating Worlds"—not to mention the bizarre possibility that the world has become Atlas' elephant-sized head. Perhaps he, and so the Earth, shows

55. *Night Thoughts,* design no. 475.

that "mysterious way" of Cowper's God—"He plants His footsteps in the sea"—or perhaps, as imaginative vision, his feet are planted on the margin of the design, the frame. The overarching zodiac is curious also, not least for the perspective it entails. While Libra precedes Scorpio, the trailing motion of these scales indicates motion in the opposite direction, increasing the picture's disorienting effect when compared with other contemporary conceptions (fig. 56). Design no. 321 (fig. 57) summarizes the space-traveller's vision of "Worlds, on Worlds!"—the vision strangely anticipates one recorded by Earth's "Voyager" spacecraft in 1980 (fig. 58).

The association of Babylon and the bright star announcing world change is embedded in the foundation of Christianity, since the only ones who knew how

56. "Le Génie de la nature dans la contemplation de l'univers,"
from Buffon's *Histoire naturelle* (1797).

to read the star announcing Christ's birth (for which there is no historical evidence) were three kings of the east, the Magi. The Babylonian faith in stars as "the writing of the sky"[23] differs little from that of Young's apostrophe:

DIVINE INSTRUCTOR! Thy first *volume,* This,
For Man's *Perusal; All in CAPITALS!*
In Moon, *and* Stars, *(Heaven's golden Alphabet!)*
Emblaz'd to seize the Sight. . . .

[*NT* 9.1690–93]

Such are the letters with which Urizen composes his constellation books, "a Language worthy of the GREAT MIND, that speaks! / *Preface,* and *Comment,* to the *Sacred Page!*" Blake's illustration to this sentiment (fig. 59), showing the hooded angel of Night opening the Book of Stars or Constellations, offers another version of plate 5 of *The Book of Urizen* (fig. 60)—both books bear the same illegible starry message written in orange and yellow. This Book of Urizen appears in its own frontispiece as a copy of the Tables of the Law—perhaps an ephemeris, if not ephemeral (fig. 5, above). Young's "GREAT MIND" is the Heavenly Father of the Lord's Prayer that Blake saw as having been condemned to the "Substantial Astronomical Telescopic Heavens" (E658). His letter protesting the arrest of an astrologer gives us Blake's understanding of the correlation between ancient and modern stargazing: "The Man who can read the Stars is often opressed by their Influence, no less than the Newtonian who reads Not & cannot read is opressed by his own Reasonings and Experiments" (E769). That is, both are oppressed by their systems:

    Astrologer reads   stars   ∴ opressed by their   influence
    Newtonian reads not [stars]   ∴ opressed by his own Reasonings

The "influence of the stars" is functionally equivalent to the Newtonian's reasonings, and neither possessed any attraction for Blake—as John Linnell reports, "[John] Varley could make no way with Blake towards enducing him to regard Astrology with favour."[24] Blake's letter is not a reaction in defense of the art, but a defense of liberty through the mental strife of opposing cosmologies.

Stargazing is not inherently an abstracting activity. *Milton* presents a lyric passage that harks back to our mythological experience of pre-Babylonian astronomy, perhaps in the guise of Blake's recollection of his childhood at 27 Broad Street, with its flat roof over the third story:

The Sky is an immortal Tent built by the Sons of Los
And every Space that a Man views around his dwelling-place:

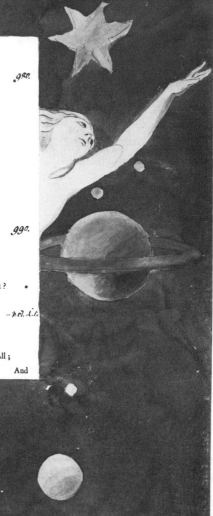

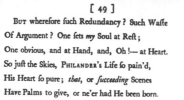

[49]

But wherefore such Redundancy? Such Waste
Of Argument? One sets *my* Soul at Rest;   .950.
One obvious, and at Hand, and, Oh!— at Heart.
So just the Skies, PHILANDER's Life so pain'd,
His Heart so pure; *that*, or *succeeding* Scenes
Have Palms to give, or ne'er had He been born.

" What an old Tale is This!" LORENZO cries.—
I grant this Argument is old; but Truth
No Years impair; and had not This been True,
Thou never hadst despis'd it for its Age.
Truth is Immortal as thy Soul; and Fable
As fleeting as thy Joys: Be wise, nor make   .990.
Heav'n's highest Blessing, Vengeance: O be wise!
Nor make a Curse of *Immortality*.

Say, know'st Thou what *It* is? Or, what *Thou* art?   •
Know'st Thou th' *Importance* of a Soul Immortal?
Behold this Midnight Glory; Worlds, on Worlds!   — *p. el. 4. l.*
Amazing Pomp! Redouble this Amaze;
Ten thousand add; add twice Ten thousand more;
Then weigh the Whole; One Soul outweighs them All;

H   And

57. *Night Thoughts*, design no. 321.

58. Montage depicting the Saturnian system, from images taken by Voyager 1,
November, 1980.

Standing on his own roof, or in his garden on a mount
Of twenty-five cubits in height, such space is his Universe;

for,

The Starry heavens reach no further but here bend and set
On all sides & the two Poles turn on their valves of gold:
And if he move his dwelling-place, his heavens also move.

[29.4–7, 10–12][25]

So in *Jerusalem*, because "all the Sons of Albion appeard distant stars, / Ascending and descending" (50.20–21), "Los all night watches / The stars rising
& setting; & the meteors & terrors of night!" and when he speaks, "the Stars
stand still to hear" (83.80–81, 85.15). But we must distinguish between seeing
the stars above, and the constellations within—for constellations, as evident by

[83]

To *Christian* Land, or *Jewry's*; fairly writ
In Language universal, to MANKIND:
A Language, Lofty to the Learn'd; yet Plain,
To Thofe that feed the Flock, or guide the Plough,
Or, from its Hufk, ftrike out the bounding Grain!
A Language, worthy the GREAT MIND, that fpeaks!
Preface, and *Comment*, to the *Sacred Page!*
Which oft refers its Reader to the Skies,
As pre-fuppofing his Firft Leffon *there*,
And Scripture-felf a *Fragment*, *That* unread.
Stupendous Book of Wifdom, to the Wife!
Stupendous Book! and open'd, NIGHT! by Thee.

BY Thee *much* open'd, I confefs, O *Night!*
Yet *more* I wifh; but *how* fhall I prevail?
Say, gentle *Night!* whofe modeft, maiden Beams
Give us a *new* Creation, and prefent
The World's great Picture, foften'd to the Sight;
Nay, Kinder far, far more Indulgent ftill,
Say, Thou, whofe mild Dominion's Silver Key
Unlocks our Hemifphere, and fets to View
Worlds beyond Number; Worlds conceal'd by Day

M 2   Behind

59. *Night Thoughts*, design no. 501.

60. *The Book of Urizen,* pl. 5, detail.

representations from Dürer's involved forms to modern stick-figures, only mirror the fashion in which the reasoning mind has chosen to organize empty space: "Los reads the Stars of Albion! the Spectre reads the Voids / Between the Stars" (*J* 91.36–37). The stars join into figures:

> *For the Chaotic Voids outside of the Stars are measured by*
> *The Stars, which are the boundaries of Kingdoms, Provinces*
> *And Empires of Chaos invisible to the Vegetable Man*
>
> . . . .
>
> *Stretchd out, compose the Mundane Shell, a mighty* Incrustation
> *Of Forty-eight deformed Human Wonders of the Almighty*
>
> [*M* 37.47–49, 53–54]

and the constellations lock together to form the Mundane Shell.[26] The nature of this operation appears in the anachronistic reference to forty-eight constellations, for Blake is not interested in the fact that his contemporaries had decided on eighty starry forms;[27] he wishes rather to explore how the mind chose to embody (even in expanding) itself within its stellar projections and, as part of *Milton's* war against memory, to annihilate this false body, "an *Incrustation*" over the immortal spirit (40.35—Blake's only other use of the word).

Though the Newtonian cannot "read" them, the *Descriptive Catalogue* says that "Newton numbered the stars" (E533). Newton's metaphorical "numbering" of the stars puts him in the position of Lucifer attempting to exalt his throne "above the stars of God" (Isa. 14:13), for only the Lord "telleth the number of the stars" (Ps. 147:4). Numbering the stars is "figuring" them, a multivalent term that covers the projection of designs onto the sky and the imposition of mathematical order on the stars. "Bring out number weight & measure in a year of dearth," says a Proverb of Hell, and the fact that quantification has been at the fore since the Garden of Eden tells the quality of our time. This history is the writing on the wall, "MENE, MENE, TEKEL UPHARSIN," "numbered, numbered, weighed and measured" (Dan. 5:25–28), and can be seen even upon the walls of heaven: Young asks us to "mark / The *Mathematic* Glories of the Skies: / In Number, Weight, and Measure, All ordain'd" (*NT* 9.1107–9). When Urizen builds his palace, the Mundane Shell, his starry children are "numb'erd all":

> *Travelling in silent majesty along their orderd ways*
> *In right lined paths outmeasurd by proportions of number weight*
> *And measure. mathematic motion wondrous. . . .*
>
> [*FZ* 33.22–24, E322]

These measures are not those that hold the foaming celestial wine.

For Blake, the long reign of quantity was emphasized by the growing realization of the astronomical nature of ancient "Druid" monuments such as Stonehenge. William Borlase cites "Cesar and Mela" as his authorities that the Druids "reason much (they say) and instruct their youth in many particulars relating to the Planets and their motion,"[28] and Edward Davies reports that the structures were thought, "not only to have been temples of the heathen Britons, but also to have been constructed upon *astronomical principles*: in short, to have represented, either the Zodiac itself, or certain *cycles* and *computations*, deduced from the study of astronomy."[29] Blake based his myth of the primacy of Albion and the Druids on the presence of such astronomical "Druid Temples . . . over the whole Earth" (*J* 27). The temples (and the values they reflect), he imagines elsewhere, "reach the stars of heaven & stretch from pole to pole" (*M* 9.15). These temples represent the apotheosis of the non-human because of the ritual sacrifice celebrated within, on the "altar" or "slaughter stone" of Stonehenge, or, nearly related, in the burning idol of "the Wicker Man," where "the Captives reard to heaven howl in flames among the stars" (*J* 47.7–8). Many of these temples, according to William Stukeley's discussion of Abury (Avebury) were built "with the form of a snake annext"; these he labels "serpentine temples, or *Dracontia*, by which they were denominated of old."[30] "The practice of building these serpentine temples," he continues, "was us'd by the patriarchs, perhaps near the beginning of the world." In *Europe* "the fiery King," the king of England but also the latest Druid high priest, seeks "his ancient temple serpent-form'd" (10.2). The temple is formed of "massy stones" which were "plac'd in the order of the stars, when the five senses whelm'd / In deluge o'er the earth-born man" (*Eur* 10.10–11). So the serpent temples mirror the dominant constellated form: Serpens, Draco, Hydra. Being "the Serpent round the tree of Mystery," Orc is also "a Serpent wondrous among the Constellations of Urizen," while, in turn, Urizen's "folding tail aspires / Among the stars the Earth & all the Abysses feel h[i]s fury."[31] This connection is illustrated in a design for Milton's "Ode on the Morning of Christ's Nativity" entitled "The Old Dragon Underground"—there stars in the night sky join and extend "the scaly Horrour of his foulded tail" (fig. 61).

To consider (which is a form of stargazing—Lat. *con-sidus*) the stars is to risk enthrallment to the Daughters of Memory, to the forms of our primitive cultural heritage. In the sky we still follow "the detestable Gods of Priam" (*M* 14.15): Jupiter, Mars, Orion, Ophicus (cf. "The Laocoön," E273). So do we entomb ourselves: the Sons of Albion peruse "Albions Tomb in the starry characters of Og & Anak" (*J* 73.16), and "the Kingdom of Og. is in Orion: Sihon is in Ophicus" (*M* 37.50). Og, Sihon, and Anak all associate in some way with the Rephaim, the race of ghosts and Giants (cf. *J* 49.56) who figure in the sky because of their size, because the preexisting race of giants was thought to have built the astrological temples,[32] and because—another version of the same—they all tried to prevent Israel from reaching the Holy Land. But these figures have no real existence; they are the on-going projection of "the ruind spirits," once the children of Urizen and Luvah, who wandered, "moping in their heart a Sun a Dreary moon / A Universe of fiery constellations in their brain" (*FZ* 70.8–9, E347). The "Constellations of Urizen" represent reason's attempt to order the universe, but reveal instead self-limitation, our enclosure in the "Starry head" of Urizen (*FZ* 30.24, E319). Where inspiration sees the Four Zoas "pervading all . . . Fourfold each in the other . . . Four Starry Universes," which "are named Life's" (*FZ* 123.37–39, E393), reason prefers to deal in its own diminutive zodiac or "circle of little sculpted animals." But reason forgets even that it created this—so Urizen, on his journey "through the abyss," "beheld the forms of tygers & of Lions dishumanizd men / Many in serpents & in worms stretchd out enormous length," but "oft would he stand & question a fierce scorpion glowing with gold / In vain the terror heard not" (*FZ* 70.31,-32, 71.1-2, E347, 348). Reason, in effect, can no longer talk to its past, which has become unconscious and so gives rise to the indefinite imaginings of the present. But after a Last Judgment we see the Eternal Man,

> *raising his heavenly voice*
> *Conversing with the Animal forms of wisdom night & day*
> *That risen from the Sea of fire renewd walk oer the Earth*
> [*FZ* 138.30–32, E406]

Our forgetting is the reason that fall and fault lie not in the stars, but in ourselves. Boehme reminds us that:

> The Image of God in Man is so powerful and mighty, that when it wholly casteth itself into the will of God, it overpowereth nature, so that the Stars are *obedient* to it, and do rejoice themselves in the Image: for their will is that they may be freed from the vanity, and thus are kindled in Meekness in the Image, at which Heaven rejoiceth.[33]

This explains how "the lapsed Soul . . . might controll / The starry pole / And fallen fallen light renew!" ("Introduction," *SE*). The lapsed soul could become our risen Sol (see fig. 62).

The Mundane Shell, Urizen's contemplation, is a "wondrous building" with "twelve halls"— like zodiacal "houses"—constructed according to his directives as "the great Work master" (*FZ* 30.15, E319; 24.5, E314). His title reflects Bacon's fantasy in *The Advancement of Learning* that, "if that great Work-master had been of a human disposition, he would have cast the stars into some pleasant and beautiful works and order, like the frets in the roofs of houses, whereas one can scarce find a posture in square, or triangle, or straight line" (2.14.9) and also Uriel's account, in *Paradise Lost*, of "the great Work-Maister" who created the material world, including the starry sphere that "in circuit walls this Universe" (3.696, 721). This universe, the "star chamber" that Urizen orders "as he stood in the Human Brain" (*FZ* 23.12, E313), is a complicated mathematical construction of "Trapeziums Rhombs Rhom-

61. *Illustrations to Milton's "Hymn on the Morning of Christ's Nativity,"*
design no. 3, "The Old Dragon Underground."

boids / Parallelograms. triple & quadruple. polygonic" (*FZ* 33.34–35, E322) showing it to be, in fact, the creation "of a human disposition" (a disposition, Blake might say, "how altered, how changed!"). One account of Urizen's temple says that "they put the Sun / Into the temple of Urizen to give light to the Abyss," and that "Urizen namd it Pande" (96.14–15, E361, 838). So we return to Milton's Pandaemonium, "built like a Temple," where "from the arched roof / Pendant by suttle Magic many a row / Of Starry Lamps . . . yeilded light / As from a sky" (*PL* 1.726–30)—it is another version of the starry temple that has "orb'd us round in concave fires / A Hell of our own making" (*M* 12.22–23).

The result of Urizen's starry considerations and contemplations is disaster:

> *Albion gave his loud death groan The Atlantic Mountains trembled*
> *Aloft the Moon fled with a cry the Sun with streams of blood*
> *From Albions Loins fled all Peoples and Nations of the Earth*
> *Fled with the noise of Slaughter & the stars of heaven Fled*
>
> [*FZ* 25.9–12, E314]

In abbreviated form, this tells the story of the Flood and the senses "whelm'd in deluge," the dispersal of all peoples from the patriarch Albion, and the collapse into finite perception. The passage presents the first phrasing of the oft-repeated lines that characterize the fundamental perception of Blake's later work:

> *All things begin & end in Albions ancient Druid rocky shore*
> *But now the Starry Heavens are fled from the mighty limbs of Albion*
>
> [*M* 6.25–26]

To say that the stars flee is to say that they "are shrunk away" by man's shrinking perception. Here again Stonehenge supplied an example: it was imagined as an observatory and temple where priests studied the distant heavens and offered human sacrifices to their abstractions. In another reference to Urizen's architectural abilities—this recurrent association suggested by the standard eighteenth-century image of God as Architect[34]—we see the complementary structure to his stellar system as the Sons of Albion (like Urizen's Bands of Heaven before them)

> *. . . build a stupendous Building on the Plain of Salisbury; with chains*
> *Of rocks round London Stone: of Reasonings: of unhewn Demonstrations*

[41]

Tell me, ye Stars! ye Planets! tell me, all
Ye Starr'd, and Planeted, Inhabitants! What is it?
What are thefe Sons of Wonder? Say, proud Arch!
(Within whofe azure Palaces they dwell)
Built with Divine Ambition! in Difdain
Of Limit built! built in the Tafte of Heav'n!
Vaft Concave! Ample Dome! Waft thou defign'd
A meet Apartment for the DEITY? ——
Not fo; That Thought alone thy State impairs,
Thy *Lofty* finks, and fhallows thy *Profound*,
And ftreightens thy *Diffufive*; dwarfs the Whole,
And makes an Univerfe an *Orrery*.

BUT when I drop mine Eye, and look on Man,
Thy Right regain'd, thy Grandeur is reftor'd,
O *Nature!* wide flies off th' expanding Round:
As when whole Magazines, at once, are fir'd,
The fmitten Air is hollow'd by the Blow;
The vaft Difplofion diffipates the Clouds,
Shock'd Æther's Billows dafh the diftant Skies;
Thus (but far more) th' expanding Round flies off,
And leaves a mighty Void, a fpacious Womb,

G   Might

62. *Night Thoughts,* design no. 459.

In labyrinthine arches. (mighty Urizen the Architect.) thro which
The Heavens might revolve & Eternity be bound in their chain.

[*J* 66.2–5]

Stonehenge is a smaller version of the earlier work whose "pillard halls & rooms recievd the eternal wandering stars" and where "within its walls & cielings / The heavens were closd" (*FZ* 32.9, 12–13, E321)—but its firm mental foundations are now explicitly identified: "The Building is Natural Religion & its Altars Natural Morality" (*J* 66.8).[35]

Blake's cosmology is not without its difficulties.[36] "Chaos" exists "beyond the stars" (*M* 23.21), but it appears a chaos of the mind against which the Mundane Shell protects (as it imprisons) us. Blake does not fight a quixotic battle against the starry mill or crystalline spheres, but rather struggles to explode the Newtonian universe, "at once infinite and constrained," as Jacob Bronowski puts it. Blake *felt* that "celestial mechanics" must have an end or limit—it simply does not feel adequate to mental perception ("the same dull round even of a univer[s]e would soon become a mill with complicated wheels" [*NNR*b]). He said that he saw the spiritual sun, and we who are coming to envision quasars and invisible black holes may yet see the same. Young, in one of the more endearing instances of his rhetorical style, argues typically that the Newtonian temple continues forever:

Where, ends this mighty building? Where begin
The suburbs of Creation? Where the wall
Whose battlements look o'er into the vale
Of non-existence? Nothing's strange abode!

[*NT* 9.1519–22]

But the building itself is for Blake "an allegorical abode where existence hath never come" (*Eur* 6.7):

. . . built when the moon shot forth,
In that dread night when Urizen call'd the stars round his feet;
Then burst the center from its orb, and found a place beneath;
And Earth conglob'd, in narrow room, roll'd round its sulphur Sun.

[*Am* b.4–7]

The awful symmetries in Blake's larger conception proliferate: Urizen/Satan fell, taking that part of heaven with which he built the Mundane S/hell/skull,

which is to say men fell and organized the sky into constellations or mathematical principles and the immediate and tangible became distant and abstract. Chaos exists beyond the stars because the interdimensional relations of
space-time, matter, anti-matter, and energy defeat conceptualization.

Taken individually, stars can have their powerful and positive associations:
opposed to the stars of Urizen are "the Stars of God" (*J* 58.49), and a Proverb
of Hell warns that, "He whose face gives no light, shall never become a star."
This emphasis on "face" harks back to the classical belief in the "*os sacrum*," the
planet or star "conceived as a 'head' or 'face'";[37] related were the beliefs that
genius manifested itself in flame and that heroes become stellar deities after
death. Blake gives Milton such attributes, seeing him "in the Zenith as a falling
star, / Descending perpendicular" (*M* 15.47–48), a phrase also evoking the
heavenly smith of *Paradise Lost*, who once "dropt from the Zenith like a falling
Star" (1.745), and Blake's early, Spenserian conception of "Mercurius," who,

> . . . *laden with eternal fate, dost go*
> *Down, like a falling star, from autumn sky,*
> *And o'er the surface of the silent deep dost fly.*
>
> [E421]

Catching a falling star is a recurring refrain in *Milton*, emphasized by the
complementary full-page illustrations of "William" and "Robert," each
thrown back as the star descends. The star entering William Blake's foot was
identified as Milton, but the symmetrical mirroring that joins his image with
that of his dead, beloved brother (figs. 63, 64), encourages us to think of the star
as signifying union with the *astral* body[38]—that is, both Robert Blake and John
Milton are projections of William (and vice versa). Blake's union with Milton
prefigures his encounter with Los as "a terrible flaming Sun" who enters into
his soul. The falling star, the soul descending to rebirth, emblematizes the
possibility of crossing the boundaries of time and space that limit fallen
imagination. The Zoas themselves are quasi-stellar beings: we read that "Los
was the fourth immortal starry one" and that together "they are named Life's
[i.e., Zoas] in Eternity / Four starry Universes going forward (*FZ* 3.9, E301;
123.39–40, E393). As falling stars are to our eyes, so perhaps the falling Zoas
were to stars. At the end of *The Four Zoas*, we see the "expanding eyes of man"
replace the stars:

> *His eyes behold the Angelic spheres arising night & day*
> *The stars consumd like a lamp blown out & in their stead behold*

63. *Milton*, pl. 32.   64. *Milton*, pl. 37.

The Expanding Eyes of Man behold the depths of wondrous worlds
One Earth one sea beneath nor Erring Globes wander but Stars
Of fire rise up nightly from the Ocean & one Sun
Each morning like a New born Man issues with songs & Joy

[138.23–28, E406][39]

It is a picture of Being after we have passed the stages of our world, entering the vortex.

CHAPTER TEN

Word and Text: Vortex and Wheel

The ordinary account of this vortex by no means prepared me for what I saw.
Edgar Allan Poe, "Descent into the Maelström"

JOHNSON's *Dictionary* defines "vortex" simply as "any thing whirled round," and the primary entry for the word in the early editions of the *Encyclopaedia Britannica* refers to "a whirlwind" and "an eddy or whirlpool," conditions that appear throughout Blake's writing connected with vortexes. The "whirling motion" of vortical phenomena leads to the wheel: Urizen refers to his universe with "many a Vortex" as "this world of Cumbrous wheels" (*FZ* 72.22, E349), and in *Jerusalem* Hyle works "to draw Jerusalems Sons / Into the Vortex of his Wheels" (74.29–30). True to its subject, our discussion will have to circulate.

The etymology of "vortex" offers a forceful illustration of a word's assimilating power as it spirals through the collective imagination and perception encoded in semantics. "Vortex" and "vertex" go directly to Latin *vertex*, which was itself the classical form of the older usage *vortex*. Its root means "to turn," and the primary significance was a whirl, eddy, or whirlpool. Yet the word also came to signify the head, the peak of a mountain, and the north pole—and diversifies in English to the vertex of an angle and verticality.[1] The explanation must be that the heavens suggest the quintessential "turning," centering on the pole, which in turn represents "height," "overheadness," "upwardness." Mythologically, the firmament was thought to rest on and revolve from the top point of the northern world-mountain, the vertex of its triangular form. More than merely turning or wheeling, the stars seem to be spinning in a giant whirlpool whose gate or drain—valve—is the pole (fig. 65). The pole is thus ground zero for our universe: when the reader is directed "beyond this Universal Confusion," it is "beyond the remotest Pole / Where their vortexes begin to operate" (*FZ* 119.24–25, E388). Blake's association of gate and pole appears through the rare word "keeper," twice applied to Urthona as "keeper of the gates of heaven" and to Arthur—"a name for the constellation Arcturus, or Bootes"—as "keeper of the North Pole" (*DC*, E542). The vortex offers the gate of entry to our world.[2] "Several mythologies," E. J. Aiton relates in his history of the vortex theory, "suggest that the constellation of the Great Bear, controlling the seasons, was kept revolving by a celestial whirlpool or whirlwind."[3] Spirits descending to generation, or ascending out of our world, take a spiral track (fig. 66), a trajectory demanded by the increasing velocities of nearer planetary spheres: so *Europe* imagines "the ever-varying spiral ascents to the heavens of heavens" (10.13).

"Vortex," like "fibre," shows itself as a somewhat indeterminate word, though evoking great power and energy. Young speaks of being "fired in the vortex of Almighty Power" (*NT* 9.1628), Smollett's *Humphry Clinker* criticizes those who allow themselves "to be sucked deeper and deeper into the vortex of extravagance and dissipation," and Burke worries about those drawn into the "vortex" of the French Revolution. The word proliferates in associations, enacting, as a word-text, the phenomenon it names in Blake: while some words reveal themselves in a flash of light, or slowly twist into a fibre, this one turns in an endless vortex, trying to name that which is beyond the situation of language.[4] So Ezra Pound appropriated "vortex" for his suggestion that "the image is not an idea. It is a radiant node or cluster . . . a whirlwind of force and emotion."[5] In the terms of this book, the vortex is one experience of the nodal point, the *Knotenpunkt*. Some of the word's force and emotion comes, no doubt, from its assimilation of intimidating meanings stemming from the Latin root *vorare*, "to devour," which merges with *vortex* in "voraginous" or "vorago." These combined associations appear when, "in the Caverns of the Grave & Places of human seed / The nameless shadowy Vortex stood before the face of Orc" (*FZ* 91.1–2, E363), where it is evident from context and formula (cf. *Am* 1.1) that "vortex" is a translation of "female." The lines that follow develop the transposition, explaining her presence: "That he might lose his rage / And with it lose himself." One inference anticipates a psychoanalytic interpretation of the vortex as the vagina. George Devereux cites instances from his clinical experience in which "the hairy vulva is fantasied as a *vortex* which, by *suction*,

65. A vortex: Polar star trails.

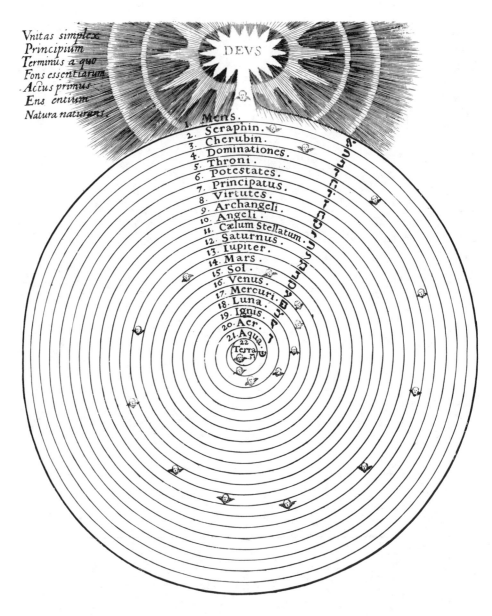

66. Robert Fludd, *Utruisque cosmi . . . historia,* vol. 2, p. 217 (1617).

draws the victim into the vagina."[6] This archaic male fear must join the intellectual/astronomical projection of the "whirls of generation"; Charles Cotton's late seventeenth-century double entendre, ΕΡΩΤΟΠΟΛΙΣ, warned that a man, "if he have not a care, he may chance to lose a limb, swallowed up in a whirl-pit, not without the Effusion of the choycest part of the blood." The nameless, shadowy, metonymic "Vortex" takes greater form as "Vala now become Urizens harlot / And the harlot of Los & the deluded harlot of the Kings of Earth" (*FZ* 91.14–15, E363). The vortex manifests the suction and seduction of veiling, spectral nature: Vala as virago, consumer, devourer, and consummation.

The instinctual response to the whirling vortex lies in our fear of being swallowed or "drawn in"—fear of utter loss of being, plunged in that abortive gulf (*PL* 2.440–41). Thel imagines her ear as an uncontrollable "whirlpool fierce to draw creations in" (6.17), while in the stellar, "attractive north"—attraction meaning "to draw towards" (*ad-traho*)—"a raging whirlpool draws the dizzy enquirer to his grave" (*Eur* 10.31). We repeatedly meet spirits or spectrous life being "drawn into" a vortex. The falling of the mind into its sunken state opens a gap that occasions a vortex or whirlpool, like water falling through a drain: "like the silent grave / Mighty was the draught of Voidness to draw Existence in" (*FZ* 23.17–24.1, E313). The mind rushes toward matter (and things that seem to matter: the grave, gravity, *mater*), drawing existence in behind it. The reason, as it was for Plato, is bodily pleasure and desire; Los and Enitharmon are "drawn down by their desires," just as "beauty & delusion . . . draw the souls of the Dead into the light" (*FZ* 34.1, E322; *J* 79.78–79). Paradoxically, the desire to be forms the ultimate "ground" of Non-Existence, the Abyss; for Being as we know it, being as we are, is always predicated—*of* some thing, genitive—and, like the devourer, we only consume portions of existence and fancy that the whole (*MHH* 16). The unanswerable question posed to our Urizen is the fact of the body, which in its vortex creates the question of its own fact.[7] Even "turning" these formulations round in our thought, we participate in the vortex. We are "drawn down into a Vegetated body" (*FZ* 105.13, E378) just as, by the same process, existence is "drawn" into the vortex, into the artist's embodiments of word and image. Each exerts its own attraction, like signifiers drawing in signifieds through the reader's attention.

The vortex is a constituting aspect of time-space consciousness (binary sleep), whose operations figure in texts that do not name it directly. *Milton*, for instance, tells that "Satan is Urizen / Drawn down by Orc & the Shadowy

Female into Generation . . . the Space." The ensuing description of the space also describes the effects of being drawn into the vortex:

> *The nature of a Female Space is this: it* shrinks *the Organs*
> *Of Life till they become Finite & Itself seems Infinite*
> *And Satan vibrated in the immensity of the Space! Limited*
> *To those without but Infinite to those within: it fell down and*
> *Became Canaan. . . .*
>
> [*M* 10.6–10]

This gives a version of the effects of penetrating, being drawn into our vale, which is, as the end of *Milton* and the frontispiece of *Jerusalem* suggest, "a Void, outside of Existence, which if enterd into / Englobes itself & becomes a womb" (cf. the text in fig. 62), in other words, "Albion's Lovely Land," or Canaan, the Promised Land. Once caught by such promises or beauty, the quest is how to escape, to return, "to rise from generation free." The success of this ultimate desire seems to hinge on attitudes toward the vortex and void: if one is "drawn in," objecting, then one "shrinks" in an attempt to compact a hard-core of identity; but if we "enter" and "commit ourselves" to the void (*MHH* 17), the possibilities are without end. In this spirit, we follow Milton into one of the most travelled "passages" in Blake.

Directly preceding the famous lines comes the description of Milton seen by the shades of hell, "in a trail of light as of a comet / That travels into Chaos: so Milton went guarded within." The proximity of "comet" to the upcoming "vortex" reminds us of Cartesian cosmology, an important supposition of which was that comets, themselves the collapsed remains of previous vortexes or stars, travelled irregularly through space, being spun from one stellar vortex or whirlpool to the next. The discovery of the regular movement of comets became a powerful argument against the idea: "For if these imaginary vortices carried the planets from west to east, by means of their particular circulations, the comets, which traverse those spaces in various directions . . . could never move according to any determinate law, as they would be constantly impeded and turned out of their course by so many contrary and opposite motions" (John Bonnycastle, *Introduction to Astronomy*, pp. 78–79). Milton the comet "travels into Chaos" (his unique track, like that of a Cartesian comet, breaking the bounds of Newtonian possibility) as Milton, by the vortexes, will be a "traveller thro' Eternity." "Chaos," the poem says, is "beyond the stars," and similarly, in Night the Ninth, it is "beyond the remotest Pole" that the "vortexes begin to operate" (*FZ* 119.24–25, E388). "Chaos," then, can name the collective system of vortexes, as it can also name the initial response to Blake's text: as David Worrall notes, what "seems chaos to some appears as the gate from or to heaven to others"[8]—a vortex.

The transition the comet Milton makes is between different states of being (and different texts), so in his course toward Earth he passes spectres "swift as lightning," reminding us that Jesus "beheld Satan as lightning fall from heaven" (Luke 10:18). Whether we imagine Milton as descending from heaven travelling through eternity, or satanically ascending from hell and travelling through chaos, in either event he enters the "Sea of Time & Space" that is the local system:

> *The nature of infinity is this: That* every thing *has its*
> *Own Vortex; and when once a traveller thro' Eternity*
> *Has passd that Vortex, he percieves it roll backward behind*
> *His path, into a globe itself infolding; like a sun:*
> *Or like a moon, or like a universe of starry majesty,*
> *While he keeps onwards in his wondrous journey on the earth*
> *Or like a human form, a friend with whom he livd benevolent.*
> *As the eye of man views both the east & west encompassing*
> *Its vortex; and the north & south, with all their starry host;*
> *Also the rising sun & setting moon he views surrounding*
> *His corn-fields and his valleys of five hundred acres square.*
> *Thus is the earth one infinite plane, and not as apparent*
> *To the weak traveller confin'd beneath the moony shade.*
> *Thus is the heaven a vortex passd already, and the earth*
> *A vortex not yet pass'd by the traveller thro' Eternity.*
>
> [*M* 15.21–35]

The first section is straightforward if we remember that the Eternals have closed us off from eternity. The traveller is like one of the souls described by Porphyry descending from the northern gate (the same Thel briefly crossed) or north pole; and, like someone lowered down into a giant cave (perhaps one of "the Polar Caves" or "the dark & intricate caves of the Mundane Shell" [*M* 25.53, 23.22]), he sees his past path englobe itself, in this case, "like a sun." In the reprise of this scene, it is by Milton's advent, "like the black storm, coming out of Chaos," that "the Sun rolls into Chaos" (*M* 23.21, 24). As "each . . . Cloud Meteor & Star / Are Men Seen Afar" (E718), so to vision these englobed forms may be "like a human form, a friend" (cf. fig. 62). The

second portion of the passage is more complicated, for the vortex is now attributed to the eye's infolded globe.[9]

In lines 28–35, the calm assertions of the preceding section are replaced by
the indefinite similitudes of "as" and the unconvincing conclusion "thus,"
which together couch a series of "views" rather than vision. The point is not, as
Frye suggests, that we "are unable to see that the Earth is 'one infinite
plane,'"[10] but precisely that we poor Earth wanderers *do* so see it. *Milton* says
later of a similar scene, "every Space that a Man views around his dwelling
place . . . such space is his Universe" (29.5, 7)[11]—but in fact we only "view a
small portion & think that All" (*J* 65.27) when "with our vegetable eyes we
view" (*M* 26.12). Swedenborg's *True Christian Religion* (which Blake praises
highly as late as the 1809 *Descriptive Catalogue*) offers a pertinent comment on
what we see with our "vegetable eyes":

> It appears to the bodily Eyes as if the Sun performed a daily and annual
> Revolution about the Earth; hence it is common to say that the Sun rises and sets
> . . . when, nevertheless, the Sun continueth immoveable, being an Ocean of Fire,
> round which the Earth performeth her daily and annual Revolutions. . . .
> whosoever confirmeth the Sun's apparent Motion by Reasonings of the Natural
> Man, particularly if he supporteth such opinion by the Authority of the Word,
> which speaks of the Sun's rising, and setting, he invalidates the Truth and
> destroys it. . . . That the Sun moveth is then as apparent Truth, but that it doth
> not move is a genuine Truth, nevertheless everyone speaketh according to ap-
> parent Truth, saying that the Sun rises, and sets, which indeed is allowable,
> because it is impossible to use any other Mode of Expression; but still in Con-
> formity with such a Mode of Expression, to think that the Fact is really so, and to
> confirm such a Thought, this dulls and darkens the rational Understanding.
>
> [1: 318–19]

Milton, to be sure, later seems to speak directly to this point in a different tone:

> *As to that false appearance which appears to the reasoner,*
> *As of a Globe rolling thro Voidness, it is a delusion of Ulro*
> [29.15–16]

This is evidently what appears to "the weak traveller confin'd beneath the
moony shade," that is, confined to the "Ulro beneath Beulah's moony shades"
(cf. *M* 21.7, 30.5). On the other hand, the view of the Earth as "one infinite
plane" (not planet) shows it to be a "vortex not yet pass'd by the traveller thro'
Eternity." Thus the Earth, as it is usually, plainly perceived, is only one

particular infinite surface (surrounding the center of the circle we have gone into), but, as always in Blake, we have to see beyond plane perception. Such perception does not appear as a parent to the weak traveller, who, "beneath" Beulah, is not yet even "as the beloved infant in his mothers bosom round incircled" (*M* 30.11); it offers, rather, a vortex for "the traveller thro' Eternity" to pass to yet another consummation inseminating time and space. This weak traveller prefigures Blake, who binds on "this Vegetable World" as a sandal "to walk forward thro' Eternity" (21.14, 22.5). "Walking *thro'*" distinguishes him from the "traveller *to* Eternity" who must "*pass* inward to Golgonooza," itself not to be seen "till *having passd*" the Ulro "it is *viewed* on all sides by a Four-fold Vision" (*M* 17.30; 35.22, 23). The strangeness of the "vortex passage" in *Milton* arises from its implicit statement that when the traveller does *pass* the earthly vortex, he will perceive that infinite plane "roll backward behind His path, into a globe itself infolding," which is, ostensibly, the way the Earth appears to the confined, weak traveller. The distinction must be that the Ulro traveller infers or reasons a globular Earth, while the expanding eyes of the "traveller thro' Eternity" really do see it so, "passing the planetary visions, & the well adorned Firmament" (*M* 23.23; cf. the space-travellers in figs. 52 and 57, and the view from Voyager, fig. 58).

The conclusion of the passage returns to Milton's journey. He sees Albion upon "the Rock of Ages" in "the Sea of Time & Space," and:

> *Hovering over the cold bosom, in its vortex Milton bent down*
> *To the bosom of death, what was underneath soon seemd above.*
>
> [*M* 15.41–42]

Milton's shadow falls, "as a wintry globe descends precipitant thro' Beulah bursting" and Blake sees him "as a falling star" (15.44, 47). The cold bosom of "Albion the Vortex of the Dead!" is also "the bosom of Time & Spaces womb" (*J* 48.54, 85.28) in which the dead may be planted as (word-) seeds. The curved interior of the bosom marks it as an animate version of the Mundane Shell. The strange and unique description of Milton's vortical descent, "as a wintry globe," recalls the descent of Luvah and Vala "swift as the winters setting sun" (*FZ* 42.9, E328)—they go "down the Human Heart" while Milton falls "thro Albions Heart" (*M* 20.41). Even more germane is plate 3 of *Europe*, titled "A Comet" by Cumberland in one copy:[12] "The deep of winter came; / What time the secret child, / Descended" (3.1–3). Susan Fox observes that Milton's descent establishes "another dimension" of the vortex: "it is the conical womb through which we beings pass from eternity into time."[13] The womb offers not only the passage, but the whole system of space and time (like the field surrounding a supergravitational object). Milton's descent can be paralleled with that which Blake/Los remembers:

> *I am that Shadowy Prophet who Six Thousand Years ago*
> *Fell from my station in the Eternal bosom.*
>
> [*M* 22.15–16]

The revealing word is the astronomical "station."[14] Star-souls, even the Prince of Heaven who fell "from his station" (*M* 11.19), enter the realm of time and space (and language) by the vortex: they lapse, according to Thomas Taylor in "Concerning the Cave of the Nymphs," "into the whirls of generation"[15] or into the "Voticall *Motion*" that, Henry More writes, was for Pythagoras and Democritus "*the cause of the generation of all things.*"[16]

Plate 1 of *Milton* (fig. 3, above) presents another vision of entering the vortex, here, in David V. Erdman's words, "a vortex of billowing smoke."[17] Existing interpretations do not seem to have recognized, however, that the "smoke" in fact emanates from the figure's left palm and, to a lesser extent, from his right wrist; indeed the entire figure can be seen as a compaction of the lines making up the vortex. The composition suggests the first emblem of a series that often accompanied versions of "The Smaragdine Table" (cf. *J* 91.34) in the seventeenth century (fig. 67), illustrating the line, "The wind hath carried it in its belly." The wind—anima, spiritus—carries its potential for dynamic expression to term, as the Word bears its vortex. Like the Lord in the whirlwind of *Job*, pl. 13 (where lines of his left foot merge into the lines of wind energy), Milton is (in) his vortex, one which the reader of *Milton* is about to enter.

There is another form of vortex travelling (to/by/with/through), one Blake writes of physically experiencing:

> *For when Los joind with me he took me in his firy whirlwind*
> *My Vegetated portion was hurried from Lambeths shades*
> *He set me down in Felphams Vale & prepard a beautiful*
> *Cottage for me that in three years I might write all these Visions*
>
> [*M* 36.21–24]

Blake relives what happened to Ezekiel, who saw "visions of God" and to whom "a whirlwind came . . . and a fire infolding" (Ezek. 1:1, 4).[18] One strange aspect of Ezekiel's whirlwind is that "out of the midst thereof came the likeness of four living creatures"—zoas or cherubim—each of which is mysteriously

67. Michael Maier, *Atlanta fugiens*,
pl. 1 (1618).

associated with a wheel, sometimes "as it were a wheel in the middle of a
wheel" (1:16). In any event, "the spirit of the living creature was in the
wheels," and, most strange, "the likeness of the firmament [was] upon the
heads of the living creature" (1:21, 22). However obscure, the wheels are a
central part of Ezekiel's vision as it has come down to us: later they are seen
"full of eyes round about," and "it was cried unto them in my hearing, O
wheel" (10:13). By their sound, the wheels suggest some equivalence with the
whirlwind: Ezekiel hears "the noise of wheels" as "a noise of great rushing"
(3:13), and Isaiah 5:28 speaks specifically of "wheels like a whirlwind." The
important nexus of Zoa and wheel appears in a summary of the opening and
setting of *The Four Zoas*:

Terrific ragd the Eternal Wheels of intellect terrific ragd
The living creatures of the wheels in the Wars of Eternal life
But perverse rolld the wheels of Urizen & Luvah back reversd
Downwards & outwards consuming in the wars of Eternal Death

[20.12–15, E313]

The structure and significance of Ezekiel's vision will not be reviewed here, but we may note that there are not many kinds of wheels to choose from in the Old Testament—and by far the most important and most mentioned are chariot wheels. The Lord's appearance to Elijah in a whirlwind is doubled as a "chariot of fire," an image Blake adapted as "the Fiery Chariot of . . . Contemplative Thought" (*VLJ*, E560; cf. "Elijah . . . his fiery Chariot" on the same page). Not overtly mentioned in the Bible, but already present in Old English uses of "wheel" is the concept of the turning heavens; the *OED* cites, ca. 1000, "Se firmamentum went on ðam twam steorran swa swa hweozel tyrnð on eaxe." Certainly the independently circling moon, planets, and constellations offer a readily accessible image of "wheels within wheels." Figure 68 shows Blake's vivid rendering of the conflation Young made of Ezekiel's vision and the stellar perspective:

Orb above Orb ascending without End!
Circle in Circle, without End, inclos'd!
Wheels within Wheel, Ezekiel! like to Thine!

Two of the word's principal referents are joined as we see Los and Enitharmon "drawing out sweet bliss / From all the turning wheels of heaven & the chariots of the Slain" (*FZ* 16.19–20, E310), while in "Beatrice Addressing Dante from the Car" (fig. 69), the wheel of the chariot presents a "vortex or whirlpool."[19] Very nearly a third (24 out of 74) of all Blake's poetic references to "wheels" are *explicitly* to the "wheels of heaven," or, more frequently, the "starry wheels," and these images support most of the remaining uses of the word.[20]

The heavens, says Cary's Dante, are the "eternal wheels" on which Beatrice's eyes are "fast fix'd."[21] For Blake such a universe can become "a mill with complicated wheels," like the "orreries" that were the fashionable and very expensive gentlemen's toys of Georgian England. Named after the Earl of Orrery in the early eighteenth century, these moving models of the solar system became common enough for Young to speak of the undevout imagination that "dwarfs the whole / And makes an universe an Orrery" (*NT* 9.786–87). The

[56]

Orb above Orb afcending without End !
Circle in Circle, without End, inclos'd !
Wheel within Wheel, EZEKIEL! like to Thine !
Like Thine, it feems a Vifion, or a Dream ;
Tho' *feen*, we labour to believe it *true !*
What Involution ! What Extent ! What Swarms
Of Worlds, that laugh at *Earth*, immenfely Great
Immenfely diftant from each other's Spheres !
What, then, the wond'rous *Space* thro' which they roll ?
At once it quite ingulphs all human Thought ;
'Tis Comprehenfion's abfolute Defeat.

Nor think thou feeft a wild Diforder here ;
Thro' this illuftrious Chaos, to the Sight,
Arrangement neat, and chafteft Order, reign.
The Path prefcrib'd, inviolably kept,
Upbraids the lawlefs Sallies of Mankind :
Worlds, ever thwarting, never interfere ;
What Knots are ty'd ? How foon are they diffolv'd,
And fet the feeming marry'd Planets free ?
They rove for ever, without Error rove :
Confufion unconfus'd ! Nor lefs admire
This Tumult untumultuous : All on Wing,

68. *Night Thoughts,* design no. 474.

69. *Illustrations to Dante:* "Beatrice Addressing Dante from the Car."

orreries were splendid examples of the clockmaker's art, dependent on an ingenious system of gears operating through cogged or toothed wheels.[22] Equally significant for Blake must have been "sun-and-planet gear" patented in 1781 and used on all Boulton and Watt rotative engines until 1794 (and many thereafter), notably in the first London factory powered by a steam engine, the Albion Mill.[23] Such wheels epitomized the gathering mechanization of life and thought that Blake perceived. More than industrial mechanization, it is the logical, linear, cause-and-effect organization predicated by such material improvement that Blake fears:

> *I turn my eyes to the Schools & Universities of Europe*
> *And there behold the Loom of Locke whose Woof rages dire*
> *Washd by the Water-wheels of Newton . . .*
>
>   *. . . cruel Works*
> *Of many Wheels I view, wheel without wheel, with cogs tyrannic*
> *Moving by compulsion each other: not as those in Eden: which*
> *Wheel within Wheel in freedom revolve in harmony & peace.*
>
>   [*J* 15.14–20]

70. *Jerusalem*, pl. 22, detail.

Cogged compulsion can be put to positive use:

This Wine-press is call'd War on Earth, it is the Printing-Press
Of Los; and here he lays his words in order above the mortal brain
As cogs are formd in a wheel to turn the cogs of the adverse wheel.

[*M* 27.8–10]

But otherwise "cog" is an ugly and negative word, its sound fusing into the other anathemata of "Og," as in "the Wheels of Og" (*M* 37.21–22), and "Gog," who appears in *Jerusalem* as Hyle attempts "to draw Jerusalems Sons / Into the Vortex of his Wheels. therefore Hyle is called Gog" (74.29–30). Both the item and the names are blasphemies of God. The compelling power of cogged wheels is illustrated at the bottom of *Jerusalem*, plate 22 (fig. 70), where the text asks, "Why should Punishment Weave the veil with Iron Wheels of War," and so suggests the perverse wheels of Urizen and Luvah, "consuming in the Wars of Eternal Death." These wheels are also "the Wheels of Albions Sons . . . cogs" (*J* 13.13–14), which begin "turning upon one-another / Into Non-Entity" (*J* 18.8–9). These wheeling sons are also solar and float, like Young's worlds, in the ocean of space (cf. fig. 54, above)—as "cogs" they can look very like solar emblems (fig. 71); so the setting sun on plate 35(39) of *Jerusalem*, notes Erdman, "radiates spikes that make it seem like one of the cogwheels of Plate 22" (fig. 72). At the end of *The Four Zoas*, these mill-wheels are presented as the power-source of the elements:

In his hand Tharmas takes the Storms. he turns the whirlwind Loose
Upon the wheels the stormy seas howl at his dread command
And Eddying fierce rejoice in the fierce agitation of the wheels

71. Ancient Greek solar emblems.

72. *Jerusalem*, pl. 35(39), detail.

Of Dark Urthona Thunders Earthquakes Fires Water floods
Rejoice to one another loud their voices shake the Abyss
Their dread forms tending the dire mills

[138.4–9, E406][24]

In *Jerusalem* these wheels "turn'd hoarse / Over the Mountains & the fires blaz'd on Druid Altars" (62.32–33). Here again the wheels are identified with stars, that is, power-wheels occasioning Druid worship and sacrifice.

While *Milton* says that Satan is "Prince of the Starry Wheels" (3.43), *Jerusalem* seems to introduce a more subtle distinction between the various wheels, saying that "the abstract Voids between the Stars are the Satanic Wheels" (13.37),[25] a formulation previously expressed as "the Newtonian Voids between the Substances of Creation" (*M* 37.46), i.e., between the stars. Ulro, the "Seat of Satan" (*M* 27.45) is "the space of the terrible starry wheels of Albions sons" (*J* 12.51)—it was seen before seated in the brain with its webs (*M* 20.37–38). (This connection, incidentally, would seem to hint at an ultimately revolving or "rolling" derivation for "Ulro" [cf. *J* 42.17–18: "deepest night / Of Ulro rolld round"]).[26] If the voids between the stars are to be seen as wheels in addition to the starry wheels, we are indeed creating a universe of wheels without wheels—that is, with "void-wheels" (verbal circles). The emphasis on the void nature of the interstellar space having removed the possibility of its being seen as crystalline, rotating substance, we are left to ponder in what way it is a wheel. The answer, I think, lies in its abstract or "drawn out" character. The Newtonian voids or Satanic wheels are, so to speak, the last spinnings of a great intermeshing system that originated when man first began to "cogitate" on the wheeling stars (*"cog ergo sum,"* to abbreviate the philosophical heritage). This process can be followed clearly through the longer poems. In *The Four Zoas*,

> . . . *the Sciences were fixd & the Vortexes began to operate*
> *On all the sons of men & every human soul terrified*
> *At the turning wheels of heaven shrunk away inward withring away*
> [73.21–23, E350]

The end of the poem pauses to look back at the compulsive effect of "the wheels of Dark Urthona," the wheels of the starry mills:

> . . . *Men are bound to sullen contemplations in the night*
> *Restless they turn on beds of sorrow. in their inmost brain*
> *Feeling the crushing Wheels they rise and write the bitter words*
> *Of Stern Philosophy & knead the bread of knowledge with tears & groans*
> [138.12–15, E406]

Owing to such philosophy, the places of thought, "Cambridge & Oxford & London, / Are driven among the starry wheels, rent away and dissipated" (*J* 5.3–4).

Another cog in this process appears with Jerusalem at the mills in the "Dungeons of Babylon"; there "her reason grows like / The Wheel of Hand. incessant turning day & night without rest" (*J* 60.42–43). In her despair she cries out to the "Human Imagination, O Divine Body," "thou knowest I am deluded by the turning mills" (60.63). Los, however, is not as worried, since he knows that imagination will manifest itself even through the mathematical wheels of the stars:

> *Yet why despair! I saw the finger of God go forth*
> *Upon my Furnaces, from within the Wheels of Albions Sons:*
> *Fixing their Systems, permanent: by mathematic power*
> *Giving a body to Falshood that it may be cast off for ever.*
>
> [*J* 12.10–13]

This indicates that the model for "their Systems" are "the Wheels," which are "fixed" as the sciences are "fixed" in *The Four Zoas*. Here, though, a quite different conclusion anticipates "Demonstrative Science piercing Apollyon with his own bow!" (12.14), revealing that "God is within, & without!" (12.15), just as the laborers in the Furnaces "appeard within & without incircling on both sides / The Starry Wheels of Albions Sons, with Spaces for Jerusalem" (*J* 12.17–18). How is Apollyon pierced with "his own bow"?[27] Since God and the laborers at the furnace are "within & without" the "starry wheels" with "spaces," and since these spaces "reachd from the starry heighth, to the starry depth," the "falshood" of the wheels is that they are solid, separating boundaries. Astronomically this would seem to say that Blake is merely asserting the spaciousness and plurality of worlds in Newtonian cosmology against medieval ideas. But Blake wants more than Newton, and a constructive analogy is the fate of the Newtonian universe at the hands of modern cosmology, which has liberated us, "demonstratively," from the "constrictive infinity" of the Newtonian system. Blake could, for example, consider an anticipation of "Big Bang" cosmology in Erasmus Darwin's idea that "all the suns, and the planets which circle round them, may sink again into one central chaos; and may again, by explosions, produce a new world, which, in process of time, may resemble the present one, and at length again undergo the same catastrophe!" (*The Temple of Nature* 4.457 n.). With such concepts, "Demonstrative Science" transcends itself and the mindless wheels of rude celestial mechanics. As we learn to see through what we took as the givens of a time and space anchored in the stars, we see that they, like the conceptions they support and the consciousness perceiving them, are "the mercy of Eternity," a space for Jerusalem.

The beginning of the last chapter of *Jerusalem*, "To the Christians," presents an important sermon on the wheel:

> *I stood among my valleys of the south*
> *And saw a flame of fire, even as a Wheel*
> *Of fire surrounding all the heavens: it went*
> *From west to east against the current of*
> *Creation and devourd all things in its loud*
> *Fury & thundering course round heaven & earth*
> *By it the Sun was rolld into an orb:*
> *By it the Moon faded into a globe,*
> *Travelling thro the night: for from its dire*
> *And restless fury, Man himself shrunk up*
> *Into a little root a fathom long.*
> *And I asked a Watcher & a Holy-One*
> *Its Name? he answerd. It is the Wheel of Religion*
> *I wept & said. Is this the law of Jesus*
> *This terrible devouring sword turning every way*
> *He answerd; Jesus died because he strove*
> *Against the current of this Wheel: its Name*
> *Is Caiaphas, the dark Preacher of Death*
> *Of sin, of sorrow, & of punishment;*
> *Opposing Nature! It is Natural Religion*
>
> [77.1–20]

There are many remarkable formulations here. "A Watcher & a Holy-One" comes directly from Daniel 4:13, where such a one descends from heaven to the prophet. S. H. Hooke reminds us of the Babylonian parallel "that the planets, not being fixed, but having definite orbits, were regarded as interpreting to men the purposes of the gods, and were called 'Interpreters' or 'Watchers.'"[28] A somewhat similar usage can be found in late sixteenth-century English, where certain stars are referred to as "those Guards or Watchers" (*OED*, s.v. "watcher"). As Blake probably would not have known any of this material, it is all the more intriguing to find, as the first of Blake's five "watcher/s," the following passage in *The French Revolution*:

> *When the heavens were seal'd with a stone, and the terrible sun*
> *   clos'd in an orb, and the moon*
> *Rent from the nations, and each star appointed for watchers of night*
>
> [211–12]

And *Milton* tells of "the heavens round the Watchers . . . the Watchers of the Ulro" (20.46, 50).

The astral nature of the watcher suggests a similar possibility for the wheel. The Book of Daniel describes the throne of "the Ancient of days" as being "like the fiery flame, and his wheels as burning fire" (7:9). But more pertinent is the history of "the Divine Vision" some ten plates earlier in *Jerusalem*, which relates another version of what happened when "Man himself shrunk up":

> . . . *as their eye & ear shrunk, the heavens shrunk away*
> *The Divine Vision became First a burning flame, then a column*
> *Of fire, then an awful fiery wheel surrounding earth & heaven:*
> *And then a globe of blood wandering distant in an unknown night*
>
> [66.40–43]

The lines we are considering from plate 77 begin three-fourths of the way into this evolution. The wheel goes from west to east, or against the (apparent) motion of the sun and stars, but with the motion of the planets. In their very names "the detestable Gods of Priam," the circling planets offered some of the earliest objects of worship. The resulting wheel of religion, or "natural religion," and science reflects also the interior mental wheel. It moves against the current of creation, reflecting the manner in which motion is communicated—cogitated—from the drive wheel to a gear. The East is the source of creation, "the Center, unapproachable for ever" (*J* 12.56; this, Blake says, Ezekiel saw "by Chebars flood"), and Jesus predicts that "as the lightning cometh out of the east, and shineth even unto the west; so shall the coming of the Son of man be" (Matt. 24:27). Jerusalem is consistently associated with the East,[29] so it is surprising to see in Golgonooza:

> *The Eastern Gate, fourfold: terrible & deadly its ornaments:*
> *Taking their forms from the Wheels of Albions sons; as cogs*
> *Are formd in a wheel to fit the cogs of the adverse wheel.*
>
> [*J* 13.12–14]

The current from the wheels of Albion's stellar sons and the wheel of religion are adversary to those of creation.

The double reference to opposing currents in *Jerusalem* plate 77 poses another possibility. For, as we read in Buffon's 1791 *Natural History*, "It is well known, that, when water runs in two directions, the combination of these motions produces a whirling, and exhibits the appearance of a void space in the middle. . . . Whirlpools, then, are occasioned by contrary currents, and whirlwinds by contrary winds" (1:397). A modern writer notes that a vortex may occur "whenever any qualitative differences in a flowing medium come together"[30]—differences, for example, in direction, speed, temperature, and "state." For Blake, "spiritual" and "material," the "Preachment of Life and of Death," are also qualitative differences that meet to form a vortex around a void, "which if enterd into / Englobes itself & becomes a Womb" (*J* 1). The vortex may be seen as the dynamic form of dialectic: the synthesis (perception) out of opposing thesis and antithesis, like Blake's text out of the words of Caiaphas and Jesus. Without contrary currents, there is no "transcendence," no shift of levels or *aufhebung*. (According to Erasmus Darwin, the vortex—as "whirlpool or tornado"—"has not only its progressive velocity, but its circular one also, which thus lifts up or overturns everything within its spiral whirl."[31]) To put it another way, the vortex is the "result" of perceiving difference, which, after the fall, is all we ever perceive.[32]

The wheel and its delusion become a manifestation of the "flaming sword which turned every way" instituted to keep man from the tree of life (Gen. 3:24). The repetition of devourd/devouring in the few lines of *Jerusalem* 77 (5, 15) is notable, for the word is the most common representative of the root concept *vorare* referred to earlier. The opening of the following plate reemphasizes the idea: "The Spectres of Albions Twelve Sons revolve mightily / Over the Tomb & over the Body: ravning to devour / The Sleeping Humanity" (78.1–3). The flaming sword and vortical motion reappear in the dense context of "the Keys of the Gates" where the "dark Hermaphrodite" says:

Rational Truth Root of Evil & Good
Round me flew the Flaming Sword
Round her snowy Whirlwinds roard
Freezing her Veil the Mundane Shell
[16–19][33]

The snowy whirlwind, the opposite of the fiery whirlwind of God, is a cold, contracting vortex whose effect mirrors that of "the wheel of religion."

The "flaming sword" or "terrible devouring sword turning every way" deserves closer consideration. Boehme devotes a chapter of *Mysterium Magnum* to the flaming sword of Genesis 3:24 and concludes that it is the "sword of the anger of God," which had "its raising and original in the corruption of Lucifer."[34] The fire-sword, which "is in man," occupies a strategic position between Boehme's first principle of wrath and second principle of mercy, cutting away the sins of those standing under its "reach and swing" who are "drawn quite through." So, though this sword waves at the gate of Paradise, we "might, by the new regeneration in the spirit of Christ, enter in again through this fire-sword. This mystery is exceedingly great." Although the fire-sword is now turned against him, it was Lucifer who "changed it from the pure clear light into fire, wherewith he willed to domineer and rule as God." This dynamic is repeated when "Orc began to Organize a Serpent body / Despising Urizens light & turning it into flaming fire," becoming "a Self consuming dark devourer rising into the heaven" (*FZ* 80.44–45, 48, E356). As early as *Europe,* we read that "thought chang'd the infinite to a serpent; that which pitieth: / To a devouring flame," and all is divided "into earths rolling in circles of space" (*Eur* 10.16–17, 19). As Morton Paley observes, "with the serpent and flame images, we have a fall into Wrath,"[35] that is to say, into the tyger's fire-world, the system of physical light. Not only visible light, but revolvings are essential to this whorled world:

> *The eternal mind bounded began to roll*
> *Eddies of wrath ceaseless round & round*
> [*BU* 10.19–20]

Eddies and whirls—vortexes—are an expression, an embodiment, of wrath and anger; in an early picture of Orc:

> *The horrent Demon rose, surrounded with red stars of fire*
> *Whirling about in furious circles round the immortal fiend.*
> [*Eur* 4.15–16][36]

The flaming sword is yet another representation of this vortical force, "turning affection into fury & thought into abstraction" (*FZ* 80.47, E356). The "flaming brand" above Adam and Eve in Blake's illustration to "The Expulsion from Paradise" (fig. 73) is thus more than a "stylized whirlpool of color":[37] it is a vision of the "devouring sword turning every way," a vortex. The fall into individual identity—into the little, self-defining eddy[38] of free-floating anxiety and wrath that commences with our being drawn through the vagina—is a fall into language with its words and texts. The vortex both keeps us from the Paradise of the Word and also offers the medium (words, texts, pictures) that could, as Boehme suggested, draw us to it.

73. *Illustrations to "Paradise Lost":*
"The Expulsion from Paradise" (ca. 1807).

Wheels, following the biblical associations, are parts of a chariot. Ezekiel's vision resolves into a picture of the *merkābā*, the divine chariot, the throne with wheels, the "chariot of the cherubim" that became a central focus of Jewish mystical speculation.[39] Cowper directly taps the astronomical overtones of this association, imagining a God who "wheels his throne upon the rolling worlds" (*The Task*, 5.814). Henry Boyd's Dante, describing the vision of the chariot of the church, refers to

> . . . *the glories of the heav'nly Car*
> *EZEKIEL sung, when, from the frozen Pole,*
> *He saw its whirling wheels in tempest roll,*
>   *Amid the shock of elemental War.*
>
> [*Purgatorio*, 29.18.3–6]

74. *The Four Zoas*, p. 83, detail.

75. *Jerusalem*, pl. 20, detail.

This image figures in Blake's illustration to the canto "Beatrice Addressing Dante from the Car" (fig. 69, above), where the whirling wheel of the chariot is a vortex. Blake adds the open book supported by the cloud of bluish smoke emanating from the vortex, which, remarkably enough, centers on the outline of a horizontal human ear (that "whirlpool fierce to draw creations in"). The smoky cloud fades into the gryphon while another strand, after passing through the head of the center figure, makes a halo around the gryphon and terminates in Dante's mind. There is, clearly, a misty connection between the word in the text the woman interprets for Dante and the vortex into which feminine faces have been drawn. The reverse spiraling vortexes, one centered on the eye of the gryphon, the other on the ear of the chariot wheel, join at a word in the text—the center of the larger vortex that is Blake's reading.

Other graphic vortexes are just as strange. In *The Four Zoas* manuscript, we see the "wheel of nature"[40] or "circle of destiny" being turned round by a feminine spirit (fig. 74). In addition to the hint of a cup or goblet lying on its side, we can see the figure's extended arms as the sides of a vortex funneling down to her womb. This figure may serve to elucidate a strange and obscure

76. Henry Fuseli, "The Tornado," engraved by Blake (1795).

sequence of images on plate 20 of *Jerusalem* (fig. 75). On the left, men seem to be pulling a vortex-chariot; in the center is a humanized comet, the vortex-traveller; on the right, a figure rolls the vortex circle of destiny, through which star-seeds are passing into globular worlds or spherical souls as " 'bubbles' of consciousness."[41] In another guise, as Northrop Frye observes, the visual iconography of the vortex "is often serpentine."[42] A key here may be Blake's engraving of Fuseli's "Tornado," included in the 1795 edition of Erasmus Darwin's *Botanic Garden* (fig. 76). The serpent represents the circular velocity or "spiral eddy" of the vortex. In plate 5 of *America*, the vortex-serpent forms a giant question mark, and we see a figure beginning his passage through its coils to the point of the question (fig. 77).

The vortex "draws"—or, spectrelike, "sucks" (note the spectrelike wings of "Tornado")—the beholder into itself, the dizzy enquirer to his grave and to Blake's engraving. But there is the other method of approach: "*if the Spectator could Enter* into these Images in his Imagination approaching them on the Fiery Chariot of his Contemplative Thought . . . *then* he would be happy" (*VLJ*, E560). A wheel is a vortex seen in cross section, a vortex is the act or body of perception itself: as every wheel becomes a vortex if entered into and pushed through to another plane, every vortex literally imagined becomes a chariot. So *Jerusalem* twice tells of "words . . . in Chariots in array," "words . . . On Chariots of gold & jewels, with Living Creatures" (55.34, 98.41–42).

77. *America,* pl. 5, detail.

CHAPTER ELEVEN

Son of Myth, Sun of Language

Jesus said to them: When you make the two one, and when you make the inner
as the outer and the outer as the inner and the above as the below . . . when you
make eyes in the place of an eye, and a hand in the place of a hand, and a foot
in the place of a foot, an image in the place of an image, then shall you enter.

The Gospel According to Thomas

HOW ARE WE TO READ Blake's literal imagination? Which is to say, how we are
to enter the vortex that Blake's work defines/constructs/reveals/engenders?
Blake, unlike Dante, never offers his sense of how the "four folds" of his vision
are to be unravelled or coordinated—the plies or folds of his text are inextric-
ably joined. All Blake says is that we should "enter the image" and "be one
with him," suggesting that experience where, after months or years of hard
study at a new language, we suddenly find ourselves in its terms. Perception,
as Blake tells us repeatedly, is a function of expectation. And our deepest
expectations—that the sun will rise tomorrow, for example—lie far below our
conscious sense of what we consider expectation. Our great expectation and
assumption is that discourse is founded in some universal bedrock that makes
possible and enforces meaning, representation of something, to be present—a
rockbed that ensures or demands, like a kind of gravity, that meaningful
discourse of necessity be continuous, consistent, congruent not necessarily with
itself, but with the comprehensive structure of our expectation, by which and
to which it may communicate its perhaps contradictory or even nonsensical
meaning. We expect representation to refer to some original presentation, to

our spectre selves and our expectations as we have known them. One consequence is that we expect communication to be in some way "logical." Even
literature, which we allow a more complicated, variously individuated logic,
must inhabit the realm of expectation.

Since Blake's words and pictures have from the beginning attracted all kinds
of responses, we cannot say that his discourse is universally discontinuous and
incoherent. The difficulty appears to be the larger syntax or lack of it—the
mythos as a whole. We read from line to line and from plate to relatively
comprehensible plate, but the whole does not add up to an intensifying light of
ever-widening comprehension for a long time. Leaving aside the real changes
in Blake's own development, this is the question of language and imagination
to which we have continually returned: why don't the discrete sequences we
behold hold all together in our perception? The answer must be that we do not
(perhaps cannot) imagine the nature of their manifold continuity. The trans-
formations of this grammar are not those we expect, since, as Sigurd Burckhardt observes, "by intellectual temper, if not by philosophical persuasion, we
are nominalists."[1] Our language is primarily digital, and so turns our expectation to the fantasy analogue of representation, mimesis, which is also an-
amnesis: "Nature ⟨Memory⟩" (E689).

Let us return to plate 23 of *The Book of Urizen*, which shows Urizen carrying
his globe of fire flashlight as he explores his dens (fig. 78). Or, rather, not
"carrying," since Urizen's hand has no real connection to the sphere or to any
evident handle: they just happen to be contiguous. The globe of fire—no
surprise here—must be the Sun. As always, the question of relative scale is part
of the message—here, about our conception of who and what the "giant form"
Urizen is, and how the Sun looks and works. In the plate itself, the association
is made clear by the otherwise laboriously explained lion or tyger (see above,
chapter 9). The animal, unnoticed by Urizen, focuses (disgruntledly) on its
encapsulated, "orb compelld" form: a pertinent quotation from *The Four Zoas*
tells of "the Sun reddning like a fierce lion in his chains." And now we begin to
enter the continuity of the apparent discontinuity. For it is the previous plate
of text in *The Book of Urizen* that tells of the chaining of Orc. And Orc is the fiery
red sol of Los bound down to an orb with the chain of jealousy, the chain of
gravity. He is the wreath of wrath, glowing in fury and anger like a spirit or gas
compressed in a transparent sphere. The poem, significantly, avoids referring
to Orc as Los's son—but, after his chaining, we read, "The dead heard the voice
of the child / And began to awake from sleep" (20.26–27), and we know we are
in the light of the Son. (In John 5:25–28, Jesus says: "The hour is coming, and

78. *The Book of Urizen,* pl. 23, detail.

now is, when the dead shall hear the voice of the Son of God: and they that hear shall live. For as the Father hath life in himself; so hath he given to the Son to have life in himself. . . . all that are in the graves shall hear his voice, And shall come forth.") By not being named a son, Orc can all the more be associated with the quickening, orbed Sun and the revolutionary energy of the Son of man. Enitharmon's invocation to the "lion Rintrah," "second to none but Orc," also uses the interplay between son and sun:

Arise my son! . . . O thou King of fire.
Prince of the sun I see thee with thy innumerable race:
Thick as the summer stars:
. . . each ramping his golden mane . . .

[*Eur* 8.8–11]

The Four Zoas tells of Urthona and "within his breast his fiery sons chaind down" (59.12, E340), and in *The Book of Ahania* we encounter the "Son of Urizens silent burnings" (2.9). We have, then, a homonym identifying what has occurred to Orc: son is sun. Two are made one. Linear, sequential relation becomes a gloss on lateral imagination, and the presence we sense is not meaning so much as the being of the Poetic (making, engendering) Genius. Meaning stalls in the apparent discontinuity, the blind spot of our expectation. The existing name for this encounter, this effect, is myth—and as real, experienced myth, it entails momentarily forgetting our metaphysical, mimetic, metaphorical selves.

Blake's offspring, his songs—including *The Four Zoas,* "The Song of the Aged Mother" (*FZ* 4.1), and "The Song of Jerusalem" (*J* 99.6)—make "as it were a new song before the throne, and before the four beasts [zoas], and the elders: and no man could learn that song" (Rev. 14:3). The Sun of Blake's songs has, of course, its fibres of intertextuality, linking it, for example, to Swedenborg's central vision of the spiritual, living Sun of which the material one is but a dead shadow ("sunk with fright a red round Globe"). To this idea, however, Blake adds Erasmus Darwin's vision of the Sun kindling out of Chaos and the planets then thrown out of the Sun (as Urizen will be rent from the side of Los). Darwin writes, "If these *innumerable and immense suns rising* out of Chaos are supposed to have thrown out their attendant planets by new explosions, as they ascended; and those their respective satellites, filling in a moment the immensity of space with light and motion, a grander idea cannot be conceived by the mind of man."[2] Three years later, *The Book of Urizen* opens with a defiantly grander conception as Blake's Eternals perceive such fallen risings and say, "Lo a shadow of horror is rizen" (3.1). So Los forms "an *immense* Orb of fire . . . . his Furnaces endur'd / The chaind Orb in their infinite wombs," and then, directly after "Los was born," we see "the *innumerable sons* & daughters of Luvah closd in furnaces" (*BL* 5.34, 39–40; *FZ* 16.2 E309). Here again we see conventional meaning stall, as for Blake all these songs sung of sons of suns are the same: the vision of the rising of our son/sun, reason, risen as a result of the horizon of our eyes in our rise in self-contemplation. Back at plate 23, we see that the globe of fire is enveloped by its background—this sun has become the simple light of reason, whose rays do not extend beyond its rational backdrop. It is eternity's turned-around image of our image of the Sun and so naturally impossible to recognize; as in plate 5, it is "like a black globe / View'd by *sons* of Eternity" (33–34). The homonym joins together erstwhile separate frames of reference, and as the differences coalesce to form a new perceptual ground, we see that we have entered on a new fold or level of vision (where, in this case, suns are sons). This *experience* both asserts the "reality" of folds or levels of vision as forms of thought, perceptual organization, codes, and also the possibility of traveling among them.

"It is vain, then, to imagine that the Lord will appear in the clouds of heaven in person; He will appear in the Word, which is from Him and is Himself," wrote Swedenborg,[3] suggesting that the Second Coming would not occur *in persona*, but with man's reexperiencing the Word in its literal and internal senses. Blake transforms this belief, noting in his copy of Swedenborg's *Divine Love and Divine Wisdom* that it is "the Poetic Genius which is the Lord." Revelation is not a wordless, transcendent moment, but the act and practice of expression, making (*poiesis*) use of and perceiving the Other immanent in language. True poetry is self-less work, revealing itself not with, but through the "I"; *speaking* with personality (through a *persona*) masks the poet's obligation to his source in "the true Man." Blake, wrote Samuel Palmer, "was a man without a mask," and so, as Yeats concluded, "a literal realist of the imagination." And the literalist is one who uses literal images, the "wondrous art of writing" (*J* 3). The "Poetic Genius" or "Spirit of Prophecy" does not "do" or "say" or "symbolize" anything—it writes its own incarnation, which is in language, to form us with its information. And, it identifies things; when we read at the end of *Jerusalem* that

> *All Human Forms identified even Tree Metal Earth & Stone. all*
> *Human Forms identified, living going forth & returning wearied*
>
> [*J* 99.1–2]

we behold all those forms identified each with its unique name and identified at the same time into one identical name. "Identified" here presents the literal imagination of uniqueness in unity, of sameness in difference: the name for all human forms will be homo-nymic. The name, then, will be in language, that unnatural Human Form Divine where all being (*bios* and *zoa*) may all be one, Albion. The realization of this unceasing process, "going forth & returning wearied," offers the ground of the indifferent, polysemous "edenity" we have not yet become (and can only become as we come to behold). The end of *Jerusalem* is its own name; and then . . . its communication is over, the information redundant: it is time for something else ("To go forth to the Great Harvest & Vintage of the Nations," the last line of *Milton* suggests). From reminding us only of Golgotha, "the place of the skull" and the (reader's) crucifixion of the Word, Los's poetic city of Golgonooza now reveals its inner form of *logon zooas* (λόγον ζωῆς), the "living word" (Phil. 2:16).

One of the most difficult moments in Blake's language occurs in *Milton* when we see the servants of the mill, "drunken with wine," rioting

> *With ecchoing confusion, tho' the Sun was risen on high.*
>
> *Then Los took off his left sandal placing it on his head,*
> *Signal of solemn mourning*

[8.10–12]

"Ecchoing confusion" here indicates the manner in which the words that follow are to be understood. Thus "Sun" becomes the "sandal," which is in turn the "signal of solemn mourning." This is another version of what appears in *Jerusalem* as "that Signal of the *Morning* which was told us in the Beginning" (*J* 93.26), the beginning in which was the Word, the *logon zooas* of Golgonooza. As the Sun was risen *"on hi*gh," so Los places the sandal *"on hi*s head" and announces, "the *Sun is on* high" (8.16). The sandal is the signal the servants behold, and its rising initiates the mourning, the awareness of Loss. The sandal would be the sun if we could only step into it. Through its "aggressive strangeness," the passage discloses a level of organization distinct from the odd picture offered by the narrative; indeed, the description seems to be intentionally "unfortunate" in order to draw attention to the process of literal transformation at work.[4] Thus in this passage *sun* becomes ri*sen*, becomes *Los*, or *sol* anagrammatically, and then becomes *sandal* becomes *signal* becomes *sol*/em*n*—and all ending with morning. The underlying theme, literally, is the Sun. This theme may be called the "hypogram," a term introduced by Saussure to characterize "the inducing word": the word or small group of words that he supposed "led, by way of phonetic paraphrase to the elaboration of the poem."[5] While the idea of such an arbitrary (and never attested) principle of composition is almost incredible, it does seem that in the passage at hand the Poetic Genius (not to be identified with the conscious poet) elaborates a pre-text concerning the Sun. The effect of such literal play parallels that which Maureen Quilligan posits for wordplay in allegory: it makes us "self-conscious of reading by indicating the primary importance of the verbal surface rather than the imagined action."[6] Such expanded considerations make the reader more conscious of the various paths to the production of meaning: the reader becomes part of the myth, realizing that how Los's action is beheld reflects what he or she will become. The glimmering indication that there are worlds of delight closed by our common sense, our expectation, our criticism, awakens another sense for that delight, the sense that "Reason or the ratio of all we have already known is not the same that it shall be when we know more." S-u-n perhaps serves in such a generating position in the passage from *Milton* since, to follow some Swedenborgian traces, the Lord is the Word, which is the spiritual Sun, which is the only real existence and the conjunction between man and itself:[7] the Poetic Genius centers on the word "sun" as another name for the Word, for itself, and for its birth. "Then the Divine Vision like a silent Sun appe*ard*. . . . and in the Sun, a Human Form appeard"; "And the Divine Appearance was the likeness & similitude of Los" (*J* 43[29].1, 4; 96.7). So, "in the Nerves of the Ear. . . . On Albions Rock Los stands creating the glorious Sun each morning" (*M* 29.40–41). We become what we behold, Blake tells us, so we must start beholding how we behold—for as the *OED* records, the transitive sense, "implying active voluntary exercise of the faculty of vision," has become archaic as the word has "passed imperceptibly into the resulting passive sensation."

The concept of the inducing or engendering word is relevant for what appear as some theme-words or key-words—*Knotenpunkte*—in Blake's poetry. Striking is the high incidence of polysemy in these words, most dramatically in the more obvious homonyms. Rather than seizing on a word only for its particular sound—following some unconscious cathexis—certain words were seized by (or perhaps seized) Blake that induce questions about the structure of perception and the nature of reality. The relations of sadness to dawn, manacles to metamorphosis, curtains to vallies, or our central star to Jesus are stimulating questions for the individual imagination. But when they appear in the homonyms *morning* or *change* or *veil* or *sun* (to mention a few), they cease to be questions and become statements, English messages from the Divine Imagination, the Poetic Genius: literal images.

If we describe the situation of the lexical sign as consisting of signifier, signified, and referent, then one referent of the polysemous, Blakean word is the entire vision of words in which each particular exists. And so we come to contemporary limit-questions concerning the origins and telos of language, of "the structurality of its structure," of its role in the evolution of consciousness. Blake's answer is Los of Eden, that greater man who "must *Create* a System" and who "*built* the stubborn structure of the Language" (*J* 10.20, 36[40].59). Experiencing the system and structure of Los, we find ourselves creating and building, beginning and ending in an activity of literal imagination that will itself be obliterated when Albion rises from his dread repose, even now as the Four Zoas wake from our slumbers of six thousand years.

Some Polysemous Words in Blake

ALAS

Three Virgins at the break of day

. . . .

Alas for woe! alas for woe!

> ["The Golden Net," 1, 3]

What are these? ALAS! the Female Martyr Is She also the Divine Image?

> [*For the Sexes: The Gates of Paradise*, pl. 7]

"Lass" appears several times on its own, so it is evident that Blake was comfortable with the word. In "The Golden Net," particularly with the second line addressed to a "young Man," it seems that the three young women are not only bemoaning the fact of sorrow, but identifying themselves each as "a lass" either "destined for" or "supporting" woe. This identification is more blatant in the *Notebook*, where "Alas for wo!" is repeated three times, once for each lass. Such a strong emphasis on "lass," together with the preceding "young Man," suggests a back-formation from "woe" to "woman."

The text surrounding the simple "ALAS!" of *For Children: The Gates of Paradise* was added some twenty-five years later. The additional text in "The Keys" identifies the prostrate and exposed spirit as female and "dead," and moreover, that her still airborne companion will not suffer this fate ("One is slain & One is fled"). In the mostly male cycle of *The Gates*, it is a doubly somber moment—the figure lying at the lad's foot is a lass, and alas this is our condition.

ALTAR/ALTER

The Building is Natural Religion & its Altars Natural Morality

. . . .

But they cut asunder his inner garments: searching with
Their cruel fingers for his heart, & there they enter in pomp,
In many tears; & there they erect a temple & an altar:

. . . .

The Human form began to be alterd by the Daughters of Albion

[*J* 66.8, 27–29, 46]

The Eye altering alters all
["The Mental Traveller," 62]

Reading the description in *Jerusalem* of the daughters, all tears, all tearing Albion—"the Senses of Men shrink together under the knife" (66.83)—together with the emphasis on sacrifice and Stonehenge, we may justly fear that this action reflects an image of the body as sacrosanct and mysterious. The body is objectified and so becomes incomprehensible. As a result, in "The Mental Traveller," "Stars Sun Moon all shrunk away" (l. 65), whereas in *Jerusalem*, "the Sun is shrunk: the Heavens are shrunk / Away" (66. 50–51). The altar is the high (*altum*) place, so Blake asks, "O Christians Christians! tell me Why / You rear it on your Altars high" (*For the Sexes: The Gates of Paradise*). Here "rear" is both "raise" and "nourish." Stanley Fish notes that the altar-alter pun "is not beyond Herbert" (*Self-consuming Artifacts* [Berkeley: University of California Press, 1972], p. 212).

APPALLS/APPALL'D

The aged sun rises appall'd from dark mountains, and gleams a dusky beam

[*FR*, 270]

How the Chimney-sweepers cry
Every blackning Church appalls
["London," 9–10]

Even from other poems in the *Songs*, it is clear that no church—certainly not the main church "of Pauls" (cf. "Holy Thursday" [SI])—is concerned, still less appalled by the "blackning" urchins' cry. Rather the cries (see below, *WEEP*), borne on the wind like incessant soot, are darkening every church, revealing them to be dead and awaiting a pall-bearer. Their *cry* could initiate the reign of Christ. Realizing the moral façade of the first reading offers a paradigm for the deepening vision the poem presses toward—it is the church's lack of social concern that is truly appalling. The obvious question "How do these lines make sense?" mirrors the social question.

The earlier instance, with the unsettling conception of an aged rising Sun with an already dusky dawn-beam, offers a nice example of referents fusing into polysemy. Prepared by the unusual personification "aged" (and the context), the Sun and the French "sun-king" tradition it represents is imagined as "appall'd" at the sight of the rising lights of the republican army. The old light is giving out—to the people as a pall before the new day, to the aristocrats as appalling, and for the reader as both.

AVOID

all avoid
The petrific abominable chaos
[*BU* 3.25–26]

While the Eternals are busy skirting Urizen's place, the melodramatic intensity of the poem cannot avoid reminding us for the third time in thirty lines that his location is "void, solitary," an "abominable void" (2.4, 3.4). More profoundly, the fact that the Eternals "avoid" the void is precisely what "voids" it, makes it chaotic—unlike the void at the end of *Milton* and the beginning of *Jerusalem*, which if entered becomes an ovoid womb.

BABYLON/BABY LONDON

Babylon again in Infancy Calld Natural Religion
[*FZ* 111.24, E386]

Here is Jerusalem bound in chains, in the Dens of Babylon
[*M* 38.27]

Dungeons of Babylon
[*FZ* 25.31, E317; *J* 60.39]

Babylon, the mother of harlots, also shows herself as a babbling ("aga*in in* I*n*fancy"), inarticulate (*in-fans*) baby. She is, by a reflexive formation, the infant form of London (Baby*lon-Den*; Baby*lon-Dung*eon) and its mind-forg'd manacles. So "I behold Babylon in the opening Streets of London" (*J* 74.16), or, conversely, "I see London blind & age-bent begging thro the Streets / Of Babylon" (*J* 84.11–12).

BOUND/BORN

For now thou art bound;
And I may see thee in the hour of bliss, my eldest born

[*Eur* 4.13–14]

Europe presents an extended meditation on binding and bounding, beginning with the question "Who shall bind the infinite?" (2.13). Soon the Sons of Urizen will "bind / Their warbling joys to our loud strings / Bind all the nourishing sweets of earth / To give us bliss" (4.3–6). Binding—political, imaginative, sexual—in this night of Nature is the prerequisite for the bliss of Female Will. Indeed, Blake seems to identify himself as a victim in "William Bond." In the neo-Platonic conception, one severe form of bondage is being born to temporal incarnation. And the great and golden rule of incarnating, of giving form in art as well as in life, is that "the more distinct, sharp, and wirey the bounding line, the more perfect the work of art" (*DC*, E550). So "the soft hand of Antamon draws the indelible line" and the Spectre "is born" (*M* 28.16, 26). Nevertheless, such binding form exists to be superseded, for "the bounded is loathed by its possessor" (*NNR*b). Blake's emphasis on definite, organized form seems to come from the realization that definite, "bounded" form is the best for being comprehended and then dialectically or contrarily left behind (loathed). Such binding is imaginative service on the part of the individual; as in *Milton*: "Therefore you must bind the Sheaves" (25.26).

CAST

In the fifth chamber were Unnam'd forms, which cast the metals into the expanse..

[*MHH* 15]

. . . Los heated the glowing mass, casting
It down into the Deeps: the Deeps fled
Away in redounding smoke; the Sun
Stood self-balanc'd.

[*BL* 5.42–45]

Cast thou in Jerusalems shadows thy Loves! silk of liquid
Rubies Jacinths Crysolites: issuing from thy Furnaces

[*J* 87.19–20]

To cast is to throw something and to form molten metal in a mold, and sometimes both. Los, Blake's smith of imagination, "casts" the Sun—just as in *The Four Zoas* we see "brass & molten metals cast in hollow globes" (100.29, E373)—and at the same time occasions our wonder at his location in being able to cast the Sun down. How metals are cast in such vast molds as "the expanse" or "the Deeps" offers another tantalizing question. In *Jerusalem*, Los's "lap full of seed" has become liquid metal to be ejaculated in and into "Jerusalems shadows": "In the shadows of a Woman & a secluded Holy Place" (*J* 30[34].33).

CHRYSALIS

In walls of Gold we cast him like a Seed into the Earth
Till times & spaces have passd over him duly every morn
We visit him covering with a Veil the immortal seed

[*FZ* 133.16–18, E401]

Blake never directly uses this word, though it is frequently implied in his poetry and designs. Yet it is evident that he knew not only the word, but its etymology. The "walls of Gold . . . a Veil" are versions of the chrysalis, a word derived from the Greek χρυσαλλίς, signifying the gold-colored sheath of butterflies; the *OED* quotes from John Rowland's edition of T. Muffet's *The Theater of Insects*, 1658: "Transformations . . . of Catterpillers . . . into Chrysallides (that shine as if leaves of gold were laid upon them)." Blake also could have acquired this information from his close friend, the entomologist and Greek scholar Fuseli. The etymological connection may influence the recurrent association of "gold" with "moth," and the images of the "couch of gold" and "cabinets . . . of gold" (perhaps we can even imagine a "Chrysal Cabinet").

CONSUMMATION

To melt the chain of Jealousy. not Enitharmons death
Nor the Consummation of Los could ever melt the chain

[*FZ* 62.27–28, E342]

> *. . . Behold how I am & tremble lest thou also*
> *Consume in my Consummation; but thou maist take a Form*
> *Female & lovely, that cannot consume in Mans consummation*
>
> [M 18.27–29]

> *But no one can consummate Female bliss in Los's World without*
> *Becoming a Generated Mortal, a Vegetating Death*
>
> [J 69.30–31]

Consummation is sexual, spiritual, and ultimately the medium of apocalypse, when both elements are joined. The quotation from *The Four Zoas* is noteworthy in its deliberate use of other standard English sexual images like "death" and "melt." The futility of this almost mechanical attempt at excitement is an index of the omnipotence of the chain of jealousy. The second and third examples are more complex, but the general sense is the warning that one cannot mate on earth without being consumed. The distinction between "male" and "female" consummation reflects Blake's use of those genders to characterize "spiritual" and "physical-sexual," Eden and Beulah. The mortal body and generative bliss must be "consummated in Mental fires" (*FZ* 85.46, E368), that is, realized, perfected, and burned away.

COVERING CHERUB/SELFHOOD

> *Jerusalem is his Garment & not thy Covering Cherub O lovely*
>
> [M 18.37]

> *I saw he was the Covering Cherub & within him Satan*
> *And Raha[b], in an outside which is fallacious! within*
> *Beyond the outline of Identity, in the Selfhood deadly*
>
> [M 37.8–10]

> *Thus was the Covering Cherub reveald majestic image*
> *Of Selfhood*
>
> [J 89.9–10]

The Marriage of Heaven and Hell, in a revision of Genesis 3:24, says that "the cherub with his flaming sword is hereby commanded to leave his guard at the tree of life, and when he does, the whole creation will be consumed, and appear infinite. and holy whereas it now appears finite & corrupt" (pl. 14). Thirteen of the remaining seventeen "epic" instances of the word refer to "the Covering Cherub," a figure appearing only once in the Bible. It is evident that the Covering Cherub is important not only for its mention in Ezekiel 28:16 (and as the "cherub that covereth," 28:14) but more so because its name identifies it as a "covering"—a useful clarification of the original "cherub" who covered the infinite. Banishing the cherub, as plate 14 continues, is identical with "melting apparent surfaces away, and displaying the infinite which was hid." This cherub offers the parallel to Blake's Boehme-influenced vision of "selfhood," where the suffix "-hood" has become, in Blake's vision, an expression of the covering, a part of the garment. This verbal felicity is probably the major motivating force behind Blake's widespread yet "isolated" (*OED*, s.v. "self-hood") use of the word. In Spenser, for example, a priest of Isis tells Britomart, "in queint disguise":

> *How couldst thou weene, through that disguized hood,*
> *To hide thy state from being understood?*
> *Can from th'immortall Gods aught hidden bee?*
> [*The Faerie Queen*, 5.7.21.4–6]

The self and selfhood, we see, are two different things. In *The Four Zoas*, the most common covering is the "covering veil," a slightly different hood. Covering is concealing, whether with a "husk," "opake hardnesses," or "Bacon, Locke & Newton" (*J* 98.19; 65.5; *M* 51.5). One of the marvelous touches in *Milton*, plate 16, where Milton steps through and out of the word "self-hood," is that the Urizenic figure before him on the plane of the page surrounds his head like a hood to be lifted off. In Ezekiel, the "Covering Cherub" is invoked only for comparison to the commerical giant, "the prince of Tyrus," the quintessence of selfhood: "Thine heart was lifted up because of thy beauty, thou hast corrupted thy wisdom by reason of thy brightness" (28:17).

DELIGHT

> *Energy is Eternal Delight*
> [*MHH* 4]

> *To the holy light*
> *Naked in the sunny beams delight*
> ["A Little GIRL Lost," 8–9]

These nostrils that Expanded with delight in morning skies
[*FZ* 105.36, E379; *J* 67.49]

. . . my Shadow of Delight
[*M* 36.31; 18.38; 42.28]

"D" to "th" is an easy phonetic transformation for the Indo-European ear and appears in Blake with the double name "Thiralatha"/"Diralada" (*Eur* 14.25, *SL* 3.31). Delight may be heard cognate with "the light." Physical light, of course, evokes any number of things powerful and positive; in Swedenborg, for example, "the Light in the natural World corresponds to the Truth of Faith in the Spiritual World" (*Divine Love and Divine Wisdom*, p. 69). That is not exactly Blake's idea, but it is clear that light and delight are different qualities of the same radiance: "He whose face gives no light, shall never become a star" (*MHH* 7), and while "some are Born to Endless Night," the happier and more luminous "are Born to sweet delight" (*AugI* 122–23). Light and delight are complementary states (like quanta of energy) by which imagination illuminates our existence. In connection with Blake's image of his wife as a "Shadow of Delight" we may remember his annotation to Lavater, "The female life lives from the light of the male" (E596). The "d"/"th" interchange may perhaps be applied to some other contexts (e.g., "His fall into Division" [a basic word that also manages to envision the plural of *deus*, the foreknowledge of death, and a variant of Zion]).

EAR / EARTH

. . . in the Auricular Nerves of Human life
Which is the Earth of Eden, he his Emanations propagated
[*FZ* 4.1–2, E301]

The ear represents a primary means of taking in words. In the Old and New Testaments, the emphasis is overwhelmingly on the acoustic presence of the Lord, the heard word. So the ear is the organ of imagination within whose "unfathomd caverns" the acoustic word is transformed to the spiritual, the Earth where word-seeds are planted to grow in time (like the Madonna's conception through the ear). "Auricular" also suggests "aureate," golden (*aurum* is aural). The ear's "hammer" and "anvil" are also those of Los's forge; and, perhaps via the "porches of mine ear" in *Hamlet*, the ears are also the "golden porches" or "labyrinthine porches" of Urizen's cerebral temple. The ear, then, is a staging ground for poetry:

And in the Nerves of the Ear (for the Nerves of the Tongue are closed)
On Albions Rock Los stands creating the glorious Sun each morning

[*M* 29.40–41]

ETERNAL/INTERNAL

Every thing in Eternity shines by its own Internal light

[*M* 10.16]

. . . to open the immortal Eyes
Of man inwards into the Worlds of Thought: into Eternity

[*J* 5.18–19]

According to Luke 17:21, "the kingdom of God is within you." For Blake, eternity is the mutual interaction of internals: just as everything outside us has a bosom which, having entered, we walk in heaven and on the Earth, so "in your own Bosom you bear your heaven / And Earth, & all you behold, tho it appears Without it is Within / In your Imagination" (*J* 71.17–19). Eternity is a dimension "expanding inwards" that meets, in a kind of Einsteinian curved space, the outside.

The Four Zoas live "in the Brain of Man . . . & in his circling Nerves." So when Bromion demands at the end of his rhetorical outburst in the *Visions of the Daughters of Albion* (4.23–24):

And is there not eternal fire, and eternal chains?
To bind the phantoms of existence from eternal life?

we expect that, fleeing from self-recognition, Bromion is speaking of internal fire and chains, and the inner phantoms he would wish to bind.

GORGEOUS

[*The Covering Cherub*] *. . . stretchd over Europe & Asia gorgeous*
In three nights he devourd the rejected corse of death

[*J* 89.12–13]

The Covering Cherub is magnificent and showy, but ever hungering to gorge himself.

HOREB/ORBED

Her shadowy Sisters form the bones, even the bones of Horeb:
Around the marrow! and the orbed scull around the brain!

[*M* 19.51]

By moral laws and physical anatomy man is bound "into horrible forms of
deformity"(*BU* 13.43). Horeb is generally identified with rocks or as a rock
(*M* 17.28, 19.58), which makes it additionally appropriate for this horrible, os-
sifying situation (bones are rocks). A visual correlative to this image appears
at the bottom of *Milton*, plate 4, where a tremendous rock in the shape of an
orbed skull rises out of the ground—one daughter sits atop the rock/skull, bowed
over, perhaps still forming it into shape.

HORSE/HOARSE

79. *The Marriage of Heaven and Hell,* pl. 27, detail.

Chorus

[*MHH* 27, see fig. 79]

Go down with horse & Chariots & Trumpets of hoarse War

[*FZ* 134.9, E402]

The final plate of *The Marriage of Heaven and Hell* offers an example of visual-
verbal interaction: a horse-chorus. The point is emphasized by two smaller
horses toward the top of the plate and by the reference, three lines before, to the
son of fire "loosing the eternal horses from the dens of night." Two lines into
the chorus, we read that the priests will no longer "with hoarse note curse"; no
longer, since wrath has loosed the "horses of instruction" from their control.

The second quotation occurs during Tharmas's apocalyptic identification of
"Mystery Fierce" and reflects Blake's intimate sense of the vocabulary of the
Authorized Version; as *Cruden's Concordance* notes, "The most striking feature of
the notices of this animal in the Bible is that it invariably means a warhorse."
The cavalry was still the elite of the army in Blake's day, and he has some
words on the fate of those who "train the Horse to War" (*AugI* 41–42).

This heading also presents an example of Blake's use of "formula," with the sense that that word has acquired in the study of oral tradition. In addition to Blake's repeating, or repeating with slight alteration, whole sections of verse from one poem to another, we sometimes find a particular word-combination (formula) used in varying contexts. One such formula is *THUNDERS HOARSE*:

> . . . *soon her woes appalld his thunders hoarse*
> [*VDA* 1.17]

> [*The Spectre of Urthona*] *writhd*
> *His cloudy form in jealous fear & muttering thunders hoarse*
> [*FZ* 49.24–25, E333]

> [re *The Twelve Sons of Albion*] *their thunders hoarse appall the Dead*
> [*J* 18.9]

Reading these instances, we cannot escape the idea of equine thunder, an image confirmed by *Europe* 14.28: "Still all your thunders golden hoofd, & bind your horses black." Remembering further that *The French Revolution* describes "Dark cavalry like clouds fraught with thunder" (291), we may begin to sense the outlines of one small structuring dimension of Blake's imagination, which links clouds, horses, and thunder. David Erdman, recording a deletion of "steeds" in favor of "clouds" in Night the Seventh of *The Four Zoas*, notes parenthetically that it offers "a clue to Blake's transpositions" (E838). The consistency of these connections further suggests the nature of Blake's vision. That vision has assimilated and reduplicated various aspects of the Western imaginative constellation of cloud-horse-thunder, as manifest in the myth of the cloud-born centaurs; Shaddai, the Thunderer riding on clouds; cloud-armies fighting in the sky; thundering hooves; and more. In Blake's vision these archaic realities move again into the present, summoned up, in part, by polysemous spells within the language.

IN ARTICULATE

> *And thus the Shadowy Female howls in articulate howlings*
> [*M* 18.4]

> . . . *Enion wanders like a weeping inarticulate voice*
> [*M* 19.42]

The first quotation allows a grimly humorous perspective on the howled lamentation that follows—it is "articulate" because Blake wants us to read on, but we are warned in advance that it is senseless. Enion's voice proves easier to understand.

INFINITE / INFANT

And who shall bind the infinite with an eternal band?
To compass it with swaddling bands? and who shall cherish it
With milk and honey?
I see it smile . . .

[*Eur* 2.13–16]

The infinite is an infant, particularly in this case where the "secret child" is parodying "On the Morning of Christ's Nativity." But we have already seen the opposing forces: to be born is to be bound. *Europe*, plates i, 1, and 3, offers a visual expansion of these verbal dimensions. Plate i is the famous design of "The Ancient of Days" orbed in a sun, in stellar clouds, his hand reaching down with a divider "to compass it." The bottom of plate 1 depicts the clutched head of an agonized man descending in a bat-winged orb to become, on the margin of plate 3, the orbed fetus surrounded by flames, but covering his eyes with his hands. The sequence can be compared to the closing images of Stanley Kubrick's film *2001*.

MAN

And the fury of Man exhaust in War! Woman permanent remain
[*J* 82.35]

Some of Blake's verbal devices serve as a kind of counterpoint emphasis to the lines in which they appear. In this case we hear by dint of repetition that "woman," triumphing in cunning domination, is turning into "man," permeating "man."

ME / METALS / REMEMBRANCE

Here alone I in books formd of metals
[*BU* 4.24]

Though not so represented by any of the editors, Blake's line ends with "me-," "tals" being carried over to the following line. The complete word would have

made for a squeezed line, no doubt—though no more so than the same thir-
ty-nine unit spaces of line 2 in the same column. Urizen's book, as has often
been noted, not only concerns, but is made of himself: The Book *of* Urizen.
Here he tells (tals?) "the secrets of dark contemplation" (4.26), which we know
to be the labor of his "self-contemplating shadow" (3.21). The illustration of
his book in plate 5 is labeled (in the *Small Book of Designs*) "The Book of my
Remembrance."

MYSTERY/MIST-TREE

Conferring times on times among the branches of that Tree
Thus they conferrd among the intoxicating fumes of Mystery
[*FZ* 85.4–5, E361]

The tree is the root (and branch) of mystery, exuding clouds, smoke, mists, and
fumes that confuse understanding: "Rolling volumes of grey mist involve
Churches, Palaces, Towers: / For Urizen unclaspd his Book!" (*Eur* 12.3–4; the
"book" being one of the "volumes"). This mystery appears to be a conifer.

OBJECTING

. . . it is the Reasoning Power
An Abstract objecting power, that Negatives every thing
[*J* 10.13–14]

A capsule dose of philosophy: the concept of "objecting" reveals the twin
birth of individualism and alienation. To say "no" is to objectify; when
"I object," I make myself something thrown in the way (Lat. *ob-iceo*). Negations are passive, reasoning, ultimately selfish, while contraries are active
and wrathful, so asserting their existence and that which they oppose (not
object). Los says that "Exceptions & Objections & Unbeliefs / Exist Not"
(*J* 17.34–35)—the negation, the world of objects and objectors is "as a distorted
& reversed Reflexion in the Darkness" (17.42).

ORGANIZING

. . . there grew
Branchy forms: organizing the Human
Into finite inflexible organs.

. . . .

Incessant the falling Mind labour'd
Organizing itself
                    [*BL* 4.43–45, 49–50]

In its primary sense, "to organize" was "to supply with organs"—"to form into a systematic whole" was a meaning only gaining currency in Blake's lifetime. A similar adaption had prepared "organic" for its important role in Romantic aesthetics, but Blake sees "natural or bodily organs" as capable only of "natural or organic thoughts" (*NNR*a). We participate in a system of organization whose complexity far surpasses our individual awareness, hence individual "organic perceptions" (*NNR*a) necessarily exclude "the Poetic or Prophetic character" of events: "For thou art but a form & organ of life & of thyself / Art nothing being Created Continually by Mercy & Love divine" (*FZ* 86.2–3, E368).

PHYSIC/FISSIC

This heading is used to present two lists from *An Island in the Moon* as examples of Blake's delight in words and the tricks they can play on the signified. Obtuse Angle describes Phebus as:

> . . . the God of Physic, Painting, Perspective Geometry Geography Astronomy, Cooking, Chymistry [Conjunctives] Mechanics, Tactics Pathology Phraseology Theolog Mythology Astrology Osteology, Somatology in short every art & science adorn'd him as beads round his neck
>
>   [E451]

Rambling through this list, the reader begins to find his or her own significance in the deeper connections summoned up by local relationships like "Cooking, Chymistry" or "Theolog Mythology Astrology." Simultaneously, the words themselves condense into small hard beads, dull and meaningless on the arts and sciences they adorn. This catalogue of significance is darkly mirrored two pages later when Aradobo, asked to "say some thing," answers that:

> . . . Chatterton was clever at Fissic Follogy, Pistinology, Aridology, Arography, Transmography Phizography, Hogamy HAtomy, & hall that but in the first place he eat wery little wickly that is he slept very little which he brought into a consumsion, & what was that that he took Fissic or somethink & so died.
>
>   [E453]

Believing Aradobo to suffer from some sudden speech impediment, the reader will strain to organize meaning, forgetting Blake's confession at the top of the page, "I was only making a fool of you." But persisting in our folly we become wise—if Transmography did not exist for the reader at the beginning of the chapter, the struggle for conceptualization that the word occasions confirms it at once.

RE-REVOLUTION

> *. . . those that remain*
> *Return in pangs & horrible convulsions to their bestial state*
> . . . .
> *. . . when the revolution of their day of battles over*
> *Relapsing in dire torment they return to forms of woe*
> *To moping visages returning*
>
> [*FZ* 102.1–2, 6–8, E374]

"Revolution" signifies the amount of time it takes a celestial body to revolve, to return to an original point (from Lat. *revolution-em*). The word in its political sense becomes common in the eighteenth century via the secular application of the poetic idea of an ultimate astronomical revolution that would return the world's great age. But after Robespierre and Napoleon had successively seized the Great Revolution, it was evident that "the iron hand crushed the Tyrants head / And became a Tyrant in his stead" (E490) and that political revolution was just another turn of the wheel. Blake's image, with its emphasis on the "day of battles," states implicitly that social change takes much more than a day or battles. We cannot revolt out of human nature, rather we can only work continually to transform ourselves by forgiveness.

RESPONSING

> *With doubling Voices & loud Horns wound round sounding*
> *Cavernous Dwellers fill'd the enormous Revelry, Responsing!*
> *And Spirits of Flaming fire on high, govern'd the mighty Song.*
>
> [*FZ* 14.3–5, E308]

Blake here coins a neologism for "answering in song." The first line of the quotation is a playful example of Blake's skill in making words embody their significance, supplying the "doubling Voices" while twisting the sounds to suggest the circular shape of the horns.

SPIRITS

Spirits are Lawful but not Ghosts especially Royal Gin is Lawful Spirit No
Smuggling ⟨real⟩ British Spirit & Truth

[Annotations to Thornton, E668]

Bitter play in the fields of the word. Blake's only use, here, of "smuggling"
indicates that it associates with "Royal Gin." Real British Spirit cannot be
smuggled because it cannot be hid, the law does not care about it, and no one
would bother.

TRAVEL/TRAVELLER

I am faint with travel!
[*Eur* 1.6]

"The Mental Traveller"
[title]

The poem begins as a report of what the mental traveller "heard & saw" in the
land of men and women, and ends with his claim that "all is done as I have
told." The possibility arises that his report is, in fact, a "Birth of Intellect"
(*VLJ*, E562) brought forth out of his imagination—"I am faint with travel!"
cries the Shadowy Female as she gives birth "in shady woe, and visionary joy"
(the *OED* cites "travel" as a form of "travail" in both substantive and verb,
and gives examples from 1650 and 1658; "traveler" was used by Wyclif of a woman
in labor). The traveller may have produced a fantasy which he imposes upon
us: his "I" altered all.

TYPES

Therefore I print; nor vain my types shall be
[*J* 3.9]

At the beginning of *Jerusalem*, Blake sites us firmly in the universe of his
engraver's "types" and his visionary typology (the inscription on one etched
plate, the "Chaining of Orc," read, "Type by W Blake" [E682]).

URIZEN

No discussion of Blake's vision of words would be complete without an example of his inventiveness in naming characters. "Urizen," the most remarked,

suggests "your reason"; the "horizon," our physical-perception limit; "your eyes in," a form of self-contemplation; "ur-reason," a primary model; "you risen," marking the ascendancy of the faculty that even now reads; "err-reason," this is only too human—to forgive is to reason not. This list is, of course, not complete: Urizen, like "Reason" (*NNR*b), is not the same that he shall be when we know more.

VAIN

O Urizen . . . thy labour vain, to form men to thine image
[*VDA* 5.3, 4]

. . . nor vain my types shall be
[*J* 3.9]

The self in and for itself is empty and powerless. Vanity, like Satan, exerts great influence in this world—"Selfish! vain, / Eternal bane!" ("Earth's Answer," 23–24)—but, like "object" above, it is a non-entity in the eyes of eternity. Oothoon's lamenting accusation to Urizen takes additional poignance from the fact that in the same breath she recognizes him as "Creator of men!"

WEEDS

. . . the Sea of Time & Space thunderd aloud
Against the rock, which was inwrapped in the weeds of death
[*M* 15.39–40; *FZ* 108.30, E384]

While Shakespeare sets up this wordplay several times with reference to terrestrial weeds, Blake's use simply presents "black sea weed & sickning slime" (*FZ* 74.22, E351) as a type of clothing. Such images suggest that Blake was greatly struck by "the Rocks of Bognor" (*M* 39.49) that reached out from the shore near Felpham. They would have been glistening with weaving weedy vegetation and "washd incessant by the for-ever restless sea-waves" (*J* 94.5)—a vision of Albion in that larger and more encompassing sea. He must also have remembered Jonah 2:5: "The waters compasseth me about, even to the soul: the depth closed me round about, the weeds were wrapped about my head."

WEEP

When my mother died I was very young,
And my father sold me while yet my tongue,
Could scarcely cry weep weep weep weep.

["The Chimney Sweeper" (*SI*), 1–3]

A little black thing among the snow
Crying weep, weep in notes of woe!

["The Chimney Sweeper" (*SE*), 1–2]

How the Chimney-sweepers cry . . .

["London," 9]

The condition of the chimneys' weepers, as Blake and some reformers saw, reflected the neglect and insensitivity of the nation. Blake saw their existence and relationship to society centered in the street-cry of their trade (like the sailor's "Huzza!" mentioned in chapter 1). The changing emphasis in the word traces the development of a voice crying in the wilderness. The (s)weeper grows into the burden of sorrow beginning almost from a state of shock. But he is forced to go on, and—if he survives—out of his experience comes a true knowledge of sorrow. That knowledge, totally devoid of self-pity and having nothing to lose, daily expresses itself like Jesus on the road to Calvary: "weep not for me, but weep for yourselves, and for your children" (Luke 23:28).

The first quotation offers a moving example of word-action through overstressing in repetition; by the third weep we realize that, though he could "scarcely cry," an upwelling release is beginning.

WILL

Printed by Will: Blake

[*Eur*]

Printed by Will   Blake

[*BU*]

O Albion why didst thou a Female Will Create?

[*J* 56.43]

A study of the different ways Blake identifies himself as "Author and Printer" suggests, as we might expect, that he was as interested in the possibilities of his name as Shakespeare or Donne were in theirs. Theodore Thass-Thienemann cites a case where "a patient with the name William asserted 'Will I am'" (*Symbolic Behavior*, p. 183). Since Blake could say in 1798 that "I have been commanded from Hell not to print" (his annotations to Bishop Watson's *An Apology for the Bible*), it is easy to imagine that, conversely, some of the prophecies were "Printed by Will," Blake being no other "than the Secretary; the Authors are in Eternity." *Jerusalem* 39[44] comments that "the Will must not be bended but in the day of Divine / Power" (18–19). Seeing "the Female hid within a Male" (*J* 75.18), perhaps Blake's great concern for the "Female Will" has some personal reference.

Concerning his surname, if Blake read Jeremiah Milles's edition of (Thomas Chatterton's) *Poems, Supposed to Have Been Written at Bristol, in the Fifteenth Century, by Thomas Rowley* (1782), he might have noticed with interest that:

> In the two following passages of Rowley we are to understand *Blake* in this sense:
> > Blake *standeth future doome.*
> i.e. my future fate is *open* and *exposed* to my view. So
> > *The* Blakied *forme of kinde*
> signifies the *naked* and *undisguised* manners of men.

WHITHER

Whither young Man whither away
["The Golden Net," 2]

The three virgins, provoking and then consumed by "ungratified desires," Lamia-like urge the man to "wither" away, a process which begins with indecision. In *Jerusalem* we read: "By Laws of Chastity & Abhorrence I am witherd up" (49.26). Emily Brontë offers a parallel: "Wither, Brothers, wither, / You were vainly given" ("Heavy Hangs the Raindrop," 33–34).

YEW

. . . mournful lean Despair
Brings me yew to deck my grave
["My Silks and Fine Array," 4–5]

"Brings me you," the beloved to whom the poem is addressed, and ourselves, the memorializing readers—despair, evidently, brings the author to write "yew."

Lamentations in English Poetry

The following table lists appearances of the word group in the complete works of selected poets and the Authorized Version (counted from respective concordance citations):

	Lamentation/s	Lament/ed/s	Lamenting/s	Lamentable	Total
Chaucer	4	0	0	0	4
Spenser	1	54 (4 nouns)	14	16	85
Shakespeare	12	38 (5 nouns)	9	16	75
Bible (AV)	26	11 (-ed only)	0	1	38
Milton	3	10	1	2	16
Dryden	0	43 (not available)	1	4	48
Pope	0	7	0	0	7
Goldsmith	0	2	0	0	2
Collins	0	1	0	0	1
Gray	0	0	0	0	0
Cowper	0	5	0	0	5
Burns	0	8 (1 noun)	2	1	11
BLAKE (not counting letters)	*46*	*26*	*18*	*1*	*91*
Wordsworth	6	9 (2 nouns)	5	7	27
Coleridge	0	8 (4 nouns)	3	1	12
Shelley	3	20 (5 nouns)	2	0	25

"Lamentation" as *Knotenpunkt*

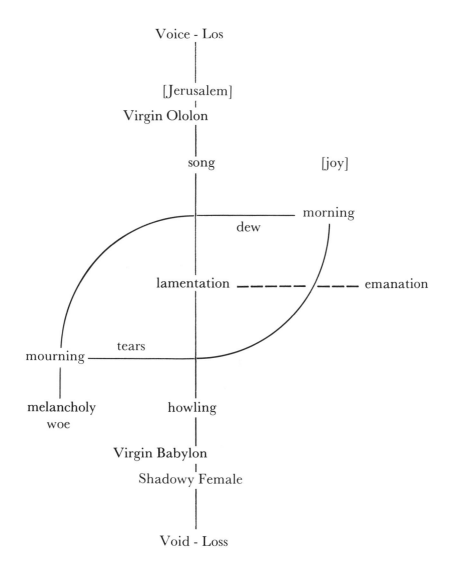

"Veil"/"Vale" as *Knotenpunkt*

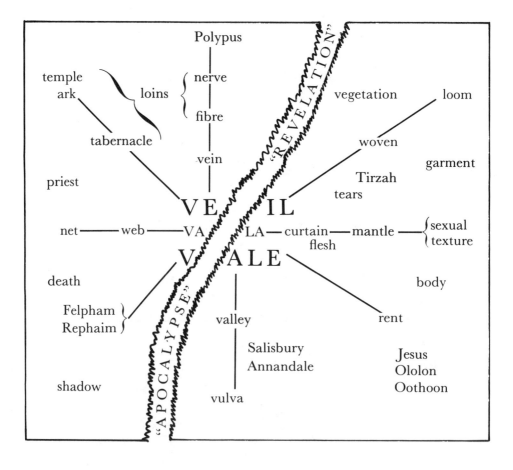

Notes

1. IN WORDS INTO THE WORLDS OF THOUGHT

1. W. B. Yeats, "William Blake and His Illustrations to *The Divine Comedy*," in *Essays and Introductions* (New York: Macmillan, 1968), p. 119.

2. Northrop Frye, *Fearful Symmetry*, p. 427.

3. See David V. Erdman, ed., et al., *A Concordance to the Writings of William Blake*, 2: 2181. The *Concordance* of course omits a number of higher-frequency articles, pronouns, conjunctions, etc. (1: xii).

4. As the engraver of his own words and letters, Blake would have been especially conscious of mirror-writing and the consequences of letter-recombination. The rearranging of letters within a word to uncover other words secretly related is known in the Kabala as *Temurah*; though not listed in the *OED*, the first edition of the *Encyclopaedia Britannica* (1771) says that *Thĕmura* "consists in changing a word, and the letters of which it is composed" (3: 537).

5. See David V. Erdman, "The Suppressed and Altered Passages in Blake's *Jerusalem*," *Studies in Bibliography* 17 (1964): 51–54. Erdman continued his discussion in "Dating Blake's Script: The 'g' Hypothesis," *Blake Newsletter* 3 (June 1969): 8–13, and "Dating Blake's Script: A Postscript," in the following issue (September 1969), p. 42. In the latter issue, G. E. Bentley, Jr., took up the question with "Blake's Sinister 'g', from 1789–93 to ?1803" (pp. 43–45).

6. John W. Wright, "Blake's Relief-Etching Method," *Blake Newsletter*, 9 (Spring 1978): 114.

7. The last *OED* reference to that spelling is 1645, though we find Defoe using it as late as 1720.

8. "The literal . . . is, after all, nothing but the 'transcription' of another literality, that of the symbol," writes Roland Barthes in *S/Z* (p. 120). For Owen Barfield, "what we call literalness is a late stage in a long drawn-out historical process," and, moreover, in a factual sense, "there is indeed no such thing as literalness" ("The Meaning of the Word 'Literal,'" in *Metaphor and Symbol*, ed. L. C. Knights and Basil Cottle [London, 1960], p. 57). Paul Ricoeur suggests that "we call literal sense *whatever* sense may occur among the partial meanings enumerated in the dictionary" ("Metaphor and the Main Problem of Hermeneutics," in *The Philosophy of Paul Ricoeur*, p. 138). Jacques Derrida writes of a need for "determining the 'literal' meaning of writing as metaphoricity itself" (*Of Grammatology*, p. 15).

9. A recent detailed study of the psychology of reading argues:

We see that a word possesses many kinds of information, features of the word itself, which may or may not be extracted in the perceptual process. To capture this notion, a word will be defined as a *complex of features*, a composite representation of five classes of information: graphic, phonological, orthographic, semantic, and syntactic. . . . Full recognition of a word depends on extraction of all these kinds of information. It should be emphasized again that they are features of the word itself, whether they are extracted by the perceiver or not. [Eleanor J. Gibson and Harry Levin, *The Psychology of Reading*, pp. 193–94]

10. *The Language of Allegory*, p. 68.

11. Locke, *An Essay Concerning Human Understanding*, 3.10.15.

12. Cf. Bacon, "Although we think we govern our words . . . certain it is that words, as a Tartar's bow, do shoot back upon the understanding of the wisest, and mightily entangle and pervert the judgment" (cited in Ian Hacking, *Why Does Language Matter to Philosophy?*, p. 5).

13. Quilligan, *The Language of Allegory*, p. 42.

14. In "An Acre of Grass" (1938), lines 14–18:

Myself must I remake
Till I am Timon or Lear
Or that William Blake
Who beat upon the wall
Till Truth obeyed his call.

15. "Uncertainty of meaning is incipient poetry," writes George Steiner in *After Babel* (p. 234). William Empson's *Seven Types of Ambiguity*, first published in 1930, began the revaluation of ambiguity, which for him comprised "any verbal nuance, however slight, which gives room for alternative reactions to the same piece of language" (p. 1). In his wise essay on "The Poet as Fool and Priest," Sigurd Burckhardt summarizes: "For Empson, ambiguity became all but synonymous with the essential quality of poetry; it meant complexity, associative and connotative richness, texture .and the possibility of irony." In opposition, Burckhardt chooses rather to insist "that many meanings can have *one word*" (*Shakespearian Meanings*, p. 32).

16. Paul Ricoeur, "Creativity in Language: Word, Polysemy, Metaphor," *The Philosophy of Paul Ricoeur*, pp. 124, 125.

17. Northrop Frye, *Anatomy of Criticism*, p. 72.

18. J. Laplanche and J.-B. Pontalis, *The Language of Psychoanalysis*, s.v. "Over-determination" and "Association."

19. "What is now proved was once, only imagin'd." "Every thing possible to be believ'd is an image of truth." "Truth can never be told so as to be understood, and not be believ'd."

20. Jacques Derrida, "Structure, Sign, and Play in the Human Sciences," in *The Structuralist Controversy*, p. 247.

21. Peter J. Gillett, "Tennyson's Mind at the Work of Creation," *Victorian Poetry* 15 (1977):324; the quotations following are taken from pp. 324 and 323.

22. Sigmund Freud, "The Unconscious," in *The Standard Edition*, 14:199.

23. Anthony Wilden, *System and Structure*, p. 190.

24. Bacon, *The Advancement of Learning*, sect. 2.15.11; the next quotation is from 1.4.4.

25. Thomas Sprat, *The History of the Royal Society* (London, 1667), p. 113.

26. Arthur Sherbo, ed., *Johnson on Shakespeare*, p. 74.

27. Alexandre Koyré, *La Philosophie de Jacob Boehme*, p. 80 (my translation).

28. William Law, trans. and ed. *The Works of Jacob Behmen* (1764–81), 1:4; the following reference is also to this edition.

29. Wolfgang Kayser, "La doctrine du langage naturel chez Jacob Boehme et ses sources" (1930), trans. Jean Launay, *Poétique* 11 (1972):366.

30. Swedenborg, *True Christian Religion*, 1:267.

31. G. E. Bentley, Jr., *Blake Records*, pp. 35–36.

32. Swedenborg, *An Hieroglyphic Key* etc., p. 4; *A Theosophic Lucubration* etc., p. 9.

33. Swedenborg, *True Christian Religion*, 1:276.

34. Cited by Inge Jonsson, *Emanuel Swedenborg*, p. 17.

35. Swedenborg, *Arcana Coelestia*, 12 vols. (New York, 1951), sect. 8943.

36. Raymond Lister, ed., *The Letters of Samuel Palmer* (Oxford: Clarendon, 1974), 2:669.

37. Alexander Gilchrist, *The Life of William Blake*, pp. 151, 328.

38. Northrop Frye makes the denigrating remark that "when he speaks of reading Greek fluently he means New Testament Greek, where he knew the crib by heart. With Blake, as with other poets, proof that he knew something about a language is not proof that he could read it, and proof that he could read it is not proof that he habitually did so" (*Fearful Symmetry*, p. 436, n. 14). But Tatham, writing a few years after Blake's death, tells us that "it is a remarkable fact, that among the volumes bequeathed by Mrs. Blake to the Author of this Sketch, the most thumbed from use are his Bible & those books in other languages" (Bentley, *Blake Records*, pp. 526–27).

39. Here, as throughout, I am obviously completely unsympathetic to critics who argue that "words, then, for Blake are the fallen and hence error-ridden versions of the mental or imaginative realities which in eternity require no formulation other than their own essences," or that Blake "has little interest in words for their own sake" (Robert F. Gleckner, "Romanticism and the Self-Annihilation of Language," *Criticism* 18 [1976]:184; Leopold Damrosch, Jr., *Symbol and Truth in Blake's Myth*, p. 73).

40. Noted by Frye, *Fearful Symmetry*, p. 368.

41. Bentley, *Blake Records*, p. 324.

42. So Mallarmé writes a friend to say that he has "cast the outline for my entire work, after having found the key to myself . . . where I rest like a sacred spider on the principal threads emanating from my spirit, at the *intersection* of which I will weave the marvellous lace that I intuit, and which already exists in the bosom of beauty" (July 28, 1866), quoted in Michel Pierseens, *The Power of Babel*, p. 3.

43. Michel Bréal, *Semantics*, p. 141.

44. Ronald Clayton Taylor, "Semantic Structures and the Temporal Modes of Blake's Prophetic Verse," *Language and Style* 12 (1979): 40.

45. See Gleckner, "Blake's Verbal Technique," in *William Blake*, ed. Alvin H. Rosenfeld, p. 330; Damrosch, *Symbol and Truth in Blake's Myth*, p. 70; Désirée Hirst, *Hidden Riches*, p. 8; J. Walter Nelson, "Blake's Diction—An Amendatory Note," *Blake*

Studies 7 (1975): 175; Karl Kroeber, "Delivering *Jerusalem*," in *Blake's Sublime Allegory*, ed. Stuart Curran and J. A. Wittreich, p. 349; and Edward J. Rose, "Visionary Forms Dramatic: Grammatical and Iconographical Movement in Blake's Verse and Designs," *Criticism* 8 (1966): 120.

46. Thomas Gunter Browne, *Hermes Unmasked*, p. 51.

47. Sam. 6:7; Blake refers to the story of Uzzah in an annotation to Lavater (E596) and again at *J* 68.51.

48. As the *OED* notes, "It is mentioned by many 17–18th c. writers as being originally a sailor's cheer or salute" (s.v.); Blake can also use the cry in praise: "Amen! Huzza! Selah!" (*J* 27). The wretched conditions of the common sailor need little comment; they stand in vivid contrast to the rhetoric of eighteenth-century recruiting posters, which declare that the sailors will return "to spend their Days in PEACE and PLENTY. HUZZA!!!"

2. ENTERING THE GRAVE

1. John Wilkins, . . . *Language*, pt. 1. ch. 4.6.1.

2. Homer, *Odyssey* (trans. Pope) 18.156.

3. Robert N. Essick, *William Blake, Printmaker*, p. 208.

4. *OED*, s.v. "sentence," 3c (1769).

5. James Hervey, *Meditations and Contemplations*, p. 43.

6. Technically, Blake's illuminated books are usually the result of relief etching rather than engraving; however, "engraving" seems to have been, even for Blake, an acceptable term for the process—note his reference to his designs "re-engrav'd Time after Time" later in the text.

7. David B. Morris, *The Religious Sublime*, p. 213.

8. See David V. Erdman, ed. *The Notebook of William Blake*, p. 22.

9. "As Time One Day By Me Did Pass" (line 23), in *The Works of Henry Vaughan*, p. 512.

10. "Ode: To the Hon. Sir William Temple" (lines 35–38), in *Swift, Poetical Works*, p. 19.

11. "As Blake etches channels into the plate, the words rise in relief above the surrounding 'graves.' . . . irrigating the copper with a lake of acid causes a garden of poetry and art to spring from the barren plate" (Essick, *William Blake, Printmaker*, p. 208).

12. Theodore Thass-Thienemann, *Symbolic Behavior*, p. 89.

13. *Romeo and Juliet*, 2.3.239–40; Thomas Denton is more explicit in his "monody" on *Immortality; or, The Consolation of Life* (1755): "Ope, ope thy pond'rous Jaws, thou friendly Tombs, / Close the sad deathful Scene, and shroud me in thy Womb!" (11.9–10).

14. *VDA* 3.10; *M* 21.10; *FZ* 113.22, E377; *J* 3. For Young, the world of the grave is more real than this Earth:

How populous? how vital is the Grave?
This is Creation's melancholy Vault,

The Vale funereal, the sad Cypress *gloom;*
The Land of Apparitions, empty Shades:
All, all on earth is Shadow, *all beyond*
Is Substance. . . .

[*Night Thoughts* 1.115–20]

15. We read in Young's *Night Thoughts:*

Grave *Minds you praise, nor can you praise too much;*
If there is weight in an Eternity,
Let the Grave *listen;—and be* graver *still.*

[7.1478–80]

The last line almost reads as an injunction for Death to be even more serious. The grave are also the self-righteous "aged men wise guardians of the poor" ("Holy Thursday" [*SI*]) showing another aspect of how "Blake's general symbol of experience is the grave" (Robert F. Gleckner, *The Piper and The Bard,* p. 48). For Blake, the "graver" represented his livelihood: "Even Johnson & Fuseli have discarded my Graver" (E704).

16. Essick, discussing "Blake and the Traditions of Reproductive Engraving" in his *The Visionary Hand,* offers another interpretation: "If this is a portrait of Milton, then it is surely the poet bound to conventions as potentially misleading as those dominating the representation of his body" (p. 511).

17. *Night Thoughts* 3.478–79.

18. Essick, *The Visionary Hand,* p. 509.

19. In "The Title-page of *The Book of Urizen*" in *William Blake,* ed. Morton D. Paley and Michael Phillips, pp. 225–30, Morris Eaves notes that "the horizontal tablets on which the patriarch is writing with one hand and etching with the other are also sepulchral, and they may be seen in several ways: as two separate and more or less square tablets, as a single long tablet extending from left to right. . . ." (p. 225). Erdman suggests that it may be "a single coffin lid" (*The Illuminated Blake,* p. 183).

3. LAMENTATION, MOURNING, AND MORNING

1. See David V. Erdman, "Textual Notes," E802.

2. George Quasha, "Orc as a Fiery Paradigm of Poetic Torsion," in *Blake's Visionary Forms Dramatic,* ed. David V. Erdman and John E. Grant, p. 283.

3. W.T., *The Countries Sense of Londons Sufferings In the Late Most Lamentable Fire* (London, 1667), ch. 1.

4. Jer. 22:29, "O earth, earth, earth, hear the word of the LORD"; and Hosea 14:1–2, "O Israel, return unto the LORD thy God. . . . Take with you words, and turn to the LORD."

5. Cf. *FZ* 62.3, E342.

6. Northrop Frye, *Fearful Symmetry,* p. 223.

7. This first instance of Blake's common formula, "Daughters of Albion" (expanded in the longer poems to include "Daughters of Beulah," "of Moab," and a few

others), again draws attention to the Prophets' widespread use of this imagery to personify Israel and to the special connection of women with lamentation (cf. Judges 11:39–40; Ezekiel 32:16; Luke 23:28–29).

8. *VDA* 2.20, 5.2, 8.13 (the last line). On the myth of Narcissus and Echo in the *Visions*, see Kathleen Raine, *Blake and Tradition*, 1:176.

9. See Louis I. Bredvold, *The Natural History of Sensibility*, pp. 51–73.

10. See E819; in a letter of 1803 Blake refers to his own "Dirge-like lamentation" (E737).

11. 5.8, E302; 17.2–18.8, E310; 35.1–36.14, E324–25; 45.15–26, E330; 37.3–10, E326; 6.3, E303; 44.23–45.8, E330; 31.4–17, E320; 28.22, E318.

12. Both "lament" and "howl" appear for the Septuagint θρηνέιν. "Howl" was generally used for Septuagint ὀλολύζω, which was the usual translation of the onomatopoetic Hebrew *yalal*.

13. *FZ* 93.34, E365.

14. Basil Willey, *The Seventeenth Century Background*, p. 100.

15. "Commentary," E923.

16. John Bunyan, *The Pilgrim's Progress*, p. 265.

17. Peter Fisher first touched on this, suggesting "Ololon, a name probably derived from a Greek word (ὀλολύζειν) which signified the crying of women to the gods" (*The Valley of Vision*, p. 248). Susan Fox also suggests the past perfect of ὀλλύμι, "ὠλώλειν, 'to have lost' or 'to have perished'" (*Poetic Form in Blake's Milton*, p. 93); the possibility here might be better translated as "to have self-annihilated," thus further linking Ololon and Christ.

18. This seems to invoke the "Dirge" or "Song of the Aged Mother" that begins *The Four Zoas* "Hearing the march of *long resounding* strong heroic Verse" (*FZ* 3.2, E300), the only other instance of that formula.

19. Frye, *Fearful Symmetry*, p. 143.

20. "Incommensurability and Interconnection in Blake's Anti-Newtonian Text," *Studies in Romanticism* 16 (Summer 1977):298.

21. Compare 36.29, "What am I now to do," with Acts 9:6, "And he trembling and astonished said, Lord, what wilt thou have me to do?" "Trembling & astonishment" are also key terms in *Milton* (39.17, 31; see also 22.9, 42.25).

22. Samuel Johnson, *Lives of the English Poets*, 1:109. Hayley, appropriately enough in Blake's later view of him, rejected this view in his *Life of Milton* (1796). He attacks "the enemies of Milton" for having "laboured to fix upon him a fictitious and most unamiable character of austerity and harshness"; quoting Johnson's image of "Turkish contempt," Hayley labels it as "assuredly the intemperate language of hatred, and very far from being consonant to truth" (p. 197) and continues this defense for four pages.

23. In his discussion of "The Female Awakening at the End of Blake's *Milton*," John E. Grant concludes that "despite hard Miltonic-sounding things he says elsewhere about the perils of female dominance, Blake shows us at the end of *Milton: A Poem* that the leadership of a women is necessary to the fulfillment of time" (*Milton Reconsidered*, ed. John Karl Franson, p. 99).

24. Note also the verbal play: the "catterpillar" was engendered by a moth-mother, so the words already remind the reader of what it will become.

25. S. Foster Damon, *A Blake Dictionary*, p. 307; Frye, *Fearful Symmetry*, p. 354.

26. *Paulys Real-Encyclopädie der klassischen Altertumswissenschaft* (1937), vol. 17, col. 2493.

27. Johnson, *Lives,* 1:75.

28. "Virgin Ololon" appears at 36.18, 27; 39.58; and 41.29; "Virgin Babylon" appears once previously, 5.27. The transposition of these epithets suggests the hypothetical composites "Babylolon" and "Holylon"; perhaps Ololon disappears at the end of the poem to become a spiritual, fourfold "Ololondon": "Their clouds roll over London with a south wind; soft Oothoon" (42.32), where the sudden appearance of "Oothoon" makes us wonder what happened linguistically to "the Clouds of Ololon folded" (42.12, the last appearance of her name as such).

29. According to Henry Crabb Robinson, Blake "had learned from the Bible that wives should be in common"; however, in the same breath "he affirmed that he had committed many murders" (G. E. Bentley, Jr., *Blake Records,* p. 548).

30. Gerhard von Rad, *The Message of the Prophets,* p. 174.

31. *J* 56.32; cf. Ezekiel 3:17, "Son of man, I have made thee a Watchman unto the house of Israel." See Harold Bloom, "Blake's *Jerusalem*: The Bard of Sensibility and the Form of Prophecy," in *The Ringers in the Tower,* pp. 64–79.

32. Martin Buber, *The Prophetic Faith,* pp. 186, 187.

33. *J* 36[40].51; after "The Lamb" of *Songs of Innocence* and Enion's compelling image of the lamb naively offering up its wool, we now hear the "lamb" in "lamentation."

34. In particular, dew is the seminal essence of spring, evidenced by the mythological conception of dew as Zeus' semen (Géza Róheim, *Animism, Magic, and The Divine King,* p. 95). Emile Benveniste discusses lexical relationships in Greek suggesting that, imaginatively, "tiny new born animals are like dew, the fresh little drops which have just fallen" (*Indo-European Language and Society,* p. 22). William Harvey equated dew with "the Primigenial Moisture" from which "Seed" is made (*Anatomical Exercitations* [1653], pp. 462–63), and the English ballad tradition offers a rich mine of sexual associations for "sweet May dews" and "the foggy foggy dew" (see James Reeves, *The Everlasting Circle,* pp. 85, 238–39, 263, and *The Idiom of the People,* pp. 45–57). Blake identifies dew with semen in *Jerusalem* 30[34].3–4: "O how I tremble! how my members pour down milky fear! / A dewy garment covers me all over, all manhood is gone!"

35. I.i.131–132; *The Rape of Lucrece,* line 1829.

36. Cf. John Dyer, *The Fleece* 1.363–65:

The crystal dews, inpearl'd upon the grass,
Are touch'd by Phoebus' beams, and mount aloft,
With various clouds to paint the azure sky.

37. "Resolution and Independence," lines 22–26.

38. In his edition of *Beowulf,* Howell D. Chickering, Jr. notes that since battles usually begin at dawn, "By extension, 'morning' in [Old English] poetry has the connotation 'sorrowful'" (*Beowulf: A Dual-Language Edition* [Garden City, N.Y.: Doubleday, 1977], p. 286).

39. "The dews of death" may be compared with the description of Jerusalem falling "in groans & Dewy death / The dew of anxious souls the death-sweat of the dying" (*FZ* 25.14–15, E314).

40. Reminiscent of the new, material earth, the "delightful land" of Paradise twice presented as "Glist'ring with dew" in *Paradise Lost* (4.645, 653).

41. Eleanor M. Sickels, *The Gloomy Egoist,* pp. 79–80.

42. Sigmund Freud, "Mourning and Melancholia," in *The Standard Edition,* 14:250.

43. Bentley, *Blake Records,* p. 517.

44. Cf. *The French Revolution,* l. 21: "seiz'd with howlings, despair, and black night," and *The Four Zoas* 94.55, quoted later in the text.

45. *J* 48.24–25; cf. 48.42; *M* 8.12; 30.5; *FZ* 21.13, E311.

46. See C. A. Moore, *Backgrounds of English Literature, 1700–1760,* pp. 179–235.

47. Thomas Hood, *Selected Poems,* p. 51.

48. "Resolution and Independence," lines 84, 117, 28.

49. "The Nightingale," lines 15, 97, 108–109.

50. Fox, *Poetic Form in Blake's Milton,* p. 18.

4. CHAINS OF BEING (THE LINE, 1)

1. Arthur O. Lovejoy, *The Great Chain of Being,* p. 183. Donald Greene argues, however, that Lovejoy's emphasis on the "great chain" is misleading: "on the whole, the century was certainly not under its spell" (*The Age of Exuberance,* p. 126).

2. *Essay on Man* 1.237–39, 245–46, emphasis added.

3. "Review of A Free Enquiry into the Nature and Origin of Evil," in *Johnson,* ed. Mona Wilson, pp. 361, 355, 356, 372.

4. Northrop Frye, *Fearful Symmetry,* p. 38.

5. Samuel Rogers, *The Pleasures of Memory,* in *The Pleasures of Memory, with Other Poems* 1.170; the quotations following in the paragraph are from: Edmund Burke, *A Philosophical Enquiry into the Origin of Our Ideas of the Sublime and Beautiful,* p. 120; J. M. Servan, *Discours sur l'administration de la justice criminelle* (Geneva, 1767), p. 35 (my translation); Hume, *A Treatise of Human Nature* 1.4.6; Young, *The Complaint; or Night Thoughts* 8.1062; Darwin, *The Temple of Nature* 1.8; Dewhurst Bilsborrow, "To Erasmus Darwin," in *Zoonomia* 1.43; Hannah More, "Sensibility: A Poetical Epistle," in *Sacred Dramas,* 6th ed. (London, 1789), p. 282; Boswell, *Life of Johnson,* p. 425; Hobbes, *Leviathan* 1.7; Haller, *Historia stirpium indigenarum Helvetiae* (1768), quoted in Norwood Russell Hanson, *Patterns of Discovery: An Inquiry into the Conceptual Foundations of Science* (Cambridge, Eng.: Cambridge University Press: 1958), p. 69; Jean Jacques Rousseau, *An Inquiry into the Nature of the Social Contract* (London, 1791), p. 3; William Godwin, *Enquiry Concerning Political Justice,* p. 149.

6. Bacon, *The Advancement of Learning* 2.14.11; Thomson, *Summer,* lines 1545–47, 1549 in *Poetical Works,* ed. J. Logie Robertson.

7. W. K. Wimsatt, "One Relation of Rhyme to Reason," in *The Verbal Icon,* p. 153.

8. *The Remonstrance of Shakespeare,* lines 23–24, 47, and 63, in *The Poems of Mark Akenside, M.D.* (London, 1772). In the prologue to *The Mysterious Mother,* first publicly

printed in 1781, Horace Walpole also criticizes the "French model," asking, "Can crimes be punish'd by a bard enchain'd?"

9. See James T. Boulton, "An Eighteenth-Century Obsession," *Studies in Burke and His Time* 9 (1968):905–26.

10. *Essay* 1.1.15; cf. Wordsworth, *The Prelude* [1804] 2.228.

11. Johnson, *Dictionary*, 6th ed. (London, 1785), s.v. "charter." E. P. Thomson's astute essay, "London," offers an illuminating and detailed commentary on the social context and implications of "charter'd" (*Interpreting Blake*, ed. Michael Phillips, pp. 5–31).

12. Stanley Gardner also argues that the "'mind-forged [sic] manacles' are the dominant sequences of word, thought and reaction. . . . Blake began by breaking the shackles of language" (*Blake*, p. 41).

13. Gavin Edwards, "Mind-Forg'd Manacles: A Contribution to the Discussion of Blake's 'London'," *Literature and History* 5 (1979): 88, 87, 96, 102.

14. W. J. T. Mitchell, *Blake's Composite Art: A Study of the Illuminated Poetry*, p. 75. In a Swedenborgian pamphlet published at the time of his greatest involvement with the New Church, Blake could have read "that in the Word, and in every Part thereof, there is a Divine Marriage and a Celestial Marriage. . . . That this Marriage is in every particular Part of the Word in its internal Sense, and therefore the Lord is therein as to Divine Good and Divine Truth" (Emanuel Swedenborg, *Concerning the White Horse Mentioned in the Revelation*, pp. 41–42).

15. Harold Bloom, *Poetry and Repression*, p. 40; the next quotation is from p. 44.

16. Hazard Adams, "Blake and the Philosophy of Literary Symbolism," *New Literary History* 5 (1973):137,138.

17. Edward Young, "Conjectures on Original Composition," in *The Works of Dr. Edward Young*, 5 vols. (London, 1783), 4: 85.

18. *The Works of Plato*, trans. Thomas Taylor and Floyer Sydenham, 4 vols. (London: Printed for T. Taylor, 1804), 1: 357 [*Republic* 514a].

19. So Ambrosio, in Matthew Lewis's *The Monk* (1796), curses "the weight of Religion's chains" (ed. Howard Anderson, p. 269).

20. *SL* 4.13–15; cf. Hobbes, "they made Artificiall Chains, called *Civill Lawes*" (*Leviathan* 2.21).

21. See Richard Broxton Onians, *The Origins of European Thought*, p. 206; George Sandys discusses the idea in a note to book 15 of his translation of Ovid's *Metamorphoses*, ed. Karl K. Hulley and Stanley T. Vandersall, p. 706; see also Thomas Browne, *Hydriotaphia; or, Urne Buriall* 3.41, in *The Prose of Sir Thomas Browne*, ed. Norman Endicott, p. 270.

22. Pope, *Homer's Iliad, Books I–IX*, ed. Maynard Mack et al., pp. 396–97.

23. Erasmus Darwin, *The Botanic Garden*, pt. 1, *The Economy of Vegetation* 2.91–92. Robert E. Simmons proposes that "the rending of Urizen from Los's side suggests . . . a geophysical theory of the origin of the earth as a chunk of matter thrown off by the sun, just as Enitharmon, the moon, is born . . . after 'Los's bosom earthquak'd with sighs'" ("*Urizen:* The Symmetry of Fear," in *Blake's Visionary Forms Dramatic*, ed. David V. Erdman and John E. Grant, p. 153). This geophysical theory, right down to the

"earthquakes," can be amply illustrated with quotations from Darwin and adds a new twist: not only Urizen's rending, but also his chaining are—on one of many levels—the story of our Earth's relation to Sol (see David Worrall, "William Blake and Erasmus Darwin's *Botanic Garden*," *Bulletin of the New York Public Library* 78 [1975]: 407–13).

24. *The Four Zoas* 96.9 ff., E361, offers a somewhat different version; there Urizen takes "the Sun reddning like a fierce lion *in his chains*" and hangs it in his "temple . . . to give light to the Abyss."

25. Knowing these stellar chains to be freezing cold and bound into the same dull round, one can see in "numb'ring" a minute instance of Blake multiplying the content of a word to carry his vision. Peggy Meyer Sherry, "The 'Predicament' of the Autograph: 'William Blake'" (*Glyph* 4 [1978]: 141), remarks of his passage: "That these chains refer not just to the linear measurement of post-lapsarian time but also to the order of language and the structure of the body is the kind of trope we would expect."

26. Francis Webb, *Poems*, quoted in William Powell Jones, *The Rhetoric of Science*, p. 225.

27. The pun is noted by Raine, *Blake and Tradition*, 2:161.

28. See John Toland, *A Critical History of the Celtic Religion and Learning*, pp. 122–23.

29. *The Gentleman's Magazine*, August 1790, p. 680 [for 684], notes "those delicate links and chains that unite mankind together in the various relations of husband and wife, of parent and child, of brother and sister." Erasmus Darwin's *Temple of Nature*, canto 2, discusses "Storgè goddess of Parental Love; First chain of Society," and "sexual love . . . Second chain of Society" (p. 42).

30. Frye, *Fearful Symmetry*, p. 214.

31. *Soma/sema*; Blake could have encountered this venerable formulation of an old debate in Thomas Taylor's 1793 translation of the *Cratylus*; there Socrates argues that "according to some, [the body, "soma"] is the *sepulchre* of the soul, which they consider as buried at present; and because whatever the soul signifies, it signifies by the body; so that on this account it is properly called σῆμα, a sepulchre [sema]" (*The Cratylus, Phaedo, Parmenides and Timaeus of Plato*, p. 37).

32. *Of the Danger His Majesty (Being Prince) Escaped in the Road at St. Andero*, lines 168–70: "The Chain that's fixed to the throne of Jove, / On which the fabric of our world depends, / One link dissolved, the whole creation ends" (in *The Poetical Works of Edmund Waller and Sir John Denham* [Edinburgh, 1857], p. 6). Urizen's opening declaration resonates with Cowper's description of "the pride of letter'd ignorance, that binds / In chains of errour our accomplish'd minds" (*Hope* 483–84).

33. The other definitions are "1. A series of links fastened one within another; 2. A bond; a manacles; a fetter; something with which prisoners are bound"; and "4. A series linked together, as of causes or thoughts; a succession; a subordination." Significantly, in the preface to the *Dictionary*, Johnson writes that "to enchain syllables and to lash the wind are equally the undertakings of pride, unwilling to measure its desires by its strength."

34. William Duff, *An Essay on Original Genius* (1767), writes of "the various ideas conveyed to the understanding by the canal of sensation" (p. 7).

35. *Prometheus Unbound* 2.4.20–21.

36. Christopher Small, *Ariel Like A Harpy: Shelley, Mary, and Frankenstein* (London: Gollancz, 1972), p. 238.

5. FIBRES OF BEING (THE LINE, 2)

1. G. S. Rousseau, "Nerves, Spirits, and Fibres: Towards Defining the Origins of Sensibility," in *Studies in the Eighteenth Century 3*, ed. R. F. Brissenden and J. C. Eade, pp. 144, 140, and 155 (twice). Sir Geoffrey Keynes notes that Willis should more properly be referred to as a "physician" rather than as a "scientist" (personal communication). See also Rousseau's discussion of "Science" in *The Eighteenth Century*, ed. Pat Rogers, where he further develops the point that "no topic in physiology was more important than the precise workings of the nerves. . . . nothing was of greater interest to the popular imagination than 'the state of the nerves'" (pp. 192, 189).

2. The word "fibre" goes unused by Gray, Collins, and Goldsmith, as well as by Milton, Shakespeare, and the Authorized Version. The concept, if not the word, becomes more important for the Romantics, whose "organic Harps, diversely fram'd" are essentially fibre-visions.

3. Karl Kroeber argues in "Delivering *Jerusalem*" that "Blake's central term for the hardened world is 'fibre'" (in *Blake's Sublime Allegory*, ed. Stuart Curran and J. A. Wittreich, Jr., p. 359).

4. Quoted in Rousseau, "Science," p. 189.

5. Edwin Clarke, "The Doctrine of the Hollow Nerve in the Seventeenth and Eighteenth Centuries," in *Medicine, Science, and Culture*, ed. Lloyd G. Stevenson and Robert P. Multhauf, pp. 123–24.

6. Thomas Blount, *Glossographia; or a Dictionary*, 5th ed. (1681), s.v.

7. See *OED* s.v. (citing Sandys' 1626 *Metamorphoses*).

8. Tacitus, *Annales* 14.30, in Pennant, *The Journey to Snowdon* (London, 1781), pp. 232–33. Cf. William Borlase, *Antiquities . . . Cornwall*: "The victim being offered, they prayed most solemnly to the gods with uplifted hands, and great zeal, and when the entrails had been properly examined by the Diviners, Pliny thinks that the Druids eat part of the human victim" (p. 127).

9. Morton D. Paley and Deirdre Toomey, "Two Pictorial Sources for *Jerusalem* 25," *Blake Newsletter* 5 (1971–72):186.

10. Laurence Sterne, *Tristram Shandy* 7.31; Emanuel Swedenborg, *Divine Love and Divine Wisdom* (1788), p. 365.

11. See Edward J. Rose, "Blake's Human Root: Symbol, Myth, and Design," *Studies in English Literature* 20 (1980):575–90. Rose notes "the relation of the root to the worm . . . based in part upon the shape of each and the fact that they begin in the earth" (pp. 578–79)—or grave.

12. Jacques Derrida, *Of Grammatology*, p. 102.

13. "Evolution and William Blake," *Studies in Romanticism* 4 (1965):110–18, p. 115.

14. Erasmus Darwin, *The Economy of Vegetation* 4.425–27. This passage is also quoted in connection with *The Book of Urizen* by David Charles Leonard, "Erasmus Darwin and William Blake," *Eighteenth-Century Life* 4 (1978):79–81. My discussion of Darwin

and Blake, "The Spectre of Darwin," appears in *Blake: An Illustrated Quarterly* 15 (1981):36–48.

15. Swedenborg, *Divine Love and Divine Wisdom*, p. 286.

16. Cf. William Harvey's early but influential *Anatomical Exercitations*, pp. 471, 484, 519; the *OED*'s first instance of the phrase, "breaking of the water," dates from 1680. The *Encyclopaedia Britannica*, 1st ed. (1771), speaks of the placenta, "in which the child swims" (2: 209).

17. "The Polype as a Symbol in the Poetry of William Blake," *Texas Studies in Literature and Language* 2 (1960):198–205, p. 205.

18. Richard Bruxton Onians, *The Origins of European Thought*, p. 39.

19. 1st ed. (1771), 2:670; 2nd ed. (1779), 5:3243; the image is also used by Harvey and Buffon.

20. *Anatomical Exercitations*, p. 468.

21. P. 369; the quotations following are from pp. 425, 369, and 413, italics added. This material is partially quoted on E608, although the necessarily selective quotation there limits the reader's appreciation of Swedenborg's minutely particular "technical" and literal analogies.

22. 4.49–50; four lines later "the *Lungs* heave *incessant.*"

23. This image offers itself as a deliberate reversal of normal development, for, as Albrecht von Haller reported, the newly-born infant's lungs "being dilated from the air, change from a small dense body, sinking even in salt water, into a light springy floating fabric, extended to a considerable bulk with air, and of a white colour" (*First Lines of Physiology*, para. 948).

24. S. Foster Damon, *A Blake Dictionary*, p. 332.

25. *Encyclopaedia Britannica*, 1st ed., s.v. "polypus."

26. See Henry Knight Miller, *Essays on Fielding's Miscellanies: A Commentary on Volume One* (Princeton, N.J.: Princeton University Press, 1961), pp. 316–26.

27. G. L. Leclerc de Buffon, *Natural History* 2. 14–15.

28. Aram Vartanian, "Trembley's Polyp, La Mettrie, and Eighteenth-Century French Materialism," *Journal of the History of Ideas* 11 (1950):259–86, p. 283.

29. In the "Biography" prefixed to John (William's brother) Hunter's posthumous *A Treatise on the Blood, Inflammation, and Gun-Shot Wounds* (London, 1794), p. xl. Kreiter, "Evolution and William Blake," speculates that Blake was acquainted with William Hunter and "could have seen" his Anatomical Theatre (p. 114).

30. *Ovid's Metamorphoses*, ed. Karl K. Hulley and Stanley T. Vandersall, p. 181, n. 39. The word, notably enough, is used in this single occurrence to describe how Hermaphroditus is held by Salmacis:

> *So clasping Ivy to the Oake doth grow;*
> *And so the* Polypus *detains his foe.*
> *But* Atlantiades [*Hermaphroditus*], *relentless coy,*
> *Still struggles, and resists her hop't-for joy.*
> *Invested with her body: foole, said she,*
> *Struggle thou mai'st, but never shalt be free.*

[4.336–71, p. 181]

Blake seems to draw on this description in *Jerusalem,* plate 66, where the Daughters of Albion alter the Sons of Albion (who would each be *Atlantiades* after a fashion, as Albion is identified with Atlas) into "a mighty Polypus nam'd Albions Tree," and:

> *As the Mistletoe grows on the Oak, so Albions Tree on Eternity: Lo!*
> *He who will not comingle in Love, must be adjoind by Hate*

> [66.55–56]

31. Richard Payne Knight, *A Discourse on the Worship of Priapus and its Connection with the Mystic Theology of the Ancients* (1786), p. 36.

32. Blake, we might remember, never uses the form "polyp" or "polype."

33. Pp. 14–15; the quotations that follow are taken from pages 248–50, and page 16.

34. Damon does little service to stress the Polypus as a "tumorous growth (particularly in the nose)" (*A Blake Dictionary,* p. 333). Applying the Swedenborgian correspondences of heart and lungs, we can see that the Polypus is situated to strangle both will and understanding.

35. Cf. the Spectre of Urthona's version of his birth:

> *I sunk with cries of blood issuing downward in the veins*
> *Which now my rivers were become rolling in tubelike forms*
> *Shut up within themselves descending down I sunk along*
> *The goary tide even to the place of seed*

> [*FZ* 84.18–21, E359]

The expression was common throughout the century; for Erasmus Darwin, "Through each new giand the purple current glides, / New veins meandering drink the refluent tides" (*The Economy of Vegetation* 4.429–30).

36. Deciduous trees do spend the winter as bare "fibrous" forms (see *America,* pl. 16), and a common classical *adynaton* or "impossibility" imagined trees as nets in which fish were caught (usually after the deluge: *Metamorphoses* 1.296; Horace, *Odes* 1.2.9–12). Tennyson also associates these themes on the root level (including "you," the reader):

> *Old yew, which graspest at the stones*
> *   That name the under-lying dead,*
> *   Thy fibres net the dreamless head,*
> *Thy roots are wrapt about the bones.*

> [*In Memoriam* 2.1–4]

37. (London, 1733), p. 62. Similar descriptions are standard throughout the century; see, for example, the *Encyclopaedia Britannica,* 2nd ed., s.v. "fibre"; von Haller, *First Lines of Physiology,* ch. 1; and Darwin, *Zoonomia,* ch. 1.

38. "Bone," for instance, which Partridge's *Dictionary* identifies as nineteenth-century Cockney slang for the erect penis (p. 1008), and the fact that the fibres are "drawn" out—as in *The Four Zoas,* "craving the more the more enjoying, drawing out sweet bliss"—into the loom or womb (this is discussed further in the next chapter). Jean H. Hagstrum comments parenthetically that "fibre" can be "a sexual term" ("Babylon Revisited, or the Story of Luvah and Vala," in *Blake's Sublime Allegory,*

ed. Stuart Curran and J. A. Wittreich, Jr., p. 107). John Webster equates semen with the fibre of "thread" in *The White Devil*:

> CAMILLO. Vittoria, I cannot be induced, or, as a man would say, incited—
> VITTORIA. To do what, sir?
> CAMILLO. To lie with you to-night. Your silk-worm useth to fast every third day, and the next following spins the better for it. To-morrow at night I am for you.
> VITTORIA. You'll spin a fair thread, trust to't.

[1.2.194–201]

39. *Encyclopaedia Britannica*, 1st ed., p. 270; cf. *J* 80.74–76:

> *She wove two vessels of seed, beautiful as Skiddaws snow;*
> *Giving them bends of self interest & selfish natural virtue:*
> *She hid them in his loins. . . .*

40. See Clarke, "Doctrine of the Hollow Nerve," pp. 130–31; cf. Swift, *A Tale of A Tub*, sect. 9.

41. See Partridge, *Dictionary*, s.v. "Shoot" and "Root." In other contexts Blake refers to "the sportive root" and the "delving root" and, in particular, in *The Four Zoas* (98.7–8, E362):

> *So Enitharmon cried upon her terrible Earthy bed*
> *While the broad Oak wreathd his roots round her forcing his dark way.*

As with "Conwenna sat above," quoted before, the description "seize therefore in thy hand / The small fibres as they shoot around me draw out in pity / And let them run on the winds of thy bosom" bears, in part, a graphically sexual interpretation: who is to draw out what in pity?

42. Albrecht von Haller, *First Lines of Physiology,* sect. 882. Buffon refers to "spermatic worms," the "small worms in the semen . . . [which] turned round, and twisted like serpents" (*Natural History* 2:135, 133). Apparently neither "seminal worms" nor "spermatic worms" are recorded in the *OED*. Buffon reports that (as with Orc's metamorphosis) "the spermatic worm . . . becomes a real foetus" (p. 137).

43. Cheyne, pp. 65, 88; the "Mental Traveller" sees the "Woman Old . . . number every Nerve" (1. 17), which is elsewhere a numbering of "fibres" (*M* 19.48–49; *J* 22.20).

44. "Knot" was a common image for ganglions; cf. James Johnstone, *An Essay on the Use of the Ganglions of the Nerves* (Shrewsbury, 1771), pp. 1–2.

45. *Divine Love and Divine Wisdom,* p. 400.

46. See *OED* s.v. "sinew," 4b; "nerve," 2a.

47. Robert Burton, *The Anatomy of Melancholy,* sect. 1.1.2.4.

48. Cf. Cowper, *The Task* 4.134–37:

> *Where now the vital energy that mov'd*
> *While summer was, the pure and subtile lymph*
> *Through th' imperceptible meand'ring veins*
> *Of leaf and flow'r?*

49. See Onians, *Origins*, αἰών, ψυχή, in index.

50. See above, p. 40, where this image is related to tears; it had traditionally been believed that the brain produced tears (Clarke, "Doctrine of the Hollow Nerve," p. 133; Samuel Richardson's Clarissa Harlowe writes that she has "wept away all my brain"). On the river Ololon as the "spermatic stream of the Hermeticists," see Florence Sandler, "The Iconoclastic Enterprise: Blake's Critique of 'Milton's Religion'" (*Blake Studies* 5 [1972]:21).

51. Onians, *Origins,* p. 216.

52. "Glandous" is a form not recorded in the *OED.*

53. G. S. Rousseau quotes a similar passage from Henry Brook's *Universal Beauty*:

Quick, from the Mind's imperial Mansion shed
With lively Tension spins the nervous Thread
With Flux of animate Effluvia stor'd,
And Tubes of nicest Perforation bor'd,
Whose branching Maze thro' ev'ry Organ tends,
And Unity of conscious Action lends;
While Spirits thro' the wandring Channels wind,
And wing the Message of informing Mind;
Or Objects to th' ideal Seat convey;
Or dictate Motion with internal Sway.

By the time this was written in 1735, observes Rousseau, "'Animal spirits' winding through the empty 'Channels' of the nerves were . . . as valid a *topos* for the didactic or satiric poet as 'memory' and 'imagination'—the 'secondary stage' of nervous physiology in Locke's system—were to become later in the century" ("Science," p. 194). But for later use of this imagery, indicative of its general accessibility and use, see Samuel Law, *A Domestic Winter-Piece; or, A Poem* 2.165–70, 235–40 (Leeds, 1772).

54. A vital fluid present in the mixed human possibilities of "sap-head" and "sapience" (cf. Onians, *Origins,* pp. 61–63). Blackmore also supplies material for the correspondence of nerve and vegetable fibre; compare the lines just quoted in the text with the following:

But every tree from all its branching roots
Amidst the glebe small hollow fibres shoots;
Which drink with thirsty mouths the vital juice,
And to the limbs and leaves their food diffuse:
Peculiar pores Peculiar juice receive,
To this deny, to that admittance give.

[*Creation* 2.827–32]

55. Buffon writes, "Animals seem to partake of the nature of flame; their internal heat is a species of fire" (*Natural History* 2:37).

56. Newton, *Opticks,* query 12, p. 319.

57. Query 14, p. 320; query 15, p. 320; query 23, 24, p. 328. For the suggestion that this concept enters into Blake's idea of "single vision & Newton's sleep," see Martin K. Nurmi, "Negative Sources in Blake," in *William Blake,* ed. Alvin H. Rosenfeld,

pp. 304–05. Blake could have known Joseph Priestley's report in *The History and Present State of Discoveries relating to Vision, Light, and Colours* that "Dr. Porterfield shews, from observation of several anatomists, that the optic nerves do not mix" (2:663).

58. Cf. Joseph Priestley, *History .. Vision.* "The following calculation of M. De Lattire gives us an idea of the extreme sensibility of the optic nerves. One may see very easily, at the distance of 4000 toises [approx. 7600 m.], the sail of a wind-mill, 6 feet in diameter, and, the eye being supposed to be an inch in diameter, the picture of this sail, at the bottom of the eye, will be 1/8000 of an inch. . . . So small, therefore, must one of the fibres of the optic nerve be, which he says is almost inconceivable, since each of these fibres is a tube that contains spirits" (1:208).

59. Tom Vogler first pointed out this connection to me.

60. David Hartley, *Observations on Man, His Frame, His Duty, and His Expectations,* 1:17; another scientific-philosophic work published by Joseph Johnson in the 1790s (it had been first published in 1749). The quotation following is from p. 214.

61. Donald Ault, *Visionary Physics,* p. 147.

62. Quoted in Clarke, "Doctrine of the Hollow Nerve," p. 135. In his *Essays on the Intellectual Powers of Man* (Edinburgh, 1785), Thomas Reid argues: "As to the vibrations and vibratiuncles, whether of an elastic aether, or of the infinitesimal particles of the brain and nerves, there may be such things for what we know; and man may rationally enquire whether they can find any evidence of their existence; but while we have no proof of their existence, to apply them to the solution of phaenomena, and to build a system upon them, is, what I conceive, we call, building a castle in the air" (p. 87). Von Haller notes the controversy, concluding: "But the phenomena of wounded nerves will not allow us to imagine the nervous fibres to be solid" (sect. 376).

6. SPINNING AND WEAVING (THE TEXT, 1)

1. *Ovid's Metamorphoses,* ed. Karl K. Hulley and Stanley T. Vandersall, p. 291.

2. Jonathan Swift, *A Tale of a Tub,* etc., ed. A. C. Guthkelch and D. Nichol Smith, p. 231.

3. Georges Poulet, *The Metamorphoses of the Circle,* p. 55. Leland E. Warren's elementary discussion, "Poetic Vision and the Natural World: The Spider and His Web in the Poetry of William Blake" (*Enlightenment Essays* 6 [1975]:50–62), also notes the relevance of Poulet.

4. Laurence Sterne, *Tristram Shandy,* ed. Howard Anderson, 4.19.

5. Poulet, *The Metamorphoses of the Circle,* p. 55; he is quoting from a poem of Hugo's, and offers another example from Tommaso Guadiosi. Robert Briffault, *The Mothers: A Study of the Origins of Sentiments and Institutions* (New York: Macmillan, 1927), 2:642, offers a number of examples relating the moon to a weaving spider.

6. Northumberland, Pa., 1799; quoted in Kathleen Raine, *Blake and Tradition,* 2:52.

7. Harold Bloom, "Commentary," E958.

8. On the rare Blakean word "squadrons," used only here and slightly before at 75.23, compare the "philosopher's" description of our solar system in M. de Fontenelle's *Conversation on the Plurality of Worlds* (London, 1783): "here all the planets are got

round their sun, in form of a little squadron" (p. 109). A more likely "intertext" is Milton's image that "all the spangled host keep watch in squadrons bright" ("On the Morning of Christ's Nativity," line 21).

9. Morton D. Paley, "The Figure of the Garment in *The Four Zoas, Milton,* and *Jerusalem,*" in *Blake's Sublime Allegory,* ed. Stuart Curran and J. A. Wittreich, Jr., p. 120. This article offers a valuable complement to the present discussion.

10. Paul Mantoux, *The Industrial Revolution in the Eighteenth Century,* p. 191.

11. Jenny is the feminine of "Jack" and so a name for everywoman; the name illustrates both the inevitable association of women and spinning, and their depersonalization into engines. These associations and their history govern Yeats's haunting fragment:

> *Locke sank into a swoon;*
> *The Garden died;*
> *God took the spinning-jenny*
> *Out of his side.*

12. See, further, Julia de L. Mann, "The Textile Industry: Machinery for Cotton, Flax, Wool, 1760–1850," and W. English, "The Textile Industry: Silk Production and Manufacture, 1750–1900," in *A History of Technology,* vol. 4, *The Industrial Revolution, ca. 1750 to ca. 1850,* ed. Charles Singer et al. (London: Oxford University Press, 1958), pp. 277–307, 308–27.

13. These figures are taken from Mantoux, p. 252; the quotation following appears on p. 251.

14. George Rudé, *Hanoverian London, 1714–1808,* p. 140.

15. *Thomas Taylor the Platonist: Selected Writings,* ed. Kathleen Raine and George Mills Harper, p. 305. "Concerning the Cave of the Nymphs" was published by 1789.

16. Sigmund Freud, *Totem and Taboo,* in *The Standard Edition* 13:132.

17. Quoted in Raine, *Blake and Tradition,* 1:92, n. 41.

18. Deirdre Toomey notes that the position of the women in this plate is taken from an engraving of *Le Tre Parche* after Il Rosso Fiorentino (Morton D. Paley and Deirdre Toomey, "Two Pictorial Sources for *Jerusalem* 25," *Blake Newsletter* 5 [1971–72]:188–89).

19. Cf. Blake's illustration to Gray's "Ode on the Death of a Favorite Cat," no. 4, which shows behind the cat an old woman about to cut its thread; note also *The Arlington Court Picture,* lower left.

20. Quoted in Jacob Grimm, *Teutonic Mythology,* trans. James Steven Stallybras (1883; rpt. New York: Dover, 1966), 1:406.

21. Note that **teks,* "weaving," perhaps via woven "wicker or wattle work" (cf. the "Wicker Idol woven round," *J* 38[43].65), is also the root for building and craft generally: architect, tectonic, technique.

22. The importance of "The Fatal Sisters" for Blake was first seen by Paul Miner, who concludes:

> The direct and connotative relations between Blake's symbols and those of Gray's *The Fatal Sisters* are striking. Blake's Albion has twelve daughters who weave at a loom of

blood and death; these twelve females weave a crimson web of war; the web of the fatal weavers is composed of viscera. Blake's "daughters" often have a Valkyrie-like role, combining the slaughter and the rescue of warriors. Gray's poem appears to have had a crucial place in the development of Blake's later symbolism.

["William Blake: Two Notes on Sources," *Bulletin of the New York Public Library* 62 (1958):206]

23. This material would have been available to Blake through Charles Cordiner's English translation of Gray's source, in "Extracts from Torfaeus," *Antiquities and Scenery of the North of Scotland*, etc. (London, 1780), pp. 128-69; Cordiner identifies the women further as "spectres employed about a loom" (p. 143).

24. Reproduced in Raine, *Blake and Tradition*, 1:90.

25. For Paley also, "Cathedron must have a degree of personal reference" ("The Figure of the Garment," p. 125). Perhaps "Dranthon" (*FZ* 63.11, E343) offers a near anagram of "Cathedron."

26. *The Temple of Nature* 3.420–22.

27. Elmer G. Suhr, *The Spinning Aphrodite: The Evolution of the Goddess from Earliest Pre-Hellenic Symbolism Through Late Classical Times*, p. 5, the quotations following are taken from pp. 92 and 52.

28. Erdman, *The Illuminated Blake*, p. 379.

29. *Encyclopaedia Britannica*, 1st ed., s.v. "shuttle."

30. *The Illuminated Blake*, p. 379. Note the position of the moon parallel with Enitharmon's womb, just as the sun adjoins the head of the Spectre of Urthona. The vital mediating function of the moon is discussed by Hugo Rahner, S.J. in *Greek Myths and Christian Mystery*; he writes that the moon "receives the light of the sun, transforms it after the manner of a mother and so, as mistress of all waters upon the earth, brings new life into the world" (p. 161).

31. In *Jerusalem* we see "the Distaff & Spindle in the hands of Vala" (*J* 64.32).

32. This suggests, of course, the important Swedenborgian idea of a "spiritual sun" that operates through its manifest correspondences in the physical world.

33. I discuss this in more detail in "The Sweet Science of Atmospheres in *The Four Zoas*," *Blake* 12 (1978): 80–86.

34. Norman O. Brown, *Love's Body*, p. 74; he quotes this passage.

35. *All's Well That Ends Well*, act 4, sc. 3, lines 71–72.

36. Cf. William Hayley, *The Triumphs of Temper* 5.279–82:

Rapture and agony in nature's loom
Have form'd the changing tissue of their doom;
Both interwoven with so nice an art,
No power can tear the twisted threads apart.

37. Cf. Erasmus Darwin, *The Temple of Nature* 2.297–304:

Erewhile the changeful worm, with circling head,
Weaves the nice curtains of his silken bed;
Web within web involves his larva form,
Alike secured from sunshine and from storm;
For twelve long days He dreams of blossom'd groves,

Untasted honey, and ideal loves;
Wakes from his trance, alarm'd with young Desire,
Finds his new sex, and feels ecstatic fire.

See also Edward J. Rose, "Blake's Human Insect: Symbol, Theory, and Design," *Texas Studies in Literature and Language* 10 (1968): 215–32.

38. This issue is one of intentionality and emphasis. For Rose, "Man the human insect can never escape the womb-tomb *he* has woven round himself in the nightmare sleep of space-time and history, can never be hatched from the mundane egg *unless the artist* broods over that womb-tomb-egg in order to bring forth the winged life *according to the image of imagination or divine vision*" ("Blake's Human Insect," p. 217; emphasis added). My point is that the "womb-tomb-egg" is, in a word, a chrysalis, and so inherently destined for ultimate (nuclear, perhaps) transformation; not even the artist can assume the "Universal Characteristics" (*J* 90.32) and imagine being after the transformation; he only sees the weaving into which he also was born and from that perceives *some* outlines of a larger design.

39. Why is the characterization of an association as being "far-fetched" a criticism? Are we only to credit those modest, close-to-home connections falling entirely within our own assumptions?

40. One "intertext" is the account of the "mystical dance" of the planets in *Paradise Lost* (5.620–24), which was borrowed by Young for *Night Thoughts:*

Their dance perplex'd exhibits to the sight
Fair hieroglyphic of His peerless power.
Mark how the labyrinthine turns they take,
The circles intricate, and mystic maze,
Weave the grand cipher of omnipotence;
To gods, how great! how legible to man!

[9.1157–62]

41. Robert Fludd, *Mosaicall Philosophy* (London, 1659), speaks of "this Dedalian labyrinth the seminall form" (p. 167), while Blackmore praises Harvey as "Albion's pride" that "didst first the winding way, / And circling live's dark labyrinth display" (*The Creation* 6.479–80).

42. *Essay on Man* 2.42; "An Epilogue, To Be Spoken at the Theatre-Royal" (line 37).

43. Brown, *Love's Body,* p. 74.

44. John Dyer, *The Fleece* 4.141–42.

45. Mary Dorothy George, *London Life in the Eighteenth Century,* p. 183; Place (1824) is quoted on p. 195.

46. On this point and its complicated context, see Lawrence Stone's essential study, *The Family, Sex and Marriage In England 1500–1800* (New York: Harper & Row, 1977).

47. W. H. Stevenson, annotator, *The Poems of William Blake,* p. 750 (regarding *J* 59.35).

48. Quoted by Mantoux, *The Industrial Revolution in the Eighteenth Century,* p. 238.

49. Great Britain, *Minutes of Evidence Taken before the Select Committee on the State of Children employed in the Manufactories of the United Kingdom* (ordered by the House of

Commons, 1816), p. 9. The working conditions were such that another witness remarked that, put to the choice, he would rather send his four daughters to prison for seven years than to the cotton-mill (p. 122). Blake might have taken a somewhat personal interest in this hearing as one of the principal witnesses was Josiah Wedgewood, Jr., whom Blake had met and corresponded with the preceding year, and drawings for whose catalogue he was in the process of engraving (see G. E. Bentley, Jr., *Blake Records,* pp. 238–41).

50. "Memoires of William Hawes, M.D.," quoted in George, *London Life in the Eighteenth Century,* p. 187. For a detailed study of the weavers during these decades, see E. P. Thompson, *The Making of the English Working Class,* pp. 269–313.

51. This single instance of "needle" in *Jerusalem,* together with Albion's following remark to Jerusalem, "I look into thy bosom / I discover thy secret places" (21.18–19), evokes Lowth's commentary on Psalm 139:15:

> In that most perfect ode, which celebrates the immensity of the Omnipresent Deity, and the wisdom of the divine Artificer in forming the human body, the author uses a metaphor derived from the most subtile art of the Phrygian workman:
>
> *"When I was formed in the secret place,*
> *"When I was wrought with a needle in the depths of the earth."*
>
> Whoever observes this, (in truth he will not be able to observe it in the common translations) and at the same time reflects upon the wonderful mechanism of the human body, the various implications of the veins, arteries, fibres, and membranes; the "undescribable texture" of the whole fabric; may, indeed, feel the beauty and gracefulness of this well-adapted metaphor, but will miss much of its force and sublimity, unless he be apprized that the art of designing in needlework was wholly dedicated to the use of the sanctuary, and, by a direct precept of the divine law, chiefly employed in furnishing a part of the sacerdotal habit, and the veils for the entrance to the tabernacle. Thus, the poet compares the wisdom of the divine Artificer with the most estimable of human arts, that art which was dignified by being consecrated altogether to the use of religion.
>
> [*Lectures on the Sacred Poetry of the Hebrews* (1787), 1:175–76]

52. Cf. Poulet, *The Metamorphoses of the Circle,* p. 67.

53. Pope, trans., *Odyssey* 8.324 regarding Vulcan's net.

54. Cf. Thomas Taylor's opaque translation of *The Cratylus* (p. 9):

> soc. A name, therefore, is an instrument endued with a power of teaching, and distinguishing the essence of a thing, in the same manner as a shuttle with respect to the web.
> herm. Certainly.
> soc. But is not the shuttle textorial?
> herm. How should it not?

See also Geoffrey H. Hartman's essay, "The Voice of the Shuttle: Language from the Point of View of Literature," *Beyond Formalism* (New Haven, Conn.: Yale University Press, 1970), pp. 337–55.

7. VEIL, VALE, AND VALA (THE TEXT, 2)

1. *De Iside et Osiride: Graece et Anglice*, Samuel Squire, trans. (Cambridge, 1744), p. 11.

2. Ralph Cudworth, *The True Intellectual System of the Universe* (London, 1678), p. 343.

3. *The Mystical Initiations; or, Hymns of Orpheus* (1787), in *Thomas Taylor the Platonist*, ed. Kathleen Raine and G. M. Harper, p. 221; note the central figure of Athena-Minerva in the Arlington Court picture (fig. 24), one of Blake's most dramatic veiled goddesses.

4. Charles Blount took his cue from this for his title, *Great Is DIANA of the EPHE-SIANS: or, The Original of IDOLATRY, Together with the Politick Institution of the Gentiles Sacrifices* (London, 1680).

5. Michael Sandivogius, *A New Light of Alchymie* (London, 1650), p. x.

6. Eighteenth-century feminine "charms" are usually sexual, as, for example, in Hayley's incredible lines about a youthful "festive night" remembered by Sir Gilbert:

> When Ch——h's charms amaz'd the public sight;
> When the fair kind one, in a veil so thin
> That the clear gauze was but a lighter skin,
> Mask'd like a virgin just prepar'd to die,
> Gave her plump beauties to each greedy eye!

> [*The Triumphs of Temper*, 4.86–90]

7. Florence Sandler, "The Iconoclastic Enterprise: Blake's Critique of 'Milton's Religion,'" *Blake Studies* 5 (1972):15.

8. John Robinson, *Proofs of a Conspiracy against All the Religions and Governments of Europe* (1797–98), cited in Irwin Primer, "Erasmus Darwin's *Temple of Nature*: Progress, Evolution, and the Eleusinian Mysteries," *Journal of the History of Ideas* 25 (1964):70–71.

9. Neville Rogers, *Shelley at Work: A Critical Inquiry*, 2nd ed. (Oxford: Clarendon Press, 1967), p. 120.

10. Richard Harter Fogle, *The Imagery of Keats and Shelley: A Comparative Study* (Chapel Hill: University of North Carolina Press, 1949), p. 239; Jerome J. McGann, "Shelley's Veils: A Thousand Images of Loveliness," in *Romantic and Victorian: Studies in Memory of William H. Marshall*, ed. W. Paul Elledge and Richard L. Hoffman (Rutherford, N.J.: Fairleigh Dickinson University Press, 1971), p. 216.

11. *Prometheus Unbound* 4.81–82; the quotation in the following sentence is from the sonnet, "Lift not the painted veil. . . ."

12. One might also think here of Coleridge's "Abyssinian maid" and the entwined deep themes of poetic and sexual creation that she represents.

13. Freud, "The Uncanny," in *The Standard Edition*, 17:245.

14. A possibility supported by the standard association of "curtain" and "bed" owing to the design of the latter: "The curtains of their beds" (E436).

15. Robert F. Gleckner writes of "A Little Girl Lost," "The whole is a dramatization of the 'curtain of flesh' which is ever 'on the bed of our desire' (*Thel*). For the first time Ona sees that curtain; the fear she lost momentarily in the secret amour now returns tenfold in the face of the real reason for that fear" [i.e., her sire] (*The Piper and The Bard*, p. 261).

16. William Wollaston, *The Religion of Nature Delineated,* 8th ed. (London, 1759), p. 338. On the same page Wollaston argues that Herodotus' opinion "'that a woman should put off modesty with her cloaths' ought not to be true."

17. Cf. Fanny Hill's observations on prostituting herself as a "virgin": "it is incredible how little it seemed necessary to strain my natural disposition to modesty higher, in order to pass it upon him for that of a very maid: all my looks and gestures ever breathed nothing but that innocence which the men so ardently require of us, for no other end than to feast themselves with the pleasures of destroying it, and which they are so grievously, with all their skill, subject to mistakes in" (John Cleland, *Memoirs of Fanny Hill* [1779], p. 159).

18. Robert J. Stoller, *Sexual Excitement* (New York: Pantheon Books, 1979), p. 17.

19. Winifred Jenkins's pun in the last letter of Smollet's *The Expedition of Humphry Clinker* (1771).

20. "His [God's] snows fall on me and cover me, while in the Veil I fold / My dying limbs" (*J* 23.35–36); cf. "On the Morning of Christ's Nativity," where Nature "woos the gentle Air / To hide her guilty front with innocent Snow, / And on her naked shame . . . The Saintly Vail of Maiden white to throw" (38–40, 42).

21. With the exception of the Song of Solomon 5:7, "vail" is the spelling used throughout the AV Old Testament; with the exception of 2 Cor. 3:13 ff. (referring to Moses' vail), "veil" is the spelling in the AV New Testament.

22. Raphael Patai relates a tradition from the *Tosefta* that "the staves that were used to carry the Ark during the wanderings grew longer in the sanctuary, until they reached the curtain that separated The Holy of Holies from the Holy Hall before it and caused the Veil to protrude as the two breasts of a woman" (*Man and Temple In Ancient Jewish Myth and Ritual,* 2nd ed. [New York: Ktav Publishing, 1967], p. 91).

23. Eric Partridge, *A Dictionary of Slang and Unconventional English,* 5th ed., s.v. "Holy of Holies."

24. See, in particular, Paul Miner's article, "William Blake's 'Divine Analogy'," *Criticism* 3 (1963):46–61, which discusses in detail "the rich 'enamel' of sexual context that Blake overlaid upon the symbolism of ark, tabernacle, and covenant."

25. Hence the importance Blake attaches to the *linen* clothes left behind in the sepulchre after the resurrection (*MHH* 3; *Am* 6.2; *M* 32.42).

26. Modern scholars have realized that "Paul is . . . attempting to introduce into congregations on Greek soil a custom which corresponds to oriental and especially Jewish sensibility rather than Greek" (Albrecht Oepke in *The Theological Dictionary of the New Testament,* ed. Gerhard Kittel and Gerhard Friedrich, 3:563). A young Iranian, quoted in the Los Angeles *Times,* July 9, 1980, epitomizes the "oriental" attitude: "We want an Islamic covering for women, one that will not stimulate men, that will cover the curves of a woman's body and hide her hair" (p. 26). This position is little different from that of the Church "Fathers" as represented by Tertullian: "Oro te, sive mater, sive soror, sive filia virgo . . . vela caput . . . omnes in te aetates periclitantur. Indue armanturam pudoris, circumdue vallum vercundiae, murum sexui tuo strue, qui nec tuo emmitat oculos, nec admittat alienos" ("*De virginibus velendis,*" in *Patrologiae Cursus Completus,* series latinae, ed. J.-P. Migne, 221 vols. [Paris, 1844], 2:911 ["I pray of you, whether mother or sister or virgin daughter . . . veil your head . . . all ages are perilled in

your person. Put on the armour of modesty; surround yourself with the rampart of bashfulness; build a wall around your sex, through which you cannot glance, nor admit the glances of others"]).

27. Florence Sandler makes the key point that "the sexual power of women should be taken not as the content of the Mystery but rather as another manifestation, along with the temple, of the perverse self-will and the false claim to ultimacy asserted by the contingent that frustrate Spirit and Imagination" ("The Iconoclastic Enterprise," p. 40).

28. Cf. Alberti's *On Painting,* where he tells of his invention of the "veil," which is set up "between the eye and the object to be represented, so that the visual pyramid passes through the loose weave of the veil. . . . this veil affords the greatest assistance in executing your picture, since you can see any object that is round and in relief, represented on the flat surface of the veil" (section 31). Appropriately for Blake's concept of veils, Alberti is considered "the inventor of the theory of fixed-point perspective in painting"—seeing with, not through, the veil (Leon Battista Alberti, *On Painting and On Sculpture,* ed. and trans. with notes by Cecil Grayson [London: Phaidon, 1972], pp. 69, 13).

29. Philo and Josephus recount in detail the supposed correspondences; Josephus in particular observes, "The curtains with the four colours of their materials represent the four elements. The linen may signify the earth from whence it was derived, and the purple the sea. . . . The violet colour is a symbol of the air, and the scarlet of the fire" (*Jewish Antiquities* 3.7, in *The Whole Genuine and Complete Works of Flavius Josephus,* trans. G. H. Maynard, p. 41—this work had three engravings by Blake).

30. Note again Winifred Jenkins in *Humphry Clinker,* who asks, "What is life but a veil of affliction?" and refers to the "veil of tares" (pp. 188, 381).

31. In a passage from *Paradise Lost* that evidently impressed Blake (cf. also *N* 91), flames driven back from Satan "leave i' th' midst a horrid Vale" (1.224).

32. Helkiah Crooke, ΜΙΚΡΟΚΟΣΜΟΓΡΑΦΙΑ: *A Description of the Body of Man* (London, 1651), etymologizes: "*Vulva,* as it were *vallis,* a valley" (p. 175). Cf. John Cleland's *Fanny Hill*: "Her posteriours . . . splendidly filled the eye, till it was commanded down the parting or separation of those exquisitely white cliffs, by their narrow vale, and was there stopped, and attracted by the embowered bottom-cavity" (pp. 145–46).

33. Sandler speculates on the possibility of a pun with "Vale" ("The Iconoclastic Enterprise," p. 15).

34. See S. Foster Damon, *A Blake Dictionary,* p. 428.

35. Pope, *The Odyssey of Homer,* Books 1–12, pp. 30, 175.

36. Letter, Oct. 18, 1801, in Bentley, *Blake Records,* p. 84; Hayley uses the phrase again in a letter of January 1802 (p. 89); Blake's observations are in letters of Sept. 23, 1800 and May 10, 1801.

37. See *Paulys Real-Encyclopädie der klassischen Altertumswissenschaft* (1937), vol. 10, pt. 2, cols. 1772–99; see also Hermann Güntert, *Kalypso: Bedeutungsgeschichtliche Untersuchungen auf dem Gebiet der indogermanischen Sprachen* (Halle, 1919), pp. 31 ff., 61 ff.

38. Leon E. Seltzer, ed., *The Columbia Lippincott Gazetteer of the World* (New York: Columbia University Press, 1952), s.v. "Dovedale." In "The Wonders of the Peake,"

Charles Cotton characterizes the area around Mam-Tor as "a country so deform'd, the Traveller / Would swear those Parts Nature's Pudenda were" (*The Genuine Poetical Works of Charles Cotton Esq.,* 6th ed. [London, 1771], p. 299).

39. Cf. Thomas Denton's *Immortality* (1755):

> *This fibrous Frame by Nature's kindly Law,*
>   *Which gives each Joy to keen Sensation here,*
> *O'er purer Scenes of Bliss the Veil may draw,*
>   *And cloud Reflection's more exalted Sphere.*

[27.1–4]

8. SPECTRES (THE TEXT, 3)

1. Susan Fox, *Poetic Form in Blake's Milton,* p. 4.

2. "The Giants & the Witches & the Ghosts of Albion" (*J* 63.13); the word also appears in the title and stage direction of *The Ghost of Abel.*

3. Cf. Nathan Drake, writing "On Superstition" in 1798: "Of the various kinds of superstition which have in any age influenced the human mind, none appear to have operated with so much effect as what has been termed the Gothic. Even in the present polished period of society, there are thousands who are yet alive to all the horrors of witchcraft, to all the solemn and terrible graces of the spectre" (*Literary Hours,* 1: 137–38).

4. W. H. Stevenson notes that the word "does not hold one meaning at all times. It is an image with many connotations, rather than an exact symbol" (*Blake: The Complete Poems,* p. 635).

5. Pierre Le Loyer, *A Treatise of Spectres; or, Straunge Sights,* etc., trans. Zachery Jones (London, 1605), p. 1.

6. *Essays on the Intellectual Powers of Man,* p. 26; the sensible species of Aristotle, by contrast, were "in the mind itself . . . mere forms without matter" (pp. 25–26). Lucretius, *De Rerum Natura* 4.26 ff., offers a detailed discussion of these films or "*membranae.*" Note that the concept of "being sent forth" also governs the operation of "emanation."

7. The *OED* cites the "Spectre of the Brocken" (1801), an atmospherically produced optical illusion. Hobbes refers to "the Apparitions men see in the Dark, or in a Dream, or Vision; which the Latines call *Spectra,* and took for *Daemons*" (*Leviathan* 4.45).

8. I quote from *The Monk* by Matthew Lewis (p. 169) not only because of its considerable popularity in the last years of the eighteenth century, but also because we can assume that William and Catherine read it (a painting of a scene from the novel, "Agnes and her baby," by Catherine and dating to 1800, is in the collection of Sir Geoffrey Keynes).

9. *Letters on a Regicide Peace* (1796), in *The Works and Correspondence of the Right Honorable Edmund Burke,* new ed., 8 vols. (London, 1852), 5:256.

10. Patricia Meyer Spacks, *The Insistence of Horror,* pp. 113, 183.

11. Note that there are no "spectres" in Night the Second or Night the Third and that a single instance of "spectrous" is an added revision. The two references in Night

the Seventh (b) as against the thirty-six in Night the Seventh (a) are additional evidence of the later date of (a).

12. Cf. *PL* 1.490, 679; 2.44; 4.793; Blake's Satan later becomes a spectre.

13. Compare also Hercules' "grim visage" (11.760) and Urthona's "dread visage" (75.16); when Hercules departs, he "stalk'd with giant strides away" (11.774).

14. Blake uses analogous imagery annotating Robert Thornton: "Spirit is the Ghost of Matter or Nature & God is The Ghost of the Priest & King who Exist whereas God exists not except for [*them*] ⟨their Effluvia⟩" (E669).

15. See David V. Erdman, "The Suppressed and Altered Passages in Blake's *Jerusalem*," p. 24, n. 23 (quoting Karl Kiralis). The Bible uses "feet" as a euphemism for both male and female genitals (Deut. 28:57; Ruth 3:4; Song of Songs 5:3; Judges 3:24).

16. *FZ* 113.7, E376; this imagery may be associated with Urizen's prophecy, "When Thought is closd in Caves. Then love shall shew its root in deepest Hell" (*FZ* 65.12, E344)—as the caves evoke the skulls of thought, so the "root" suggests the organ and origin of fallen love.

17. G. E. Bentley, Jr., *Blake Records*, p. 259.

18. Edward J. Rose, "Blake and the Double: The Spectre as *Doppelgänger*," *Colby Library Quarterly* 13 (1977):127–39, discusses "Blake's anticipation of Romanticism's interest in the double" and characterizes the spectre as "the dark half of the soul divided into a seemingly separate and independent being" (pp. 138, 130).

19. On this issue, see also Leopold Damrosch's illuminating remarks in *Symbol and Truth in Blake's Myth*, pp. 268–72.

20. Morton D. Paley, "The Truchsessian Gallery Revisited," *Studies in Romanticism* 16 (1977):165–77, reviews the pictures Blake would have seen in the gallery and discusses Blake's experience in the face of "the Continent" as a reconfirmation of "his artistic faith" in his own uncompromising style. Paley points to the "associative process at work" in the letter, which, he argues, takes off from a reference to a Mr. Hawkins, who had tried to raise money to send Blake to Rome in 1784.

21. The spectre becomes another of those reciprocal relations (like Orc and Urizen, above, chapter 4) that characterize Blake's vision; like other reciprocal elements, they are both part of the same class.

22. Cf.: "Why should the Divine Vision compell the sons of Eden / to forego each his own delight to war against his Spectre" (*FZ* 12.27–28, E307); the spectre of Urthona argues, "be assurd I am thy real Self / Tho thus divided from thee" (*FZ* 85.35–36, E368).

23. John Sutherland also notes this connection, observing that, "It seems possible that Blake, after his father's death, may have moved a perceptible step further away from the visionary openness of his youth" ("Blake and Urizen," in *Blake's Visionary Forms Dramatic*, ed. David V. Erdman and John E. Grant, p. 246).

24. Alexander Gilchrist, *Life of William Blake*, p. 37; Bentley considers this to be "unreliably reported" (*Blake Records*, p. 24). Blake married in 1782.

25. Cf. Leopold Damrosch, Jr.: "But the son's guilt at hostility toward his father might well have been intensified by the recognition that his father was well-meaning and kind, for it is precisely the loving father, according to Blake, who imposes guilt" (*Symbol and Truth in Blake's Myth*, p. 270).

26. Ronald Paulson, "The Spectres of Blake and Rowlandson," *The Listener* 90 (2 August 1793):140; for John Sutherland, "the chief antagonists in Blake's psychological dramas" for the twenty years up to 1804, "can be generalized as repressive father figures of one sort or another" ("Blake and Urizen," p. 247).

27. Adam Smith, *The Theory of Moral Sentiments*, etc., 6th ed., 2 vols. (London, 1790), 1:77, 286, 287, 337, 360–61, and 465. Blake would also have encountered the idea of the "impartial spectator" through William Godwin's frequent reference to it in the *Enquiry Concerning Political Justice* (1st ed. London, 1793). P. Berger, *William Blake, Poet and Mystic*, trans. Daniel H. Conner (1914; rpt. New York, 1968), discusses the spectre as "conscience": "Little by little, he has become our conscience, has gained such possession of us that he has stifled all that made our own personality; and now he seems actually to be the whole man" (p. 113).

28. Morton D. Paley, "Cowper as Blake's Spectre," *Eighteenth-Century Studies* 1 (1968):236–52, argues that the spectre in plate 10 of *Jerusalem* presents "a Calvinist who believes himself irrevocably damned by a God of wrath and doomed to suffer forever" (p. 236), a type best represented by Cowper.

29. The fallen zoas exclaim, "Why should we enter into our Spectres, to behold our own corruptions" (*J* 38[43].10)—through spectre-perception we see our "moral failings."

30. In "Authority, Guilt, and Anxiety in *The Theory of Moral Sentiments*," R. F. Brissenden remarks that "Almost alone among eighteenth-century moral theoreticians [Adam Smith] has an awareness of guilt; and this awareness of guilt is related, to use the Freudian terminology, to 'tension between the demands of conscience and the actual performances of the ego'" (p. 951). Norman O. Brown notes the larger implications of the spectre in *Love's Body*:

> Christian personality remains a self-dramatization of the son enacted before the eyes of the heavenly father. In the sight of this spectator, personality ceases to be a social or political role (we take from our earthly fathers to give to our heavenly father); all performers are immediate and unique, the distinction between public and private disappears; we are on stage all the time. Christianity will not be rid of the performance principle, will not become a pure principle of invisible grace, until it gets rid of the spectre of the Father, Old Nobodaddy, the watching institution. [p. 106]

31. Lewis, *The Monk*, p. 160. Patricia Spacks observes that eighteenth-century spectres "frequently have 'eyes that blast the sick'ning moon'" (*The Insistence of Horror*, p. 85). In Dryden's *Aeneid*, "the spectre stares . . . with erected eyes" (1.487–88), while in James Ralph's *Night* (London, 1729) we see "rising *Spectres* with a dreadful glare" (p. 66).

32. *The Theory of Moral Sentiments*, 1:482; Brissenden believes that Smith's "major contribution to the development of moral theory lies in the use he made of the notion of sympathy. It was, he asserted, a basic fact of existence that the individual human being is able somehow to enter imaginatively into the feelings of his fellows. Indeed to a great extent this imaginative participation is involuntary" ("Authority, Guilt, and Anxiety in *The Theory of Moral Sentiments*," p. 946).

33. Knight offers a typical description in *A Discourse on the Worship of Priapus*: "It was the celestial or aetherial principle of the human mind, which the ancient artists

represented under the symbol of the butterfly, which may be considered as one of the most elegant allegories of their ancient religion. . . . The Greek artists, always studious of elegance, changed this, as well as other animal symbols, into a human form, retaining the wings as the characteristic members, by which the meaning might be known" (pp. 194–95). For another retelling of the image, see my discussion in "The Spectre of Darwin," *Blake: An Illustrated Quarterly* 15(1981):43.

34. "Filthy thoughts, which evil spirits inflict"; G. P. Valeriano Bolzani, *Hieroglyphica* (1602), The Renaissance and the Gods, no. 17, ed. Stephen Orgel (New York: Garland Publishing, 1976), p. 252. Goya's famous design, "El sueño de la razón produce monstruos" (1796–98) is dominated by bats coming to roost on the sleeper.

35. Geoffrey Keynes, ed., *William Blake's Water-Colour Designs for the Poems of Thomas Gray* (Paris: Trianon Press, 1971), p. 3.

36. 1st ed. (1771), s.v. "vespertilio."

37. Erdman, *Prophet Against Empire*, p. 234.

38. Bentley, *Blake Records*, p. 48.

39. Stedman, *Narrative*, 2:298, 299 (no such blood-sucking bat is, in fact, known).

40. Erdman notes, "the red-winged spectre still darkens communication; indeed vision can transpose his bat wings and ravenous head into the dove wings and red globe supporting Albion's right foot" (*The Illuminated Blake*, p. 312).

41. Erdman describes it as "fatuously kissing or nibbling at the toes" (*The Illuminated Blake*, p. 350).

42. Ernest Jones, *On the Nightmare* (New York: Liveright, 1971), p. 120; Knight, *Discourse on the Worship of Priapus*, p. 18. Jones relates that "according to Quedenfeldt, south of the Atlas mountains there prevails the belief that there are old negresses who at night suck blood from the *toes* of those asleep. The Armenian mountain spirit Dachnavar similarly sucks blood from the *feet* of wanderers" (pp. 119–20).

43. Cf. in the *Illustrations to Gray*, "Ode on the Death of a Favorite Cat," design no. 7; *Jerusalem*, pl. 25 (fig. 11, above), and *America*, pl. 6.

44. Erdman, *The Illuminated Blake*, p. 279, and George Wingfield Digby, *Symbol and Image in William Blake* (Oxford: Clarendon Press, 1957), p. 53.

45. *Midsummer Night's Dream*, 3.2.364–65.

46. John Wolcott ("Peter Pindar"), "The Lousiad," canto 3, in *The Works of Peter Pindar, Esq.* (London, 1794), 1:269.

47. Róheim, *The Gates of the Dream* (New York: International Universities Press, 1952), p. 58.

48. Janet Warner, "Blake's Figures of Despair: Man in His Spectre's Power," in *William Blake*, ed. Morton D. Paley and Michael Phillips, observes that "Blake came to associate Despair with a reasoning power cut off from Imagination," and that "the Spectre is both the 'Reasoning Power in Man' and the Despair which such reasoning brings about" (p. 214).

49. Michel Foucault, *Language, Counter-Memory, Practice*, trans. and ed. Donald F. Bonchard (Ithaca, N.Y.: Cornell University Press, 1977), p. 168.

50. *King Lear*, 3.4.156; cf. Blake's own "spectrous Fiend," discussed above.

51. In one of his "Illustration to Melancholy. Pensieroso," Blake writes that "the Spirits . . . are seen under the domination of Insects" (E685).

52. Rose correctly stresses this: "[Blake's] training and occupation as a printer, taken together with his insights into human psychology, makes him keenly aware of the doubleness and the relation of that doubleness to the idea of the other self. Furthermore, the process by which the image on the copper plate is reversed as it is transferred to the paper is never far removed from his consciousness. Every image has its inverted counterpart, every world a shadow world, every man his spectre" ("Blake and the Double," p. 127).

9. STARS AND OTHER BRIGHT WORDS

1. For a sampling, see Winston Weathers, ed. *The Tyger*, Literary Casebook Series (Indianapolis: Bobbs-Merrill, 1969).

2. Cf. Jacob Boehme, *Aurora* 25.19, in the Law ed. 1:218; "deeps" and "skies" suggest the analogy of Latin *altum*, which could be used to translate them both. In Blake's "To Summer," noon rides "o'er the deep of heaven," and in *The Book of Los*, the sun is cast "down into the Deeps" but "the Deep fled away . . . and left an unform'd / Dark vacuity" (5.43, 48–50).

3. On the questions as exclamations, see E. L. Epstein's discussion of "The Tyger" in "The Self-Reflexive Artefact: An Approach to a Theory of Value in Literature," in *Style and Structure in Literature: Essays in the New Stylistics*, ed. R. Fowler (Ithaca, N.Y.: Cornell University Press, 1975):40–78.

4. John E. Grant, "Reading Blake's Lyrics: 'The Tyger,'" in *Discussions of William Blake*, ed. John E. Grant (Boston: Heath, 1961), p. 70.

5. *Mysterium Magnum* 12.24–27, 10.32.

6. Jacob Boehme, *The Threefold Life of Man* 7.73, in *Works*, ed. William Law, 2:77.

7. "To the Evening Star" concludes with just this idea:

The fleeces of our flocks are cover'd with
Thy sacred dew: protect them with thine influence.

[E410]

A more subtle semantic expansion here is "cover'd": "protect" (from Lat. *protegere*, to cover).

8. Oswald Crollius, *Philosophy Reformed*, p. 30; Michael Sandivogius, *A New Light of Alchymie*, trans. J. F. (London, 1650), p. 88.

9. Crollius, *Philosophy Reformed*, p. 30; cf. Boehme, *Threefold Life* 11.38.

10. E. D. Hirsch, Jr., *Innocence and Experience: An Introduction to Blake* (New Haven, Conn.: Yale University Press, 1964), p. 251.

11. Frederick A. Pottle, *The Explicator* 8 (March 1950), item 39. Kathleen Raine followed this four years later: "The tyger grew on earth because the stars rained down their influence—threw down beams of light like 'spears'" ("Who Made the Tyger?", *Encounter* 2 [June 1954], p. 49). This formulation is omitted in her revision of the article for *Blake and Tradition*, 2:3–31.

12. Paul Miner, "'The Tyger': Genesis & Evolution in the Poetry of William Blake," *Criticism* 4 (1962):59 (emphasis added).

13. Newton had suggested that comets had an important role in the economy of the universe, refueling stars and replenishing atmospheres by importing cometary material, an idea versified by Thomson, who speculates that each comet "his long ellipses winds," "to lend new fuel to declining suns . . . and feed the eternal fire" (*Summer* 1727–29). Thus when we read of the comets "falling with Wheel impetuous down among Urthonas vales / And round red Orc returning back to Urizen gorgd with blood" (*FZ* 75.28–31, E352), we see that "Terrible Orc" has been subdued into a stellar power plant supplying life-giving "blood" to its local system.

14. Henry More cites Paracelsus for the information "that the Stars are as it were Pots in which the *Archeus* or heavenly *Vulcan* prepares pluvious matter, which exhaled from thence first appears in the form of clouds, after condenses to rain" ("A Brief Discourse of Enthusiasm" in *A Collection of Several Philosophical Writings of Dr. Henry More,* 2nd ed., separate pagination [London, 1662], sect. 45, p. 32).

15. "On Nebulous Stars, Properly So Called," appeared in *Philosophical Transactions* 81 (1791); this is edited and reprinted in Michael A. Hoskin, *William Herschel and the Construction of the Heavens,* Oldbourne History of Science Library (London: Oldbourne, 1963), p. 118; the quotations following are from pp. 125 and 128. This connection was first suggested by William S. Doxey in "William Blake and William Herschel: The Poet, The Astronomer, and 'The Tyger,'" *Blake Studies* 2 (Spring 1970): 5–11. Doxey urges "that the descriptions and arguments of 'The Tyger' lend themselves to a significant astronomical interpretation which questions the nature of the universe" (p. 6).

16. Erdman, "Textual Notes," E791, considers "The Tyger" to have been composed "between 1790 and late 1792."

17. Andrew Marvell, "Eyes and Tears": "Stars shew lovely in the Night, / But as they seem the Tears of Light" (lines 43–44).

18. "Concerning the Cave of the Nymphs," in *Selected Writings,* ed. Kathleen Raine and George Mills Harper, p. 333.

19. Franz Cumont, *Les Religions orientales dans le paganisme romain,* 4th ed. (Paris, 1929), p. 160, my translation.

20. George Stanley Faber, *The Origin of Pagan Idolatry Ascertained from Historical Testimony and Circumstantial Evidence,* 3 vols. (London, 1816), 1:37–38.

21. Marjorie Hope Nicolson, *Mountain Gloom and Mountain Glory: The Development of the Aesthetics of the Infinite* (New York: Norton, 1963), p. 362, observes: "No poet was ever more 'space intoxicated' than Edward Young, nor did any other eighteenth-century poet or aesthetician equal him in his obsession with the 'psychology of infinity'—the effect of vastness and the vast upon the soul of man."

22. William Powell Jones, *The Rhetoric of Science,* pp. 99–103, quotes a number of examples.

23. Ernst Robert Curtius, *European Literature and the Latin Middle Ages,* trans. Willard R. Trask, (New York and Evanston: Harper & Row, 1963), p. 304.

24. G. E. Bentley, Jr., *Blake Records,* p. 263.

25. The last two lines, it might be noted, recognize that the world is not to be imagined as the "flat Earth" mentioned in the intervening lines (29.9) and so often cited as an example of Blake's eccentricity. Macrobius states the obvious fact

that "because the roundness of the earth makes the aspect of localities different, the same part of the sky is not over the heads of all men; so all will not be able to have the same meridian directly overhead" (*Commentary on the Dream of Scipio,* trans. W. H. Stahl, 1.15.16, p. 161).

26. Cf. S. H. Hooke, "The Myth and Ritual Patterns in Jewish and Christian Apocalyptic," in *The Labyrinth:* "We also find the conception that the various territorial divisions of the world in the apocalyptist's time were represented in heaven by angels who, in their relation to one another, reflected the relations, friendly or hostile, that existed between the nations who they represented. . . . This conception corresponds to the early belief in Babylon that the terrestrial divisions of the time were represented in heaven by special stars" (pp. 219–20).

27. See John Bonnycastle, *An Introduction to Astronomy,* p. 331.

28. William Borlase, *Antiquities . . . of Cornwall,* p. 92; see also John Toland, *A Critical History of the Celtic Religion,* pp. 121–22.

29. Edward Davies, *The Mythology and Rites of the British Druids,* p. 302.

30. William Stukeley, *Abury, A Temple of the British Druids,* p. 9. See also Ruthven Todd, *Tracks in the Snow,* pp. 48 ff.

31. *FZ* 93.24, E365; 101.1 ff., E373; 107.2–3, E382.

32. According to Stukeley, the old name of Stonehenge was *choir gaur,* "which some interpret *chorea Gigantum,* or Giant's Dance" (*Concise Account,* p. 7).

33. *The Threefold Life of Man* 11.38, in *Works,* ed. Law, 2:116.

34. See the examples in Jones, *The Rhetoric of Science,* pp. 23, 88, 172; Young praises "the glorious Architect, / In this his Universal temple" (*NT* 9.769–70).

35. See, for example, William Whiston's *Astronomical Principles of Religion, Natural and Revealed,* 2nd ed. (London, 1725).

36. Cf. Jacob Bronowski, *William Blake and the Age of Revolution* (New York: Harper and Row, 1969): "Since Blake made his picture by analogy, we cannot be sure what his universe was. If he drew the analogy from a flat world, his construct is a solid which is an analogue of the surface of a ring. If he drew it from a spherical world, his construct is the solid which is the analogue of the surface of a sphere. Either solid is strikingly such a universe as Blake sought: for both are finite, but have no bounding surfaces" (p. 139).

37. Richard Broxton Onians, *The Origins of Eruopean Thought,* p. 164.

38. See the discussions by D. P. Walker, "The Astral Body in Renaissance Medicine," *Journal of the Warburg and Courtauld Institutes* 21 (Jan.–June 1958): 119–33, and E. R. Dodds, ed., Proclus, *The Elements of Theology,* 2nd ed. (Oxford: Clarendon Press, 1963), appendix 2, "The Astral Body in Neoplatonism," pp. 313–21.

39. The expression "Erring Globes wander" seems a learned play on the etymology of 'planet," from the Greek πλάνητες, meaning "wanderer," and the Latin, *errantes.*

10. WORLD AND TEXT: VORTEX AND WHEEL

1. 'Vertex is also used in astronomy for the point of heaven perpendicularly over our heads, properly called the zenith" (*Encyclopaedia Britannica,* 1st ed. [1771], s.v.). Note that when Milton enters the "vortex" he is seen "in the Zenith" (*M* 15.41, 47).

2. Cf. the following non-Western example: "The Chukchees say that at the Pole Star there is a hole, through which it is possible to pass from one world to another. There are several levels or storeys of worlds, one above the other, and all these worlds are connected with each other by holes situated directly under the Pole Star" (E. A. S. Butterworth, *The Tree at the Navel of the Earth*, p. 4).

3. E. J. Aiton, *The Vortex Theory of Planetary Motions*, p. 34.

4. See Mark Greenberg, "Blake's Vortex," *Colby Library Quarterly* 14 (1978): 198–212. He argues that the term is "polysemous," and suggests that such "symbols are charged with multiple meanings, and their diverse significance must be realized by—indeed, exists only within—the perceiving mind," adding that, "in creating the significance of the symbol for ourselves, we connect abstraction and experience" (pp. 199, 205).

5. *Gaudier-Brzeska: A Memoir* (London, 1916), p. 106.

6. George Devereux, *Dreams in Greek Tragedy: An Ethno-Psycho-Analytical Study* (Oxford: Basil Blackwell, 1976), p. 334. Devereux also cites instances where the "female pubic hair is fantasied as *behaving* like the tentacles of certain marine animals, or like the arms of cephalopods, which sweep their victims into their maw" (p. 334). Erasmus Darwin's *The Temple of Nature* describes the "Vorticella," which "whirls her living wheels" (1.290); the footnote on microscopic organisms explains, "the Vorticella has wheels about its mouth, with which it makes an eddy, as is supposed thus to draw into its throat invisible animalcules" (p. 25).

7. For Leopold Damrosch, Jr., Blake symbolizes "the experiencing self . . . as the 'vortex' of fallen perception" (*Symbol and Truth in Blake's Myth*, p. 33).

8. "William Blake and Erasmus Darwin's *Botanic Garden*," p. 410.

9. "The eye . . . its vortex"; this has occasioned much discussion on the mechanics of vision, beginning with Northrop Frye's analogy of the vortex as "an angle of vision opening into our minds with the apex pointing away from us" (*Fearful Symmetry*, p. 350). This is more properly "parallax," a word that shows up in *Ulysses* as one of *its* perceptual hints to the reader. Donald Ault makes better use of the analogy to vision with his suggestion that "the conical angle of the eye becomes the optical analogue to the cosmological vortex" (*Visionary Physics*, p. 160). The lens of the eye, as could be seen in numerous contemporary diagrams, is the center of a vortex, which indeed changes what is underneath to the above.

10. *Fearful Symmetry*, p. 350.

11. Or, rather, such space is his vortex. In his discussion of Cartesian cosmology, *A Conversation on the Plurality of Worlds*, M. de Fontenelle writes, "I think I have said enough for a man that was never out of his own vortex" (p. 109). In our condition, observes Susan Fox, "all is vortex. The earth itself, the center of our fallen vision, is merely our vortex point . . . a providential calm, the space erected by the eternals" (*Poetic Form in Blake's Milton*, p. 73). Cf. Ronald L. Grimes's image of Urizen living "in the eye of his private hurricane" ("Time and Space in Blake's Major Prophecies," in *Blake's Sublime Allegory*, ed. Stuart Curran and J. A. Wittreich, p. 80).

12. Copy D, British Museum. Cumberland's fascinating annotations are reproduced in S. Foster Damon, *William Blake: His Philosophy and Symbols* (1924, rpt.; Gloucester, Mass.: Peter Smith, 1958), pp. 348–51; see also G. E. Bentley, Jr., *Blake Books*, pp. 158–59.

13. *Poetic Form in Blake's Milton*, p. 74; she concludes "that the womb is in the bosom of Albion reflects Los's giving birth to the Bard's Song."

14. In *The Four Zoas* each of the "stars of heaven . . . took his station" (33.16, 18, E322), while the conclusion to *The Ghost of Abel* sees "the Elohim . . . each in his station fixt in the Firmament" (2.25–26; cf. *PL* 7.563).

15. *Selected Writings*, ed. Kathleen Raine and George Mills Harper, p. 316.

16. Quoted in Hirst, *Hidden Riches*, p. 159.

17. *The Illuminated Blake*, p. 217.

18. This is in turn somewhat analogous to Elijah's assumption in 2 Kings 2:1; Los "in his firy whirlwind" is "the Vehicular terror" who "enterd into my soul" (*M* 17.31, 22.13), reminiscent of Ezekiel 3:24: "Then the spirit entered into me. . . ."

19. Albert S. Roe, *Blake's Illustrations to the Divine Comedy*, p. 165.

20. In his article, "Wheels Within Wheels in Blake's *Jerusalem*," *Studies in Romanticism* 11 (1972): 36–47, Edward J. Rose takes the opposite tack. He begins with the assumption that, "by using the Scriptural tropology of Ezekiel's wheels, Blake develops the theoretical basis of biblical symbolism while also expanding upon it." Other wheels (like the "Starry Wheels"), Rose insists on three occasions, must be recognized as Blake's "demonic parody of Ezekiel's wheels" (p. 36, cf. pp. 38, 39).

21. Henry Francis Cary, trans., *The Vision: or, Hell, Purgatory, and Paradise of Dante Alighieri* (1814; rpt. New York: D. Appleton, 1850), *Paradise* 1.62. In an earlier translation, *The Divina Commedia of Dante Alighieri* (London, 1802), Henry Boyd translates the same passage showing Beatrice, "as if she meant to watch in museful mood / The mighty mundane wheel" (1.16.1–2).

22. Cf. Dante in Boyd's translation: "As in a horologe the circles play, / Some running speeding round, while some delay; / So seem'd the glorious Orbs to mix above" (*Paradiso* 24.3.1–3). Fontenelle's *Conversation on the Plurality of Worlds* begins with "the Lady" stating that she values the universe the more "since I know it resembles a watch; and the more plain and easy the whole order of Nature seems, to me it appears to be the more admirable"; we discover that a universe, even of vortexes, can be most mechanical: the vortexes "take hold of one another, like the wheels of a watch, and mutually help each other's motion" (pp. 22, 113).

23. See John Lond, *Capital and Steam-Power, 1750–1800*, 2nd ed. (London: Frank Cass & Co., 1966), pp. 161, 164–65. On the Albion Mill, which ran from 1786 to 1791, when it burned down, see also Bernard Blackstone, *English Blake* (Cambridge: Cambridge University Press, 1949), p. 19, and David V. Erdman's remarks in *Prophet Against Empire*, p. 396, n. 7.

24. This passage may remind us of Urizen's voyage "into the Abyss":

> *Thro lightnings thunders earthquakes & concussions fires & floods*
> *Stemming his downward fall labouring up against futurity*
> *Creating many a Vortex fixing many a Science*

[*FZ* 72.11–13, E349]

25. Cf. Jacob Boehme, *Threefold Life* 10.23, in *Works* (ed. William Law, 2:105): "Thus the Devil dwelleth near us, and yet hath a Princely Dominion much deeper,

nearer towards the Constellations, in the midst (amongst them,) where it is darkest: for he may not come near the shining luster of the Stars: and so he is a Prisoner."

26. At its first appearance, Ulro is a space for the "Circle of Destiny," which is "Round rolld" (*FZ* 5.25, E302).

27. This in itself raises a question, for Apollyon, mentioned once in the Bible as the king over the locusts with scorpion tails, an angel of the bottomless pit (Rev. 9:11), is nowhere associated with a bow. Since the early seventeenth century, however, the name has usually been taken as a play on "Apollo," which opens up the possibility of an association with the memorable, plague-spreading bow that Apollo wields in the opening of the *Iliad*. Blake refers to a heavenly bow for Urizen (a solidification of the rainbow), who sometimes resembles "Phoibos Apollon."

28. "The Myth and Ritual Pattern in Jewish and Christian Apocalyptic," in *The Labyrinth*, p. 220.

29. S. Foster Damon, *A Blake Dictionary*, p. 113.

30. Theodore Schwenk, *Sensitive Chaos: The Creation of Flowing Forms in Water and Air*, trans. Olive Whicher and Johanna Wrigley (New York: Schocken Books, 1978), p. 47.

31. *The Economy of Vegetation*, p. 86, n. 33.

32. Phillip Slater presents a contemporary example: "Sometimes it seems that everything I see is the center of an elaborate pattern—like a magnetic field—that radiates out to infinity. And each of those patterns is formed around a conflict, like a whirlpool formed in a stream by opposing currents. Every shape we see is such a whirlpool—an interruption in the flow of energy, a hanging-on. Some ambivalence makes an elegant little disturbance in the stream—a little eddy—and each has a unique fantastic pattern that radiates and reverberates through the whole universe in an exquisite dance" (*The Wayward Gate: Science and the Supernatural* [Boston: Beacon Press, 1977], p. 193).

33. The strange image of "snowy Whirlwinds" may owe something to Boyd's eccentric translation of *Paradiso* 27.67 ff.: "Soon, as around the snowy whirlwind flies" (15.1); that is, as snow flakes fall on the Earth, so the *"fioccar di vapor triunfanti"* ascend to the heavens. Immediately afterwards, Beatrice tells Dante to look around, to see that his "feet had trac'd the PRIMAL Sphere"—a sphere he is just about to leave ("I rent the veil where the dead dwell," "The Keys of the Gates," line 20).

34. *Mysterium Magnum*, ed. C. J. B., 25.24, p. 169; 25.21, p. 169; the quotations following are from 25.5, 25.6, 7, and 25.17.

35. Morton D. Paley, *Energy and the Imagination*, p. 92.

36. Cf.: "Great Henry's soul shuddered, a whirlwind and fire tore furious from his angry bosom" (*FR* 200); "Perturbed Immortal mad raging / In whirlwinds" (*BU* 8.4–5); "Round the flames roll as Los hurls his chains / Mounting up from his fury, condens'd / Rolling round & round" (*BL* 3. 33–35); "Tharmas like a pillar of sand rolld round by the whirlwind / An animated Pillar rolling round & round in incessant rage" (*FZ* 107.23–24, E383).

37. W. J. T. Mitchell, *Blake's Composite Art*, p. 19.

38. Schwenk nicely characterizes the vortex as a form "enclosed within itself and yet bound up with the whole" (*Sensitive Chaos*, p. 44).

39. Cf. Gershom G. Scholem, *Major Trends in Jewish Mysticism,* 3rd ed. (New York: Schocken Books, 1961): "The earliest Jewish mysticism is throne-mysticism. Its essence is not absorbed contemplation of God's true nature, but perception of His appearance on the throne, as described by Ezekiel, and cognition of the mysteries of the celestial throne-world" (p. 44); see also the same author's *Jewish Gnosticism, Merkabah Mysticism, and Talmudic Tradition,* 2nd ed. (New York: The Jewish Theological Seminary of America, 5725/1965).

40. "*The outward Wheel is the* Zodiac, *with the* Constellations" (Boehme, *Threefold Life* 9.68, in *Works,* ed. Law, 2:94).

41. Mitchell, *Blake's Composite Art,* p. 63.

42. Northrop Frye, "Notes for a Commentary on *Milton,*" in *The Divine Vision,* ed. Vivian De Sola Pinto (London: Gollancz, 1957), p. 133 n.

II. SON OF MYTH, SUN OF LANGUAGE

1. *The Drama of Language* (Baltimore: Johns Hopkins University Press, 1970), p. 1.

2. *The Economy of Vegetation* 1.105 n., italics added.

3. *True Christian Religion,* sect. 777.

4. The quotations are from Leopold Damrosch, Jr., *Symbol and Truth in Blake's Myth,* p. 94, and W. H. Stevenson, annotator, *The Poems of William Blake,* p. 494.

5. Jean Starobinski, *Les Mots sous les mots: Les Anagrammes de Ferdinand de Saussure* (Paris: Gallimard, 1971), p. 152, my translation.

6. *The Language of Allegory,* p. 254.

7. Emanuel Swedenborg, *Concerning the White Horse,* pp. 59–61.

Select Bibliography

Adams, Hazard. "Blake and the Philosophy of Literary Symbolism." *New Literary History* 5 (Autumn 1973):135–46.

Aiton, E. J. *The Vortex Theory of Planetary Motions.* New York: American Elsevier, 1972.

Arthos, John. *The Language of Natural Description in Eighteenth-Century Poetry.* Ann Arbor: University of Michigan Press, 1949.

Ault, Donald. "Incommensurability and Interconnection in Blake's Anti-Newtonian Text." *Studies in Romanticism* 16 (Summer 1977):277–303.

———. *Visionary Physics: Blake's Response to Newton.* Chicago: University of Chicago Press, 1974.

Bacon, Francis. *The Advancement of Learning and New Atlantis.* Edited by Arthur Johnson. Oxford: Clarendon Press, 1974.

Baillie, Matthew. *The Morbid Anatomy of Some of the Most Important Parts of the Body.* London: J. Johnson, 1793.

Barthes, Roland. *Critical Essays.* Translated by Richard Howard. Evanston, Ill.: Northwestern University Press, 1972.

———. *S/Z: An Essay.* Translated by Richard Howard. New York: Hill and Wang, 1974.

Bentley, G. E., Jr. *Blake Books: Annotated Catalogues of William Blake's Writings in Illuminated Printing, in Conventional Typography and in Manuscript and Reprints Thereof, Reproductions of His Designs, Books with His Engravings, Catalogues, Books He Owned, and Scholarly and Critical Works about Him.* Oxford: Clarendon Press, 1977.

———. *Blake Records.* Oxford: Clarendon Press, 1969.

———. *William Blake: Vala or The Four Zoas: A Facsimile of the Manuscript, a Transcript of the Poem, and a Study of Its Growth and Significance.* Oxford: Clarendon Press, 1963.

Benveniste, Emile. *Indo-European Language and Society.* Translated by Elizabeth Palmer. London: Faber and Faber, 1973.

Bishop, Morchand [Oliver Stoner]. *Blake's Hayley: The Life, Works, and Friendships of William Hayley.* London: Gollancz, 1951.

Blackmore, Richard. *Creation: A Philosophical Poem.* 4th ed. London, 1718.

Blake, William. *Blake: Complete Writings with Variant Readings.* Edited by Geoffrey Keynes. 1966; rpt. London: Oxford University Press, 1971.

———. *The Notebook of William Blake: A Photographic and Typographic Facsimile.* Edited by David V. Erdman. With the assistance of Donald K. Moore. Oxford: Clarendon Press, 1973.

———. *The Complete Poetry and Prose of William Blake.* Edited by David V. Erdman.

Commentary by Harold Bloom. Revised edition. Berkeley: University of California Press, 1982.

Bloom, Harold. *Poetry and Repression: Revisionism from Blake to Stevens*. New Haven, Conn.: Yale University Press, 1976.

―――. *The Ringers in the Tower: Studies in the Romantic Tradition*. Chicago: University of Chicago Press, 1971.

Blount, Thomas. *Glossographia; or, A Dictionary Interpreting All Such Hard Words, Whether Hebrew, Greek, Latin . . . As Are Now Used in Our Refined English Tongue*. 5th ed. London, 1681.

Boehme, Jacob. [Böhme, Jakob]. *Mysterium Magnum: An Exposition of the First Book of Moses called Genesis*. Translated by John Sparrow (1652). Edited by C. J. B. London: John M. Watkins, 1965.

―――. *The Works of Jacob Behmen*. Translated [*sic*] and edited by William Law. 4 vols. London, 1764–81.

Bonnycastle, John. *An Introduction to Astronomy*. London, 1786.

Borlase, William. *Antiquities, Historical and Monumental, of the County of Cornwall. Consisting of Several Essays on the First Inhabitants, Druid-Superstition, Customs, and Remains of the Most Remote Antiquity*. 2nd ed. London, 1769.

Boswell, James. *Life of Johnson*. Edited by R. W. Chapman. 1953; rpt. London: Oxford University Press, 1969.

Bréal, Michel. *Semantics: Studies in the Science of Meaning*. Translated by Mrs. Henry Cust. 1900; rpt. New York: Dover, 1964.

Bredvold, Louis I. *The Natural History of Sensibility*. Detroit: Wayne State University Press, 1962.

Brissenden, R. F. "Authority, Guilt, and Anxiety in *The Theory of Moral Sentiments*." *Texas Studies in Literature and Language* 11 (1969):945–62.

Brown, Norman O. *Love's Body*. New York: Vintage Books, 1966.

Browne, Thomas. *The Prose of Sir Thomas Browne*. Edited by Norman Endicott. Garden City, N.Y.: Doubleday, 1967.

Browne, Thomas Gunter. *Hermes Unmasked; or The Art of Speech*. English Linguistics 1500–1800, no. 201. 1795; rpt. Menston, Eng.: Scholar Press, 1969.

Buber, Martin. *The Prophetic Faith*. Translated by Carlyle Witton-Davies. 1949; rpt. New York: Harper & Row, 1960.

Buffon, G. L. Leclerc de. *Natural History, General and Particular*. Translated by William Smellie. 3rd ed. 9 vols. London, 1791.

Bunyan, John. *The Pilgrim's Progress from This World to That Which Is to Come*. Edited by James Blenton Wharey. 2nd ed. by Roger Sharrock. Oxford: Clarendon Press, 1967.

Burckhardt, Sigurd. *Shakespearean Meanings*. Princeton, N.J.: Princeton University Press, 1968.

Burke, Edmund. *A Philosophical Enquiry into the Origin of Our Ideas of the Sublime and Beautiful*. Edited by J. T. Boulton. Notre Dame, Ind.: University of Notre Dame Press, 1968.

Butterworth, E. A. S. *The Tree at the Navel of the Earth*. Berlin: De Gruyter, 1970.

Cheyne, George. *The English Malady; or, a Treatise of Nervous Diseases of all Kinds*. London, 1733.

Clarke, Edwin. "The Doctrine of the Hollow Nerve in the Seventeenth and Eighteenth Centuries." In *Medicine, Science, and Culture: Historical Essays in Honor of Owsei Temkin*, edited by Lloyd G. Stevenson and Robert P. Multhauf, pp. 123–41. Baltimore: Johns Hopkins University Press, 1968.

Cleland, John. *Memoirs of Fanny Hill*. Introduced by J. H. Plumb. 1779; rpt. New York: New American Library, 1965.

Cohen, Murray. *Sensible Words: Linguistic Practice in England, 1640–1785*. Baltimore: Johns Hopkins University Press, 1977.

Corti, Maria. *An Introduction to Literary Semiotics*. Translated by Margherita Bogat and Allen Mandelbaum. Bloomington: Indiana University Press, 1978.

Cowper, William. *Cowper: Poetical Works*. Edited by H. W. Milford. 4th ed., rev. Corrected and additions by Norma Russell. London: Oxford University Press, 1967.

Crollius, Oswald. *Philosophy Reformed & Improved in Four Profound Tractates*. Translated by H. Pinnell. London, 1657.

Cruden, Alexander. *Cruden's Complete Concordance To the Old and New Testaments*. Edited by C. H. Irwin, A. D. Adams, and S. A. Waters. Rev. ed. Guildford and London: Lutterworth Press, 1954.

Cudworth, Ralph. *The True Intellectual System of the Universe*. 1678; facsimile rpt. Stuttgart: Friedrich Frommann Verlag, 1964.

Curran, Stuart, and Wittreich, Joseph Anthony, Jr., eds. *Blake's Sublime Allegory: Essays on the Four Zoas, Milton, Jerusalem*. Madison: University of Wisconsin Press, 1973.

Damon, S. Foster. *A Blake Dictionary: The Ideas and Symbols of William Blake*. 1965; rpt. New York: E. P. Dutton, 1971.

Damrosch, Leopold, Jr. *Symbol and Truth in Blake's Myth*. Princeton, N.J.: Princeton University Press, 1980.

Darwin, Erasmus. *The Botanic Garden: A Poem, in Two Parts. Part I. Containing The Economy of Vegetation. Part II. The Loves of the Plants. With Philosophical Notes*. 1791; facsimile rpt. Menston, Eng.: Scholar Press, 1973.

———. *The Temple of Nature; or, The Origin of Society: A Poem, with Philosophical Notes*. London: J. Johnson, 1803.

———. *Zoonomia; or, The Laws of Organic Life*. 2 vols. London: J. Johnson, 1794–96.

Davies, Edward. *The Mythology and Rites of the British Druids*. London, 1809.

Denton, Thomas. *Immortality; or, The Consolation of Life: A Monody*. London, 1755.

Derham, W. *Physico and Astro Theology: or, A Demonstration of The Being and Attributes of God*. 1713, rpt. London, 1786.

Derrida, Jacques. *Of Grammatology*. Translated by Gayatri Chakravorty Spivak. Baltimore: Johns Hopkins University Press, 1976.

———. "Structure, Sign, and Play in the Human Sciences." In *The Structuralist Controversy: The Languages of Criticism and the Sciences of Man*, edited by Richard Macksey and Eugenio Donato, pp. 247–72. Baltimore, Johns Hopkins University Press, 1972.

Drake, Nathan. *Literary Hours*. 2nd ed. 2 vols. London, 1800.

Duff, William. *An Essay on Original Genius*. London, 1767.

Dyer, John. *The Fleece: A Poem. In Four Books*. London, 1757.

Edwards, Gavin. "Mind-Forg'd Manacles: A Contribution to the Discussion of Blake's 'London'." *Literature and History* 5 (1979):87–105.

Eliade, Mircea. *Patterns in Comparative Religion*. 1958; rpt. New York: World Publishing Co., 1963.

Empson, William. *Seven Types of Ambiguity*. 3rd ed. New York: New Directions, 1966.

Encyclopaedia Britannica. 1st ed. 3 vols. Edinburgh, 1771.

Erdman, David V. *Blake: Prophet Against Empire*. Rev. ed. Garden City, N.Y.: Doubleday, 1969.

————. ed., et al. *A Concordance to the Writings of William Blake*. 2 vols. Ithaca, N.Y.: Cornell University Press, 1967.

————. annotator. *The Illuminated Blake*. Garden City, N.Y.: Doubleday, 1974.

————. "The Suppressed and Altered Passages in Blake's *Jerusalem*." In *Studies in Bibliography*, vol. 17, edited by Fredson Bowers, pp. 1–54. Charlottesville: University Press of Virginia, 1964.

————, and Grant, John E., eds. *Blake's Visionary Forms Dramatic*. Princeton, N.J.: Princeton University Press, 1970.

Essick, Robert N., ed. *The Visionary Hand: Essays for the Study of William Blake's Art and Aesthetics*. Los Angeles: Hennessey & Ingalls, 1973.

————. *William Blake, Printmaker*. Princeton, N.J.: Princeton University Press, 1980.

Farber, George Stanley. *The Origin of Pagan Idolatry Ascertained from Historical Testimony and Circumstantial Evidence*. 3 vols. London, 1816.

Fawcett, Thomas. *The Symbolic Language of Religion: An Introductory Study*. London: SCM Press, 1970.

Fenichel, Otto. *The Psychoanalytic Theory of Neurosis*. New York: W. W. Norton, 1945.

Fisher, Peter. *The Valley of Vision: Blake as Prophet and Revolutionary*. Edited by Northrop Frye. University of Toronto, Department of English, Studies and Texts, no. 9. Toronto: University of Toronto Press, 1961.

Fontenelle, M. de. *A Conversation on the Plurality of Worlds, to Which Is Added Mr. Addison's Defense of the Newtonian Philosophy*. Translated. 6th ed. London, 1783.

Fox, Susan. *Poetic Form in Blake's Milton*. Princeton, N.J.: Princeton University Press, 1976.

Freud, Sigmund. *The Standard Edition of the Complete Psychological Works of Sigmund Freud*. Translated under the general editorship of James Strachey. 24 vols. London: Hogarth Press, 1953–74.

Frye, Northrop. *Anatomy of Criticism: Four Essays*. 1957; rpt. Princeton, N.J.: Princeton University Press, 1971.

————. *Fearful Symmetry: A Study of William Blake*. 1947; rpt. Princeton, N.J.: Princeton University Press, 1969.

Gardner, Stanley. *Blake*. New York: Arco, 1969.

George, Mary Dorothy. *London Life in the Eighteenth Century*. Harmondsworth, Eng.: Penguin Books, 1966.

Gibson, Eleanor J., and Levin, Harry. *The Psychology of Reading*. Cambridge, Mass.: MIT Press, 1975.

Gilchrist, Alexander. *The Life of William Blake*. Edited with an introduction, notes, and bibliography by Ruthven Todd. New York: E. P. Dutton, 1945.

Gleckner, Robert F. *The Piper and The Bard: A Study of William Blake*. Detroit: Wayne State University Press, 1959.

The Gospel According to Thomas. Coptic text established and trans. by A. Guillaumont et al. New York: Harper, 1959.

Grant, John E. "The Female Awakening at the End of Blake's *Milton*: A Picture Story, with Questions." In *Milton Reconsidered: Essays in Honor of Arthur E. Barker*, edited by John Karl Franson. Salzburg Studies in English Literature, Elizabethan and Renaissance Studies 49, pp. 78–99. Salzburg: Institut für Englische Sprache und Literatur, Universität Salzburg, 1976.

Great Britain. *Parliamentary Papers* (Commons). *Minutes of Evidence Taken before the Select Committee on the State of Children in the Manufactories of the United Kingdom*. 1816.

Greene, Donald. *The Age of Exuberance: Backgrounds to Eighteenth Century English Literature*. New York: Random House, 1970.

Hacking, Ian. *Why Does Language Matter to Philosophy?* Cambridge: Cambridge University Press, 1975.

Haller, Albrecht von. *First Lines of Physiology*. Translated by William Cullen. The Sources of Science, no. 32. 2 vols. in 1. 1786; facsimile rpt. New York: Johnson Reprint, 1966.

Hartley, David. *Observations on Man, His Frame, His Duty, and His Expectations*. 3 vols. 1749; rpt. London: J. Johnson, 1791.

Harvey, William. *Anatomical Exercitations: Concerning the Generation of Living Creatures*. Translated. London, 1653.

Hayley, William. *The Life of Milton*. 2nd ed. Introduction by Joseph Anthony Wittreich, Jr. 1796; facsimile rpt. Gainesville, Fla.: Scholars' Facsimiles and Reprints, 1970.

———. *Poems and Plays by William Hayley*. 6 vols. London, 1788.

Hervey, James. *Meditations and Contemplations: Containing Meditations Among the Tombs, Reflections on a Flower Garden, A Descant on Creation, Contemplations on the Night, Contemplations on the Starry Heavens, and a Winter-piece*. New and corrected edition. Liverpool, n.d. [ca. 1815].

Hilton, Nelson. "The Sweet Science of Atmospheres in *The Four Zoas*." *Blake: An Illustrated Quarterly* 12 (Summer 1978):80–86.

Hirst, Désirée. *Hidden Riches: Traditional Symbolism from the Renaissance to Blake*. London: Eyre & Spottiswoode, 1964.

Hobbes, Thomas. *Leviathan*. Edited by C. B. Macpherson. Harmondsworth, Eng.: Penguin Books, 1969.

Homer. [George] *Chapman's Homer: The Iliad, The Odyssey, and The Lesser Homerica*. Edited with notes, commentary, and glossary by Allardyce Nicoll. Bollingen Series no. 41. 2 vols. Princeton, N.J.: Princeton University Press, 1956.

Hood, Thomas. *Selected Poems of Thomas Hood*. Edited by John Clubbe. Cambridge, Mass.: Harvard University Press, 1970.

Hooke, S. H., ed. *The Labyrinth, Further Studies in the Relation between Myth and Ritual in the Ancient World*. New York: Macmillan Co., 1935.

Hume, David. *A Treatise of Human Nature*. 2nd ed. Edited by L. A. Selby-Bigge, revised by P. H. Nidditch. Oxford: Clarendon Press, 1978.

Jenyns, Soame. *The Works of Soame Jenyns, Esq*. 4 vols. London, 1790.

Johnson, Samuel. *A Dictionary of the English Language*. 4th ed. London, 1773.

————. *Johnson on Shakespeare.* Edited by Arthur Sherbo. The Yale Edition of the Works of Samuel Johnson, vol. 8. New Haven, Conn.: Yale University Press, 1968.

————. *Johnson: Prose and Poetry.* Edited by Mona Wilson. Cambridge, Mass.: Harvard University Press, 1950.

————. *Lives of the English Poets.* Introduction by Arthur Waugh. 2 vols. 1906; rpt. Oxford: Clarendon Press, 1952.

Jones, William Powell. *The Rhetoric of Science: A Study of Scientific Ideas and Imagery in Eighteenth-Century English Poetry.* Berkeley and Los Angeles: University of California Press, 1966.

Jonsson, Inge. *Emanuel Swedenborg.* Translated by Catherine Djurklou. Twayne's World Authors Series, no. 127. New York: Twayne Publishers, 1971.

Josephus. *The Whole Genuine and Complete Works of Flavius Josephus.* Translated by George Henry Maynard. References and notes by Edward Kempton. London, n.d. [ça. 1785].

Jung, Carl G. *Psychology and Alchemy.* Translated by R. F. C. Hull. 2nd ed. rev. The Collected Works of C. G. Jung, vol. 12. Bollingen Series, no. 20. Princeton, N.J.: Princeton University Press, 1968.

Kittel, Gerhard, and Friedrich, Gerhard, eds. *Theological Dictionary of the New Testament.* Translated and edited by Geoffrey W. Bromiley. 8 vols. Grand Rapids, Mich.: Eerdmans Publishing Co., 1968–72.

Knight, Richard Payne. *A Discourse on the Worship of Priapus and its Connection with the Mystic Theology of the Ancients.* 1786; rpt. in *Sexual Symbolism: A History of Phallic Worship,* introduced by Ashley Montagu. New York: Julian Press, 1957.

Koyré, Alexandre. *La Philosophie de Jacob Boehme.* Paris: Vrin, 1929.

Kreiter, Carmen S. "Evolution and William Blake." *Studies in Romanticism* 4 (1965):110–18.

Kristeva, Julia. *Desire in Language: A Semiotic Approach to Literature and Art.* Edited by Leon S. Roudiez. Translated by Thomas Gora, Alice Jardine, and Leon S. Roudiez. New York: Columbia University Press, 1980.

Laplanche, J., and Pontalis, J.-B. *The Language of Psycho-Analysis.* Translated by Donald Nicholson-Smith. New York: W. W. Norton, 1973.

Lewis, Matthew. *The Monk.* Edited by Howard Anderson. London: Oxford University Press, 1973.

Locke, John. *An Essay Concerning Human Understanding.* Edited by Peter H. Nidditch. Oxford: Clarendon Press, 1975.

Lovejoy, Arthur O. *The Great Chain of Being: A Study in the History of an Idea.* 1936; rpt. New York: Harper & Row, 1960.

Lowth, Robert. *Lectures on the Sacred Poetry of the Hebrews.* Translated by G. Gregory. 2 vols. London: J. Johnson, 1787.

McLuhan, Marshall. *The Gutenberg Galaxy: The Making of Typographic Man.* Toronto: University of Toronto Press, 1962.

Macrobius. *Commentary on the Dream of Scipio.* Translated with notes by William Harris Stahl. New York: Columbia University Press, 1952.

Mantoux, Paul. *The Industrial Revolution in the Eighteenth Century.* Rev. ed. Preface by T. S. Ashton. London: Jonathan Cape, 1961.

Miles, Josephine. *Eras and Modes in English Poetry.* 2nd ed., rev. Berkeley and Los Angeles: University of California Press, 1964.

Milton, John. *The Complete Poetry of John Milton.* Edited with notes and translations by John T. Shawcross. Rev. ed. Garden City, N.Y.: Doubleday, 1971.

Miner, Paul. "William Blake's 'Divine Analogy'." *Criticism* 3 (1963):46–61.

Mitchell, W. J. T. *Blake's Composite Art: A Study of the Illuminated Poetry.* Princeton, N.J.: Princeton University Press, 1978.

Moore, C. A. *Backgrounds of English Literature, 1700–1760.* 1953; rpt. New York: Octagon Books, 1969.

More, Henry. *A Collection of Several Philosophical Writings of Dr. Henry More.* 2nd ed. London, 1662.

Morris, David. B. *The Religious Sublime: Christian Poetry and Critical Tradition in Eighteenth-Century England.* Lexington: University Press of Kentucky, 1972.

Nelson, J. Walter. "Blake's Diction—An Amendatory Note." *Blake Studies* 7 (1975): 167–75.

Newton, Isaac. *Opticks; or, A Treatise of the Reflections, Refractions, Inflections and Colours of Light.* 2nd ed. London, 1718.

Nicolson, Marjorie Hope. *Mountain Gloom and Mountain Glory: The Development of the Aesthetics of the Infinite.* 1959; rpt. New York: W. W. Norton, 1963.

Onians, Richard Broxton. *The Origins of European Thought: About the Body, the Mind, the Soul, the World, Time, and Fate.* 1951; rpt. New York: Arno Press, 1973.

Ovid. *Ovid's Metamorphoses, Englished, Mythologized, and Represented in Figures by George Sandys.* Edited by Karl K. Hulley and Stanley T. Vandersall. Lincoln: The University of Nebraska Press, 1970.

Paley, Morton D. *Energy and the Imagination: A Study in the Development of Blake's Thought.* Oxford: Clarendon Press, 1970.

———, and Phillips, Michael, eds. *William Blake: Essays in Honour of Sir Geoffrey Keynes.* Oxford: Clarendon Press, 1973.

Partridge, Eric. *A Dictionary of Slang and Unconventional English.* 5th ed. New York: Macmillan Co., 1961.

Percival, Milton O. *William Blake's Circle of Destiny.* 1938; rpt. New York: Octagon Books, 1970.

Phillips, Michael, ed. *Interpreting Blake.* Cambridge: Cambridge University Press, 1978.

Pierseens, Michel. *The Power of Babel: A Study of Logophilia.* Translated by Carl R. Lovitt. London: Routledge & Kegan Paul, 1980.

Plato. *The Cratylus, Phaedo, Parmenides and Timaeus of Plato.* Translated by Thomas Taylor. With notes on *The Cratylus* and an explanatory introduction to each dialogue. London, 1793.

———. *The Works of Plato.* Translated by Thomas Taylor and Floyer Sydenham. 4 vols. London, 1804.

Plotinus. *The Enneads.* Translated by Stephan MacKenna. 2nd ed. rev. B. S. Page. London: Faber & Faber, 1962.

Pope, Alexander, trans. *Homer's Iliad and Odyssey.* Edited by Maynard Mack, et al. The Twickenham Edition of the Poems of Alexander Pope, vols. 7–10. New Haven, Conn.: Yale University Press, 1967.

————. *The Poems of Alexander Pope*. Edited by John Butt. New Haven, Conn.: Yale University Press, 1963.

Poulet, Georges. *The Metamorphoses of the Circle*. Translated by Carley Dawson and Elliott Coleman. Baltimore: Johns Hopkins University Press, 1966.

Priestley, Joseph. *The History and Present State of Discoveries relating to Vision, Light, and Colours*. 2 vols. London: J. Johnson, 1772.

Quilligan, Maureen. *The Language of Allegory: Defining the Genre*. Ithaca, N.Y.: Cornell University Press, 1979.

Rad, Gerhard von. *The Message of the Prophets*. Translated by D. M. G. Stalker. New York: Harper & Row, n.d. [ca. 1970].

Rahner, Hugo, S. J. *Greek Myths and Christian Mystery*. Translated by Brian Battershaw. London: Burns & Oates, 1963.

Raine, Kathleen. *Blake and Tradition*. Bollingen Series, no. 35, vol. 11. 2 vols. Princeton, N.J.: Princeton University Press, 1968.

Reeves, James. *The Everlasting Circle: English Traditional Verse*. London: Heinemann, 1960.

————. *The Idiom of the People: English Traditional Verse*. London: Heinemann, 1958.

Ricoeur, Paul. *The Philosophy of Paul Ricoeur: An Anthology of His Work*. Edited by Charles E. Reagan and David Steward. Boston: Beacon Press, 1978.

Roe, Albert S. *Blake's Illustrations to the Divine Comedy*. Princeton, N.J.: Princeton University Press, 1953.

Rogers, Samuel. *The Pleasure of Memory, with Other Poems*. New and enlarged ed. London, 1799.

Róheim, Géza. *Animism, Magic, and the Divine King*. London: Kegan Paul, Trench, Trubner & Co., 1930.

Rose, Edward J. "Visionary Forms Dramatic: Grammatical and Iconographical Movement in Blake's Verse and Designs." *Criticism* 8 (1966):111–25.

Rosenfeld, Alvin H., ed. *William Blake: Essays for S. Foster Damon*. Providence, R.I.: Brown University Press, 1969.

Rousseau, G. S. "Nerves, Spirits, and Fibres: Towards Defining the Origins of Sensibility." In *Studies in the Eighteenth Century, vol. 3: Papers Presented at the Third David Nichol Smith Memorial Seminar, Canberra*, edited by R. F. Brissenden and J. C. Eade, pp. 137–57. Toronto: University of Toronto Press, 1976.

————. "Science." In *The Eighteenth Century*, edited by Pat Rogers, pp. 153–207. New York: Holmes & Meier, 1978.

Rudé, George. *Hanoverian London, 1714–1808*. Berkeley and Los Angeles: University of California Press, 1971.

Sandler, Florence. "The Iconoclastic Enterprise: Blake's Critique of 'Milton's Religion'." *Blake Studies* 5 (1972):13–57.

Santillana, Giorgio de, and Von Dechend, Hertha. *Hamlet's Mill: An Essay on Myth and the Frame of Time*. Boston: Gambit, 1969.

Saussure, Ferdinand de. *Course in General Linguistics*. Edited by Charles Bally and Albert Sechehaye, in collaboration with Albert Riedlinger. Translated by Wade Baskin. 1959; rpt. New York: McGraw-Hill, 1966.

Schorer, Mark. *William Blake: The Politics of Vision.* 1946; rpt. New York: Vintage Books, 1959.

Shelley, Percy Bysshe. *Shelley: Poetical Works.* Edited by Thomas Hutchinson. New ed. corrected by G. M. Matthews. London: Oxford University Press, 1970.

Sickels, Eleanor M. *The Gloomy Egoist: Moods and Themes of Melancholy from Gray to Keats.* New York: Columbia University Press, 1932.

Singer, Charles, ed., et al. *A History of Technology.* vol. 4, *The Industrial Revolution, ca. 1750 to ca. 1850.* 7 vols. London: Oxford University Press, 1932.

Smith, Adam. *The Theory of Moral Sentiments; or, An Essay towards an Analysis of the Principles by Which Men Naturally Judge Concerning the Conduct and Character, First of Their Neighbours, and Afterwards of Themselves.* 6th ed. 2 vols. London, 1790.

Smollett, Tobias. *The Expedition of Humphry Clinker.* Edited by Angus Ross. Harmondsworth, Eng.: Penguin Books, 1967.

Spacks, Patricia. *The Insistence of Horror: Aspects of the Supernatural in Eighteenth-Century Poetry.* Cambridge, Mass.: Harvard University Press, 1962.

Stedman, John Gabriel. *Narrative of a Five Years Expedition Against the Revolted Negroes of Surinam in Guiana on the Wild Coast of South America from the Years 1772 to 1777.* Introduction and notes by R. A. J. van Lier. 2 vols. 1796; rpt. Barre, Mass.: Imprint Society, 1971.

Steiner, George. *After Babel: Aspects of Language and Translation.* London: Oxford University Press, 1975.

Stempel, Daniel. "Blake, Foucault, and the Classical Episteme." *PMLA* 96 (May 1981):388–407.

Sterne, Laurence. *Tristram Shandy.* Edited by Howard Anderson. New York: W. W. Norton, 1980.

Stevenson, W. H., annotator. *The Poems of William Blake.* Text edited by David V. Erdman. London: Longman, 1971.

Stone, Lawrence. *The Family, Sex and Marriage in England 1500–1800.* New York: Harper & Row, 1977.

Stukeley, William. *Abury, A Temple of the British Druids.* London, 1743.

———. *A Concise Account of the Most Famous Antiquity of Great Britain, Vulgarly call'd Stonehenge.* London, n.d. [ca. 1750].

Suhr, Elmer G. *The Spinning Aphrodite: The Evolution of the Goddess from Earliest Pre-Hellenic Symbolism Through Late Classical Times.* New York: Helios Books, 1969.

Swedenborg, Emanuel. *Concerning the White Horse Mentioned in the Revelation, chap. xix, with Extracts from the Arcana Coelestia, concerning the Word and its Spiritual or Internal Sense.* Translated. London, 1788.

———. *An Hieroglyphic Key to Natural and Spiritual Mysteries, by way of Representation and Correspondences.* Translated by R. Hindmarsh. London, 1792.

———. *A Theosophic Lucubration On the Nature of Influx, As It Respects the Communication and Operation of Soul and Body.* Translated. London, 1780.

———. *True Christian Religion; Containing the Universal Theology of the New Church: Which Was Foretold by the Lord, in Daniel, chap. vii. 5, 13, 14, and in the Apocalypse, chap. xxi, 1, 2.* Translated. 2 vols. London, 1781.

————. *The Wisdom of Angels concerning Divine Love and Divine Wisdom.* Translated. London, 1788.

Swift, Jonathan. *Swift: Poetical Works.* Edited by Herbert Davis. London: Oxford University Press, 1967.

————. *A Tale of a Tub, To Which Is Added The Battle of the Books and The Mechanical Operation of the Spirit.* Edited by A. C. Guthkelch and D. Nichol Smith. 2nd ed. Oxford: Clarendon Press, 1958.

Taylor, Ronald Clayton. "Semantic Structures and the Temporal Modes of Blake's Prophetic Verse." *Language and Style* 12 (1979):26–49.

Taylor, Thomas. *Thomas Taylor the Platonist: Selected Writings.* Edited with introductions by Kathleen Raine and George Mills Harper. Bollingen Series, no. 87. Princeton, N.J.: Princeton University Press, 1969.

Thass-Thienemann, Theodore. *Symbolic Behavior.* New York: Washington Square Press, 1968.

Thompson, E. P. *The Making of the English Working Class.* New York: Vintage Books, 1963.

Thomson, James. *James Thomson: Poetical Works.* Edited with notes by J. Logie Robertson. London: Oxford University Press, 1908.

Todd, Ruthven. *Tracks in the Snow: Studies in English Science and Art.* London: Grey Walls Press, 1946.

Toland, John. *A Critical History of the Celtic Religion and Learning: Containing An Account of the Druids; or the Priests and Judges of the Vaids, or the Diviners and Physicians; and of the Bards, or the Poets and Heralds; of the Ancient Gauls, Britons, Irish and Scots. With the History of Abaris, the Hyperborian, Priest of the Sun.* London, n.d. [ca. 1740].

Tucker, Susie B. *Protean Shape: A Study in Eighteenth-Century Vocabulary and Usage.* London: Athlone Press, 1967.

Vaughan, Henry. *The Works of Henry Vaughan.* Edited by L. C. Martin. 2nd ed. Oxford: Clarendon Press, 1957.

Vries, Ad de. *A Dictionary of Imagery and Symbolism.* Amsterdam: North-Holland Publishing, 1974.

Wilden, Anthony. *System and Structure: Essays in Communication and Exchange.* 2nd ed. London: Tavistock Publications, 1980.

Wilkins, John. *An Essay towards a Real Character, and a Philosophical Language.* English Linguistics 1500–1800, no. 119. 1668, facsimile rpt. Menston, Eng.: Scholar Press, 1968.

Willey, Basil. *The Seventeenth Century Background: The Thought of the Age in Relation to Religion and Poetry.* 1934; rpt. Garden City, N.Y.: Doubleday, 1953.

Wimsatt, W. K. *The Verbal Icon.* Lexington: University of Kentucky Press, 1954.

Wollstonecraft, Mary. *A Vindication of the Rights of Woman.* London: J. Johnson, 1791.

Wordsworth, William. *The Complete Poetical Works of William Wordsworth.* Edited by Andrew J. George. Boston: Houghton, Mifflin & Co., 1904.

Worrall, David. "William Blake and Erasmus Darwin's *Botanic Garden.*" *Bulletin of the New York Public Library* 78 (1975):397–417.

Young, Edward. *The Complaint; or Night Thoughts.* New York, 1853.

Subject Index

Index of Quotations from Blake's Works

Alphabetically ordered, except for short manuscript poems grouped at end.

Designer: Barbara Llewellyn
Compositor: Dharma Press
Text: 11/14 Baskerville
Display: Baskerville
Printer: Malloy Lithographing, Inc.
Binder: John H. Dekker and Sons